Medical Malpractice and the U.S. Health Care System

Medical malpractice lawsuits are common and controversial in the United States. Since early 2002, doctors' insurance premiums for malpractice coverage have soared. As Congress and state governments debate laws intended to stabilize the cost of insurance, doctors continue to blame lawyers and lawyers continue to blame doctors and insurance companies. This book, which is the capstone of three years' comprehensive research funded by The Pew Charitable Trusts, goes well beyond the conventional debate over tort reform and connects medical liability to broader trends and goals in American health policy. Contributions from leading figures in health law and policy marshal the best available information, present new empirical evidence, and offer cutting-edge analysis of potential reforms involving patient safety, liability insurance, and tort litigation.

William M. Sage received his medical and law degrees with honors from Stanford University in 1988 and has been a member of the faculty of Columbia Law School since 1995. In 1993, he headed four working groups of the President's Task Force on Health Care Reform in the Clinton White House. He recently served as principal investigator for the Project on Medical Liability in Pennsylvania. He is also the recipient of an Investigator Award in Health Policy Research from the Robert Wood Johnson Foundation and has published more than sixty articles in legal, health policy, and clinical journals. He is an elected Fellow of the Hastings Center on bioethics and is a member of the editorial board of *Health Affairs*. He is married with two children and lives near New York City.

Rogan Kersh received his B.A. from Wake Forest University and his M.A., M.Phil., and Ph.D. from Yale University. He has taught political science and public administration at Syracuse University since 1996; his extensive political experience includes internships in the U.S. Senate and British Parliament as well as work in the Washington tax-policy office of Coopers & Lybrand and think tanks in Washington and Tokyo. His book *Dreams of a More Perfect Union* was published in 2001, and he is currently completing two books on health policy. He is a board member of the Critical Review Foundation and associate editor of the *Journal of Health Politics, Policy and Law*.

Medical Malpractice and the U.S. Health Care System

Edited by

WILLIAM M. SAGE
Columbia University

ROGAN KERSH
Syracuse University

CAMBRIDGE
UNIVERSITY PRESS

CAMBRIDGE UNIVERSITY PRESS
Cambridge, New York, Melbourne, Madrid, Cape Town, Singapore, São Paulo

Cambridge University Press
40 West 20th Street, New York, NY 10011-4211, USA

www.cambridge.org
Information on this title: www.cambridge.org/9780521849326

First published 2006

Printed in the United States of America

A catalog record for this publication is available from the British Library.

Library of Congress Cataloging in Publication Data

Medical malpractice and the U.S. health care system / edited by
William M. Sage, Rogan Kersh.
  p. ; cm.
Includes bibliographical references and index.
ISBN-13: 978-0-521-84932-6 (hardback)
ISBN-10: 0-521-84932-2 (hardback)
ISBN-13: 978-0-521-61411-5 (pbk.)
ISBN-10: 0-521-61411-2 (pbk.)
  1. Physicians – Malpractice – United States.   2. Insurance, Physicians' liability – United States.
3. Medical care – United States.   I. Sage, William M.   II. Kersh, Rogan.
  KF2905.3.M4393   2006
  344.7304'121 – dc22   2005037931

ISBN-13   978-0-521-84932-6 hardback
ISBN-10   0-521-84932-2 hardback

ISBN-13   978-0-521-61411-5 paperback
ISBN-10   0-521-61411-2 paperback

Contents

Contributors

Jennifer Arlen is the Norma Z. Paige Professor of Law at New York University School of Law and is codirector of the NYU Center in Law and Economics. Arlen received her B.A. from Harvard University (*magna cum laude*) and earned both a J.D. (Order of the Coif) and a Ph.D. in economics from New York University. Her main research interests include medical malpractice liability and the use of legal rules to deter corporate wrongdoing. Her recent scholarship on medical malpractice liability includes "Torts, Expertise, and Authority: Liability of Physicians and Managed Care Organizations," *RAND Journal of Economics* 36 (2005) (with W. Bentley MacLeod), and "Malpractice Liability for Physicians and Managed Care Organizations," *New York University Law Review* 78 (2003) (with W. Bentley MacLeod).

Tom Baker is the Connecticut Mutual Professor and Director of the Insurance Law Center at the University of Connecticut School of Law. His research examines issues of risk and responsibility in the fields of torts and insurance from an interdisciplinary perspective. His recent book, *The Medical Malpractice Myth* (U. Chicago Press, 2005), attacks the misperceptions behind the tort reform movement and proposes an evidence-based approach to medical liability reform. He is the coeditor of *Embracing Risk: The Changing Culture of Insurance and Responsibility* (U. Chicago Press, 2002) and the author of more than twenty articles and essays relating to insurance, risk, and responsibility, as well as a leading insurance law textbook, *Insurance Law and Policy* (Aspen Publishing, 2003).

David J. Becker is assistant professor at the University of Alabama–Birmingham's Department of Health Care Organization and Policy. Prior to his graduate studies, Becker was a researcher at the National Bureau of Economic Research (Stanford, CA; 1997–9) and a health care consultant with The Lewin Group (1996–7). Becker specializes in health, labor, and regulatory economics. His current research interests include the effect of reimbursement policy on treatments and health outcomes, medical malpractice and defensive medicine, Medicare fraud and abuse, and quality reporting initiatives. Becker has recently published in journals including the *Journal of Health Economics* and the *Journal of the American Medical Association*.

Robert Berenson is a senior Fellow at the Urban Institute in Washington, D.C. He is an expert in health care policy, particularly Medicare, with experience practicing medicine, serving in senior positions in two Administrations and helping to organize and manage a successful preferred provider organization. Berenson is a board-certified internist who practiced for twelve years in a Washington, D.C., group practice and a Fellow of the American College of Physicians. Berenson is also adjunct professor at the University of North Carolina School of Public Health. For ten years he was medical director of the National Capital PPO, a large rental PPO serving the Washington, D.C., metropolitan area, and he was coauthor, with Walter Zelman, of *The Managed Care Blues and How to Cure Them* (1998). Berenson's current research focuses on modernization of the Medicare program to improve efficiency and the quality of care provided to beneficiaries.

Randall R. Bovbjerg is a principal research associate in the Health Policy Center of the Urban Institute in Washington, D.C. In more than thirty years of research, practical, and teaching experience in health policy, one of his specialties has been medical injury, liability, and reform. Bovbjerg has served on the malpractice and quality workgroup of the Clinton Administration's transition team, JCAHO's taskforce on alternatives to tort, and the Patient Safety taskforce of the Federation of State Medical Boards. He and Robert Berenson recently coauthored "Surmounting Myths and Mindsets in Medical Malpractice," an issue brief available on the Institute's Web page www.urban.org, with more than a hundred of Bovbjerg's other professional publications. Before coming to the Institute, he was a state insurance regulator in Massachusetts.

Troyen A. Brennan is chief medical officer of Aetna. Through 2005, he was in academic medicine as professor of medicine at Harvard Medical School, professor of law and public health at Harvard School of Public Health, and chief executive officer of the Brigham and Women's Physician Organization. He is a graduate of Oxford University and of Yale Medical School and Yale Law School. He is past chair of the American Board of Internal Medicine and a member of the Institute of Medicine.

Charles E. Eesley is a doctoral student at the MIT Sloan School of Management, specializing in technological innovation and entrepreneurship. He received his B.S. from Duke University in 2002. During the past two years he has worked for Neurocog Trials and as a research assistant at the Duke University Medical Center, focusing on cognition in schizophrenia and neuroimaging studies. He has also worked at Duke's Fuqua School of Business on research related to business strategy and innovation.

Chris Stern Hyman is a health care lawyer and a mediator. In 1998 she formed Medical Mediation Group LLC with Marc Fleisher, J.D., which provides mediation services to resolve disputes in health care. Medical Mediation Group conducts training and mediates medical malpractice lawsuits and other conflicts arising in health care facilities. Hyman has written on state medical boards' pain management policies and on mediation and health care. She received her undergraduate degree from the University of Chicago and her law degree from Brooklyn Law School. Hyman was coprincipal investigator for the Demonstration Mediation and ADR Project of the Project on Medical Liability in Pennsylvania and principal investigator of the New York City Pilot Project for Mediation of Medical Malpractice Claims, funded by a grant to Columbia Law School.

Peter D. Jacobson is professor of health law and policy in the Department of Health Management and Policy, University of Michigan School of Public Health, and director of the Center for Law, Ethics, and Health. Before coming to Michigan, Jacobson was a senior behavioral scientist at the RAND Corporation in Santa Monica, California. His current research interests focus on the relationship between law and health care delivery and policy, law and public health systems, public health ethics, and health care safety net services. Jacobson's most recent book is *Law and the Health System*, coauthored with Lawrence O. Gostin (Foundation Press, 2005). He is also a coauthor on the forthcoming book *False Hope vs. Evidence-Based Medicine: The Story of a Failed Treatment for Breast Cancer* (Oxford University Press, 2006). Jacobson is currently writing a book on the history of free clinics.

Rogan Kersh is associate professor of political science and public administration at Syracuse University's Maxwell School. He is currently a Fellow at Yale's Rudd Center for Health Policy and Nutrition Politics, where he is completing a book on obesity politics. He has published on health policy in such journals as *Health Affairs*, the *Journal of Health Politics, Policy and Law*, and *Studies in American Political Development*. As a Robert Wood Johnson Scholar in Health Policy, he began a study of health care lobbying that has yielded several articles and will be published in book form in 2007. His extensive political experience includes internships in the U.S. Senate and British Parliament as well as work in the Washington tax policy office of Coopers & Lybrand and think tanks in Washington and Tokyo.

Daniel P. Kessler is a professor at the Stanford University Graduate School of Business, a senior Fellow at the Hoover Institution, and a research associate at the National Bureau of Economic Research. He has a J.D. from Stanford Law School and a Ph.D. in economics from MIT. His research interests include antitrust law, law and economics, and health economics. Among his recent publications are, with Mark McClellan, "The Effect of Hospital Ownership on Medical Productivity" (*RAND Journal of*

Economics) and "Designing Hospital Antitrust Policy to Promote Social Welfare" (*Frontiers in Health Policy Research*). Kessler's current research focuses on the effects of organizational form in health care on the cost and quality of care.

Eleanor D. Kinney is professor of law and codirector of the Center on Law and Health at Indiana University–Indianapolis, where she teaches courses in health law and administrative law. A widely published author and respected lecturer on the subjects of America's health care system, medical malpractice, health coverage for the poor, and issues in administrative law, Professor Kinney recently published *Protecting American Health Care Consumers* (Duke University Press, 2002) and edited the *Guide to Medicare Coverage Decision-Making and Appeals* (ABA Publishing, 2002). She currently chairs the Patient Safety Subcommittee of the Indiana Commission on Excellence in Health Care, as well as the American Bar Association's Section on Administrative Law and Regulatory Practice.

Carol B. Liebman is a clinical professor at Columbia Law School, where she is director of the school's Mediation Clinic and teaches negotiation and professional ethics. She has mediated cases involving discrimination, medical malpractice, family issues, public agencies, community disputes, business conflicts, and educational institutions and is a nationally recognized speaker and trainer in conflict resolution. She has designed and presented mediation training for a variety of groups including the Albert Einstein College of Medicine; Association of the Bar of the City of New York; and high school students, parents, and teachers; she has also taught about negotiation and mediation in Vietnam, Israel, China, and Brazil. Liebman is the author with Nancy Dubler of *Bioethics Mediation: A Guide to Shaping Shared Solutions*, published by the United Hospital Fund. She is also a member of New York City's Civilian Complaint Review Board.

Maxwell J. Mehlman is Arthur E. Petersilge Professor of Law and director of the Law-Medicine Center, Case Western Reserve University School of Law, and professor of biomedical ethics at Case Western's School of Medicine. He received his J.D. from Yale Law School in 1975 and holds bachelors degrees from Reed College and Oxford, which he attended as a Rhodes Scholar. Prior to joining the faculty at CWRU in 1984, Professor Mehlman practiced law with Arnold & Porter in Washington, D.C., where he specialized in federal regulation of health care and medical technology. Professor Mehlman served from 1987 to 1990 as a member of the Committee to Design a Strategy for Quality Review and Assurance in Medicare of the Institute of Medicine National Academy of Sciences. From 1988 to 1994, he served as special counsel to the Special Committee on Medical Malpractice of the New York State Bar. In 1992, he was a consultant on medical malpractice to the American Association of Retired Persons. He recently served as an advisor and a researcher on the Project on Medical Liability in Pennsylvania of The Pew Charitable Trusts.

Michelle M. Mello conducts empirical research into issues at the intersection of law, ethics, and health policy. She is the author of more than fifty articles and book chapters on the medical malpractice system, medical errors and patient safety, research ethics, mass tort litigation, the obesity epidemic, pharmaceuticals, bioethics, and other topics. Recent projects include an analysis of the efficacy and fairness of leading medical malpractice reforms, a study of legal relationships between academic investigators and industry sponsors of clinical trials, and an analysis of patient safety regulation. Dr. Mello is presently studying ethical issues in the pharmaceutical industry as a Greenwall Faculty Scholar. She teaches courses in Public Health Law and the Ethical Basis of the Practice of Public Health at the Harvard School of Public Health.

Mark V. Pauly is Bendheim Professor at the Wharton School of Management, University of Pennsylvania, where he is also professor of Health Care Systems, Business and Public Policy, Insurance and Risk Management, and Economics. Pauly is a widely respected expert on medical economics, health policy, health and other insurance, public finance/public choice, and regulation; among his recent publications are *Health Benefits at Work* (Michigan, 1997) and *Pooling Health Insurance Risks* (AEI Press, 1999, with B. Herring). He has served in an advisory capacity to the National Advisory Council, Agency for Healthcare Research and Quality; Committee on Evaluation of Vaccine Purchase Financing in the U.S., Institute of Medicine/National Academy of Sciences; and the Medicare Technical Advisory Panel. Pauly is currently on the editorial board of *Public Finance Quarterly*, advisory editor of the *Journal of Risk and Uncertainty*, and coeditor of the *International Journal of Health Care Finance and Economics*.

William M. Sage received his medical and law degrees with honors from Stanford University in 1988 and has been a member of the faculty of Columbia Law School since 1995. In 1993, he headed four working groups of the President's Task Force on Health Care Reform in the Clinton White House. He recently served as principal investigator for the Project on Medical Liability in Pennsylvania. He is also the recipient of an Investigator Award in Health Policy Research from the Robert Wood Johnson Foundation, and he has published more than sixty articles in legal, health policy, and clinical journals. He is an elected Fellow of the Hastings Center on bioethics and is a member of the editorial board of *Health Affairs*.

Catherine M. Sharkey is an associate professor at Columbia Law School. She teaches, researches, and writes in the areas of torts, punitive damages, class actions, remedies, and product liability. Her articles have been published in the *Journal of Empirical Legal Studies, Maryland Law Review, New York*

University Law Review, *Texas Law Review*, *UCLA Law Review*, and *Yale Law Journal*. Sharkey received her B.A. in economics, *summa cum laude*, from Yale, her M.Sc. in economics for development, with distinction, from Oxford, where she was a Rhodes Scholar, and her J.D. from Yale Law School, where she was executive editor of the *Yale Law Journal*. She served as a law clerk to the Hon. Guido Calabresi of the U.S. Court of Appeals for the Second Circuit and to the Hon. David H. Souter of the U.S. Supreme Court.

Frank A. Sloan is the J. Alexander McMahon Professor of Health Policy and Management and professor of economics at Duke, where he is also director of the Center for Health Policy, Law, and Management. Sloan did his undergraduate work at Oberlin and received his Ph.D. in economics from Harvard. Before joining the faculty at Duke in July, 1993, he was a research economist at the RAND Corporation and on the faculties of the University of Florida and Vanderbilt University. He was chair of the Department of Economics at Vanderbilt from 1986 to 1989. His current research interests include alcohol use prevention, long-term care, medical malpractice, and cost-effectiveness analyses of medical technologies. Sloan also has a long-standing interest in hospitals, health care financing, and health manpower. He has served on several national advisory public and private groups. He is a member of the Institute of Medicine of the National Academy of Sciences and was recently a member of the Physician Payment Review Commission.

Catherine T. Struve is a professor of law at the University of Pennsylvania Law School. In addition to studying procedural reforms in the context of medical liability litigation, she has analyzed similar issues with respect to product liability claims concerning FDA-approved pharmaceuticals. She serves as co-reporter to a task force preparing model jury instructions for use in civil cases within the Third Circuit, and her current research explores the effect of jury procedures and instructions on the functioning of the civil justice system.

David M. Studdert is associate professor of law and public health at the Harvard School of Public Health, where he teaches courses in health law and medical ethics. His research focuses on legal and regulatory issues in the health care sector. He holds degrees in law, public health, and health policy. Before joining the public health school faculty, he held positions as a policy analyst at RAND, a policy advisor to the Minister for Health in Victoria, Australia, and a practicing attorney. In 2004, Studdert received the Alice S. Hersh New Investigator Award from AcademyHealth.

Introduction

William M. Sage and Rogan Kersh

With the United States embroiled in its third major medical malpractice crisis in the past thirty years, this volume brings together an array of experts from law, medicine, social science, and business to explore the public policy of medical liability. As malpractice premiums continue to rise, doctors and lawyers engage in bitter debates across the country, and legislators struggle to comprehend and consider a myriad of proposed medical liability reforms, this volume provides an explanation of malpractice policy past and present – and a set of promising paths forward.

The major failing of the current debate over malpractice reform is that it ignores the relationship between medical malpractice policy and core characteristics of American health care. For reasons both deliberate and circumstantial that this book describes, conventional approaches to medical liability barely pay lip service to the persistent inequities of access to health care and health insurance in the United States, to the recent revelation of serious safety and quality problems in medical "systems," or to the decades-long battle being waged against rising public and private health care expenditures. Yet these forces are largely responsible for the severity of the current malpractice crisis and point the way to solutions far more promising than the measures – little changed since the 1970s – on which malpractice reformers and their opponents both fixate. The authors' collective purpose is to close the gap between malpractice policy and health policy.

The book encapsulates and extends a substantial body of empirical research and expert analysis funded by The Pew Charitable Trusts. The Project on Medical Liability in Pennsylvania (www.medliabilitypa.org) is a program of research, consultation, and communication that seeks to provide decision makers with objective information about the ways in which medical, legal, and insurance-related issues affect the medical liability system; broaden participation in the debate to include new constituencies and perspectives; and focus attention on the relationship between medical liability and overall health and economic prosperity. The Project was commissioned by The Pew Trusts in 2002 in response to a contentious and accusatory political debate – conducted primarily through mass media campaigns – between physicians and trial lawyers over proposed legislative reform in Pennsylvania.

The Pew Trusts hoped that accurate information from a neutral source would help public officials, health professionals, patients, and citizens find their way past harsh anecdotes and partisan rhetoric to sound policy solutions. The Pew Trusts selected Columbia Law School to oversee the Project, with Professor William Sage, M.D., J.D., as principal investigator. Over the next three years, the Project's researchers produced eight reports and published approximately twenty articles in professional journals arrayed across academic disciplines and research methodologies. The unifying themes of the Project's work, captured in this volume, were to identify ongoing trends in American health care that alter the public policy impact of medical liability and to connect malpractice reform to measurable improvement in the experiences of those who provide and receive health services.

PART ONE: FRAMING MEDICAL MALPRACTICE AS A
HEALTH POLICY ISSUE

The book's three opening chapters introduce medical malpractice as a health policy concern. Two chapters – one by Michelle Mello and David Studdert and the other by William Sage – provide a sound theoretical and factual basis for assessing malpractice reform. They explain the three components of the malpractice system: liability insurance markets, legal processes for filing claims and resolving disputes, and the patient safety aspects of health care financing and delivery. They also attest to a foundational truth about the present malpractice regime: The current insurance crisis reflects modern medicine's successes far more than its failures.

To complete the introduction, Rogan Kersh's chapter approaches malpractice as an explicitly political topic, an unusual angle in contemporary studies of the subject. Malpractice is part of a "new politics of health care," the author argues, comparing it to other long-private health topics thought to be off limits to government regulation. An uneasy public/private tension continues to mark malpractice politics today, along with other characteristics that bring into clearer focus both the intensity of the ongoing malpractice debate and the recurring failure of Congress to pass malpractice reform at the federal level.

PART TWO: THE HEALTH POLICY IMPACT OF
MEDICAL MALPRACTICE

Mark Pauly's chapter opens the discussion of malpractice's policy impact by asking the deceptively simple question, "who pays when malpractice premiums rise?" Although much debate during the present crisis is framed around the financial pain experienced by physicians (and, to a lesser extent, hospitals and other medical institutions), Pauly finds that patients, consumers, and taxpayers still bear most of the cost of rising premiums. Pauly utilizes both theoretical and empirical approaches to reach this compelling conclusion.

David Becker and Daniel Kessler also proceed from a vital question: What are the medical liability system's effects on cost and quality of health care? Their contribution summarizes the massive body of research generated over the past three decades, then focuses on a specific reform: liability protection for quality improvement initiatives and for physicians who comply with clinical practice guidelines. These innovations, the authors conclude, are a promising source of reduced health care costs and improved quality.

Michelle Mello and David Studdert, joined by Troyen Brennan, return in the book's sixth chapter with a comprehensive analysis of current trends in medical safety enhancement and liability reform. Combining literature review and original empirical research, this trio of experts concludes that, of the different state approaches to compensate and deter injuries arising from medical errors or negligence, perhaps the most rational is increased reporting of adverse events to public authorities and disclosure to patients. Yet this route is likely to increase malpractice claim frequency and therefore raise premiums for physician and hospital liability insurance.

A vitally important influence on malpractice policy – indeed, on U.S. health policy in general – is medical technology. Peter Jacobson's tightly focused chapter examines the short- and long-term effects of technological innovations on medical liability and the reciprocal effects of liability on technology. His grim but persuasive conclusion: Society's insatiable demand for technological innovation will inevitably continue to affect physicians' liability exposure, all but ensuring further cycles of malpractice crisis unless a more explicit public debate occurs.

PART THREE: MALPRACTICE REFORMS THAT SOLVE
THE RIGHT PROBLEMS

The macro-level intransigence of American health policy that emerges from the preceding chapters meets its match in the form of potentially workable smaller-scale malpractice reforms described in the book's third part. Maxwell Mehlman's important transitional chapter uses a key health policy construct, fairness, to shift the book's tone from problem to solution and to guide the reader through the complex landscape of proposed malpractice reforms. Melhman demonstrates that the traditional malpractice system performs poorly on most measures of procedural and substantive failure and evaluates a range of proposed changes.

Caps on damages for "pain and suffering" in malpractice cases have been a holy grail for physicians and other stakeholders since the 1970s malpractice crisis. California's Medical Injury Compensation Reform Act (MICRA), adopted in 1975, served as the model for legislative responses to the crisis of the 1980s and remains the primary focus of today's tort reformers. Opponents of noneconomic damage caps often question the relationship between tort reform and liability insurance premiums. Catherine Sharkey's chapter evaluates the debate over damage caps from an unusual angle: She hypothesizes that, in an environment of rising yet unpredictable health care spending, limiting noneconomic damages might increase the *economic* component of compensatory awards. Sharkey's analysis indeed suggests a "crossover" effect, whereby judges and juries boost economic damage awards to make up for capped noneconomic damages.

Catherine Struve's chapter, like Mehlman's, develops the sprawling landscape of malpractice reform along a single principle, in her case expertise. Struve investigates proposals to improve the ability of malpractice decision makers to evaluate medical mishaps. Expertise-enhancing reforms such as certificates of merit, screening panels, and medical courts often find favor among physicians because they purport to return control over the determination of misconduct to the medical profession. Struve criticizes these reforms for oversimplifying the malpractice problem and points out their operational complexities. She concludes, however, that expertise rightly deployed could improve both patient safety and compensation for injury and offers feasible suggestions for modifying the litigation process – such as jury education, expert witness reform, and a modified standard for remittitur – that could yield substantial dividends in accuracy and consistency of outcomes.

Carol Liebman and Chris Stern Hyman bring patients – the obvious link between malpractice policy and health policy – into the reform equation by presenting the results of a demonstration project to improve information flow surrounding the occurrence of medical errors. Their approach emphasizes immediate disclosure, apology when appropriate, and early mediation of disputes. Because most health care professionals will only experience medical errors occasionally, Liebman and Hyman urge hospitals to train error consult teams that can provide advice and assistance in difficult circumstances. As Liebman and Hyman note, most malpractice reforms require legislative approval; their alternative dispute resolution program is open to immediate implementation by hospitals.

PART FOUR: IN SEARCH OF A "NEW PARADIGM"

The book's concluding section considers more sweeping malpractice reforms, which have attracted widespread interest in the academic community but have found scant support among politicians and organized interest groups.

Randall Bovbjerg and Robert Berenson examine one such approach: assigning health plans, hospitals, and other health care institutions greater responsibility for avoiding and compensating medical injuries. The authors find enterprise liability to have been a promising project in the early 1990s but conclude that changes in market trends and governmental policy have rendered enterprise liability, especially if applied to health plans, less appealing as a widespread reform.

Free market advocates often favor voluntary private bargaining over one-size-fits-all rules such as the "standard of care" applied to professional negligence. Jennifer Arlen's study of contractual alternatives to the existing malpractice regime builds on preceding chapters' discussions of information, evaluating the legal and political implications of allowing health care providers and patients to modify or opt out of medical malpractice law. Working from within the law and economics perspective, Arlen reaches a surprising conclusion given that school of thought's usual recommendations. Contractual liability is not necessarily better than tort liability, she reasons, because health care providers who expect customers to waive their tort rights will underinvest in acquiring expertise that can make all patients safer.

Comprehensive approaches to malpractice reform require novel approaches to financial risk-bearing as well as to patient safety and compensation for injury. Noting that all three modern medical malpractice crises were triggered by sharp increases in medical liability insurance premiums, Tom Baker reminds us that malpractice is an insurance problem first and foremost and argues that tort reforms are an incomplete and inefficient response. His "insurance solution" reprises Bovbjerg and Berenson's discussion with a twist. Instead of enterprise liability, Baker favors "enterprise insurance" and sets out the details of this innovative proposal.

The periodic failure of private liability insurance markets raises an obvious question: Should government supplement or supplant commercial malpractice insurance with public coverage? A comprehensive response comes in Frank Sloan and Charles Eesley's chapter. Ranging across both recent history and states' diverse experiences with malpractice insurance, the authors examine direct government provision of malpractice coverage and explore the connection between such coverage and systematic medical liability reforms. Although public provision of insurance can advance the public interest, the authors note, success is predicated above all on program design. A poorly structured program of public insurance may be worse than no program at all.

A concluding chapter by William Sage and Eleanor Kinney proposes a novel fusion of health policy and malpractice policy: having Medicare take the lead on malpractice reform. Noting the centrality of Medicare policy (and Medicare politics) to the structure and financing of American health care, and the limited recourse to litigation for elderly victims of medical error in the current regime, Sage and Kinney urge the federal government to sponsor demonstration projects of comprehensive malpractice reform in selected hospitals and physician organizations. Their proposed Medicare demonstrations, which are similar to state-based reforms recommended by the Institute of Medicine (IOM) in 2002, emphasize patient safety, error disclosure, mediation, timely compensation for avoidable injury, and "no-trial" resolution of disputed cases using an administrative system similar to the one that Medicare already employs for benefits determinations.

AFTER THE MALPRACTICE CRISIS

Surgeons have a saying: "All bleeding stops." Less certain is the patient's condition when it stops. This book is intended as a long-term treatment plan for the medical liability system, not merely a postmortem on the first malpractice crisis of the twenty-first century. Indeed, as the "insurance cycle" returns liability carriers to nominal profitability and legislative energy is diverted elsewhere, many will claim that the crisis is over. This is not surprising. But turning a temporary corner says little about the overall condition of the liability system or about the core public health components of access, cost, and quality of health care that both influence and are influenced by liability. The goal of this book is to evaluate that condition, confirm or revise the original diagnosis of crisis, and recommend preventive measures to avoid a relapse, or at least reduce its severity should one occur.

Of the many lessons emerging from the book's analysis, four bear additional comment. Three involve distinctions current malpractice policy fails to make; the fourth involves distinctions it makes but probably should not. First, malpractice insurers and legal counsel treat patient-claimants no differently from any other adversary; in a word, as strangers. Recognizing the special character of the therapeutic relationship by encouraging honesty, open communication, compassion, and provision for needs can help patients, families, and health care providers. It can also improve patient care and, yes, reduce litigation. Second, malpractice politics increasingly has become captive to the politics of general tort reform. As a result, each malpractice crisis becomes a referendum on trial lawyers, and opportunities to improve the malpractice system for both physicians and patients are missed because they do not confer partisan advantage in the larger fight.

Third, conventional malpractice reform treats all physicians (and hospitals) as if they have the same current competence and the same capacity for improvement. Decades of research on small-area variations and patient safety – what the IOM labels the "quality chasm" – reveal major differences in how medical practice is organized and performs. Rather than serving the lowest common denominator, an important option for reformers is to create a more responsive malpractice system for providers able to succeed in it, while offering incentives for the rest to perform to the same level. Fourth, liability insurance markets must be included in malpractice reform. Practices such as rating physicians based solely on specialty and practice location perpetuate small risk pools and accentuate downturns of the insurance cycle in today's collaborative, industrialized health care system. This invites periodic crises by rendering the system vulnerable even when the diversified, aggregate risk it poses would be manageable.

ACKNOWLEDGMENTS

We extend heartfelt thanks to The Pew Charitable Trusts for sponsoring the Project on Medical Liability in Pennsylvania, which literally made this volume possible. We are particularly grateful to the following Pew Trusts leaders: Rebecca Rimel, president and CEO; Donald Kimelman, director, Information Initiatives; Sue Urahn, director, Policy Initiatives and the Education Program; Lori Grange and Lawrence White, program officers; and Cindy Jobbins, public affairs associate.

Within Pennsylvania, which was the primary focus of the Pew Project, our profound thanks go to a long roster of willing guides. In particular, we thank Rosemarie Greco, director of the Office of Health Care Reform; Robert Muscalus, D.O., former physician general; Carolyn Scanlan and Jim Redmond from the Hospital and Healthcare Association of Pennsylvania; Roger Mecum and Elizabeth Metz from the Pennsylvania Medical Society; Andrew Wigglesworth from the Delaware Valley Hospital Council; Clifford Rieders and Mark Phenicie from the Pennsylvania Trial Lawyers Association; the members and staff of the Joint State Government Commission; the members and staff of Governor Edward Rendell's Task Force on Medical Liability; and the members and staff of the Pennsylvania legislature. We are also indebted to many others, too numerous to name, who so generously gave of their time and expertise to help us outline the dimensions, complexities, and possible solutions to the medical liability crisis in Pennsylvania.

At Cambridge University Press, Ed Parsons was the model of an engaged editor, politely overlooking missed deadlines while shepherding the book to its timely completion. Much appreciation to him and to Faith Black, editorial assistant extraordinaire, as well as to Katie Greczylo, who kept the production process moving along.

Other aiders and abettors of this book deserve a grateful salute as well. They include Barbara Beck of Sage Communications, Inc.; Michael Nardone; Anna Bartow, M.D., J.D.; Karen Miller, David Thornburgh, and LeeAnne Rogers at the Pennsylvania Economy League; Susan Liss, Esq., executive director of the Project on Medical Liability in Pennsylvania; and Deans David

Leebron and David Schizer and assistants Julie Poll Blitzer and Mirlande Mersier at Columbia Law School. Our thanks also to a superb team of research assistants, without whom this book would be far more factually challenged: Marco Castillo, Nathaniel Becker Chase, Caitlin Friedemann, Ari Greenberg, Erin Hurley, Rebecca Levin, Jodie Ralston, and Elizabeth Schloesser.

ONE

FRAMING MEDICAL MALPRACTICE AS A HEALTH POLICY ISSUE

I

The Medical Malpractice System

Structure and Performance

Michelle M. Mello and David M. Studdert

Few aspects of American law provoke as impassioned a public debate as medical liability. Physicians, insurers, lawyers, consumer groups, and politicians frequently clash over the effectiveness, fairness, and costs of the medical liability system, with the din reaching a crescendo during periods of "malpractice crisis." Notwithstanding the high degree of civic engagement on this issue, evidence suggests that the medical liability system and its effects on health care are not well understood by the public. In a recent poll, a majority of respondents expressed a belief that malpractice suits were effective in preventing medical errors and making doctors take better care of their patients, but a majority also felt that too many lawsuits were brought and that providers' liability should be limited.[1]

This snapshot of public opinion nicely captures the cognitive dissonance about the malpractice system that characterizes the broader policy debate about tort reform. It also illuminates the need for empirically informed analyses of the system and its performance. In this chapter, we describe the structure of the medical liability system – what happens when a lawsuit is filed, what the system costs, and where the money comes from. We then review the best available evidence on how well the system performs its primary functions of compensation, deterrence, and corrective justice and how it affects the way health care is delivered in the United States.

STRUCTURE OF THE AMERICAN MEDICAL LIABILITY SYSTEM

The Litigation Process

American medical malpractice law revolves around the concept of negligence. A plaintiff in a malpractice case has the burden of proving by a

Portions of this chapter are reprinted from Mello and Brennan 2002.
[1] Kaiser Family Foundation 2003.

preponderance of the evidence that (1) the relationship between the plaintiff-patient and the defendant-physician gave rise to a duty, (2) the defendant-physician was negligent – meaning that her care fell below the standard expected of a reasonable medical practitioner, (3) the plaintiff-patient suffered an injury, and (4) the injury was caused by the defendant-physician's negligence. Medical malpractice is a matter of state law, and some differences in the standard of care exist across states. Traditionally, the standard of care in a medical malpractice case has been based on customary medical practice. Now, however, many states are moving to a more objective "reasonable prudence" standard. The standard of care in an informed consent case varies across states: In most jurisdictions, the scope of a physician's duty to inform patients about material risks associated with proposed treatments is defined by what a reasonable physician would disclose, but a minority of states have moved to a patient-based standard, requiring physicians to disclose all risks that a reasonable patient would expect to be told before undergoing the treatment.[2]

Physicians are the primary targets of malpractice claims. Although the law in most states provides that physicians and health care facilities may be jointly and severally liable for medical malpractice, in practice, individual physicians are the central defendants in a majority of claims. Health care organizations are frequently named as codefendants, but the circumstances in which a hospital or other organization will itself be held liable are quite limited. Courts have generally limited theories of "corporate negligence" to cases in which the hospital acted negligently in its performance of certain oversight responsibilities, such as making staff credentialing decisions or setting staffing levels.

A more common basis for claims against hospitals, clinics, and other health care institutions is the allegation that they are indirectly (or "vicariously") liable for the acts of their employees. Institutions may also face vicarious liability for the acts of physicians who are affiliated with but not employed by the institution if the institution exerts a degree of control over the care or practice environment at issue in the claim. The latter form of vicarious liability is particularly salient because many physicians operate as independent contractors rather than employees of hospitals.

Each defendant in a malpractice case is responsible for arranging for his or her own defense. Multiple defense attorneys therefore may be involved and may mount separate defenses. Each is paid by the defendant he or she represents (typically, through the client's malpractice insurance), and legal costs are not reimbursed if the defendant prevails in the case. Plaintiffs retain their own private attorneys, generally through contingency-fee

---

[2] Brennan 1991.

arrangements, in which the attorney receives a proportion of any damages recovered (up to 40% of the award). Because the plaintiff's attorney receives nothing if the case is resolved in the defendant's favor, he has a theoretical incentive to screen potential cases and accept only those that have a high probability of resulting in a payout that exceeds the attorney's litigation costs.

Obtaining a reliable estimate of the number of malpractice claims brought nationwide each year is difficult, as there is no centralized repository of information on all filed claims. A reasonable estimate is probably in the 50,000 to 60,000 range.[3] Available figures suggest that approximately 70 percent of malpractice claims do not reach trial. Those that do are heard by a jury, although plaintiffs may choose to waive their constitutional right to a jury. Plaintiffs prevail in approximately 30 percent of trials. Considering settlements and verdicts together, about 30 percent of all claims are closed with a payment to the plaintiff.[4]

The average payout among paid claims is also difficult to pinpoint, but hovered somewhere in the $260,000 to $310,000 range in 2003.[5] Multiplying by the estimated number of claims nationally, we estimate total annual outlays on compensation at approximately $5.8 billion nationwide. This is less than 0.3 percent of the $1.7 trillion in total health spending in 2003. When administrative costs are included, the total costs rise considerably, but still represent a tiny fraction – less than 1 percent – of the total amount spent on health care in the United States. Some commentators and policy makers argue that the sum of compensation and administrative costs still underestimates the costs of the medical liability system because the costs of defensive medicine – that is, additional services of marginal or no medical value motivated primarily by liability pressures – are not included. Published estimates of such "shadow" costs range as high as $15 billion in 1991 dollars,[6] potentially pushing total system costs as high as 1.5 percent of health care spending, but the methods used to derive these estimates of systemwide defensive medicine costs are weak.[7]

Insurance Arrangements

Most physicians are required by law to carry professional liability insurance. Except for those who are directly employed by a hospital or health plan,

[3] Studdert et al. 2006.
[4] Stevenson and Studdert 2003.
[5] National Practitioner Data Bank 2004; Smarr 2003.
[6] R. Rubin and Mendelson 1994, 7–15.
[7] U.S. Congress, Office of Technology Assessment 1994; U.S. General Accounting Office 2003a; Studdert, Mello, and Brennan 2004, 283–92.

physicians obtain and pay for their own insurance. A standard primary-layer physician insurance policy provides $1 million in coverage per incident, up to a maximum of $3 million per year. Hospitals have separate insurance, and many choose self-insurance arrangements. Both physicians and hospitals may opt to supplement their primary-layer policies with excess-layer insurance, which covers them in the event of a judgment that exceeds their policy limits. In recent years, excess-layer insurance has become increasingly important to physicians and hospitals, due to rising awards, but also much more expensive and thus less prevalent.

Historically the professional liability insurance market was dominated by commercial carriers, but the past thirty years have witnessed the ascendance of physician-owned mutual insurance companies. The past five years in particular – a time of "malpractice crisis" – have seen the retreat of some of the major commercial carriers, who no longer find malpractice to be a profitable line of business. In their place, new organizational forms created by health care providers have emerged, including new mutuals, captive insurers, and risk retention groups.[8]

Malpractice insurance premiums reflect the degree of risk involved in the provider's specialty or subspecialty as well as expected litigation costs in the local area in which the provider is located. The degree of experience rating (the degree to which premiums vary according to the insured's claims experience) is lower in malpractice insurance than in other forms of insurance, such as automobile insurance.[9] Hospital insurance premiums are frequently experience rated to some degree (up to 20–25% above or below the average premium). Physician insurers consider it infeasible to individually experience rate their subscribers. Physicians are sued too infrequently, and their claims experience varies too much over each three- or five-year period, to make experience rating actuarially feasible. A few states and many major insurers have experimented with experience rating for physicians but have generally found it to be unworkable. Insurers found that instead of being chastened by the imposition of higher premiums, physicians tend to simply switch to another carrier if one is available.[10]

Unlike health or automobile insurance, malpractice insurance usually does not impose deductibles or copayments on insureds. Primary-layer policies generally provide first-dollar coverage up to the policy limits. In some states, secondary-layer coverage is provided by a state-run patient compensation

---

[8] Mello, Kelly, et al. 2003, 225–33. A mutual insurance company is an entity owned by policy-holders rather than investors. A risk retention group is a corporation or other limited liability association established under federal law for the purpose of pooling risk among a group of member-owners who are all in the same line of business. A captive also insures member-owners in a common line of business but may be formed by a single institution (for example, a teaching hospital) and is often incorporated offshore.

[9] Danzon 2000, 1341–404, 1360.

[10] Sloan 1990, 128–33.

fund, into which providers contribute an annual premium based on their location, specialty, and range of services provided.

PERFORMANCE OF THE SYSTEM

There are a number of criteria on which the performance of the medical liability system can be evaluated. First, how well does it direct compensation toward its intended beneficiaries, patients injured because of negligence? Second, how effective is it in deterring health care providers from rendering substandard care – in other words, sending a signal that such care will result in the economic and psychological costs of litigation? Third, does it fulfill a meaningful "corrective justice" function, giving injured patients and their families an opportunity to exact restitution and retribution from those who have wronged them? Fourth, how efficient is the system, in terms of minimizing transaction costs and avoiding waste? Finally, what collateral effects does the system have on health care providers and the quality of care? We consider each of these criteria in turn.

Compensation

An optimal liability system would provide fair compensation to a high proportion of patients injured by negligence.[11] It would provide no compensation to patients who lacked a cognizable injury or whose injury was not attributable to negligence. The optimal system should erect no substantial obstacles in the path of those injured by negligence, either in terms of deterring them from claiming or in failing to respond to their claim with an appropriate damages award. It should contain some mechanism for screening out nonmeritorious claims, either at the point of adjudication or (preferably) at the point of initiating the claim.

A body of evidence from three major studies demonstrates that the actual functioning of the system departs significantly from this model. In the mid-1970s, at the height of the tort crisis in California, the California Medical Association sponsored a study of the costs of medical injuries.[12] The investigators asked nurses and then physicians to review nearly 21,000 medical records in twenty-three California hospitals and identify patients who had suffered an iatrogenic injury. Raters also evaluated the likelihood of a jury finding of liability. They determined that 4.65 percent of people

---

[11] Some might argue it should compensate all such patients, but allowances should be made for the preferences of some patients who, despite their understanding that they were injured because of substandard care, opt not to sue because of a personal feeling that their provider should not be held responsible for the lapse. In addition, some would argue that in cases of relatively minor injury, from a societal perspective, the transaction costs associated with delivering compensation outweigh the benefits of the compensation.

[12] Mills et al. 1977.

hospitalized suffered an adverse event and that 0.79 percent suffered an adverse event for which the provider would likely be found liable. Patricia Danzon matched the California data on adverse events with malpractice claims data from the National Association of Insurance Commissioners' survey of claims closed by private insurers from July 1975 to December 1978.[13] She found that only about 10 percent of the victims of negligent injuries filed a malpractice claim. Furthermore, of these claims, only 40 percent resulted in a payment to the plaintiff. Thus, the overall ratio of paid claims to injuries in the Danzon study was 0.039. In other words, in this sample, a physician who committed an error leading to injury had only a 4 percent chance of having to compensate the patient.

A second study was conducted in New York in the 1980s. The Harvard Medical Practice Study (HMPS) was modeled after the California study but involved a more comprehensive review of malpractice claims. The investigators undertook a review of 30,000 medical records while concurrently evaluating more than 67,000 litigation records held by the New York Department of Health and conducting in-depth reviews of 3,500 claims. The study estimated that 3.7 percent of New Yorkers suffered adverse events and 1 percent suffered adverse events due to negligence.[14]

As in California, the researchers found a poor fit between negligent injuries and claims in the New York sample. The total number of malpractice claims filed was about 14 percent of the total number of negligent injuries.[15] However, this figure masks the tiny overlap between the group of patients injured by negligence and the group who brought suit: Less than 2 percent of persons injured because of negligence filed a claim, and only about a sixth of the claims that were filed involved both negligence and a cognizable injury.

Subsequently, a subgroup of the investigators undertook a validation study in Utah and Colorado. Using data from twenty-eight hospitals from the early 1990s, they found rates of medical injuries and negligence that were quite similar to the New York findings, although there were many fewer deaths due to the negligent injuries. They determined that adverse events occurred in about 3 percent of all hospitalizations, and that 33 percent and 27 percent of adverse events were due to negligence in Utah and Colorado, respectively.[16] Thus, about 1 percent of hospitalizations involved a negligent injury. Matching these data against records of malpractice claims filed through 1996 relating to incidents from 1992 showed that only 2.5 percent of the patients who were injured because of negligence filed a malpractice

---

[13] Danzon 1985.
[14] Brennan 1991, 370–6.
[15] Localio et al. 1991, 245–51.
[16] Thomas et al. 2000, 261–71.

claim.[17] In total, the group of patients represented in the sample of medical records reviewed for adverse events filed eighteen malpractice claims. Fourteen of these claims were found not to involve negligence and ten involved no cognizable injury. Only four claims (22%) actually involved a negligent injury.

These studies show that the system does not perform well either in compensating eligible patients or in avoiding claims by those who are not eligible. Evidence regarding the system's accuracy in sorting meritorious from nonmeritorious claims once filed, in terms of directing compensation to appropriate plaintiffs, is mixed but somewhat more encouraging. When the HMPS investigators tracked the disposition of the forty-six claims closed within a ten-year period, they found that ten of the twenty-four cases that expert reviewers judged to have no evidence of an adverse event resulted in a payoff to the plaintiff (mean payment $28,760), as did six of thirteen cases judged to involve an adverse event but not negligence (mean payment $98,132). Conversely, four of the nine cases judged to involve negligent injuries resulted in no payoff to the plaintiff. In a multivariate analysis, the severity of the plaintiff's injury was a much stronger predictor of the outcome than negligence,[18] but the negative finding regarding negligence must be interpreted with caution because the small number of claims included in the analysis limits the statistical power of the model to detect a relationship. The Utah/Colorado study did not examine payoff amounts and their correlation with negligence. At least one other study has also found a weak relationship between negligence and compensation,[19] but others have found more encouraging results.[20] Overall, however, the weight of the evidence points to a liability system that is deeply flawed in terms of its ability to direct compensation to its intended beneficiaries.

Deterrence

Deterrence is the primary theoretical rationale for the tort liability system.[21] If compensation were the only objective, there would be much more straightforward and less costly ways of delivering it than tort litigation.[22] The appeal of the tort approach is that the threatened costs of litigation, both economic and psychological, will create an incentive to take safety precautions. In a world of perfect deterrence, there would be no negligence in medicine. Iatrogenic injuries would still occur, but only those due to circumstances that could not be prevented by taking reasonable care. In economic terms,

---

[17] Studdert and Brennan 2000b, 250–60.
[18] Brennan et al. 1996, 1963–7.
[19] Cheney et al. 1989, 1599–603.
[20] Taragin et al. 1992, 780–4; Vidmar 1995; Sloan 1990, 997–1039; White 1994, 75–87.
[21] G. Schwartz 1994, 377–8.
[22] Danzon 2000, 1343.

injuries would only occur where the marginal cost of the precautions necessary to prevent them exceeds the marginal benefit in terms of reduction of injury-related costs.[23]

This theory rests on several assumptions. First, it assumes that health care providers understand what the law requires of them, in terms of precaution taking. Second, it assumes that providers are rational actors who determine their optimal level of precaution taking on the basis of a careful weighing of the risks, costs, and benefits of the various alternatives. Third, it assumes that providers actually internalize a significant proportion of the costs of their own negligence – an assumption called into question by the inaccuracy and insufficiency of claiming and the prevalence of liability insurance among physicians and hospitals.

There is little evidence to suggest that the system actually deters negligence in medicine or improves the quality of care. In obstetric care, the best-studied field, research has failed to identify any differences in the quality of care rendered by obstetricians with varying histories of malpractice claims. A review of obstetric-care medical records for sentinel markers of errors and other indicators of substandard care found no relationship between the provider having been "punished" by the malpractice system and having fewer future deviations from the standard of care.[24] Other studies examined the effect of malpractice threat on a range of birth outcomes and found no systematic improvement in any of the outcomes associated with a physician's prior claims experience.[25]

Studies have also been conducted of the relationship between physicians' past malpractice claims experience and their chances of being sued again.[26] It is tempting to view these as deterrence studies because a positive finding would suggest that the experience of being punished for negligence reduces the likelihood of further negligence. However, the deterrence question cannot be answered by these studies for two reasons. First, because only a tiny fraction of patients injured because of negligence file a claim, an absence of lawsuits against a physician does not imply an absence of negligence, only the absence of a claim. Second, it might be the case that physicians' perceived malpractice risk exerts a stronger influence on their practice behavior than their actual claims experience. If so, then studies that focus on the actual claims experience rather than perceived litigation risk as the variable of interest may miss the mark.

Perhaps the most thorough deterrence analysis to date is that performed as part of the HMPS. The investigators undertook a relatively sophisticated econometric analysis of the association between a hospital's past claims

[23] Ibid.
[24] Entman et al. 1994, 1588–91.
[25] Sloan et al. 1995, 700–14; Dubay et al. 1999, 491–522.
[26] Taragin et al. 1995, 550–6.

experience and its current patterns of care and adverse events rates. They determined that hospitals facing the highest tort risk had per-patient hospital care costs that were higher than the statewide average, whereas hospitals with the lowest tort risk had significantly lower per-patient costs, suggesting a deterrent effect. However, when other measures of the impact of tort risk on medical practice were tested, the result proved unstable. Although the variable representing malpractice risk was negatively associated with the proportion of hospitalizations involving adverse events and the proportion of adverse events involving negligence, the association did not achieve statistical significance at the conventional level. The HMPS investigators struggled with how to interpret these results and ultimately settled on this conclusion: "Although we did observe the hypothesized relationship in our sample – the more tort claims, the fewer negligent injuries – we cannot exclude the possibility that this relationship was coincidental rather than causal."[27]

The lack of robustness of the estimates of deterrence is a critical issue. The one HMPS model that did show a pronounced deterrent effect used measures of the intensity of services provided as the dependent variable. Increased per capita quantity or cost of services does not necessarily reflect better quality care or lower error rates, however. It may reflect one or more different phenomena: (1) increased ordering of services that are not medically necessary (defensive medicine), (2) ordering of services that are medically indicated and improve the overall quality of care but do not effect a reduction in the number of adverse events, (3) ordering of services that do reduce the number of adverse events (deterrence), or (4) ordering of services necessitated by an adverse event. Of these, only the third possibility is an indicator of deterrence.

Recognizing the limitations of the initial HMPS analysis, a different subgroup of the investigators later took a second stab at modeling deterrence, incorporating more sophisticated measures of deterrence. They ran a number of different models, which again produced mixed results. A statistically significant negative association (i.e., a deterrent effect) was found for a model using the number of claims against the hospital per 1,000 discharges as the malpractice-risk measure and the number of adverse events per 100 hospitalizations as the outcome variable. However, none of the other models evinced a statistically significant deterrent effect. In the end, the investigators were unable to agree on which of the several models was correctly specified or on how to interpret the group of results as a whole. As a result, the findings were not submitted for publication.

The overall picture that emerges from the existing studies of the relationship between malpractice claims experience and medical errors is that evidence of a deterrent effect is (1) limited and (2) vulnerable to methodological

---

[27] Weiler et al. 1993.

criticism. The findings, although far from solid, are provocative enough to suggest that further empirical study would be appropriate. The findings also raise a question as to why the existing evidence does not provide stronger support for deterrence theory. Why is the deterrent signal so weak?

One problem is that the legal standard of care is not always clear to physicians. Variations in the legal standard of care across states (medical custom versus objective reasonableness), variations in clinical standards of care across and even within medical communities, and variations in judicial decisions in malpractice decisions all muddy the waters. Law-and-economics scholarship explains that unclear legal standards tend to cause the deterrent signal to misfire; people may take too few or too many precautions if they do not understand what the law requires of them.[28] This is believed to be a problem for medical malpractice law.[29]

Another important factor diminishing deterrence is that physicians are nearly universally insured against medical malpractice. The existence of insurance always dampens incentives for taking safety precautions, but this is especially true where, as in physician malpractice insurance, premiums are not experience rated. Because experience rating does occur on a widespread basis for hospitals, the incentive-dampening effect of insurance is a less serious problem than for individual physicians.

Even in a world of perfect experience rating, the deterrent signal would still be blunted by the poor fit between instances of negligence and suing. As discussed previously, most instances of negligence never give rise to a malpractice claim, and many malpractice lawsuits are brought and won by patients even though expert reviewers can identify no evidence of negligent care.

Notwithstanding this disjunction, it is still the case that those injured because of negligence are more likely than those injured by nonnegligent treatment to file a claim. Data from the New York and Utah–Colorado studies show that the likelihood that any given patient will sue is at least twenty times higher if he sustains a negligent injury than if he does not (about 2% versus about 0.1%).[30] Few physicians are aware of this aspect of the data, however, and the perception reigns that suing is a near-random behavior. It is also still true that providers who are negligent face only a small risk of being sued. Thus, the system's failings on its compensation function directly lead to the system's failings on its deterrence function.

Insurance effects and the compensation problems combine to undercut deterrence by severely limiting the extent to which the tort system can force hospitals to pay the costs of negligent adverse events. There is no question that medical errors exact a profound societal toll: In addition to their

[28] Craswell and Calfee 1986, 279–303.
[29] Danzon 2000, 1349–50.
[30] Mello, Studdert, DesRoches, et al. 2004, 39–46.

human costs, preventable adverse events in the United States are estimated to produce national economic costs in the range of $17 billion to $29 billion annually.[31] These costs take several forms, including additional acute-care costs, long-term care and maintenance of the disabled, lost income, and lost household production. Researchers have attempted to spur cost-conscious hospitals to pursue error reduction by disaggregating error costs to the hospital level and arguing that reducing adverse events can save hospitals money – the so-called business case for patient safety. However, such statistics mask the fact that hospitals do not internalize all of these costs.

In fact, when the noneconomic loss components of injury costs are taken into consideration, more than 91 percent of the costs of errors accrue to other payers, including private medical insurers, Medicare and Medicaid (the government's health insurance programs for elderly, disabled, and very low-income Americans), state disability and income support programs, and injured patients and their families.[32] There exist only two mechanisms through which hospitals internalize error costs: absorbing the cost of additional medical care necessitated by adverse events, and payments associated with malpractice claims. It is unlikely that these mechanisms result in a high degree of cost internalization. Health care costs account for only about half of the total cost of errors,[33] and providers are able to obtain reimbursement for some of these care costs from insurance payers. Payments associated with malpractice claims also do not represent a large portion of the cost of errors because, as noted, only a tiny fraction of negligent injuries result in claims and less than a third of claims result in a payment.

Thus, the liability system departs considerably from the model of perfect deterrence. The three major studies of medical injury demonstrate that there is a great deal of negligence in medicine. Injuries occur that could be prevented by taking reasonable care, and that situation persists because providers remain relatively insulated from the consequences of their own negligence. Their perception that they are also barraged with nonmeritorious suits makes the liability system appear arbitrary to them, rather than an effective policer of substandard care.

Corrective Justice

The adversarial, punitive nature of the tort liability system is attractive to those who believe victims of medical negligence are entitled to corrective justice. The notion of corrective justice has two strands: a soft strand that points to the need for financial restitution to make victims "whole" after

---

[31] Institute of Medicine 2000.
[32] Mello, Studdert, Thomas, et al. 2004.
[33] Thomas et al. 1999, 255–64.

they are injured as a result of negligence, and a harder strand that points to a human need to express anger and condemnation and impose punishment for serious wrongs. Common to both strands is the interest in a public process of holding the wrongdoer accountable for his actions.

The tort system fits well with notions of corrective justice. Although few injured persons file claims, claimants do gain access to a means of learning about what happened to them (through the discovery process in the early stages of litigation), showing the defendant the impact of his behavior on them (through settlement discussions and proof of damages at trial), demanding (in pleadings and settlement talks) that the defendant accept responsibility for his actions, receiving restitution (as a settlement or damages award), and in so doing, imposing a financial, reputational, and psychic penalty on the defendant. Some evidence suggests that many of these opportunities are important to claimants: Patients tend to be motivated by feelings of anger and frustration and a desire to "get back at" providers who have not communicated appropriately with them or otherwise dealt with them in a sensitive fashion.[34]

However, other study findings suggest that the needs of patients who are injured by medical errors could be met through a less punitive process. For many, corrective justice consists – or could consist, if the patient was approached in a sensitive way – in hearing the provider acknowledge that an error occurred that hurt the patient, apologize or otherwise take responsibility for what happened, and assure the patient that attempts will be made to fix the problem so that others will not be similarly hurt.[35] Thus, although the tort system performs its corrective justice function fairly well for those who enter the system, it is a narrow (and punitive) conception of corrective justice that points to tort redress as the sole avenue for satisfying this criterion.

Efficiency

A final criterion on which the liability system is vulnerable to criticism is operational efficiency. The transaction costs associated with obtaining compensation through the liability system are simply staggering: Of every dollar spent on malpractice insurance premiums, only 40 cents reaches injured patients as compensation; the remainder is consumed by legal fees (40 cents) and insurance overhead (20 cents).[36] In contrast, administrative costs in nonjudicial compensation systems such as Social Security Disability Insurance and workers' compensation are on the order of 5 to 30 percent.[37] Much of the expense of litigation is thought to arise from the requirement of proving

[34] Beckman et al. 1994, 1365–70; Hickson et al. 1994, 1619–20; Hickson et al. 1992, 1359–63; Lester and Smith 1993, 268–72; Vincent et al. 1994, 1609–13.
[35] Gallagher et al. 2003, 1001–7.
[36] Danzon 2000, 1344.
[37] Schwartz 1994, 377.

negligence, which typically necessitates extensive discovery and testimony by multiple expert witnesses. The negligence standard is a murky and contested one; even in the controlled and nonadversarial context of research studies, expert reviewers frequently disagree about the presence or absence of negligence in a particular case of medical injury.[38] The pressures and biases of the litigation process only compound this disagreement.

PHYSICIANS' BEHAVIORAL RESPONSES TO THE SYSTEM

We noted earlier that the medical liability system should be judged on the basis of its collateral effects on health care providers and the quality of care as well as its performance on the primary criteria of compensation, deterrence, corrective justice and efficiency. Unfortunately, the collateral effects of the system appear to be predominantly negative. One major effect is inducement of "defensive medicine," a response that we previewed earlier. Another, which we call "bristling behaviors," refers to a hardening of physicians' attitudes toward patients and a focus on self-interested responses to liability risk. Yet another effect is the reinforcement of impulses to cloak medical mistakes in secrecy. These effects undermine the physician–patient relationship, quality of care, access to care, and access to compensation for medical injuries.

Defensive Medicine

Historically, defensive medicine has been described as having "positive" and "negative" forms.[39] The former refers to the overprovision of services, such as diagnostic tests, procedures, and medications; the latter refers to restrictions on practice, which at the physician level range from stopping the delivery of specific high-risk procedures to relocations to another state or leaving medicine altogether. To avoid the implication that these terms connote normative judgments about the practices in question, we prefer the terms "assurance behaviors" (in place of positive defensive medicine) and "avoidance behaviors" (instead of negative defensive medicine). Thus, defensive medicine consists of assurance and avoidance behaviors that are induced by apprehension about liability and are of little benefit (compared to their cost), no benefit, or outright harmful.[40]

There is broad consensus that the practice of defensive medicine, particularly assurance behavior, is widespread. In Chapter 6, we posit that malpractice crises elevate its frequency. Ironically, though the search for a strong deterrent signal for incentivizing quality improvements from the tort system has been largely in vain, this mutation of the deterrent signal appears

---

[38] Thomas et al. 2002, 812–16; Localio et al. 1996, 457–64.

[39] U.S. Congress, Office of Technology Assessment 1994.

[40] Detailed examples of assurance and avoidance behaviors are described in Chapter 6.

to operate quite powerfully in the health care system. What are the dimensions of the problem? Two complicating factors frustrate an easy answer to this question and consistently imbue with controversy discussions of the prevalence and cost of defensive medicine.

First, defensive medicine is a slippery concept. Its measurement is notoriously difficult.[41] The science of quality measurement, still in its adolescence, is capable of delineating appropriate from inappropriate care for selected treatments but not across the board.[42] Even more vexing is the task of disentangling liability concerns from other influences on clinical decision making. Providers' treatment decisions are driven by a collage of factors, including training, habit, colleagues, eagerness to maintain good relations with patients (independent of the possibility that they will sue), and dedication to high-quality care. Where do these influences end and defensiveness begin? The separation is further complicated by the fact that what are perceived as defensive practices today may morph into tomorrow's standard of care.

Researchers have used two basic strategies to measure defensive medicine: surveys of providers and analyses that try to link variations in liability environments to variations in practice patterns. Survey data, not surprisingly, suggest that malpractice fears exert a strong influence on clinical decision making,[43] even in countries with relatively low rates of claims, modest liability insurance premiums, and predictable awards.[44] Many of the published surveys were conducted by provider organizations, focused on single specialties, and made little attempt to guard against potential exaggerations of the importance of litigation. A few, however, have employed quite sophisticated techniques, such as clinical scenarios, to isolate the impact of liability perceptions.[45]

The alternative approach sidesteps problems of self-attribution by focusing on actual clinical decision making at the aggregate level. The best studies of this kind include a series reviewing the impact of different levels of liability exposure on cesarean section rates[46] and Kessler and McClellan's analysis of heart disease treatments among Medicare beneficiaries nationwide.[47] Results from obstetrics studies are mixed. Some have found that higher malpractice risk increased the probability of delivery by cesarean section,[48] others have found the opposite,[49] and still others have found no

---

[41] U.S. Congress, Office of Technology Assessment 1994.
[42] McGlynn et al. 2003, 2635–45.
[43] U.S. Congress, Office of Technology Assessment 1994.
[44] Veldhuis 1994, 27–9; Summerton 1995, 27–9; Coyte et al. 1991, 89–93.
[45] Glassman et al. 1996, 219–41; Klingman et al. 1996, 185–217.
[46] Baldwin et al. 1995, 1606–10.
[47] Kessler and McClellan 1996, 353–90.
[48] Localio et al. 1993, 366–73; Dubay et al. 1999, 491–522.
[49] Tussing and Wojtowycz 1992, 529–40.

association.[50] Kessler and McClellan found a positive association between "plaintiff-friendly" states and the intensity of cardiac care in those states; in addition, they found that patients in high-liability/high-treatment states had fewer complications or lower mortality.

The second major challenge to evaluating the dimensions of the problem of defensive medicine relates to its impact. Conventional definitions apply "unnecessary" or "inappropriate" as the qualifier to the type of treatment at issue. This qualifier decomposes into three types of care: care that is of little benefit (compared to its cost), care that is of no benefit, and care that is outright harmful. The latter two types – for example, imaging scans that are not indicated (no benefit) or biopsies that are contraindicated (harmful) – clearly bear a negative stamp. However, a great deal of defensive practice, perhaps the lion's share, undoubtedly falls into the first category. The service carries a marginal benefit to patients – for example, a mammogram for a thirty-two-year-old woman with no known risk factors for breast cancer – but one that is arguably too small to justify its expense.

Services in this realm summon cost-effectiveness analyses and inevitably involve a debate about what care is appropriate. A societal perspective may counsel against the wisdom of delivering such treatments. But arguments about the deleterious impact of defensive medicine must switch course and become more subtle when individual patients and physicians actually prize the benefits that flow from the treatments at issue.

Bristling Behaviors

In addition to the cost and access implications of defensive medicine, the liability system also affects patient care by influencing physicians' relationships with patients and their sense of professionalism. In particular, liability costs and pressures can lead to what we have termed bristling behaviors. Many such behaviors are a constant presence in American health care, but these types of practices become especially pronounced during periods of malpractice crisis.

One clear effect of liability worries is to lead physicians to view patients with a degree of suspicion and distrust. There is some evidence that malpractice concerns are impacting the relationship of trust between physician and patient and physicians' willingness to disclose errors, but study findings are not unequivocal. A survey by Common Good (2002) found that 38 percent of physicians reported that their relationship with patients is "less personal" because of liability concerns – but, somewhat surprisingly, the same survey found that only a minority of physicians (15%) felt that liability concerns had made them less candid with their patients. In fact, nearly half (43%) felt malpractice concerns had had the opposite effect.

---

[50] Sloan et al. 1995, 700–14; Baldwin et al. 1995, 1606–10.

Our recent survey research in Pennsylvania also shed light on some negative effects of the liability environment on patient–physician relationships, which we discuss further in Chapter 6.

A second, more tangible effect of liability pressures is to prompt physicians to take aggressive steps to protect themselves against the threat and economic consequences of lawsuits. For example, recent reports have suggested physicians are electing to practice without liability insurance coverage, a practice often referred to as "going bare."[51] This practice is not new, but anecdotal evidence suggests that interest in it has picked up in the past two years, particularly among practitioners in high-risk specialties such as neurosurgery and obstetrics and in certain regions of the country.

Three factors appear to make this strategy tenable and alluring: high or rapidly escalating liability premiums; bankruptcy laws that permit divestment and asset protection; and the absence of statutory requirements in many states that physicians carry liability insurers. Florida is widely noted as a jurisdiction that fits this description. Approximately 5 percent of Florida's physicians go bare, a proportion that has increased dramatically in recent years; in Miami-Dade County, nearly one-fifth of physicians practice without liability coverage.[52]

Deliberately underinsuring or going bare undermines the compensation goal of the malpractice system by jeopardizing the availability of damages. It also raises questions of medical ethics. A broad view of the physician's obligation to patients may regard failure to contribute to the pool of funds used to compensate injured patients as a dereliction of duty. Uninsured physicians might counter that faced with the dilemma of ceasing practice or going bare, they chose the lesser evil.

Another response involves use of contractual waivers. Reportedly, prior to rendering care, some physicians have begun asking patients to sign statements submitting to mandatory arbitration in the event of a claim, promising not to bring frivolous claims, or relinquishing the right to sue at all. Outright waivers would almost certainly carry little legal weight; courts generally take a dim view of such attempts to circumvent tort liability through contract when essential services are at stake.[53] The legality of the more limited waivers is highly questionable but untested. Though courts, most notably the Supreme Court of California,[54] have upheld binding arbitration for medical injury claims, they have done so in the context of an established arbitration program and at the point of obtaining health insurance (as opposed to the point care).

[51] Kachalia et al. 2005.
[52] Silverman 2004a.
[53] Havighurst 1995.
[54] *Madden v. Kaiser*; *Engalla v. Permanente*; *Tunkl v. Regents of University of California*.

There have been reports of a variety of other aggressive responses from physicians and organized medicine in recent years.[55] Although they are anecdotal in nature and their prevalence is unknown, they are nonetheless noteworthy because they exhibit further tensions with both the ideals of medical malpractice system and optimal health policy. These responses include the compilation of data on patients who have filed suit against a physician, which is then made available to prospective care givers on a subscription basis;[56] disciplinary action by boards of medicine and specialty societies against physicians who act as expert witnesses and testify "irresponsibly" or "negligently";[57] surcharges to contribute toward the costs of the physician's liability insurance;[58] physician protests; and work stoppages, which have been conducted in New Jersey, Pennsylvania, and West Virginia. Few physicians would suggest that these moves contribute to quality care or patient well-being; indeed, some have acknowledged that the opposite is probably true, but argue that they are desperate responses to extreme and untenable circumstances.

Cloaking Behaviors

A primary tenet of the new patient safety movement is that improvements in patient safety and medical quality can only come about if providers are willing to share information about errors and other quality problems when they occur. Traditionally, such sharing has taken place behind the closed doors of hospital peer review processes, but the new movement calls for greater transparency. Providers are asked to share information with other institutions and with government regulators through mandatory or voluntary reporting of adverse events to centralized databases. They are also asked (and in a few states, required) to disclose adverse events to the involved patients and families. Unfortunately, the rise of the patient safety movement in the United States coincides with the rise of a new medical malpractice crisis. One effect of this liability environment is that providers have been very reluctant to move toward greater transparency.

Adverse event reporting systems provide a structured means of collecting data about the prevalence of and circumstances surrounding adverse events and medical errors. Mandatory reporting systems require hospitals to report certain adverse events that are associated with serious injuries or death. Voluntary reporting systems encourage providers to report information about a range of adverse events, including those from which no serious harm to

---

[55] Kachalia et al. 2005.
[56] Silverman 2004b; Blumenthal 2004.
[57] Liptak 2004; Grow 2004.
[58] Boodman 2004.

patients resulted. About a third of the states currently mandate reporting to state agencies of adverse events by general and acute care hospitals, and recent federal legislation encourages voluntary reporting.

The more detailed the data contained in these reporting systems, the more useful they potentially are to malpractice attorneys pressing legal claims on behalf of patients injured by adverse events. The threat that reported information will be used against them in a lawsuit serves as a powerful disincentive for providers to report to these systems. Most states have adopted some form of protection for adverse event data, either by providing by statute that the data are not discoverable in legal proceedings or by implementing practical measures, such as anonymous reporting or the deletion of identifying information, that reduce the usefulness of the data to plaintiffs' attorneys. Even with these measures in place, however, there remains widespread concern on the part of providers that attorneys and patients will gain access to the data and use it in malpractice litigation.

State licensing authorities consider underreporting of adverse events to be one of the top two problems with mandatory reporting systems.[59] Although no studies have yet examined physicians' and hospitals' reasons for not reporting events to state reporting systems, studies of the Food and Drug Administration's reporting system for drug and medical device adverse reactions show that American physicians report to the database at a quarter to a half the rate of physicians in European countries,[60] and that at least a small percentage of physicians do not report to the system because of the fear that they might increase their liability.[61] Physician surveys show that an overwhelming majority of physicians believe that fear of malpractice exposure is a barrier to adverse event reporting.[62]

In addition to discouraging reporting of errors to centralized databases, tensions between tort law and patient safety have also impaired a range of other forms of communication about errors. Since July 2001, hospitals have been required by the Joint Commission on the Accreditation of Healthcare Organizations (JCAHO) to inform patients when an adverse event has occurred. Yet a survey of hospital administrators conducted a year after implementation of the JCAHO requirement found that although nearly all hospitals reported that they sometimes informed patients or their families when an adverse event occurred, only about half did so routinely.[63] Fear of malpractice litigation was the most commonly cited barrier to disclosure. Between 2002 and 2005, six states passed laws requiring disclosure of serious

[59] National Academy for State Health Policy 2000; Perez-Peña 2004.
[60] Edlavitch 1988, 1499–503.
[61] Scott et al. 1990, 1785–8; A. Rogers et al. 1988, 1596–600.
[62] A. Robinson et al. 2002, 2186–90; Blendon et al. 2002, 1933–40.
[63] Lamb et al. 2003.

adverse events to patients. No empirical evidence is yet available with which to gauge compliance with those laws.

Advocates of disclosure argue that patients who are dealt with openly and honestly will actually be less inclined to sue.[64] However, empirical evidence concerning the impact of hospital disclosure policies is scant and not generalizable to all providers.[65] So far, a "business case" for disclosure has not been established, and the liability system continues to operate primarily as a damper on disclosure of medical mistakes.

CONCLUSIONS

American health care today sits at the intersection of a perceived epidemic of medical injuries and a medical malpractice crisis. The concern over medical errors has brought demands for increased regulation in the interest of patient safety, including regulation through the tort system, but rising professional liability costs have created strong political pressure to decrease malpractice litigation. Many have begun to wonder how effective the tort system is in deterring medical errors and whether its benefits are worth its costs.

Many plaintiffs' attorneys view themselves as patient safety crusaders and believe that the threat of litigation makes providers practice more safely. But the tort approach to safety regulation – which is punitive in orientation, individualistic in focus, and adversarial in process – is in serious conflict with the nonpunitive, systems-focused, cooperative approach of the "patient safety movement." The clash between the incentive structures erected by these two approaches to safety improvement has left many providers paralyzed and unwilling to participate in error reduction initiatives.

Thus, the problems with the tort liability system run deeper than a simple failure to compensate accurately and efficiently and create positive incentives for safer health care. The punitive, adversarial, negligence-based system of medical justice gives providers strong disincentives to participate in initiatives that are likely to lead to real improvement in patient safety. In the current policy debate over appropriate responses to the medical malpractice crisis, this fact is often submerged, as discussions of the need to limit liability and better regulate insurance markets take the fore. Coinciding as it does with the ascendance of the patient safety movement, the current crisis presents an opportunity to look more deeply at the fundamental flaws of the system and experiment with far-reaching reforms.

[64] Witman et al. 1996, 2565–9; Levinson et al. 1997, 553–9; Hickson et al. 1992, 1359–63.
[65] Kraman and Hamm 1999, 963–7; Pietro et al. 2000, 794–6; Brennan and Mello 2003, 267–73.

2

Malpractice Reform as a Health Policy Problem

William M. Sage

When experts discuss health policy, they typically mean the factors that affect access to medical care, its quality, and its cost. The first medical malpractice crisis of the twenty-first century began in 2001 and continues into 2006. Previous malpractice crises occurred in the 1970s and 1980s. Until the current crisis, few connections have been drawn between the medical malpractice reform movement and overall health policy.

Malpractice crises are defined by rapidly rising liability insurance premiums for physicians, sometimes accompanied by difficulty obtaining insurance coverage at any price. Because lawsuits are upsetting as well as financially costly to physicians, and because armies of white-coated demonstrators make good political theater, hand-wringing over physicians leaving practice and hospitals closing their doors is standard fare for "tort reformers" in crisis years. During the longer intervals between crises, when insurance premiums are stable, malpractice reformers sustain momentum for their cause by suggesting that physicians' fear of litigation leads them to waste health care resources on "defensive medicine" and contributes significantly to overall medical inflation. For the most part, however, these issues have been voiced as political rhetoric and not incorporated seriously into policy making.

BARRIERS TO POLICY INTEGRATION

There are several reasons why medical malpractice has not been integrated with health policy. Malpractice insurance is an intense but intermittent agony for physicians and tends to be ignored by health care policy makers when coverage is cheap and plentiful. Malpractice litigation is so deeply enmeshed in professional rivalries that outsiders hesitate to interfere. Indeed, malpractice has been a defining issue for the American medical profession in its relationship with lawyers over nearly two centuries. For leaders of medical associations, as for rank-and-file physicians, malpractice evokes deep emotions entwined with their personal and professional reputations, setting it apart from workaday regulatory matters.[1] Malpractice law itself has been the province of the judicial branch of state government, with occasional incursions from state legislatures, but has been of little interest to federal policy makers even as the center of gravity for health care regulation has shifted to Washington, D.C. Perhaps most important, the administrative agency most important to federal policy making – the Centers for Medicare and Medicaid Services in the U.S. Department of Health and Human Services, is invisible insofar as malpractice is concerned.

In recent years, medical liability has drawn closer to national partisan politics but in many ways is even farther away from health policy. What began in the 1970s as a political battle between two well-funded professional groups – organized medicine and the personal injury lawyers who regarded malpractice litigation as a major source of income – is now merely one front in a much larger war over general tort reform. This war is being fought by major business interests on one side and the general trial bar, including powerful class action specialists who seldom sue individual doctors, on the other. The original malpractice partisans have been relegated to secondary roles in terms of funding and influence. When the national media reported shortly after the November 2004 elections on initiatives for President Bush's second term, quotes favoring malpractice reform often came from the National Association of Manufacturers, a group with little direct interest in health care, not from the American Medical Association or the American Hospital Association.

THE LIMITATIONS OF CONVENTIONAL TORT REFORM

The details of malpractice reform proposals reflect these pressures. Both long-standing antipathy between doctors and lawyers and the macro-politics of tort law tend to fixate the malpractice debate on lowest-common-denominator reforms of the legal process that are familiar to the medical profession and that translate readily to nonmedical litigation.

This is a short-sighted view of malpractice policy. The medical malpractice system consists of three activities: medical care to keep patients safe, a legal process to air and resolve complaints, and liability insurance to pay compensation when appropriate.

Nearly all the energy put into malpractice reform since the 1970s has been dissipated on the second category. Until very recently, quality assurance in medical care was regarded as best left to individual physician judgment. Malpractice liability insurers have been courted or appeased during downturns of the "insurance cycle" and neglected otherwise. Consequently, the paradigmatic reform package has been California's Medical Injury Compensation Reform Act of 1975 (MICRA), which consists of a $250,000 cap on

[1] Sage 2004b.

noneconomic and punitive damages, the possibility of reducing damages for lost wages and medical expenses by the amount available to the plaintiff from "collateral sources" such as first-party health or disability insurance, a sliding scale for plaintiff lawyers' contingent fees, and a shortened statute of limitations for filing claims. Enacting or opposing MICRA-style tort reform remains the focus of the political stakeholders.[2]

Nevertheless, a strong consensus has emerged in both the medical and legal academic communities favoring much more sweeping reforms than are typically raised in political debate. Perhaps the only good thing about a malpractice crisis is that it prompts researchers to study the medical liability system.[3] Notably, the 1970s and 1980s crises focused researchers' attention on measuring medical error and improving clinical performance. It is only a small exaggeration to say that today's active patient safety movement, which found a broad audience with the publication of the Institute of Medicine's report *To Err Is Human*,[4] owes its existence to the Harvard Medical Practice Study (HMPS) a decade earlier.[5]

The HMPS reviewed medical records of patients hospitalized in New York State in 1984, assessed the quality of care received, and attempted to correlate that care with subsequent malpractice litigation. Before the HMPS, malpractice crises were generally attributed to a single problem: frivolous claims and excessive jury awards. The HMPS radically changed the academic understanding of medical malpractice by revealing a two-sided mismatch between malpractice litigation and underlying negligence, with dramatic implications for patient safety.[6] The HMPS confirmed that malpractice awards are frequently unjustified, in that most successful claimants, though suffering from substantial physical infirmities, had not been treated negligently and often had not even been injured by medical care. However, the HMPS also showed high rates of avoidable error, producing serious injuries the vast majority of which never generated lawsuits or received compensation. These injuries – many of which can be prevented by systematic attention to patient safety – pose a significant threat to patients and impose substantial costs on the health care system.[7]

Subsequent research has echoed the findings of the HMPS that the malpractice litigation system is both a poor arbiter of medical error and an inadequate source of patient compensation. Among other things, smaller claims seem to be declining rapidly while defendants' (and presumably

[2] See, for example, W. Hamm et al. 2005.
[3] Danzon 2000.
[4] Institute of Medicine 2000.
[5] Harvard Medical Practice Study Group 1990.
[6] Brennan et al. 1996.
[7] Zhan and Miller 2003.

plaintiffs') costs of litigating cases rise.[8] Neither does the process of litigation advance medical quality.[9] Adversarial proceedings suffer from extreme delay, restricted information, limited opportunity for remedies other than cash compensation, lack of quality-related feedback to health care providers, and a misdirected focus on individual sources of medical error rather than systemic sources. Physicians also go to extreme lengths to avoid or deflect legal claims, often with perverse consequences for quality of care.[10]

Moreover, it is increasingly clear that short-term litigation trends do not explain liability insurance crises.[11] Aggregate payments in malpractice cases have risen markedly in recent decades, but the trend approximates the increase in society's expenditures on health care over the same period.[12] Controlling for medical expenditures, population growth, or available health care providers, malpractice claims and payouts appear steady or declining.[13] Nonetheless, litigation rates in many states are substantial. In Texas, for example, annual claims rates approximate 25 per 100 physicians, and annual paid claims average around 5 per 100 physicians.[14] Moreover, the post-2002 period has indisputably burdened physicians in "high-risk" specialties in many states with sharp, sudden increases in liability insurance premiums and has limited their access to alternative coverage.

This research suggests that the amount, character, and distribution of insurable risk consequent to medical injury are major determinants of malpractice crises. Although critiques of MICRA-style tort reform from the trial bar frequently target bad doctors and greedy or incompetent insurance companies, identifying the contributions of both medical error and liability insurance to the current crisis is more than a finger-pointing exercise. It is important for medical liability reforms to take account of specific attributes of today's health care system and of corresponding imperfections in malpractice insurance markets.

MALPRACTICE REFORM AND HEALTH SYSTEM CHANGE

Were it not for preconceptions and politics, research demonstrating the limitations of conventional tort reform would be completely intuitive. MICRA was enacted in 1975, based on knowledge gathered and expectations formed in the 1950s and 1960s. Major changes in the health care system since 1975, and in our understanding of that system, make it presumptively unlikely

---

[8] Black et al. 2005.
[9] Dauer 2003.
[10] Bovbjerg et al. 1996.
[11] U.S. General Accounting Office 2003a.
[12] Chandra et al. 2005.
[13] Black et al. 2005; Budetti and Waters 2005.
[14] Black et al. 2005.

that MICRA alone will resolve the current malpractice insurance crisis or prevent future ones. The key elements of health system change over the past forty years are medical progress, industrialization, and cost containment. These long-term factors in turn affect the prevalence and character of medical injury, claims and litigation processes, and demands on malpractice insurance markets.

Medical Progress

Scientific progress is closely connected to the law of negligence, both generally and with respect to medicine. Malpractice litigation reflects the overall success of modern medicine, not its failure. The better health care becomes, the more liability it is likely to generate. Technology in particular drives malpractice litigation, from the nineteenth-century epidemic of claims for incorrectly setting long-bone fractures that previously had required amputation, to contemporary issues of early detection and choice of treatment modality for cancers that until recently were incurable.[15] Because the "standard of care" that governs liability is based on prevailing practice, improvements in care imply that subsequent defendants are held to higher standards. As medical science advances, moreover, patients' (and jurors') expectations of success rise, and failure is more readily attributable to misadventure than to misfortune. Similarly, delays in diagnosis more plausibly cause injury when effective therapies clearly exist than when cure is speculative. It is also increasingly common to survive serious injury, bringing into dispute compensation for prolonged future suffering and future medical need that would not be present in a claim for wrongful death.

Other characteristics of modern medical transactions predispose to litigation. Advanced technologies offer a better chance of successful treatment but also create more opportunities for error through incorrect selection, misapplication, or lack of coordination among providers. Patient–physician interactions relating to these treatments tend to be more transitory and less personal, reducing opportunities to build relationships and maintain communications that will either avoid errors or mitigate their consequences. Finally, progress comes at a very steep price. Medical technology is inseparable from medical economics.[16] Patients seriously injured by medical care incur significant expenses for subsequent treatment and will have proportionately greater need and incentive to seek compensation. For this reason, even providers in states that have capped noneconomic damages can face financially crippling damage awards, particularly when young plaintiffs with serious injuries require lifetime care. One compilation of large jury awards in California between 1997 and 2002, for example, lists ten cases totaling

[15] De Ville 1998; Mohr 2000.
[16] L. Baker et al. 2003; Connor 2004.

nearly $300 million in economic damages.[17] In a comprehensive study of civil jury verdicts in tort cases of all types from 1960 to 1999, RAND researchers concluded that claimed medical losses accounted for approximately 58 percent of the observed growth in damage awards.[18]

Even a cursory review of recently litigated malpractice cases finds many that echo these themes. In *Fellin v. Long Island College Hospital*,[19] several hours' delay in diagnosing and operating on a cerebral aneurysm in a twenty-three-year-old elevator repairman resulted in quadriplegia and severe brain damage. A New York jury awarded $112 million, including $76 million for future medical care and $15 million for future pain and suffering. In a Michigan case with unidentified parties that settled for $875,000, it was alleged that an ophthalmologist using a new type of laser to prevent deterioration of macular degeneration both operated the equipment improperly and failed to disclose its experimental nature. In *Leyvas v. Paragas*,[20] a jury awarded a five-year-old child $84,750,000 because a pediatrician had not timely diagnosed neonatal jaundice, resulting in cerebral palsy with extensive medical needs. California's cap on noneconomic damages reduced the award by a mere $500,000.

Industrialized Health Care

Industrialization has accompanied technological change, reflecting both the inadequacy of cottage production of advanced health care services and the generous returns to capital available from public and private health insurance. As in other industrializing sectors of the economy, corporate medical enterprises such as hospitals face increasing liability risks as their charitable origins recede and they both function and are perceived to function as "cheapest cost-avoiders" of systematic harm to patients. The attribution of profit motives to these organizations, most of which were previously considered charitable enterprises, also exposes them to punitive damages, which are only rarely assessed against individual physicians. This effect was heightened by the expansion of (and public backlash against) financial incentives in managed care, which placed at issue health care providers' loyalty to patients as well as their technical competence. In addition, many suburban and exurban hospitals and physician practices consolidated during the 1980s and 1990s into health systems and networks affiliated with large metropolitan providers. This invited venue shopping by plaintiffs' lawyers, who previously had been constrained to bring claims in the home communities of individual physicians, where a defense verdict or a low award was more likely than among urban jurors who had no personal knowledge of the defendant.

---

[17] Californians Allied for Patient Protection 2005.
[18] Seabury et al. 2004.
[19] Kings County (NY) Supreme Court, Index No. 4129/93 (2003).
[20] Alameda County (CA) Superior Court, Case No. 798868 4OH.

Medical Cost Containment

The malpractice crisis of 2005 also differs from its predecessors because it follows two decades of cost containment by both public and private health insurers. Research from the 1980s malpractice crisis confirmed that even sudden, substantial increases in physicians' liability insurance premiums were quickly passed along to patients and health insurers as higher medical fees.[21] This may be changing. Private managed care companies now drive hard bargains with hospitals and physicians over prices, while Medicare and Medicaid reimbursement rates have been subject to broad-based budgetary constraints.[22] Cost containment has both direct and indirect implications for malpractice liability. In direct terms, many of the measures adopted by physicians, hospitals, and managed care organizations to reduce cost also increase liability exposure. In office practice, physicians spend less time with individual patients and delegate more tasks to nonphysicians. In hospital settings, patients are sicker but staffing is leaner. Less directly, health care providers no longer enjoy a financial cushion against hard liability insurance markets. Rapidly rising malpractice premiums bite deeply into reserves, especially if prompt pass-through is limited. These financial considerations increase the likelihood that volatile malpractice insurance markets will adversely affect access to medical care, at least for some specialties in some locations.[23]

EXPANDING THE REFORM DOMAIN

Health system change has persuaded many in the academic community that much more than MICRA is required to solve the problems now known to afflict the malpractice system. Caps on damages are reasonable responses to frivolous claims and excessive awards. They are irrelevant or counterproductive, however, to other shortcomings of malpractice litigation: that too many avoidable injuries occur; that compensation is frequently inadequate; that litigation is too slow, too costly, too uncertain, and too unpleasant; that premiums for primary coverage are too volatile and, for some physicians, too expensive; and that excess coverage and reinsurance are currently too costly for hospitals and other health care institutions. Put differently, MICRA-style reform perhaps yields somewhat less of a bad system, but it does not create a better system.

In *Crossing the Quality Chasm*, the sequel volume to *To Err Is Human*, the Institute of Medicine (IOM) declared its commitment to a safe, effective, patient-centered, timely, efficient, and equitable health care system.[24] The malpractice system possesses none of these characteristics. In particular,

[21] Danzon et al. 1990.
[22] J. Lee et al. 2003.
[23] U.S. General Accounting Office 2003a; Dubay et al. 2001.
[24] Institute of Medicine 2000.

patient safety has yet to improve measurably in the five years since the first IOM report,[25] in part because medical liability and patient safety mechanisms do not yet work hand in hand.[26] Academics and public policy experts therefore favor testing more sweeping reforms that would remove injuries caused by medical care from conventional civil litigation, and place them instead in a dedicated compensation system more closely connected to real-time patient care and quality assurance processes.[27] The current generation of these proposals draws on a rich literature of innovation that emerged from the 1980s crisis, including early offers in settlement,[28] accelerated-compensation events,[29] guidelines for appropriate damages,[30] specialized medical courts, both fault-based and no-fault administrative systems,[31] and enterprise liability for either provider organizations or health plans.[32] Ideally, these reforms would improve both dispute resolution and liability risk-bearing processes governing medical injury, which in turn would create clearer incentives for optimal medical treatment in the first place.[33]

Legal Process

Several aspects of the dispute resolution process demand attention from a health policy perspective. Principal among these is delay: The average malpractice claim takes roughly two years to resolve, and most large claims take five years or longer. Delay withholds information from patients for prolonged periods while defense lawyers position their cases strategically for settlement or trial, denies compensation to legitimate claimants, diminishes learning opportunities for health care providers, imposes high psychic costs on all parties, and increases uncertainty for malpractice insurers when pricing coverage. The tone throughout the proceedings is adversarial and accusatory, with both legal counsel and insurers focused on the financial implications of the case to the exclusion of opportunities for the parties to discuss the situation, offer nonmonetary expressions of sympathy or assistance, and engage in emotional healing. Awards and settlements, when conferred, vary widely in amount even for similar injuries, often reflecting the exaggerated positions argued by partisan expert witnesses who testify not only to clinical matters such as negligence but also to key economic issues such as the plaintiff's life expectancy and projected future medical expenses.

[25] Wachter 2004; Leape and Berwick 2005.
[26] Sage 2003a; Budetti and Waters 2005.
[27] Brennan and Mello 2003.
[28] J. O'Connell 1982.
[29] Tancredi and Bovbjerg 1991.
[30] Bovbjerg et al. 1989.
[31] J. O'Connell 1986; Studdert and Brennan 2001a.
[32] Abraham and Weiler 1994b; Sage et al. 1994; Sage 1997.
[33] Jacobi and Huberfeld 2001.

Liability Insurance

Flaws in the structure of malpractice liability insurance, particularly for physicians, accentuate the problematic aspects of dispute resolution.[34] All liability insurance is by definition "third-party" insurance, meaning that payments on a policy are made not to the policyholder, but to someone else to whom the policyholder becomes obligated within the scope of coverage. This third-party orientation means that, regardless of the intimacy in principle of the physician–patient bond, a patient who becomes a claimant is treated as a stranger. Because liability insurance is disconnected from both the patient's first-party health insurance and many of the settings in which the physician-defendant practices, moreover, "risk management" activities promoted by malpractice carriers are uncoordinated with other quality improvement incentives or requirements.

Large health insurers that cover comprehensive packages of health services offered by interdependent professionals and health care institutions end up inefficiently supporting the cost of selling malpractice policies piecemeal to small, undiversified groups of physicians. Commercial malpractice carriers price liability coverage based solely on physician specialty and geographic location. Even in California, which boasts a relatively stable malpractice insurance climate, an internist, anesthesiologist, or family physician paid $13,808 for standard coverage in 2004, whereas an orthopedic surgeon paid $46,128, an obstetrician paid $66,100, and a neurosurgeon paid $74,660.[35] This worsens premium volatility and results in downturns in the insurance cycle hitting some physicians much harder than other. Annual premiums for 2004 in Dade County, Florida, for example, rose to $277,242 for obstetricians and $344,162 for neurosurgeons.[36]

There is no public policy justification for maintaining small risk pools that burden a few specialties with high, volatile malpractice premiums. A chain is only as strong as its weakest link: If obstetricians or neurosurgeons cannot afford to remain in practice, the entire health care system is threatened. At the same time, it is both actuarially and politically untenable for malpractice insurers to rate physicians based on individual quality or loss experience, which significantly attenuates the deterrent effect of malpractice liability.[37] Finally, historical fragmentation of medical practice, coupled with a legal regime based on individual physician accountability for error, has resulted in physicians bearing the lion's share of liability costs notwithstanding their relatively modest share of overall health care resources and declining political influence.[38] As health care spending increases nationally, more than a

[34] Sage 2004b; T. Baker 2005b; Geistfeld 2005.
[35] W. Hamm et al. 2005.
[36] Ibid.
[37] Mello and Brennan 2002.
[38] Laugesen and Rice 2003.

trillion-dollar annual gap has emerged between the revenue flowing through the entire health care system and that available to physicians to fund liability protection.

Legal processes and insurance practices in combination place a ponderous burden on physicians. Physicians have always had strong beliefs about the harms caused by malpractice litigation.[39] Lawsuits are taken variously as personal betrayals by patients, profit-motivated opportunism by lawyers, or quasi-criminal accusations by the public that threaten physicians' personal and professional reputations.[40] Malpractice climate affects young physicians' choices of specialty and practice location and older physicians' decisions about retirement.[41]

Crisis conditions exacerbate these effects. Based on the HMPS's findings of high injury rates but low associated claims rates, one might anticipate social benefits to flow from a malpractice crisis as physicians focus more on the threat of litigation and adjust their clinical behavior accordingly. Because most safety problems in medicine have systems-based causes and solutions not within the control of individual physicians, however, malpractice pressures do not typically enhance the deterrent effect of liability but rather result in misdeterrence, which is commonly called "defensive medicine." Physicians preoccupied with the cost and availability of malpractice insurance, particularly those in specialties at high risk of litigation, tend to practice defensively. In some cases, they engage in "assurance behavior" such as ordering diagnostic tests, performing invasive procedures, and referring for second opinions. In other cases, they engage in "avoidance behavior" such as limiting their practices to routine cases and declining to treat patients with certain conditions or personalities.[42] Relatively little of this conduct demonstrably enhances quality, whereas many practices are clearly detrimental.

GETTING TO A BETTER SYSTEM

A better medical liability system would have two core elements: "no-trial" dispute resolution and a "health system" rather than an individual physician focus. The phrase "no-trial" (rather than "no-fault") is used to denote procedures that are distinct from conventional litigation but that retain, and in fact strengthen, health care providers' legal accountability for error. True no-fault systems largely accept baseline accident rates as unavoidable and seek to compensate victims at low administrative cost, often from pooled social resources. By contrast, most proposals to replace malpractice litigation

---

[39] Sage 2001.
[40] Sage 2004b.
[41] Kessler et al. 2005; Encinosa and Hellinger 2005; Mello et al. 2005.
[42] Studdert et al. 2005.

with some form of administrative compensation determine eligibility for payment based on whether the injury in question was avoidable as a matter of scientific "best practice."[43] This standard is broader than negligence but narrower than accident and places financial responsibility squarely on the responsible provider (or its liability insurer). Established lists of "accelerated-compensation events" (ACEs), adverse outcomes that do not typically occur in the absence of error, are a good starting point for classifying injuries as avoidable or unavoidable.[44] Patients would receive compensation for economic damages not covered by collateral sources, plus noneconomic damages based on a sliding scale that takes into account the character, severity, and duration of injury.[45]

"No-Trial" Reform

In the most recent formulations of a "no-trial" approach, initial dispute resolution procedures are an extension of the process of clinical care. Health care providers make immediate disclosure to patients who have suffered unanticipated harm and apologize when appropriate, mediated discussions with the patient or family begin promptly, providers offer timely compensation in all clearly eligible cases, and information about the error and its aftermath are rapidly transmitted to internal patient safety and injury prevention systems.[46] These elements are not new; a survey of malpractice plaintiffs conducted by Blum nearly a half century ago in 1958 found that "[i]n no case was a doctor sued who told the patient directly and honestly that he made a mistake and that he was sorry for it."[47] But few mechanisms exist for institutionalizing a more productive system of dispute resolution. Still, some programs exist through voluntary contractual agreements. In Colorado, for example, the dominant physicians' malpractice carrier offers error disclosure and prompt payment of limited economic damages without requiring release of claims to patients of selected physicians who participate actively in safety improvement and risk management.[48]

System Accountability

In an ideal system, financial and administrative responsibility for implementing dispute resolution and quality improvement procedures typically

[43] Studdert and Brennan 2001a.
[44] Tancredi and Bovbjerg 1991.
[45] Bovbjerg et al. 1989.
[46] Liebman and Hyman 2004; Joint Commission on the Accreditation of Healthcare Organizations 2005; J. Cohen 2000.
[47] Somers 1977.
[48] COPIC 2004.

would lie with organized health care providers such as hospitals, physician group practices, and closed-panel HMOs, not with individual physicians. These enterprises can diversify liability risk across a range of specialties and services, insure or self-insure that risk at manageable cost, engage in coordinated injury reduction activities, and enter into efficient contractual arrangements downstream with patients and upstream with health insurers regarding claims for compensation.

Bringing health and liability insurance closer together at the hospital or health enterprise level is important. Private and public decisions about the appropriate level of social investment in health care should encompass both the cost of care and the right to compensation if care goes awry, especially when one considers that patients usually need compensation primarily to pay future medical expenses. Increases in aggregate malpractice payments closely track increases in overall health care spending.[49] In many ways, therefore, universal health coverage would be the most effective malpractice reform. Health insurers also need to be on the same page as health care providers with respect to patient safety, which is best improved through organizational change involving the settings where physicians and other health professionals work.

Testing Innovative Reforms

Despite solid consensus among medical malpractice scholars and researchers regarding productive directions for liability policy, the political will to pursue comprehensive reform remains elusive. How might one go about building an improved medical liability system? The key is to embed malpractice reform within, and thereby leverage, existing regulatory and self-regulatory mechanisms that advance health care quality rather than merely creating another stand-alone, reactive institution such as a "medical court." The most promising paths involve replacing the conventional civil litigation model with an administrative law model akin to workers' compensation that interfaces with health care regulation.

Productive reform might occur under the auspices of state governmental agencies that regulate health care or patient safety, through private employers acting as sponsors of health coverage under the Employee Retirement Income Security Act of 1974 (ERISA), or through the federal Center for Medicare and Medicaid Services (CMS) using its complement of administrative law judges. The Joint Commission on Accreditation of Healthcare Organizations (JCAHO) could play an important role in reform by requiring hospitals to improve their error detection, disclosure, and dispute resolution processes. According to a JCAHO White Paper, a well-functioning liability system

---

[49] Chandra et al. 2005.

would assure (1) prompt disclosure of medical errors to injured patients, (2) apology, (3) analysis of the error to inform future prevention efforts, (4) an early offer of compensation for losses, and (5) alternative dispute resolution to bring disputed claims to a swift, fair, and efficient resolution.[50]

Testing a variety of reforms on a demonstration basis is preferable to committing in advance to a single, irrevocable model. The effectiveness of liability reform depends to a considerable extent on the clinical and administrative capacities of particular health care providers and on the responses of both malpractice plaintiffs and malpractice defendants to changed incentives and procedures. Accordingly, the Institute of Medicine in 2002 recommended federal funding for state-based demonstrations of liability reform, some of which would be limited to subsets of providers that met safety-related criteria for participation.[51] Limiting liability or publicly subsidizing the costs of malpractice insurance makes sense only if hospitals and physicians truly can provide a safe environment for patients and a prompt, compassionate response to unexpected injury.

Furthermore, debates over comprehensive malpractice reform tend to get mired in the aggregate budgetary implications of potentially surfacing and compensating significantly more claims than currently attract attention from plaintiffs' lawyers.[52] Proposals for large-scale change that emerge despite these constraints are often stacked against claimants in order to guarantee overall affordability. By testing reforms on particular providers and in particular geographic regions, sponsors could hold participants harmless for any financial burden exceeding their current liability expenses, and could measure the actual costs and benefits to patients and society. In other words, it finally would become possible to assess the health policy implications of the medical malpractice system.

---

[50] Joint Commission on the Accreditation of Healthcare Organizations 2005.
[51] Institute of Medicine 2002.
[52] Studdert et al. 1997.

3

Medical Malpractice and the New Politics of Health Care

Rogan Kersh

Among the few self-evident truths about the U.S. medical malpractice system is that it desperately needs reforming. Medical and legal academic experts, stakeholders on every side, even President Bush and his predecessor Bill Clinton, all describe the present malpractice regime in terms like "broken."[1] No shortage exists of comprehensive proposals to overhaul malpractice; indeed, several are presented or evaluated in this book. But implementing any significant reform requires coordinated effort by a set of actors outside the health professions: politicians. Since malpractice first appeared on political agendas in the 1960s, Congress and successive administrations have been unable to decisively address the issue. Officials in some states have had more success, though typically short-lived: As of mid-2005, the American Medical Association (AMA) listed forty-three states as in or nearing a malpractice crisis. Without a workable political strategy for achieving reform, the much-deplored medical malpractice system will remain essentially unchanged. Malpractice's political aspects and prospects therefore demand attention alongside more commonly studied features.

Why have successive Congresses failed to enact any meaningful legislation addressing the malpractice system? Is that record likely to change in the near future? What explains national and state lawmakers' near-exclusive focus on "first-generation" reforms like caps on damage awards, rather than such "second-generation" proposals as alternative dispute resolution, no-fault insurance plans, and enterprise liability? Why have unlikely interest-group actors, like the National Association of Manufacturers, become exponentially more involved in malpractice in recent years? And what explains the simultaneous increase in federal court involvement with malpractice issues, also over the past quarter-century or so? Approaching such questions requires, first, a review of modern malpractice politics. Sustained

---

[1] Bush quoted in Lohr 2005, Sec. 3, p. 8; Clinton in Andersen 2005, 19; Sage 2005a.

political attention to this topic began some four decades ago, intensifying in each of the malpractice system's three crisis episodes (early/mid-1970s, mid-1980s, and 2002–present). Many arguments and actors remain similar across the decades, though the present round of congressional and state malpractice politics includes novel features as well. This historical development is reviewed in the next section.

Medical malpractice cannot be understood without reference to broader changes in U.S. health care in recent years. The political features of malpractice likewise are shaped by general trends in health policy, as controversies displaying common characteristics develop in similar ways. Together, issues like HMO reform, tobacco use, obesity, and malpractice mark a "new politics of health care."[2] This wider context affecting malpractice politics is detailed in the second section of this chapter. A concluding section offers thoughts about the future of malpractice reform, in the light of its recent history and connection to other leading health policy concerns.

HISTORICAL CONTEXT: A BRIEF HISTORY OF MALPRACTICE POLITICS

Though the contemporary malpractice regime's outlines are traceable as far back as 1835, with malpractice lawsuits a "prominent and permanent feature of American medical life [by] the 1840s,"[3] national and state legislators were peripheral or absent players until comparatively recently. Periodic upsurges in malpractice claims – in the 1840s–50s, 1870s, 1920s–30s, and 1950s – drew scant response from elected officials. Abraham Lincoln, to take one notable example, variously represented physicians and plaintiffs in numerous malpractice cases, right up to the eve of his presidential election. His experience never translated into any recorded comment on the topic as president (or congressman, or Senate candidate). A few state medical societies, like Ohio's, in the late nineteenth century sought legislative changes to the malpractice system, but their model bills went nowhere. Detailed histories of medical malpractice nationally, or in individual states like New York, include scant mention of involvement by Congress, state legislatures, or executive-branch actors before the late 1960s. Physicians concerned about spiraling malpractice premiums or rising numbers of case filings instead worked to improve medical treatment and education, compiled medical-jurisprudence manuals, formed malpractice legal defense and insurance associations – and, from the mid-nineteenth century forward, railed against malpractice lawyers as "'human vampires,' 'sharks,' 'jackals,' 'legal adventurers,' 'pettifogging attorneys,' and 'shysters.'"[4]

---

[2] Kersh and Morone 2005.
[3] De Ville 1990, 224.
[4] Ibid., 195 (descriptions of lawyers); and see generally 68–91 and 187–230. Compare Hogan 2003; Cirincione 1986; Mohr 2000.

1960s–1970s

This political inattention changed in the late 1960s, owing to both general and specific factors. Medical care came under increased U.S. government scrutiny during this time; as a Department of Health, Education, and Welfare (HEW) undersecretary remarked during President Nixon's first term, "In the past, decisions on health care delivery were largely professional ones. Now the decisions will be largely political."[5] Malpractice became a focus of heightened official interest owing to a steep rise in the cost of liability insurance for some specialties, beginning around 1968–9. Suddenly, "malpractice became a dramatic story in which all the characters could be condemned: hospitals, attorneys, and even patients."[6] Subsequently, both the Senate and executive branch officially addressed malpractice for the first time.

Initial Senate action came from an unlikely quarter. In 1969 the Government Operations Committee's subcommittee on executive reorganization opened hearings on malpractice, culminating in a report issued by subcommittee chair (and liberal crusader) Abraham Ribicoff (D-Conn.). Ribicoff, though modestly characterizing his report as "nondefinitive" and "a starting point for public debate," warned that "the situation threatens to become a national crisis" and insisted "there is a definite Federal role in the malpractice problem."[7] What role this was remained unclear, in part thanks to a swift rebuttal from the AMA: "This appears to be another attempt to impose Federal regulations over the practice of medicine," the physicians' lobby declared. "The medical malpractice situation is critical in some areas in the United States. But the country does not need the establishment of Federal regulations over medicine, palmed off on an unsuspecting public as merely the solution to the malpractice problem."[8] The AMA's plain message: The only acceptable malpractice policy was short-term measures targeting premium costs.

Meanwhile, executive-branch actors also took up the subject. President Nixon in 1971 decried "the growing menace of malpractice suits" and called for "an intensive program of research and analysis in this area."[9] HEW Secretary Elliott Richardson obliged, convening a commission to study "the entire range of problems associated with professional liability (malpractice) claims." The commission's far-reaching report, issued in January 1973, addressed seventy-seven different aspects of the malpractice system, from defensive medicine and patients' rights to clinical standards and grievance mechanisms. One commission member warned that without government action to limit litigation, "the malpractice problem will surpass that of a

[5] Quoted in Starr 1982, 393.
[6] Hogan 2003, 129.
[7] Committee on Government Operations 1969, v.
[8] American Medical Association 1970.
[9] Nixon 1971, 37-A.

crisis and become that of a national standard.... some rationality must be brought to bear before our entire health care system falters under the burden which will result in ultimately harming everyone who is or ever will be a user of health care facilities or providers."[10]

Most of this federal government attention preceded the malpractice "crisis" of 1974–6. As many insurers ceased offering coverage amid the oil-shock recession, driving premiums to new heights, officials in most U.S. states actively sought policy change, transforming medical malpractice from a private matter into one for public regulation. State remedies during the 1970s came in two primary categories: (1) reforms designed to *increase insurance availability*, through joint underwriting or reinsurance plans, as well as state-run patient compensation funds, and (2) attempts to *reduce provider liability*, usually via tort reforms aimed at limiting malpractice damage awards, and also by streamlining claims resolution through case screening tribunals, restrictive statutes of limitation, and other mechanisms.[11] Most prominent among tort-reform approaches was California's Medical Injury Compensation Reform Act (MICRA), enacted in 1975. MICRA's principal provisions, which subsequently were adopted in varying combinations by several other states, included a $250,000 cap on noneconomic malpractice damage awards; collateral source reform, wherein compensation to a patient (e.g., prior payments by medical or disability insurers) could be introduced as evidence by defendants; periodic rather than lump-sum payments of jury awards; and a sliding-scale limit applied to plaintiff lawyers' contingency fees.[12]

These "first-generation" legislative changes had relatively little influence on malpractice premium levels, as subsequent research has shown.[13] A more enduring feature of 1970s-era malpractice turmoil was the reorganization of the trial bar's political arm, newly renamed the Association of Trial Lawyers of America (ATLA) in 1972. ATLA moved to Washington, D.C., five years later and emerged as a major player in malpractice politics during the next crisis – which already loomed on the horizon.

1980s

Less than a decade after the first malpractice crisis abated, liability premiums and claims frequency rose sharply in many states. (Underlying reasons are debated still; of primary concern here is the political response.) At the federal

[10] DHEW 1973, xv, 137.
[11] On the 1970s crisis, and state remedies, see Feagles et al. 1975; Bovbjerg 1989; Sloan 1985; G. Robinson 1986.
[12] The scale provides that a malpractice victim's lawyer can charge no more than 40% of the first $50,000 of any jury award, 33% of the next $50,000, a quarter of the next $500,000, and 15% of any amount over $600,000.
[13] "First generation" is Bovbjerg's term (1989; see also Kinney 1995); studies of the inefficacy of these changes include Sloan 1985; Adams and Zuckerman 1984.

level, reaction was stronger than in the 1970s. As the crisis became apparent, President Reagan demanded that Congress limit lawsuits and directed the Department of Health and Human Services to develop recommendations for reform. Reagan's successor George H. W. Bush was particularly engaged on the issue, promoting sweeping MICRA-style legislation in Congress as his presidency's health reform centerpiece; Bush also frequently critiqued the malpractice system in his presidential campaigns. In a 1992 town-meeting debate with fellow candidates Bill Clinton and Ross Perot, the president responded to a question on controlling medical spending as follows: "The number one problem with health care costs is medical malpractice rates, caused [by] lawsuits. These huge judgments need to be capped."[14]

The Democratic-controlled Congress was also more active than in the first crisis, considering in 1987 the first substantial federal legislation on medical malpractice. This 100th Congress's "National Professional Liability Reform Act" (H.R. 1955) included a number of first-generation reforms, including arbitration panels, damage caps at the MICRA $250,000 level, sliding-scale attorney contingency fees, and reduced statutes of limitations on malpractice claim filings. The plan languished in committee, but a trend was set: The next three Congresses introduced more than sixty malpractice bills, most of them first-generation tort and insurance reforms, some of which passed the House. Kinney lists several second-generation innovations proposed during the 1980s crisis, such as medical practice guidelines, mandated alternative dispute resolution, various no-fault approaches, enterprise liability, and damages scheduling. Congress exhibited little enthusiasm for any of these.[15]

Accompanying increased federal involvement was another wave of state malpractice policy making, beginning around 1985 and continuing into the mid-1990s. This round of state enactments also favored first-generation policies like shortened statutes of limitation, expert-witness requirements, and pretrial tribunals to screen liability actions. MICRA-style reforms were especially popular – though the signature feature, damage caps, encountered legal trouble in some jurisdictions; seven state courts overturned existing damage caps, usually on equal-protection grounds.[16] By the waning of the second crisis in the early 1990s, more than forty states had debated damage caps, but only twenty actually had statutory limits on noneconomic damages. (Five more would cap damages by 1995.) Perhaps more telling, by that time just four states (Arkansas, Kentucky, North Carolina, and Pennsylvania) had not enacted malpractice tort reform legislation of some type; all four would eventually fall into line.[17]

---

[14] Debate transcript, *New York Times*, Oct. 16, 1992.
[15] Kinney 1995, esp. 102–10.
[16] Haiduc 1990.
[17] Fielding 1999, 148. On legislative responses to the 1980s crisis, see Kinney 1995; Bovbjerg 1989.

Some states did implement innovative second-generation policies. Virginia and Florida, for example, both adopted limited no-fault rules for certain injuries, and Vermont mandated both alternative dispute resolution in malpractice cases and medical practice guidelines. The 1980s crisis, accompanied by similar problems with the affordability of auto insurance, also inspired another state intervention: malpractice insurance regulation. Again California led the way, with an Insurance Rate Reduction and Reform Act, passed as Proposition 103 in 1988. The reform rolled back insurance rates, installed transparency regulations (e.g., insurers proposing a rate increase had to provide detailed justification), established financial incentives for efficient insurer performance, and required insurers to cut costs described as "unnecessary," a category including "excessive expenses, bloated executive salaries, and bad-faith lawsuit costs."[18] This innovation was not nearly so widely diffused among other states as MICRA reforms; subsequent calls for insurance regulation have come not from principal stakeholders (physicians tend reflexively to side with insurers on malpractice matters; lawyers' primary focus of criticism is medical errors rather than insurance cycles) but from academics. A number of comprehensive reform proposals recommend liability insurance changes, along the lines of California's 1988 regulations, as a key to relieving the malpractice crisis.[19] But insurance regulation – like most of the second-generation reforms listed by Bovbjerg or Kinney – has been largely ignored in malpractice legislation to date, especially at the national level.

2002–Present

Existing statutory protections did little to shield most states from the current malpractice crisis, touched off by a "perfect storm" of shocks to the liability insurance market.[20] The principal causes are once more a subject of heated debate, but the symptoms were familiar: spiraling insurance premiums in certain specialties (and particularly hard-hit states), threatening providers' financial viability and some patients' access to care. Reinsurance costs rose sharply in the wake of September 11's terrorist attacks, further exacerbating the problem. As bad news mounted, malpractice reform reappeared atop political agendas nationwide. Longtime combatants – the AMA and ATLA, principally – lined up behind familiar arguments (with a few novel twists, including reports of physicians refusing treatment to trial lawyers).[21] House members and senators dusted off reform bills dating back to the 100th Congress more than a decade before. Again state legislatures went to work,

---

[18] Cal. Code Regs., tit. 10, § 2646.6; Cal. Ins. Code, § 1861.07.
[19] See, most recently, Geistfeld 2005.
[20] Sage 2004b, 13. Another concise summary is Mello, Studdert, and Brennan, 2003.
[21] See, for example, Steffy 2004, A1.

once more primarily on first-generation reforms like damage caps: Forty-four states introduced bills between 2002 and 2004 either to cap noneconomic damages for the first time or to lower existing ceilings, usually aiming at MICRA's $250,000 level. During the first half of 2005 alone, forty-eight states introduced more than 400 bills on medical liability and malpractice. More than 80 percent of these were exclusively or primarily first-generation policies, most of them conceived twenty-five years ago or more.[22]

But this third crisis episode may be distinguished from its two predecessors in certain respects. Notably, for the first time in modern malpractice history the political stars were aligned for change: The AMA, AHA, and other medical advocates found willing backers among Republican leaders in the House and Senate as well as in the Bush Administration. Most of these officials actively promoted familiar first-generation reforms, headlined by MICRA-style statutory caps on noneconomic damage awards. And second, traditional stakeholders battling to advance their preferred policy solutions were joined by a host of new actors, including such (superficially) odd malpractice-reform bedfellows as the National Association of Manufacturers, American Tort Reform Association, and U.S. Chamber of Commerce.

Despite these novel features, the outcome in Congress remains the same as in the 1980s and 1970s crises: much sound and fury, yielding no substantive policy change. The U.S. House has passed MICRA-style reforms in each year of the current crisis – most recently in July 2005 – capping noneconomic damages at $250,000 and instituting three-year time limits on litigation in individual malpractice cases. These measures have died in the Senate each year; no cloture vote to end a filibuster has managed even a fifty-vote total, much less the necessary sixty votes in support. State outcomes in the current crisis have been mixed; many passed small-bore reforms, while debating more sweeping reforms – especially damage caps. A few states reduced their cap levels after 2001, though only two more (Maine and Alaska) achieved the MICRA grail of $250,000 as of this writing. By mid-2005, twenty-five states – the same number as a decade earlier – featured statutory caps on malpractice damage awards. Especially at the national level, the contrast between expectations and legislative outcome has never been starker in U.S. malpractice politics.

POLITICAL CONTEXT: MALPRACTICE AND THE NEW POLITICS
OF HEALTH CARE

How best to account for the complex politics surrounding medical malpractice reform, both the novel features arising in the present crisis and the

---

[22] Author's analysis of data presented at the National Conference of State Legislatures 2005.

legislative record since the 1970s? Kersh and Morone (2005) describe an emerging "new politics of health care," a paradigm that helps situate malpractice politics in broader context. Three basic features are present in many recent health policy battles over tobacco control, obesity, patients' rights, and many other issues – including medical malpractice. Indeed, struggles over malpractice beginning in the late 1960s helped to establish this distinctive health politics form.

First, many nationally prominent health care issues concern the *politics of private behavior*. Instead of topics familiar among medical policy makers for the first two-thirds of the twentieth century, like expanding the U.S. health care infrastructure (think Hill–Burton) or increasing access to health care, such traditionally private concerns as smoking, eating fast food, and drug use are of greater interest to policy makers. Though public authorities' attention to personal behavior dates at least to early nineteenth-century efforts to reduce excessive alcohol consumption, the expansion in recent years of federal government action into realms once considered private (or, at least, a concern of local/state officials only) has been dramatic. It has also been piecemeal. Industry and other actors' longtime habit of resisting "big government intrusion" into their activities lingers, shaping – and limiting – policy outcomes.

Malpractice politics fits this description as well. Physicians, insurance companies, and other stakeholders argued throughout the nineteenth century and well into the twentieth century that medical malpractice was an inappropriate subject for government regulation, as "a matter for private actors – physicians, insurers, patients – to sort out in private."[23] Today, in contrast, congressional leaders and President Bush are deeply engaged in debates over how to reduce liability insurance rates, encouraged by the AMA and fellow medical professionals. This shift is part of a more general trend in health policy making.

Second, the emergent model of U.S. health politics turns on extensive *issue framing* battles, carried out in congressional hearings and presidential pronouncements, across state capitals, and among interest-group representatives. These framing contests are typically fueled by crisis rhetoric. Obesity is cast as an "epidemic," morbidity and mortality rates from smoking were portrayed as "catastrophic" beginning in the 1980s, and so on. Such apocalyptic claims may or may not reflect reality; the perception of danger is usually sufficient to propel a health policy issue up the government agenda. Malpractice has been the subject of an especially fierce framing battle in recent years, driven by recurrent crisis warnings. The roots of this exchange trace to the late 1960s, helping set the tone for a wide range of health policy issues in ensuing years.

[23] Ward 1955, 92.

Third, a distinctive policy outcome has characterized health politics in recent years. Even in cases where framing disputes have been decisively resolved – by the late 1980s, for example, public demand for restrictions on tobacco advertising and use was massive – legislative results, especially at the national level, have been minimal. On numerous health issues, seeming consensus – and strong majority-party support in Congress and the White House – have not translated into statutory action. Instead, the *judicial branch* has increasingly shaped health policy solutions where the executive and legislative branches cannot. Efforts to guarantee certain patients' rights against their HMO or other managed care organization, for example, were unable to win approval from elected officials in Congress or the White House. It took a series of Supreme Court decisions to reshape managed care. The landmark $246 billion tobacco "Master Settlement Agreement" (MSA) was likewise worked out by judicial actors – trial lawyers and state attorneys general, principally – and court orders mandated a wide range of punitive requirements, including reduced tobacco advertising and sales policies. The new politics of health care features much churning in the legislative and executive branches but little action, opening the way to a response from the courts.

Malpractice policy fits at least part of this still-evolving "script." Years of sustained effort on Capitol Hill – including frequent public demands for action from both Presidents Bush – have yielded no legislative results. State capitals have instead been the principal locus of change. And though the malpractice system has not yet been a subject of judiciary-supervised reform, malpractice cases are increasingly a subject of federal court attention.

What accounts for this record of national elective-branch inaction in recent health policy making, including (thus far) in the malpractice example? Three primary possibilities come to mind. First, a range of *political entrepreneurs* have been drawn to health policy in recent years. These relative newcomers, facing off on multiple sides of an issue, slow the decision-making apparatus in Congress and the executive branch. Jonathan Rauch describes the result as "demosclerotic" – figuratively clogging the arteries of the body politic.[24] Many of the new players also tend to favor judicial action, as seen in the monumental conflicts over tobacco policy in the 1990s. With legislative stalemate in part caused by the sheer number of groups lobbying Congress and the White House for and against tobacco restrictions, an odd-bedfellows alliance of state attorneys general, plaintiffs' lawyers, and interest groups achieved a settlement ratified in court. Medical malpractice debates feature familiar figures, especially the AMA and the trial bar, but – especially in the current crisis – additional actors are centrally involved.

[24] Rauch 1994.

A second reason for congressional and executive inaction on many health care issues in recent years might be termed *preemptive federalism*: National policy making is rendered less necessary by enactments in individual states. Sometimes this action takes place at the judicial level – state courts were the original locus for tobacco settlements, until Minnesota's supreme court issued a sweeping decision in favor of antismoking advocates that pushed tobacco companies to negotiate the MSA. Other issues, prominently including malpractice reform, have been fought out in legislatures state by state. Note that "preemption" is not alone sufficient to explain national-government inaction, as variations in state policy making can also increase pressure for a uniform national solution.

Third, the federal government may simply *lack capacity* to enact comprehensive, long-lasting reform on contemporary health issues. Such a view first emerged in the 1970s, gained credence during the Clinton health reform debate of 1993–4, and has been advanced in a number of individual cases since.[25] Whether it also applies to malpractice politics is considered later.

This chapter's next section traces malpractice politics through each of these three broad features of contemporary health policy making: public attention to once-private health topics, a massive struggle over framing the issue, and elective-branch impotence. The anomaly of Congress/Bush Administration inaction on malpractice despite determined support for change from a Republican majority, the diffusion of malpractice "solutions" across American states, the enormous resources expended on framing the issue – these and other features snap more clearly into focus when medical malpractice reform is considered in wider political context. Also highlighted are instances where malpractice debates depart from analogous health policy areas.

Private Concern? No, Public Crisis!

As the history reviewed in Section I makes clear, malpractice has only recently become a topic of widespread public concern. Though specific acts of negligence were sometimes redressed through jury trials, the malpractice system was otherwise considered a largely private matter well into the twentieth century, left to individual patients and physicians (and their lawyers) to negotiate case by case. And principal stakeholders seemed clearly to want it that way: "No Federal or State legislator," wrote a Connecticut medical-society officer in 1938, "should dream of trespassing onto the winding paths of medical malpractice."[26] Instead, "self-regulation" was the byword among health professionals, who opposed public intrusion into malpractice like most other aspects of health care. Partly this position reflected broader features of U.S.

[25] Starr 1982, 411; Steinmo and Watts 1995.
[26] Cushing 1938, 5.

medical culture. Paul Starr notes that by the mid-nineteenth century, "the state had almost nothing to do with the private transactions between medical practitioners and their patients."[27] Personal health insurance has long been organized through employers in the United States;[28] why should medical liability insurance depart from market standards?

By the 1960s, this reflexive preference for private provision and policing of all aspects of American medicine – including physician negligence, real or putative, and liability insurance – was challenged by deep concern among physicians and their allies about the malpractice system's viability. Inspired by rising public concern, as noted in the historical section earlier, legislative actors began to show interest. Once the first liability-insurance crisis hit in the mid-1970s, state legislatures were already poised to turn medical malpractice from a private matter into a public policy issue. But policy making in most states as well as in Congress was strictly limited. AMA leaders and other medical professionals, while seeking relief from rising premiums, insisted on keeping federal and state regulations to a minimum. Virtually all the policy solutions enacted in state capitals or advanced in Congress were designed to limit the size of awards or restrict legal actions (e.g., through statutes of limitations, revision of joint and several liability, or limiting plaintiff attorneys' fees). Responsibility for redressing medical error still lay with individual patients, and liability insurance rates remained – except in California and a handful of other states – largely undisturbed by public officials.

Apart from some consumer advocates and other public interest groups, none of the players in malpractice politics has an incentive to invoke the regulatory action necessary to implement and oversee more sweeping reforms to the malpractice system. Executive and legislative action would be required for such second-generation policies as restructuring malpractice as a subset of Medicare, establishing a system of "health courts," and/or opening malpractice cases to mediation, compulsory screening measures, or other alternatives to traditional dispute resolution.[29] Liability insurers, for obvious reasons, remain fiercely devoted to blocking any regulation of premium rate levels. Physicians and other medical professionals reflexively resist public officials' intrusion into their domain of expertise. The trial bar has rarely pushed for public oversight or national standardization of malpractice awards; any rational economic actor would prefer the potential rewards of case-by-case litigation.

The rise of the patient-safety movement, spurred by the Institute of Medicine's (IOM) 2000 report on medical errors and the attendant "media

---

[27] Starr 1982, 66.
[28] On the development of employer-based health insurance in the United States, see Glied 2005.
[29] Sage 2004b, 20 (on Medicare); Udell and Kendall 2005 (health courts). On mediation, see the Liebman and Hyman chapter in this volume as well as Dauer and Marcus 1997; Brown 1998.

blitz . . . [that] captured the attention of President Clinton and members of Congress," inspired efforts to deter negligence through uniform practice guidelines established by statute.[30] In summer 2005, Congress passed a limited patient-safety measure – but explicitly decoupled its protections from malpractice litigation.

Medical malpractice has been a matter of public concern since the 1960s. But most legislative solutions passed by states, or debated in Congress, leave the system within private confines. Doctors and hospitals police medical errors and negligence; liability insurers set rates largely without interference by state or federal regulators (along with Major League Baseball, insurance is one of two industries exempt from federal antitrust regulation); standards for care remain nonbinding "guidelines"; and awards vary wildly from case to case, depending on judges and juries' whims or attorneys' skill. Perhaps no other outcome is possible, in a nation that invests enormous faith in markets and other private institutions and retains healthy (some say overzealous) suspicion of government actors.

In sum, the post-1960s politicization of malpractice has laid a veneer of public involvement over a long-private system – one that essentially remains that way. The result is an awkward, incremental, fragmentary politics: "Legislate in *this* area, but not in *that* one." A key to that patchwork outcome are the massive fights over defining the issue in the first place.

This Frame Is My Frame . . .

Rochefort and Cobb note that "to name a problem's cause is to dispel its disconcerting mystery and to turn in the direction of certain kinds of remedies and away from others."[31] Framing struggles over medical malpractice reform arose during the initial modern crisis of the late 1960s to early 1970s. Public hearings, media coverage, and the detailed Ribicoff and HEW Commission reports featured strongly worded, often contrasting positions, in terms that would recur in each subsequent "malpractice crisis" (itself a powerful framing term). Almost four decades ago, the AMA and allies were already warning that physicians were forced to practice costly "defensive medicine" and even abandon practice altogether: "Some 350 physicians in California alone" had "quit medical practice because of rising insurance costs," and "large numbers" more would "retir[e] in order to escape the evil scythe of unwarranted and unjustified malpractice litigation." Consumer advocates responded with calls for "quality health care," requiring a "patients' bill of rights" to protect against "wrongs inflicted upon them through improper medical procedures, through the promotion of scientific advancement, and lack of medical care."[32]

---

[30] Leape 2005 (quote at 163); see also Hyams, Shapiro, and Brennan 1996.
[31] Rochefort and Cobb 1994, 163.
[32] LeTourneau 1970, 19; DHEW 1973, 135.

Though the principal combatants were identified in the Ribicoff report's subtitle as "The Patient versus the Physician," legal and medical representatives were the principal voices exchanging blame in public. "The serious problems of the increasing frequency and cost of medical malpractice claims," insisted AMA president Charles Hoffman, "seem clearly to have arisen because of the zealous performance of legal duties by lawyers representing injured patients as claimants."[33] Retorted former ATLA president Richard Markus, the HEW Commission had "failed to give the patient-consumer sufficient consideration," perhaps because "lobbying efforts were made [on the Commission] to assemble the allied interests of those predisposed to special favor for the health care provider." Patient advocate Norma Almanza added tartly that "medical malpractice, at present, is viewed as a 'crisis' only by the medical profession.... the breakdown of the doctor–patient relationship in recent years is a key factor in malpractice claims." Lamented HEW Commission member George Northrup, the "malpractice problem" was exacerbated by "a major area of misunderstanding and lack of mutual trust [in] the relationship between law and medicine. The misunderstanding between lawyers and doctors has surfaced several times in the course of this Commission's hearings."[34]

In succeeding years, the terms of debate changed little. Physicians and insurers continued to insist that malpractice difficulties arose from lawyers' misplaced eagerness to sue and called primarily for changes to the legal system; as noted previously, federal regulation was viewed as anathema in these circles. Lawyers responded by citing the "gross inequity" and "enduring harm to society" that would result from any effort to "deprive victims of medical malfeasance of their day in court." The IOM's report and ensuing patient-safety movement contributed to these arguments from the trial bar. Especially after 1999, ATLA presidents and other malpractice lawyers' standard arguments included messages like, "If you want to address the medical malpractice crisis in this country, do something about the medical errors. That's the real problem."[35]

During the 1970s and 1980s crises, the framing battle was usually fought to a draw.[36] That seems less true in the present. The causes, consequences, and even extent of the malpractice problem remain difficult to specify; detailed studies by academics and nonpartisan organizations like the Government Accountability Office (GAO) and Congressional Budget Office (CBO) have been unable to pinpoint the reasons for rising malpractice losses, due to incomplete data and wide variation over time and by state.[37] But few

---

[33] DHEW 1973, 121.
[34] Ibid., 131, 109, 106–7.
[35] ATLA president Todd A. Smith quoted in Lohr 2005, 8.
[36] Kinney 1995.
[37] U.S. General Accounting Office 2003a; Congressional Budget Office 2004. Both reports identify, with extensive qualifications, two principal factors behind premium hikes: increased

qualifiers or nuances mark most advocates' positions, and public opinion analyses indicate that the battle over causes and preferred solutions was at least initially "won" by physicians and their allies. Polling by Gallup, Harris, and other national organizations demonstrated strong popular support for damage caps after 2001 and that much of the public viewed physicians as victimized by a deeply flawed medical liability system. In Pennsylvania, to take one example, a nonpartisan poll found in August 2004 that 68 percent of the public supported changing the state's constitution to cap noneconomic damages, as against 24 percent in opposition.[38]

The success, in Pennsylvania and many other states, of the AMA and allied groups in framing the issue owed in significant part to an intensive public lobbying campaign, surpassing in breadth and sophistication efforts in previous crises. Some of the most successful tactics were adapted from labor-union and other grassroots action. Individual physicians, who had traditionally remained distant from malpractice lobbying, engaged in work stoppages and large-scale protests at state capitals. Some 20,000 New Jersey doctors staged a work slowdown for more than a week in February 2003; a Maryland physicians' protest in 2004 helped push the state's governor to call a special legislative session to address malpractice reform.[39] Other AMA-coordinated techniques included political messages on liability reform mailed along with patient bills, mass e-mail campaigns from patients and doctors to public officials, media buys of print and television ads (and, in some places, a thirty-minute "infomercial" deploring rising premiums and touting damage caps in response). And, as in any successful public-health framing campaign, "crisis" rhetoric abounded. In June 2002, the AMA warned that twelve states were experiencing a full-fledged malpractice crisis and another thirty faced

malpractice payouts by insurers, especially in some specialties and geographic locales, and insurance market problems including declining investment income, diminished competition after the default of several malpractice insurers (especially the national carrier St. Paul's), soaring reinsurance costs after September 11, 2001, and depleted loss reserves.

[38] In a March 2003 Harris Poll, respondents favored damage caps by 58% to 16% (Harris Interactive, Mar. 6, 2003); a Gallup Poll in January 2003 found 72% favoring caps with 25% opposed. In comparison, in a March 1993 NBC/Wall Street Journal poll – with different question wording – only 44% of respondents called limits on damages "totally acceptable" (Kaiser Family Foundation 2003, 22–5). These numbers had slipped by late 2004; in a November national poll, only 26% of respondents agreed that "reducing the number and size of jury awards in medical malpractice lawsuits" was a "top priority" for Congress, down from nearly 40% who agreed some sixteen months before. (Thirty-three percent said it was "not that important" or "should not be done at all," more than double those selecting that option in mid-2003.) Though support for damage caps declined in late 2004–5, malpractice remained a concern. In a Kaiser poll in February 2005, 84% of respondents said reforming the medical malpractice system was "very important" (53%) or "somewhat important" (National Journal Poll Track 2005).

[39] Physicians staged work stoppages over malpractice premium rates as early as the 1970s crisis but in far smaller numbers than in 2002–5.

"severe problems" with premiums; in subsequent months the number of crisis states was revised upward to nineteen. Major media outlets trumpeted these reports, with *U.S. News* profiling "Healthcare's 'Perfect Storm'" in a July 2002 piece that blamed "skyrocketing premiums" on "the increasing number of personal injury lawsuits – and high-priced damage awards." (A year later, the magazine drew a very different conclusion: that the "dramatic crisis" had been overstated, and that "it's not clear that juries or the courts are the culprits . . . . left out of [doctors and insurers'] argument is recognition that ordinary market forces may be at work instead.")[40]

One particular feature of this framing debate turns on judgments about California's landmark 1975 law, MICRA. The Act is cited approvingly, indeed almost reflexively, by advocates of damage caps and other legal reforms. A recent exchange about malpractice policy between Nevada's Republican Senator John Ensign and Diana DeGette, House member from Colorado, is typical. "Because MICRA limited non-economic damages and reined in the cost of medical liability insurance premiums," writes Senator Ensign, "patients in [California] are reaping the benefits of effective medical liability by having the access they need." Responds DeGette, "Despite the [MICRA] caps, California malpractice premiums rose 450 percent in the 13 years following the legislation. It was not until the passage of insurance reform in California . . . that premiums stabilized and declined."[41]

As with many features of the malpractice debate, the actual impact of MICRA is difficult to assess. An exhaustive RAND study of the law's effects, released in 2004, concluded ambiguously that "MICRA appears to have had the California Legislature's intended *initial* result of limiting defendants' expenditures. . . . Whether such savings have translated into reduced premiums, greater availability of coverage, and a more stable health care delivery system – which were the California Legislature's *ultimate* goals for MICRA – is a question not answered by the data in our study." The RAND analysts also note which types of claims were most affected by the $250,000 cap: those "with the severest injuries (brain damage, paralysis, or various catastrophic injuries)" and plaintiffs less than a year old.[42] Such more qualified views (including the influence of 1988's liability insurance regulations) are generally lost in the crucible of political exchange. Of fifty-two references to MICRA in newspaper articles from across the nation between January 2001 and June 2005, forty-seven referred solely to the effect of MICRA damage caps on premium levels. Through such successful messages are framing debates decided.

---

[40] American Medical Association, "Medical Liability Reform" (self-published reports; June 2002, March 2003, November 2003). Marcus 2002, 39; Schmitt 2003, 24.

[41] Ensign 2005, 14; DeGette 2005, 12. See also Anderson 2005, 349–50.

[42] Pace, Golinelli, and Zakaras 2004, 47–8. See also Studdert, Yang, and Mello 2004; Sharkey 2005.

Why the different outcome of framing disputes during the present crisis? Partly it owed to physicians' extensive direct involvement in the political arena; more sophisticated lobbying and public relations techniques also helped. But greater legitimacy also underlies physicians' claims of distress. As William Sage notes, "previous malpractice crises occurred at the high-water mark of financial success and professional independence for physicians." This permitted doctors (and hospitals) to absorb or pass on to patients the costs of spiraling insurance policies. By 2002, a raft of changes in the U.S. health care system meant this was no longer the case.[43] Physicians' anxieties were matched by patients' own worries about affordability of care, helping tip public opinion in the AMA's direction.

One final note on framing issues. As noted previously, the storm of attention following the IOM's patient-safety report initially shifted the terms of debate on malpractice policy, as medical errors rather than tort liability became the central focus. Providers and other tort-reform advocates reframed that discussion, however, by successfully arguing that "lawsuits harm patients by driving error reports underground." As the IOM report itself observed, patient safety was "hindered through the liability system and the threat of malpractice, which discourages the disclosure of errors ... [and] encourages silence about errors committed or observed."[44]

With initial success at defining the problem on their terms, the AMA and its allies promoted a variety of policy reforms designed to reduce premium levels. Most prominent of these was noneconomic damage award caps; by summer 2003, all twelve of the states listed by the AMA as in crisis were debating caps or were seeking to reduce existing cap limits. As one summary of Washington State's lobbying battle over malpractice concluded: "For reasons of principle and politics, the entire debate centered on the issue of caps on damage awards. And neither the doctors nor the lawyers will bend on that question."[45]

Whatever damage caps' actual efficacy in reducing premiums – evidence notoriously remains mixed[46] – their appeal is undeniable. Politically, the caps solution meets three key features associated with successful health policy reforms: It is simple to understand, grounded in experience (as noted, half the states had established damage caps at various levels by 2000), and appeals to a variety of parties in the debate. As the present crisis mounted, the likelihood

---

[43] Sage 2005a, 467.

[44] Hyman and Silver 2005, quote at 896 (see generally on this successful reframing); Institute of Medicine 2000.

[45] Galloway 2004, A1.

[46] Positive accounts of caps' efficacy include Studdert et al. 2005; Thorpe 2004; U.S. General Accounting Office 2003a; Kessler and McClellan 1996. But compare Weiss Ratings 2003; Chandra et al. 2005; Black et al. 2005 – all empirical studies that find very weak relationships between caps and malpractice premiums.

of federal action establishing damage caps, along with other first-generation reforms, appeared high.

But successfully framing an issue – persuading policy makers and the public of one's position – is only a beginning.[47] To turn even a widely appealing policy idea into legislative enactment, several more steps are required. And these steps have proven very difficult to travel in the current health policy environment.

Implementation

In each year of the current malpractice crisis – as well as many of those preceding – damage caps and other first-generation reforms have been introduced in Congress, with high-profile support from other national officials. Yet these proposals died in both the 107th (2001–2) and 108th (2003–4) Congresses, the same fate met by every major malpractice bill introduced over the past eighteen years. This political failure requires explanation.

Interest Groups: Expanding the Malpractice Policy Horizon ... or Limiting It? Familiar stakeholders populate malpractice policy debates from the 1960s forward. The principal combatants, the AMA and ATLA, along with less publicly visible but still deeply engaged insurance groups like the American Insurance Association (AIA) and, more recently, Association of Health Insurance Professionals (AHIP), dominated malpractice lobbying activity into the 1990s, in terms of news coverage and reputed influence. In part this was due to spending: AMA and ATLA political action committees (PACs) have long been major sources of campaign funds and were both among the top five donors to federal candidates in 2002 and 2003.[48] They also engage in a host of other lobbying activities, from testifying before Congress to massive grassroots efforts reaching to medical and legal professionals and beyond.

Determining the extent of AMA, ATLA, or any other group's power to influence legislative outcomes is extremely difficult, given the manifold factors involved in any policy battle. A few state-level studies highlight lobbying successes and failures in tracing the fate of proposed legislation. Mello and Brennan report that their attempts to encourage adoption in Utah and Colorado of no-fault malpractice insurance rules similar to those governing auto accidents crumbled in the face of ATLA opposition and indifference on the part of malpractice liability insurers.[49] Kinney suggests persuasively that most stakeholders' strong preference for first-generation over

---

[47] Druckman and Nelson 2003.
[48] Contributions data at www.opensecrets.org (last accessed July 6, 2005).
[49] Mello and Brennan 2002.

second-generation reforms led to the former's "dominance" in both state and federal debates during the 1970s to 1990s; the same seems true for recent years as well.[50]

A similar interest-group effect is often cited for Congress's failure to pass any malpractice legislation, particularly damage caps. "Trial lawyers pursing their own agenda have continued to block this much-needed reform," asserted President Bush in 2004.[51] ATLA's power seems overstated, however. The best empirical study to date of congressional malpractice legislation, focusing on the House "HEALTH Act" (a package of first-generation reforms, centered around a $250,000 noneconomic-damages cap) in 2003, drew three intriguing conclusions. First, financial contributions had only a limited effect on legislators' votes on the HEALTH Act – and the influence of insurance/AMA contributions was roughly similar to that of ATLA. Second, the AMA's designation of "crisis states" had no measurable effect on voting – in other words, House members from the nineteen states the AMA designated in 2003 as facing a malpractice crisis were no more likely to vote for damage caps than were members from other states. Third, a significant determinant of voting was whether a House member had a law degree; lawyers were more inclined to vote against the bill, regardless of party affiliation.[52]

Thus, it is difficult to exclusively credit (or blame) the usual players for the continued national legislative standoff on malpractice. Interest groups certainly play a role – but traditional combatants are now only part of an elaborate malpractice "issue network," one featuring many additional groups active on the topic. As any issue gains salience in Washington, lobbying groups of all stripes are attracted to the action, diminishing the possibility of decisive policy action.[53] Interest groups have swarmed over the malpractice issue, with a set of entrepreneurial newcomers joining the debate in recent years. Table 3.1 provides one measure of expanded conflict in malpractice politics since the mid-1960s, by charting mentions of different groups in newspaper stories about malpractice. Thirty substantial (defined as more than five paragraphs) stories about malpractice policy were selected from a range of newspapers for each five-year period from 1966 to the present; the results display the number of different groups mentioned, total group cites, and percentage of those total cites for each of a variety of lead actors. (To take one illustrative example, a *New York Times* story titled "A Push in States to Curb Malpractice Costs," from January 14, 2005, included six cites of five different groups: the American Tort Reform Association, ATLA, AMA (twice), AIA, and Missouri Association of Trial Lawyers.) As measured in

---

[50] Kinney 1995, esp. 122–5.
[51] Compare Anderson 2005.
[52] Wolaver and Magee n.d.
[53] Heclo 1978; Rauch 1994.

TABLE 3.1. *Interest Groups in Media Coverage of Malpractice Politics,*
1966–2005

Year	Total # grps	Grp cites	AMA % cites	Other med	ATLA/law	Insurnc	Pub-int gps	Tort refrm
1966–70	8	21	43%	19%	14%	14%	5%	–
1971–75	11	37	38%	14%	22%	8%	11%	–
1976–80	10	33	36%	24%	18%	6%	15%	–
1981–85	17	48	38%	15%	19%	13%	15%	–
1986 90	32	62	31%	23%	21%	8%	16%	2%
1991–95	39	60	27%	12%	18%	13%	22%	3%
1996–2000	44	79	30%	19%	13%	8%	18%	5%
2001–05*	67	134	28%	12%	19%	7%	18%	11%

*2005: Through May 31.

N = 30 stories/5-year grouping [1966–70: 28; 1976–80: 27; 1991–95: 28][54]

Note: Row percentages do not always add to 100% because of unlisted "other" category. "Total grps" indicates the total number of different interest groups appearing in newspaper stories over each 5-year period. "Grp cites" reports how *many* times any interest group was mentioned. The remaining columns indicate individual group mentions as a percentage of total group citations. From left to right, the categories are AMA, other medical professionals like the AHA ("Other med"), ATLA and other legal groups, insurance groups like AIA, public interest advocates, and tort-reform organizations.

newspaper coverage, the expansion of stakeholders – especially during the current crisis – is dramatic.

As Table 3.1 displays, traditional stakeholders – especially the AMA – still routinely appear in news coverage of medical malpractice. Tort-reform advocates (far right column) are now frequently featured as well, comprising 11 percent of all group mentions since 2001. Most striking in the table, however, is the leap upward in total groups cited in newspaper stories (far left column). During the latter 1960s, as malpractice emerged as a political issue, the same handful of groups were quoted or mentioned again and again. In the period 2001–present, sixty-seven different organized interest-group players – a more than eightfold increase since 1970 – appear in newspaper coverage.

Of the additional stakeholders drawn to malpractice policy during the current crisis, one set comprises the private institutions responsible for health care, especially HMOs and other managed care organizations (MCOs) as well as nursing homes; also in this category are (nonmalpractice) health insurers, pharmaceutical companies, and medical device manufacturers. Common across these private entities is concern about the effects

[54] The newspapers consulted: *New York Times, Wall Street Journal, Washington Post, Chicago Tribune, Los Angeles Times, Philadelphia Inquirer, Dallas Morning News, Boston Globe, San Diego Union-Tribune.*

of malpractice politics on their own industry or profession. Various actors' interests take different forms, with a logical result the diffusion of lobbying efforts, potentially muddying the impetus for change. Yet in this round of malpractice debates, even past foes in the private/provider community have made common cause. To take one example: Health plans and other MCOs were at odds with the AMA through the 1990s, primarily because of AMA support for a patients' bill of rights that included malpractice liability for health plans. (Though no national patients' rights legislation was enacted, several states passed "right to sue" laws.[55]) Malpractice damage caps proved a means of bridging disagreements between health plans and the AMA: As AHIP (then AAHP) president Karen Ignagni remarked in 2003, "Although doctors and health plans do not always agree, AAHP is committed to supporting physicians in the fight for medical malpractice reform." AHIP lobbying in support of caps during the current crisis has been extensive; like the AMA – and most other private players listed previously – AHIP lists as a principal policy aim the passage of damage caps.[56]

As for groups like medical-device manufacturers and pharmaceutical companies, each advanced specific concerns in the malpractice debate and also joined in a larger effort to utilize malpractice as a means of advancing broader tort reform. Again as indicated in Table 3.1's far right-hand column, malpractice debates have also attracted a broader group of tort-reform players, mostly in the form of coalitions of U.S. businesses.[57] The largest of these groups, the American Tort Reform Association (ATRA), comprises familiar malpractice stakeholders (the AMA, insurance lobbyists) along with such other actors as gun manufacturers and the tobacco industry. ATRA and like groups view malpractice reform as a promising basis for more sweeping changes in liability laws and have worked both nationally and in numerous states to promote damage caps in a range of areas besides medical malpractice, such as construction liability and torts brought against state and local governments. Affirms a *New York Times* report, "limiting jury awards has long been a high priority for Republicans and business interests, who believe malpractice legislation could open the door to a broader tort reform agenda." Such an expansion of the debate arouses strong reactions from consumer and other public interest advocates, who denounce this "sophisticated lobbying campaign coordinated by Republican operatives and underwritten by business groups with little interest in the practice of medicine."[58]

These public interest actors are another set of entrants to the malpractice debate. Some long-established groups, such as Public Citizen and Families

---

[55] Bloche and Studdert 2004; Jost 2004.
[56] Belfiglio 2003, 5. AHIP's Ignagni in 2003 joined AMA president Donald Palmisano as co-chair of the American Tort Reform Association's Medical Liability Committee, a strong signal of support.
[57] On the tort-reform movement more broadly, see Feinman 2005; P. Rubin 2005.
[58] Stolberg 2003, A1; Mencimer 2003, 23. See also Boehm 2005, esp. 363–4.

USA, have added malpractice to the list of issues they lobby on. Issue entrepreneurs have formed new organizations around efforts to enhance patient safety in the wake of the movement sparked by the 2000 IOM report. Another set of consumer groups promotes liability insurance reform, such as public regulation of premium rates. Longtime advocate Consumer Federation of America has been joined by newer players like "Americans for Insurance Reform" (a coalition of consumer groups advocating insurance regulation) and the Foundation for Taxpayer and Consumer Rights. Reviewing the newspapers examined for Table 3.1, the steady growth in the number of public interest advocates cited in stories on malpractice policy is evident. Public interest organizations were a peripheral player in the 1960s; over the past decade, nearly two dozen different groups were quoted in major newspapers on the need for comprehensive malpractice reform.

In both federal and state venues, liability reform coalitions have met with mixed political success. The national tort-reform movement's single legislative victory to date, a congressional act limiting class-action lawsuits passed in February 2005, had no substantive effect on the malpractice system, where cases are argued one at a time; the outcome did lead to headlines like "Bush's Next Target: Malpractice Lawyers."[59] Elsewhere, attempts to alter malpractice laws through general tort reform have faltered. Pennsylvania, for example, debated a constitutional amendment capping damages in all civil suits during 2004. On the pivotal state Senate vote, held in the early hours of July 4, the broad-based proposal was defeated. Only the majority leader's fast legislative footwork – by stripping the bill down to medical malpractice damage caps alone – enabled an amended version to squeak through temporarily (it eventually failed as well). The broader tort-reform effort was also unsuccessful in other states; it is possible that perceived overreaching by this coalition may blunt the drive for medical malpractice legislation.

All in all, the case for interest-group gridlock hampering passage of liability reforms, especially the damage caps that appealed to many private players in the malpractice domain, is plausible but partial at best. Opponents of caps, led by the trial lawyers' association and consumer groups like Public Citizen, have mounted major state and national lobbying efforts in turn, likely helping stem the reformist tide. But a national debate initially framed around damage caps; a sustained and coherent lobbying effort by the AMA, AHIP, ATRA, and other powerful groups; a unified and determined majority on Capitol Hill and in the White House: These are the customary ingredients of policy change. Ultimately, legislative results *were* rung up – but in statehouses, not the national government.

State Action, 1960s–Present. As the history in the first section reviews, in each of the three modern malpractice "crisis" episodes, affected states were

---

[59] Lohr 2005, Sec. 3, p. 1.

the source of statutory malpractice reforms. That state officials generally are more decisive policy makers than the national elective branches on most health care matters is a standard claim of federalism analyses. Health issues at the state level, in one detailed account, "tend to be less complex, to have more singular objectives, and more predictable outcomes." Moreover, divergent interests within coalitions are "less severe at the state level," principally because "the business community is more homogeneous there.[60]

Perhaps it is simpler to achieve legislative change in states. But malpractice reformers and their foes in Olympia and Trenton and Tallahassee, among many other state capitals, have encountered unpredictability, complexity, and diverse objectives aplenty. And clashes among interest groups – even ostensible private-sector allies – are similarly widespread, as studies of Pennsylvania's malpractice battles testify. Research on state-level lobbying increasingly suggests that with vast expansions of group activity in recent years, state battles are coming to resemble those inside the Beltway in terms of scope and density of interest-group involvement.[61]

States' success in passing malpractice reforms may owe less to their ostensibly unrefined political landscapes than to the issue's urgency. Facing threats of physicians' imminent departure, states are spurred to legislate change. Do these state-level reforms reduce pressure on the federal government for action? Not necessarily. As the noted federalism scholar Daniel Elazar has observed, a collection of related state actions more often *inspires* than diminishes policy making in Washington.[62] Many participants in the current round of debates are pushing for a federal government solution to help clarify the patchwork of divergent state responses. Writing in the *Annals of Health Law*, a team of practitioners and academic observers called for "a federal statute that sets forth a bright-line rule regarding [health care] quality control privileges, immunities, and confidentiality" and further noted that "[i]t is essential that federal legislation be enacted that addresses the [malpractice] crisis .... current legislation that is pending in the Senate would be a vast departure from the state to state inconsistencies that currently prevail in this area."[63]

Yet although national political figures have for more than three years steadily sounded alarms about a malpractice crisis similar to those heard in affected states, Capitol Hill results have been scant. Could the institutional and political capacity for national reform be attenuated?

Institutional Capacity. The failure of most second-generation reforms, including comprehensive plans to control costs and enhance patient safety,

---

[60] Mintz and Palmer 2000, 354.
[61] A. Rosenthal 2001.
[62] Elazar 1972.
[63] Spaeth, Pickering, and Webb 2003, 247.

even to win committee consideration in Congress probably owes most to stakeholder opposition or disinterest. More popular MICRA-style changes, especially caps on noneconomic damages, likely have failed in Congress because of interest-group gridlock or "safety-valve" state legislation as well as to specific events that derailed the push for policy reform, especially in the Senate.[64] Abstracting from these case-by-case events and viewing malpractice politics since the late 1960s as a whole, the persistence of inertia is striking. Malpractice policy may be a victim of a wider institutional failure.

In any policy realm, the U.S. separated-powers system places formidable obstacles in the way of reformers, from multiple veto points to the three-fifths supermajority required to achieve cloture in the Senate. Incrementalism, as Charles Lindblom noted decades ago, characterizes most American policy making – including health policy.[65] Ambitious malpractice reforms, in this perspective, will almost inevitably be whittled down to minor changes, as has happened in most health care debates over the past thirty years.

And yet, even incremental adjustments to the malpractice system have thus far eluded federal officials. Beyond micro-level explanations focused on the strategic environment of each successive crisis, a deeper rationale might be the national government's depleted capacity to enact significant change. Buttressing such an explanation are the histories of particular policy debates in Washington. The "path dependent" persistence of organizational and institutional patterns exerts a powerful effect on policy making, as political scientists increasingly recognize.[66] Here the forty-year history of malpractice politics itself becomes an influential explanatory factor, as present-day actions are affected by the federal government's responses to past crises. A legacy of national inaction on malpractice constitutes a type of policy framework, with prior government moves establishing and reinforcing boundaries on legislative possibilities – affecting creative and adaptive solutions. This is not an insurmountable process – the past conditions, rather than determines, the present – but helps to illuminate the resistance to change in a given policy domain. Space precludes a fuller accounting of the distinctive features of malpractice politics in this regard, but such explanations have been persuasively offered in realms such as the provision of national health insurance.[67]

Ultimately, the U.S. national government's apparently shrunken capacity for undertaking broad-based reform returns us to both the public–private

---

[64] For example, the widely reported February 2003 death of Jésica Santillan, a seventeen-year-old recipient of a heart and lung transplant from an incompatible donor, was viewed as a setback for damage caps at the national level.

[65] Lindblom 1959.

[66] Pierson 2000.

[67] Hacker 1998. See also Kersh 2005 for a study of Pennsylvania's bounded malpractice policy regime.

divide (substantive change is all the more difficult to achieve when meaning-ful public regulation is essentially off the table) and federalism: Continued prospects for reform seem to be at the state level. Damage caps and other stopgap policies may help slow premium growth in the worst-affected states, blunting the leading edge of the crisis. And state innovations also provide a basis for comparative evaluation, contrasting premium levels in states fea-turing damage caps with those that do not. But state reforms by definition represent a patchwork solution. "Resolving" the present crisis through a series of partial state actions may be unsatisfying enough to invite judicial-branch involvement, hitherto a road not taken in malpractice politics – but increasingly a favored route in other health policy realms.

THE ROAD AHEAD

Might federal or state courts act to alter the medical malpractice regime? Reform proposals stalled for decades in Congress could be enacted by court order, much as many other health policy changes have been achieved in recent years. This possibility was floated during the first malpractice crisis, as the HEW Commission debated whether courts should instantiate practice guide-lines to provide uniform standards for malpractice litigation. An exasperated Commission physician, Paul B. Jarrett, responded that "[n]o thinking person would have the courts establishing the standard of practice rather than the medical profession, yet we are dangerously close to this situation."[68]

Judicial action is also likely if Congress were to enact legislation along the lines of a MICRA-style act, as federal court appeals would swiftly follow. One likely basis for such a challenge: the act's constitutionality. A long tra-dition of state regulation in malpractice and other tort-law realms renders suspect the national government's power to adjudicate this area of state leg-islative concern. As one legal commentary notes, "it is not clear that Congress possesses the authority to prescribe procedures that state courts must use to enforce state rights of action." Recent Supreme Court decisions limiting the reach of the Commerce Clause, under which national malpractice reform would be justified, also suggest that damage caps and other first-generation measures could be rejected by the judiciary.[69]

In fact the time may have passed for major reforms of the malpractice regime, whether legislated by Congress or judicially imposed. By the second quarter of 2005, the pressure for political action had begun to abate, as various sources suggested that the malpractice crisis was nearing resolution. Claims about "runaway jury awards" lost some of their bite after reports that total malpractice award amounts dropped after 2003, and that malprac-tice cases' share of the 100 largest jury verdicts declined sharply in 2003 and

[68] DHEW 1973, 138.
[69] Suit 2005, 219 (quote), and *passim*.

TABLE 3.2. *Trends in Largest Malpractice Jury Awards, 2001–2004*

Year	Total cases[Ψ]	Total amount[δ]	Avg. per-case payout	% Change (previous yr.)
2001	14	$695 million	$49.64 million	21.4% increase
2002	13	$761 million	$58.54 million	17.9% increase
2003	15	$560 million	$37.33 million	36.2% decrease
2004	13	$514 million	$39.54 million	5.9% increase

[Ψ] Number of malpractice cases among the 100 largest-dollar jury awards for that year.
[δ] Total dollar amount awarded in those malpractice cases, adjusted for inflation.

remained flat in 2004. Table 3.2 displays the latter figures, using inflation-adjusted data for the past four years. A few recent accounts suggest that the malpractice problem was overblown from the beginning. These include detailed academic studies of Texas and Pennsylvania, two states declared to be in "crisis" by the AMA early in 2002. Both analyses examined numerous measures – including large paid claims (total number and mean/median payouts per claim), mean/median jury verdicts in all trials won by patients, total payouts and defense costs, average paid claims per practicing physician in the state, and so forth – and concluded that 2002 (or subsequent years) did not mark the sharp increases that "crisis" rhetoric would imply.[70] Debates will continue about the extent and nature of the difficulties facing the malpractice system generally, and liability insurance premiums specifically. But for now it is enough to note that, by early 2005, the high-intensity alarms of the preceding three years had begun to abate.

If the issue's urgency continues to fade, the chances of even minor political tinkering will plummet as well. And that outcome is likely to satisfy few stakeholders in the debate. As a trio of academic experts summarize, the malpractice system's "fundamental shortcomings require more fundamental reform,"[71] but it is difficult to imagine such an undertaking in the present political climate. More likely is a resumption of familiar framing battles and legislative churning on first-generation reforms when the next round of premium increases occurs.

[70] Mello and Brennan 2002; Black et al. 2005.
[71] Studdert, Mello, and Brennan 2004, 290.

TWO

THE HEALTH POLICY IMPACT OF
MEDICAL MALPRACTICE

4

Who Pays When Malpractice Premiums Rise?

Mark V. Pauly

Malpractice premiums, as is well known, have been high and rising in recent years. Both the level and the growth in premiums vary substantially across states, due in large part to different "malpractice regimes" that either facilitate or inhibit the filing of claims and the awarding of large judgments. There has been considerable discussion of the effects of high or rising premiums, but a fundamental issue in predicting effects or judging normative claims about them is surely the consequences of premium changes on physician incomes and revenues. At one polar extreme, higher premiums may fall almost entirely on physician net incomes, prompting outflow from one state to another or retirement from the active practice of medicine. At the other extreme, if physicians could expect the fees they charge to increase on average by the amount of any premium increase, and if the quantity of services demanded remains unchanged, the full cost of premiums would be shifted forward to consumers (and taxpayers) as higher out-of-pocket payments and/or higher insurance premiums to cover those payments. In between, various divisions are possible.

The consequences of higher malpractice premiums are important regardless of their "incidence" – that is, the identity of those who finally bear the burden of the cost. This chapter first outlines the set of theoretically possible outcomes in terms of incidence, which turns out to be large indeed. It is impossible to choose a scenario based on the causal empirical evidence available. Next is a discussion of such rigorous evidence as there is on the subject, extracting both some reasonably secure conclusions and some evaluation of the large scope of remaining uncertainty. Finally, policy implications about what we know and what we need to know about the incidence of premiums are summarized as well as how the evidence on this aspect of behavior relates to other questions about malpractice policy.

THINKING ABOUT INCIDENCE

There are several different types of responses to or effects of higher malpractice premiums that potentially could affect incidence. These responses may depend as well on the reason why a medical practice's premiums rise or are higher than average, and the proportion of other physicians in the market who experience similar increases.

One useful benchmark case is the following: Suppose malpractice premiums rise equally for all physicians in a given specialty in a given market area, and suppose all insurers have reimbursement formulas that cause reimbursements to rise to offset higher premiums. We also need to assume that patient out-of-pocket payments will not increase, either because insurance coverage is complete or because cost sharing takes the form of fixed dollar copayments rather than proportional coinsurance.

If all physicians chose the same outputs and inputs after the change in premiums as before, we would expect that gross revenues would rise by an amount equal to the premium increase. For example, if premiums are 15 percent of gross practice revenues and they increase by 20 percent, prices and gross revenues would rise by 3 percent ($.20 \times .15$). If this happened, average net money income per physician would be left unchanged. In this case, the full incidence of premiums is shifted forward (to patients or their insurers) and none of the incidence falls on physicians.

Such an outcome – no change in physician net income and therefore no reason to alter any other physician behavior – requires quite restrictive assumptions. Change those assumptions, and at least some of the consequences may reduce physician incomes. However, it is more difficult to construct a model that illustrates the opposite end of the spectrum – full incidence on the physician. The reason is that, as individuals, physicians would be expected to change their behavior after an increase in premiums rather than tolerate a large decline in income. Income may still decline, but that will not be all that happens. Physicians may induce demand for services ("defensive" or not) or change nonphysician inputs to the practice in order to reduce the bite on net money income. They may change the scope of practice, location, or activity.

Which of these two behaviors (or some combination of them) is likely to occur, and any interpretation of the data we do observe, depends on two kinds of hypotheses: what we hypothesize to be the objectives of the physicians in a practice, and what we hypothesize to be the constraints they face from public and private insurers, from patients, from regulators, and from suppliers of other inputs to the practice. In the discussion that follows, the organizational form I have in mind is a multiperson, single-specialty practice, whether organized as a partnership or formal group practice, that is controlled and largely managed by the physicians in the practice. This is now the most common structure for all but the "hospital-based" practices of anesthesiology, radiology, pathology, and hospitalization. Where necessary, I consider physicians in solo practices and settings where some physicians are salaried employees of a physician practice, hospital, or clinic.

Usual assumptions about physician objectives in economic models identify three goals: money income, leisure time, and the physicians' perception of patient welfare. This conceptualization causes hypothesized practice behavior, given some set of constraints, to differ from the more familiar model of a profit-making firm in two ways. First, with the additional assumption that both leisure and patient welfare matter to physicians and are "normal" goods (in the sense that they command higher value the higher the physicians' income), one possible outcome of lower income for a given amount of physician work is a decision to "supply" less leisure and/or less patient welfare. That is, lower prospective money income might prompt the physicians to work more hours and pay less attention to possibly negative effects on a patient's welfare from suggesting larger quantities of profitable services – to induce demand. Second, in a multiperson practice the need to divide net income among partners may lead to decisions that reduce aggregate net income but divide what income there is in more acceptable ways.

Under fee for service payment, probably the main constraint on forward shifting in the short run is the reimbursement policies of insurers that pay for the practice's patients' care. Medicare and, to a considerable extent, Medicaid simply fix prices. The practice is strictly limited in its ability to balance bill for anything more than the reimbursement level or some fixed multiple of that level (e.g., 115%); the reimbursement level thus fixes the maximum price the physician is permitted to charge. However, if an insurer permits the practice to increase its fees, any coinsurance present will cause patients who lack supplemental insurance to experience higher out-of-pocket payments, which would be expected to decrease demand to some extent. So even if an insurer were to raise its reimbursement rate to fully offset any higher premiums, the increase in total revenue will be expected to be smaller than that needed to maintain net income; prices will have to go up yet further to offset any reduction in quantity demanded.

Private insurers permit balance billing. In such a case, physicians can raise the fees they charge even if insurer reimbursement levels are held constant, and now the full price increase (rather than a proportion) falls on patients. Even here, the net effects of higher patient prices should be to reduce the extent of possible forward shifting as patients cut back on their use. However, if the insurers also automatically increase their reimbursement rate when malpractice premiums rise (as Blue Cross in Pennsylvania has done), that will permit greater forward shifting.

Patients who do not have coverage for physician services will have the same response to a price increase regardless of the level of malpractice costs. For them, the reason why fees are rising will not matter.

Physicians can in theory do more than just alter prices if malpractice premiums change. They can also change their recommendations about what services patients are advised to use – both services they supply and those supplied by others. One dimension of this change is so-called defensive medicine – recommending more services thought to furnish protection against malpractice action. The other possibility is that, in an attempt to restore money income, physicians may recommend higher volumes of other profitable services they sell (unrelated to the probability of malpractice action).

Both are cases of "demand inducement," in the sense that patients are urged to consent to these additional services even though their user price has not changed and there has been no increase in patient demand. The physician cost of demand inducement is usually modeled as a reduction in physician utility associated with reductions in patient welfare (either from side effects of the unnecessary services or from higher copayments); it is also sometimes modeled as a utility cost to the physician for deviating from advice known to be correct. Finally, one can also model such increased quantities as a "packaging" response to a price limit imposed by the seller: a de facto increase in the total cost to the patient as a quid pro quo for supplying the services the patient truly seeks.[1] If the insurer has limited the explicit price, this may be a way for the physician to increase the implicit price.

In addition to the demand constraint just discussed, the physician supplies time as an input, to be combined with other practice inputs. It is possible that the ideal mix of those inputs may change when malpractice premiums rise. Most obviously, when a physician's money income falls, a way to regain it is to reduce the practice's nonphysician staff but supply more doctor time and effort to produce output. Although the physician's real income or utility is reduced, his or her money income need not be.

The final issue in modeling is the source of high or increasing malpractice premiums. The cause most relevant to most policy discussions is, of course, the legal climate, broadly defined. At least at the level of a state, higher costs to malpractice insurers should be reflected in higher average statewide premiums for a given level of coverage. Both the frequency of claims per doctor and the severity of claims as measured by awards or cost per claim are germane.

There can be reasons other than the statewide claims climate that affect why a practice pays high premiums. Because different insurers are permitted to charge different premiums, one practice may discover a lower price than another simply because it shopped more aggressively or with better luck. The extent of coverage chosen by the practice may also vary, although it generally takes on one of two standard levels. Finally, although there is relatively little explicit experience rating of a given policy, premiums may depend on especially adverse experience and/or coverage may be harder to get after bad experience.

[1] McGuire 2000.

NAÏVE STORIES AND NONINTUITIVE BEHAVIOR

To many physicians and patients, it seems obvious that higher malpractice premiums can turn immediately into higher fees, especially if the managed care presence is moderate. As long as a large insurer does not forbid it, won't physicians raise their fees and balance bill for more when premiums rise? However, if the typical small business run by physicians behaves in the same way and is subject to the same constraints as other small businesses, this will not happen. Those asked to pay higher prices, whether patients or insurers, may respond by reducing the amount of services they demand, either by consuming less in total or by switching to other practices that have yet to raise fees. Paradoxically, if a practice had a single-minded devotion to maximizing net income, it would have already set the price at the profit-maximizing level. Raising the price above this level will so depress quantity that net income will fall. Of course, a physician concerned about patients' financial well-being might set price below this level until a rise in premiums makes charity less affordable; price then can rise.

Another naïve story that can sometimes be wrong deals with managed care. Managed care plans are known to bargain for low or discounted prices, compared to what other kinds of insurers pay. But this only means that prices will be "low" and not necessarily that the response of prices to a change in cost will be lower under managed care than with other kinds of insurance. The key issue in either case is the extent to which patients are willing to forgo or to be led to forgo care when price rises – either because they are paying the price under conventional insurance or because their managed care plan wants them to economize. Resistance to restrictions by members may limit a managed care plan's ability to dampen price increases.

The next point is that the response of price to a change in malpractice costs depends on the kind of cost increase. If only malpractice premiums rise, this will mean a higher *fixed* cost for the practice, but the additional (or marginal) cost of supplying various amounts of output will be unaffected. The result is that the profit-maximizing price will not change. Despite the reduction in income from high premiums, raising price would only lower net income yet further. An increase in premiums will not open new opportunities to raise output prices.

This story changes if higher premiums accompany higher explicit and implicit marginal costs per unit of output. For example, if the risk of a malpractice action per patient encounter increases, and if physicians must spend time that could have been used in other ways defending themselves, then in a sense the expected marginal cost of seeing another patient rises, and we should expect to see an increase in price.

If the marginal cost rises by $X, by how much will fees rise? If demand is fairly responsive to price and the physician market is highly competitive across firms, the price increase will be positive but will be less than X. Some fraction of the higher cost will fall on physicians as long as total demand in the market responds to higher prices. If, in contrast, a practice has some monopoly power, price may rise by an amount equal to or even greater than X. The key to predicting what will happen to quantity demanded if the physician firm raises its price is firm-level demand elasticity. If markets are very competitive, so that an increase in price of Q percent by one practice causes a fall in its demand of many multiples of Q (because patients switch or are switched to other practices), price will still rise but by a small amount. If instead an increase in price of Q percent would reduce demand from this firm by only a small amount – say 2Q percent – then price will rise by 2X; there can be considerably *more* than 100 percent forward shifting.[2]

The key questions in pricing then are

1. the objectives of the practice,
2. the degree of competition among practices, and
3. the extent to which higher malpractice premiums reflect higher *marginal* costs.

EMPIRICAL EVIDENCE ON THE INCIDENCE OF MALPRACTICE PREMIUMS

Because a variety of outcomes could occur in theory, we now turn to evidence from empirical data. For reasons to be discussed, the question of incidence is difficult to answer empirically and has been investigated in only a small number of studies. We will therefore also examine other empirical evidence that bears on the question of incidence, "circumstantial evidence" that is not itself conclusive but may influence the probability one places on a particular hypothesis.

The general answer to the question of what a physician practice will do in response to an increase in malpractice premiums will surely depend on the reason for the increase. The most policy-relevant reason is related to what I earlier called the "malpractice climate": changes in either the likelihood of malpractice action or the damage levels per case. When either of these increases, the benefits an insurer will expect to pay out will increase, and the premium will presumably increase as well. Another reason for higher premiums is insurer decisions to raise premiums even when expected benefits remain the same; the rationale for such increases could be a reduction in returns on reserves, an increase in insurer market power that raises the equilibrium profit level, or an attempt by insurers to recoup past losses. A given practice might pay a higher premium because its insurer charged more and the practice was unable or unwilling to shop around, or it may for various reasons choose to raise the limits of its coverage.

---

[2] McCarthy 1985 provides us an estimate that suggests 150% shifting.

What one would like to be able to observe is a situation in which some practices were randomly subject to premium increases only for the reason of interest (e.g., changes in the litigation costs), and others were not. The world does not furnish us with such clean experiments, however. Instead, we can observe practices with apparently similar characteristics (specialty, size, patient insurance mix, and practice employee wage rates) paying different premiums per full-time physician, but we cannot easily know why the premiums vary. Some statistical techniques can help separate out those variations due to causes that we can identify, but they are imperfect, so some ambiguity of interpretation necessarily remains.

Most of the empirical evidence relating premiums to physician net incomes relies on data from the late 1980s.[3] These studies used the information from the Physician Practice Cost and Income Surveys (PPCIS) from 1976 through 1986; this type of data unfortunately is no longer collected. The PPCIS provided information from a random sample of physicians (not physician practices) on net incomes, malpractice premiums, and measures of fees for a small sample of common procedures. The liability "climate" was usually measured by the premium charged by one large insurer in the state where the physician was located for a basic insurance policy. These years were ones in which premiums increased significantly but before the spread of managed care.

The main result was that physician incomes were not lower in states where the "climate" (as measured by standard premiums) was more adverse. The primary basis for this conclusion was evidence that fee levels increased when premiums increased, with an elasticity sufficiently large to imply 100 percent forward shifting or even shifting of more than 100 percent. (Recall that firms with market power can raise prices in amounts that are more than proportional to cost increases.) Reimbursement levels by insurers also increased when premiums increased, but to a somewhat smaller extent than fees charged (implying that some of the higher premiums were shifted to consumers as higher balance bills). There is also some evidence, as might be expected, that the volume of some services changed with higher premiums (given fee levels), but sometimes the effect was negative. Defensive ordering of extra tests does not seem to have occurred: lab tests fell, X-rays rose, as did the average length of an office visit, even while the total volume of visits fell.

Additional work[4] showed that this forward shifting was similar across specialties but was more pronounced for surgical services than for office visits. Thurston's interpretation is that a patient is unable to shop as aggressively for lower fees for surgical procedures (which are usually rare) as for office visits (which are common), so that malpractice premiums can be more

---

[3] Danzon 1990; Danzon et al. 1990.
[4] Thurston 2001.

easily shifted to surgical fees. Another possible explanation is that higher premiums reflect higher marginal costs for surgical procedures (an additional procedure raises risk of a time-consuming suit) in a way that medical services do not. In addition, Thurston found that the effect on prices was stronger for practice-specific premium increases than for marketwide ones.

More recent studies of the effect of premiums and climate on income have had to deal with poorer data. Neither the benchmark plan premium data nor a random sample of physicians detailing their incomes, fee levels, and premiums paid is available for the 1990s. Moreover, in the modern managed care environment, posted or listed fees have much less meaning because many PPOs and HMOs get discounts of varying amounts. "Prices" are much harder to measure now. The analogous data collection effort by the American Medical Association was suspended in 1999 and resumed in smaller-scale form in 2001, but it does not take the form of a panel.

Pauly et al.[5] therefore turned to data from physician group practices, collected by the Medical Group Management Association (MGMA), covering the years from 1994 to 2002. This does offer the possibility of looking at a given group over time. Although this survey obviously omits nongroup physicians, it covers a sample that represents a sizeable proportion of medical practices that are likely to have more reliable financial data than the information self-reported by solo practices in the older surveys.

The MGMA data were also analyzed to determine the relationship between malpractice premiums and the malpractice climate and physician net incomes. Cross-sectional analysis was undertaken for 1994, 1998, and 2002. For those practices that reported in both 1998 and 2002, changes in net increases were related to changes (almost always increases, many substantial) in premiums for physicians.

The general results were highly consistent with those from the earlier period. There was no negative relationship between malpractice premiums per physician and net income per physician in a practice; the relationship was usually statistically insignificant but sometimes was positive (in the panel data), implying at least 100 percent forward shifting. Practices in a given specialty paying higher premiums did not experience lower net incomes per physician.

This analysis controlled for many practice characteristics, including the practice's specialty, which is strongly related to net income. Net income is, paradoxically, generally higher in specialties with higher average premiums, but some of that difference in income is doubtless due to longer periods of training and other costs. Other practice characteristic variables were significantly and plausibly related to net income per physician. Income tended to be lower in practices with a larger share of managed care or Medicaid patients;

5 Pauly et al. 2004.

it tended to be higher in the specialties known generally to have higher net incomes, and also when wages per full-time equivalent (FTE) employee were higher, probably reflecting cost-of-living differences across areas.

There was no effect from interacting the malpractice premium with the proportion of patients on managed care; that is, there was no evidence that forward shifting differed by the level of managed care penetration. Possible nonlinearities in effects were also explored, but there was no evidence of a negative effect on net income even of relatively high levels of premiums. A subset of practices in the surgical specialties (primarily general surgery and OB-GYN) displayed the same stability of net income in the face of higher premiums as was found for the larger sample of all specialties.

Two measures of malpractice premiums were used. One was the actual premium paid by the practice. But this variable is potentially endogenous; practices can affect the premium they pay by how much coverage they choose to buy, by how much they shop for coverage, and possibly by adding or deleting some additional services that affect the insurer's perception of risk.

To deal with this problem, the determinants of a practice's premium were analyzed. It is not, after all, a foregone conclusion that higher malpractice awards will translate immediately into increased premiums or that, conversely, higher premiums will only occur when expected payouts increase. What actually happens is an empirical matter.

It was found that premiums were significantly higher in certain specialties, as expected. Given specialty, premiums are significantly higher also in states with higher levels of malpractice claims per physician and in states in which the malpractice component of Medicare's practice cost index was higher. Thus, in contrast to the recent work of Baicker and colleagues,[6] there was a systematic relationship between state-level characteristics related to malpractice clauses and the premium that a practice in that state pays. However, there was even more variation in premiums within a state not tied to these causes.

To separate the effects of malpractice climate and overall premiums from any practice-specific effects, a measure of predicted premiums based on variation in "climate" and (Medicare) cost was developed. Using simultaneous equations techniques, such an analysis should avoid any bias due to endogeneity. The results of this analysis were virtually identical to those using the direct measure; there was no relationship between the variation in premiums due to the malpractice climate and net physician income.

Although the results in terms of shifting and net income were therefore quite similar to those in the earlier period, additional analysis suggests that the mechanism for forward shifting may have changed. In particular, although net incomes in a practice were independent of premium levels,

[6] Baicker and Chandra 2004.

gross revenue per physician was significantly higher in practices with higher premiums. The elasticity suggests that gross revenues rose by at least the addition to premium.

The MGMA data contained a measure of prices, but that measure was missing for many observations. Instead, we looked at how premiums were related to proxies for the quantity or volume of services. Malpractice premium levels were related to nonphysician expenses per physician (wage rates held constant), as a measure of practice inputs per physician. The relationship was positive and statistically significant, indicating two things: First, physicians were not sustaining their money incomes when premiums rose by cutting nonphysician practice inputs and substituting more of their own time. Second, the higher quantity of nonphysician inputs per physician associated with higher premiums suggests that volumes of services per physician were also higher for practices with higher premiums. Rather than primarily affecting price increases, as in the earlier data, this analysis suggests that physicians maintained net income by providing more services. This increased volume could either represent defensive medicine or it could represent an increase in the volume of services of all types, both in response to an inability to raise fees.

Other survey evidence from Pennsylvania, a high-premium state, similarly found that physicians reported increasing the number of patients seen as a response to higher premiums.[7] Of course, there are limits to the demand-increasing strategy. An obstetrician who claimed (in the Mello study) that, because of higher statewide premiums, "doctors are delivering more babies per month than they should be" may have been correctly describing what some practices are doing, but it is unlikely that a given number of obstetricians could respond to higher premiums by causing more babies to be born.

Unfortunately, reliable recent data on fee levels are not available that would allow a direct test of that relationship. It may well be that fees are more constrained than they were earlier, so that more of the effort to maintain income spilled over into higher quantities. It is likely that there was forward shifting both into higher fees and higher quantities of income-yielding services.

Some additional evidence also bears on this question. Empirical evidence confirms common sense; physician practices have some market power and do not lose large amounts of business when they raise prices.[8] Empirical estimates of firm-level demand elasticity are in the range of three to seven, suggesting that increments in marginal cost are marked up from 117 to 150 percent, so one would not be surprised to see both large price and quantity increases.

[7] Mello, Studdert, DesRoches, et al. 2004.
[8] Pauly and Satterthwaite 1981.

POLICY IMPLICATIONS

The first policy question is the most obvious one: If physicians generally can offset the impact of higher malpractice premiums on their net incomes, why do they complain so bitterly? One might wonder whether the cross-sectional stability of net income hides a process of supply adjustment in which the number of practices shrinks in order to rebuild net income, but the panel data results strongly suggest that increases in premiums are turned into higher incomes in less than four years' time, surely a period too short for large-scale practice migrations in response to premium changes.

Danzon[9] offers one possible explanation for complaints: A zero average effect on net income may conceal substantial individual practice variation about that average, with some quiet practices gaining more than cost but those who gain less being the ones who complain. Another possibility is that the process of increasing volume to offset higher costs may itself be wearying and upsetting to physicians who would rather have kept things as they were. Nevertheless, these results suggest that some of the more dire predictions about the effects of higher malpractice premiums may be somewhat overstated. Higher premiums may not be driving physicians in general out of practice in response to lower incomes or even providing strong incentives to relocate. (There may still be an effect on particular specialties, however.)

If we take the cost-increasing change in the malpractice climate as given, from a policy viewpoint is it better that practices respond by full forward shifting rather than by exit or relocation? The ideal response to an exogenous increase in cost would be for fees to rise by an offsetting amount and yet have no decline in demand as a result. That is, it would be efficient to have complete forward shifting, given that this cost had to be paid. That would mean that no additional distortions would be introduced by this rise in cost; the money would have been extracted from the system in the least harmful (though not necessarily the fairest) way. This could happen if insurance coverage was virtually complete and if insurers agreed to pay the higher fees. Although this situation may sometimes exist, it surely is not universal.

The late-1980s PPCIS results did not examine the overall impact of higher premiums on quantities of services, but only individual items, some of which rose when premiums rose and some of which fell. The more recent MGMA results suggest that, on balance, the overall volume of services during 1994–2002 rose when premiums rose. Higher premiums were correlated with more productive inputs being drawn into physician practices from elsewhere in the economy. Unless we have reason to believe that these additional malpractice-induced inputs were providing consumers with value greater than their cost, we would need to count this shift as inefficient. To say much more we would need more details on how the increased inputs were used

---

[9] Danzon 1990, 2000; Danzon et al. 1990.

and, as well, on where they came from and what other investments, goods, or services were forgone in order to make them available.

The apparent impact of higher premiums on total volume seems less than ideal. Those additional services use up real inputs, and the cost of those inputs means that total patient spending (directly or through insurance) must increase by a larger amount to stabilize physician income than if only prices had to rise. We do not have any empirical hints as to why the process of responding to higher malpractice costs apparently has shifted away from fees and toward quantity. The earlier studies did, however, focus much more on price than current analysis with imperfect data can do. There was no evidence that managed care penetration helped to produce this result; an alternative possibility is that the implementation of fee schedules for Medicare through Resource-Based Relative Value Scale (RBRVS, wherein payments for medical services are determined by the cost of resources required to provide them) and limits on balance billing, and through more aggressive Medicaid pricing, might be responsible.

One especially troublesome distortion still potentially in evidence is physician relocation. Even though physician money net incomes and hours of work might not be reduced by higher premiums, economists believe that physicians may suffer a "psychic" or "conscience" cost associated with inducing demand for additional services that are not of sufficient intrinsic value to patients.[10] Rather than tolerate this type of effort to maintain income in a high malpractice premium state (despite its success), the physician on the margin may choose to move to another state where such efforts are unnecessary. We do not know how large this influence is or even whether it really exists. The McGuire model of quantity-expansion as a reaction to price controls does not have an intrinsic cost to this second-best alternative. Still, introspection and common sense suggest that it might matter.

Can these results be made consistent with other findings about the impact of changes in malpractice laws or malpractice climates? For the most part, the answer appears to be yes. If capping noneconomic damages reduces claims and reduces premiums, the primary message here is that the main financial gains will go to patients or their insurers, not to physicians. Patients on average will be compensated for the loss of their "right to sue," though obviously those who previously had strong cases will lose.

The other policy question relates to adverse consequences of forward shifting when insurance coverage is not complete and/or always present. For people without full insurance coverage, higher levels of spending when they go to the doctor may increase the number of people who fail to seek physician care at all, precisely because the cost to them of the recommended regimen of care has risen. Even though the physician practice may be able to retain income by pushing up use by those who continue to see physicians,

[10] Pauly 1980.

there could be some serious and consequential attrition in access as a result of higher premiums.

If the cost of physician services is covered by insurance, those with private insurance will experience an increase in premiums, other things equal, if physician expenditures rise. At the margin, such higher premiums may cause some consumers to fail to obtain insurance.

The most recent data bear indirectly on the question of the role of class rating in malpractice insurance. Sage notes that, because premiums are not experience rated, they do not work well to deter negligent behavior.[11] But because they are not uniform across all specialties, they do potentially serve to deter entry into some specialties relative to others. The finding that changes in premiums tend to be offset by higher revenues suggests that this deterrent may not be getting more severe over time even as premiums have risen more for some specialties than for others. If the higher liability costs (and attendant chances for patients to get a higher legal reward) are shifted forward into specialty-specific patient costs, this adjustment in relative prices would improve efficiency, because it would mean that patients would be paying the cost of the higher benefits they might claim. Of course, insurance coverage for medical care costs itself greatly attenuates this incentive for the individual patient, but it still may be affecting insurer choice of network or panel specialty mix in an appropriate way. This is a topic that bears further investigation.

CONCLUSION

Based both on a priori theory and empirical evidence, one may conclude that consumers do bear much of the cost of a more adverse malpractice climate. For many practices, there is not much of a fall in net income or the probability of "losing money." That climate change increases the amount of money consumers transfer to the medical services sector, which is then transferred to the legal sector. What consumers lose physicians do not lose, so this forward shifting may serve to mitigate some of the more severe consequences of malpractice regimes on physicians themselves. Because some of this forward shifting tends to occur at the market level (perhaps by fees not being as low as they would have been in the absence of shifting), physicians may not always be aware of forward shifting; they may not know how much worse things could have been (for their net incomes) in the absence of shifting and may attribute the higher fee levels in the market to other causes. How these considerations modify the politics of changing health policy toward malpractice is therefore less than clear. Making more evident how much shifting occurs and how it happens (whether through higher prices or higher volumes) may help to keep the debate on a more solid empirical footing.

---

[11] Sage 2004b.

5

The Effects of the U.S. Malpractice System on the Cost and Quality of Care

David J. Becker and Daniel P. Kessler

In theory, the medical malpractice liability system operates according to the "negligence rule": Doctors are responsible for the costs of injuries that they negligently cause. The negligence rule should lead doctors' private decisions about whether and how to practice medicine to reflect society's overall interests, by leading them to balance the benefits of medical care, the costs of precaution, and the costs of negligence.

Imperfections in markets for health care and the liability system, however, mean that the negligence rule may not provide incentives for appropriate medical care in practice. It may lead doctors to take insufficient precautions against medical injuries or may lead to "defensive medicine" – medical practice based on fear of legal liability rather than on patients' best interests.

This indeterminacy has led to an extensive empirical debate over tort policy. What are the effects of the medical liability system on the cost and quality of care? What reforms to the system have the potential to reduce cost and improve quality?

This chapter reviews existing research on these questions. The first section outlines why understanding the effects of the liability system on the cost and quality of care is an important empirical issue. The second section summarizes the empirical evidence about the effects of the system and the effects of conventional "tort reforms" – changes to state law that seek to reduce liability. In brief, the empirical evidence supports the hypothesis that the existing system encourages defensive medicine, and that tort reforms reduce its prevalence. The third section discusses the potential of two alternative

We would like to thank Ashley Ensign for excellent research assistance and the Manhattan Institute for Policy Research for financial support. Sections of this chapter have been taken from Daniel Kessler, "The Effects of the U.S. Malpractice System: A Review of the Empirical Literature," and Daniel Kessler and Daniel Rubinfeld, "Empirical Study of the Civil Justice System," forthcoming in the *Handbook of Law and Economics*. The views expressed in this chapter do not necessarily reflect those of any of the authors' institutions.

reforms to the tort system – protection from liability for quality improvement initiatives and for physicians who comply with clinical practice guidelines – and also finds these a promising source of reduced health care costs and improved quality. The fourth section concludes with a comparison of the approaches and some suggestions for future research.

WHY ARE THE LIABILITY SYSTEM'S EFFECTS ON MEDICAL CARE IMPORTANT?

In a recent comprehensive survey, Danzon (2000) estimated the monetary costs of the malpractice liability system – including payments to malpractice claimants, attorneys, and malpractice insurance overhead – to be 1 percent of overall health care costs. In a simple model of medical decision making, physicians and patients balance the monetary costs of liability against the costs of precaution and the benefits of medical care. According to this model, the liability system is likely to be unimportant: To a first approximation, the consequences of the liability system for treatment decisions could be no larger than the magnitude of the monetary costs it creates.

However, markets for health care and the operation of the liability system deviate significantly from the assumptions underlying this simple model of behavior. Asymmetries of information or other barriers may prevent patients from filing a malpractice claim even when there is evidence of a negligent medical injury (Harvard Medical Practice Study 1990). In addition, because malpractice liability insurance is at most weakly experience-rated (Sloan 1990), physicians may bear little of the costs of patient injuries from malpractice. For these reasons, the harm to patients of medical negligence may be far greater than the monetary costs of the liability system would suggest.

At the same time, the system may lead to unnecessary precaution, or "defensive medicine." The practice of defensive medicine can take two forms: "positive" and "negative." Positive defensive medicine (also called "assurance behavior") involves the supply of care that is relatively unproductive for patients; negative defensive medicine (also called "avoidance behavior") occurs when providers decline to supply care that is relatively productive for patients. Both positive and negative defensive medicine may arise out of the fact that physicians bear significant uninsured, nonmonetary costs of patient injuries, including the value of lost time and emotional energy in responding to a malpractice claim (U.S. Congress, Office of Technology Assessment 1993). Because of this, physicians may be more cautious than the monetary costs of the liability system would suggest.

Positive defensive medicine can also be driven by the moral hazard inherent in health insurance, which means that neither patients nor physicians bear the full cost of care in any particular case. The costs of precautionary services financed through health insurance are generally larger than the uninsured cost of the physician's own effort. Doctors and patients make decisions that balance the costs of precaution that they bear against the costs imposed on them by the malpractice system. Thus, even if medical malpractice tort law allocated the burden of medical injuries with neither errors nor nonmonetary costs, insensitivity to the true costs of care would lead physicians and their patients to take socially excessive precautions against injuries. The added burden due to errors and nonmonetary costs only intensifies this effect.

Negative defensive medicine is also driven by the fact that patients reap substantial surpluses from medical care for which they cannot compensate providers, whereas providers bear malpractice risk for which they cannot charge patients. If doctors weigh the malpractice downside of a course of care against only a fraction of the upside, then they may withhold treatments that may be in patients' best interests.

Just as the harm to patients from insufficient precaution may be greater than the monetary costs of the liability system, so may be the costs of defensive medicine. For example, because the costs of precaution borne by patients and physicians account for a small share of overall costs, but the incentives created by the liability system are at least as large as its monetary costs, a $1 change in liability costs could induce a change in treatment decisions that costs much more than $1.

EMPIRICAL ASSESSMENT OF THE LIABILITY SYSTEM'S EFFECTS ON MEDICAL CARE

A significant body of empirical research investigates how treatment decisions and patient health outcomes respond to the incentives created by the liability system. Early work estimated the effect of physicians' actual exposure to malpractice claims on clinical practices and outcomes (Rock 1988; Harvard Medical Practice Study 1990; Localio et al. 1993; Baldwin et al. 1995). Rock, Localio et al., and the Harvard Medical Practice Study found results consistent with defensive medicine; Baldwin et al. did not. However, concerns about unobserved differences between providers and between small geographic areas qualify the results of all of these studies. These studies used frequency of claims or magnitude of insurance premiums at the level of individual doctors, hospitals, or areas within a single state over a limited time period to measure malpractice pressure. Because malpractice laws within a state at a given time are constant, the measures of malpractice pressure used in these studies arose not from laws but from primarily unobserved factors at the level of individual providers or small areas. For example, the claim frequency or insurance premiums of a particular provider or area may be relatively high because the provider is relatively low quality, because the patients are particularly sick (and hence are prone to adverse outcomes), because the patients had more "taste" for medical interventions (and hence more likely to disagree with their provider about management decisions), or because of many other factors. Since such factors are extremely difficult to capture fully in observational datasets, estimates from these studies represent a combination of the true effect of malpractice pressure on treatment decisions or outcomes and unobserved differences in providers, patients, and areas.

More recent work seeks to address this problem by identifying the effects of malpractice pressure with variation across states and over time in tort reforms. This technique yields unbiased assessments of the impact of malpractice pressure under the assumption that the adoption of legal reforms affects malpractice pressure but is uncorrelated with unobserved differences across states in the characteristics of patients and providers (see Danzon 2000 for a critique of this assumption).

Much of this work has investigated the consequences of malpractice pressure for positive defensive medicine. Kessler and McClellan (1996) used longitudinal data on essentially all elderly Medicare beneficiaries hospitalized with serious cardiac illness from 1984, 1987, and 1990, matched with information on the existence of direct and indirect law reforms from the state in which the patient was treated. They found that reforms that directly limit liability – such as caps on damages – reduced hospital expenditures by 5 to 9 percent in the late 1980s, with effects that are greater for ischemic heart disease (IHD) than for heart attack (AMI) patients.[1] In contrast, reforms that limit liability only indirectly, such as caps on attorneys' fees, were not associated with any substantial expenditure effects. Neither type of reforms led to any consequential differences in mortality or the occurrence of serious complications. The estimated expenditure/benefit ratio associated with liability-pressure-induced intensive treatment was more than $500,000 per additional one-year survivor, with comparable ratios for recurrent AMIs and heart failure. Thus, treatment of elderly patients with heart disease does involve defensive medical practices, and limited reductions in liability can reduce this costly behavior.[2]

Two recent studies identified the mechanism through which "direct" reforms affect physician behavior, in order to help predict the effects of existing reforms under new market conditions, or new and untried types of reforms. Kessler and McClellan (2002a) matched longitudinal Medicare data with legal reforms and data on health insurance markets to explore the ways in which managed care and liability reform interact to affect treatment intensity and health outcomes. They reported that direct reforms reduce defensive practices in areas both with low and with high levels of managed care enrollment. Managed care and direct reforms do not have long-run interaction effects that are harmful to patient health. However, at least for

---

[1] Because IHD is a less severe form of illness, IHD patients may have more "marginal" indications for intensive treatment, leading to a greater scope for defensive practices.

[2] Dubay et al. (1999) confirmed that defensive practices exist in nonelderly populations, although they reported that the costs of defensive medicine in obstetrics are small.

patients with less severe cardiac illness, managed care and direct reforms are substitutes, so the reduction in defensive practices that can be achieved with direct reforms is smaller in areas with high managed care enrollment.

Kessler and McClellan (2002b) integrated four unique data sources to illuminate how reforms affect malpractice pressure and how reform-induced changes in the incentives provided by the liability system affect treatment decisions, medical costs, and health outcomes. That paper matches by state and year the longitudinal Medicare data discussed previously (updated to include all years from 1984 to 1994) with data on law reforms, physician-level data on the frequency of malpractice claims from the American Medical Association's Socioeconomic Monitoring System (AMA SMS), and malpractice-claim-level data from the Physician Insurers Association of America on claim costs and claim outcomes. They reported that although direct reforms improve medical productivity primarily by reducing malpractice claims rates and compensation conditional on a claim, other policies that reduce the time spent and the amount of conflict involved in defending against a claim can also reduce defensive practices substantially. For example, at least for elderly heart disease patients, an untried reform that reduced the legal-defense burden on physicians and hospitals by one quarter – which is within the range of policy possibilities – could be expected to reduce medical treatment intensity by approximately 6 percent but not to increase the incidence of adverse health outcomes. In the same population, a policy that expedited claim resolution by six months across the board could be expected to reduce hospital treatment costs by 2.8 percent, without greater adverse outcomes. This finding is consistent with Kessler and McClellan (1997), who reported broad differences in physicians' perceptions of the impact of malpractice pressure in states with and without liability reforms.

Other work has investigated the consequences of malpractice pressure for negative defensive medicine. For example, Dubay, Kaestner, and Waidmann (2001) found that a decrease in malpractice premiums resulting from a feasible policy reform would lead to a decrease in the incidence of late prenatal care by between 3.0 and 5.9 percent for black women and between 2.2 and 4.7 percent for white women. However, although they found evidence that malpractice pressure was associated with greater delay and fewer prenatal visits, they found no evidence that this negatively affected infant health.

More recent work finds substantial evidence of negative defensive medicine. Kessler, Sage, and Becker (2005) matched data from the American Medical Association's Physician Masterfile on the number of actively practicing physicians in each state for each year from 1985 through 2001 with law reforms and data on health care markets. They found that the adoption of direct reforms leads to greater growth in the overall supply of physicians. Three years after adoption, direct reforms increase physician supply by 3.3 percent, controlling for fixed differences across states, population, states' health care market and political characteristics, and other differences in malpractice law. Direct reforms have a larger effect on the supply of nongroup versus group physicians, on the supply of most (but not all) specialties with high malpractice insurance premiums, on states with high levels of managed care, and on supply through retirements and entries than through the propensity of physicians to move between states. Direct reforms have similar effects on less experienced and more experienced physicians. Hellinger and Encinosa (2003) reported even larger effects, finding that the supply of physicians was approximately 12 percent greater in states with caps on noneconomic damages, as compared to states without them.

EMPIRICAL ASSESSMENT OF NEW REFORMS TO THE LIABILITY SYSTEM

Two alternative reforms to the tort system hold significant promise for reducing cost and improving quality of care: protection from liability for quality improvement systems and for physicians who comply with clinical practice guidelines.

Protection from Liability for Quality Improvement Systems

Systems of error reporting, analysis, and feedback are central to efforts to reduce costs and improve quality. Because many specific errors – especially those producing serious injuries – occur relatively infrequently within any one institution, systems of reporting and analysis are more effective when they collect events from many locations. For this reason, the Institute of Medicine (IOM 2000) endorsed the creation of multiparty quality improvement (QI) systems.

The most important impediment to the creation and success of QI systems is the discoverability of their data by potential plaintiffs in medical malpractice lawsuits. States differ in the extent to which they protect analyses of medical errors by hospitals, physician groups, and insurers from lawsuits. As Scheutzow (1999) and Liang (2000) pointed out, such analyses are generally discoverable by plaintiffs, unless the analysis falls under a state's specific statutory exception. However, even states with these statutory exceptions do not generally protect information that is shared across organizations.

There is some empirical evidence that existing laws provide less than the optimal amount of protection for QI systems. In *To Err Is Human*, the Institute of Medicine (IOM 2000) examined the experience of a few error reporting systems. Although the scope of this study was limited (in that it examined protections in only a few states at a single point in time), it recommended that Congress pass legislation to extend protection from discoverability to data collected solely for purposes of improving safety and quality. Future research could expand this study and analyze the effects of protections from discoverability on the cost and quality of care in a greater number of states over a longer time period.

Guidelines-Based Systems

Clinical practice guidelines are written statements of what constitutes appropriate treatment for a specific illness, set of symptoms, or type of patient. Proponents of guidelines argue that they promote evidence-based medicine and inform physicians of best clinical practices; opponents argue that guidelines promote "cookbook medicine" that fails to account for the significant variations in patients' conditions associated with even basic health problems. Guidelines have been developed by both public and private entities, including the U.S. Agency for Health Care Research and Quality (a division of the U.S. Department of Health and Human Services), state health departments, and large insurers. A recent survey of the health services literature (Cabana 1999) suggests that guidelines have had a limited effect on physician behavior for several reasons, including lack of awareness or familiarity, lack of agreement with guideline recommendations, lack of applicability, and inertia.

A guidelines-based malpractice system would retain most aspects of the current tort system but would change the method by which the third element of a malpractice claim – physician negligence – is adjudicated. Under common law, physician negligence is an issue of fact for the jury, informed by expert testimony. Under a guidelines-based system, physicians and hospitals who complied with a clinical practice guideline would be presumed to be nonnegligent. Although guidelines are an obvious source of information about the negligence of a given treatment decision in a medical malpractice case, courts generally bar guidelines from being admitted as evidence under the hearsay rule, which prohibits the introduction of out-of-court statements as evidence. Guidelines are sometimes admitted under the "learned treatise" exception to the hearsay rule. Under most states' common law, no one set of guidelines necessarily trumps any other, and guidelines do not carry any more weight than any other form of expert testimony (U.S. Congress OTA 1994). Thus, adoption of a guidelines-based system would require legislative action.

Several states have already experimented with legal reforms that make evidence of compliance with guidelines statutorily admissible by defendants as an affirmative defense to malpractice. For example, Florida and Maine passed laws creating demonstration projects in the 1990s that allowed physicians to opt in to a guidelines-based malpractice system (see U.S. Congress OTA 1994 for a description). Under these guidelines-based systems, physicians who complied with the guidelines had an affirmative defense against malpractice, but plaintiffs could use noncompliance with guidelines as evidence of negligence.[3] Deprez et al. (1997) evaluated the Maine demonstration project and presented two conclusions: that the Maine project had limited effects on physician practice patterns, but that this may have been due to its idiosyncratic design and administration. Future research should further investigate the potential effects of such guideline-based reforms.

CONCLUSION

This chapter reviews empirical research on two questions. First, does the U.S. malpractice system lead to too little, too much, or the appropriate level of precaution? In theory, the shortcomings of the system, combined with market failures in health care, could lead to any of these three results. Because the social costs of distortions in precautionary behavior, in terms of loss of life and the financial costs of inappropriate care, could be substantial, assessing the effects of the malpractice system is an important empirical issue. Second, if the system does provide inappropriate incentives, how might it be reformed?

The existing literature presents three main findings. First, most empirical evidence supports the hypothesis that doctors practice defensive medicine. Surveys indicate that physicians believe that the existing malpractice system leads to defensive medicine. Studies of the effects of malpractice pressure on positive defensive medicine find that decreases in malpractice pressure lead to decreases in the supply of care with minimal medical benefit – that is, to decreases in health care costs with no adverse consequences for health outcomes. Studies of the effects of malpractice pressure on negative defensive medicine find that decreases in malpractice pressure lead to increases in the supply of certain types of care, although there is no strong evidence that this additional care leads to improved health outcomes.

Second, liability-reducing tort reforms reduce the prevalence and cost of defensive medicine. In particular, reforms such as caps on damages and collateral source offsets that have a direct effect on awards reduce malpractice pressure and, in turn, defensive medicine. For example, by reducing claims rates and compensation conditional on a claim, a range of feasible policy reforms could reduce medical expenditures for elderly heart disease patients by approximately 6 percent, without any increase in adverse health outcomes.

Third, alternative approaches that seek to supplant the tort system hold significant promise for reducing cost and improving quality. In this chapter, we focus on two approaches: protection from liability for quality improvement systems and for physicians who comply with clinical practice guidelines. Other approaches also deserve attention, although many of these are

---

[3] Plaintiffs were prohibited by the Maine statute from using noncompliance with the guidelines as evidence of malpractice. However, an anomaly in the statute may have actually allowed guidelines to be used against physicians in certain cases (see Hyams et al. 1996).

intended to improve the way the liability system compensates victims of medical injury rather than alter the incentives it provides for appropriate medical care.

For example, there is evidence that medical no-fault, the most radical of the alternative approaches, would lead to faster and more equitable compensation at lower transactions costs. However, medical no-fault has two important problems. First, there is no direct evidence of how a broad medical no-fault system would affect physicians' incentives to take appropriate care; evidence from the automobile tort context shows that auto no-fault increases the auto accident rate (see Kessler and Rubinfeld 2004 for a detailed discussion of this research). Second, there is evidence that medical no-fault is politically difficult (if not impossible) to implement. Mello and Brennan (2002) reported that their attempts to encourage adoption of no-fault in Utah and Colorado crumbled against the strength of the lobby of the American Trial Lawyers Association and lack of interest on the part of malpractice insurance companies.

Policy changes that enable doctors, hospitals, and patients to voluntarily opt out of the tort system offer another alternative route to reform (see Havighurst 1995 for a comprehensive general discussion of private contracts as instruments of health reform). For example, strengthening laws that allow patients and their physicians to agree to resolve malpractice disputes by binding alternative dispute resolution may combine the efficiency gains of tort reform with the compensation improvements of no-fault in a politically feasible package.[4] Empirical evaluation of these alternative reforms is an important area for future research.

[4] For an extended discussion, see this volume's chapter by Liebman and Hyman on alternative dispute resolution.

6

Liability, Patient Safety, and Defensive Medicine

What Does the Future Hold?

Troyen A. Brennan, Michelle M. Mello,
and David M. Studdert

Approaches for dealing with medical injuries are developing quickly today. Publication of the Institute of Medicine's (IOM's) report, *To Err Is Human*,[1] in 2000 unleashed a variety of innovative ideas, some of which have already prompted policy changes. But the field of patient safety is in its infancy and policy responses to the problem of medical errors remain in flux, suggesting that significant changes lie ahead in the way we address the challenge of reducing the number of patients injured by medical care.

To help anticipate how these new policies may affect the medical profession and health care industry, it is critical to examine the recent medical malpractice "crisis."[2] The connections between strategies to reduce medical injury and the medical malpractice system are vital and often overlooked.[3] Developments in the medical liability arena will affect the evolution and eventual shape of methods used to combat error in medicine. Moreover, we believe that medical injury policy can and will significantly affect medical liability policy.

This chapter focuses on the implications of the medical injury/medical malpractice dynamic for physician behavior. It is informed by research on defensive medicine we undertook with support from The Pew Charitable Trusts in 2003 and 2004. This research was motivated in part by the ongoing national crisis in medical liability, which hit Pennsylvania particularly hard from 2001 onward.[4] The information we gleaned from physicians and policy makers in Pennsylvania provides some insights into the ways in

Portions of this chapter are adapted with permission from Studdert et al. 2005; Mello et al. 2005; and Mello, Studdert, DesRoches, et al. 2004.
[1] Institute of Medicine 2000.
[2] Mello, Studdert, and Brennan 2003.
[3] Bovbjerg, Miller, and Shapiro 2001; Studdert and Brennan 2001b.
[4] Bovbjerg and Bartow 2003.

which physicians may react to future shocks in the liability system, especially if tensions between medical injury and malpractice policy strengthen, as we suggest they might. Our findings also underscore the importance of providing timely quantitative information on malpractice issues to policy makers as they consider how to guide patient safety policy.

THE FUTURE OF MEDICAL LIABILITY

To describe the interaction of safety and malpractice, we will identify several key aspects of the relationship and then suggest four potential scenarios for the future, all of which will provide a vantage point for understanding the findings from our studies of physician responses to Pennsylvania's recent liability crisis.

The Causes of Malpractice Crises: Rival Theories

Medical malpractice crises are a subspecies of tort crises. Their precise causes are unclear. Many legal and economics scholars believe that there is a cyclical nature to hard and soft markets in the underwriting of professional liability insurance premiums.[5] Every few years, the theory goes, purchasers of insurance will be visited by rapidly rising premiums; in between, the costs of premiums slacken, and there is fierce competition among insurers for business. According to the cyclical theory, such peaks and troughs should be expected and are not cause for serious concern. "Crises," which appear every decade or so, represent unusually large peaks.

A closer look at underwriting practices over the past fifteen years lends some support to the cyclical theory. In the relatively soft market of the 1990s, with steady but not dramatic increases in either litigation rates or median costs of claims, a number of malpractice insurance companies sought to grow their market share by pricing premiums below cost. In the late 1990s and early 2000s, they found themselves in a bear market with low investment returns. This led to significant problems with liquidity and triggered the need to raise the cost of liability premiums quickly, especially among companies that had significantly underpriced their products.

Although the insurance-cycle account of the recent malpractice crisis is compelling at first glance, closer inspection reveals some holes. First, many insurers in the American professional liability market are prohibited from developing portfolios of investments that rely heavily on stocks and have to maintain a majority of their investments in bonds.

Second, the cycle explanation overlooks increases in the overall costs of providing insurance. The compensation costs of lawsuits are a function of two factors: (1) volume and (2) total payouts. There is no solid evidence

---

[5] T. Baker 2005b.

of major changes in the volume of lawsuits, but some insurers have reported a considerable rise in the median cost of paid claims during the late 1990s and early 2000s, with particularly sharp increases in the proportion of "high-cost" claims – those receiving payments of more than $1 million.[6] Of note, an analysis of claim cost trends in Texas concluded that no significant increase coincided with the run-up in liability insurance premiums, so there may be considerable state-to-state variations in the role that per-claim costs have played.[7]

Why have payouts in successful claims jumped in some jurisdictions? One hypothesis is that their value in the eyes of plaintiffs' attorneys has risen in the wake of publicity associated with medical injuries after the IOM's report; plaintiffs expect more and defendants are more reluctant than ever to argue their position before juries. However, the timeline does not provide much support for this theory: The median cost of claims had already begun to rise by the late 1990s, before the IOM issued its report. Nonetheless, the rise in compensation costs does suggest that the increase in premiums seen in many states in the late 1990s or early 2000s was not simply a matter of financing and insurance cycles but rather of real litigation demand.

This is an important point. One view of the malpractice crisis, as we have suggested, is a manifestation of inefficiencies in insurance underwriting. Alternatively, it can be seen as a barometer of underlying changes in the dynamics of the litigation itself – specifically, the total number of claims being brought and their total value. The unschooled might ask, how can costs increase unless doctors are less careful and injuring more patients? The answer, well recognized in malpractice policy circles, is that litigation costs have the potential to expand because there exists a large reservoir of injuries caused by error that do not currently lead to claims. This epidemiologic insight is the legacy of a series of studies of the relationship between medical injury and malpractice litigation that we, and others, have undertaken over the past fifteen years.[8] It is also the presumption of the various reports on quality and patient safety issued by the IOM. Thus, looking forward, it is critical to recognize that there is at least the potential for crises of even larger scale than those seen to date; such crises could tap into the large body of errors that do not prompt litigation presently and could unfold independent of insurance market cycles.

Tort Reform

Tort reform – that is, attempts to reduce the amount and cost of medical malpractice litigation by recourse to various legislative changes – continues apace. As of this writing in summer 2005, the Bush Administration is still

---

[6] Smarr 2003.
[7] Black et al. 2005.
[8] Studdert, Brennan, and Thomas 2000.

pushing for enactment of a package of reform measures at the federal level. The Administration's proposal mirrors California's Medical Injury Compensation Reform Act (MICRA), landmark tort reform legislation passed thirty years ago in that state. Limitations on punitive damages, a cap on pain and suffering awards, and the elimination of joint-and-several liability are central components in the Administration's proposed package.[9] The central objective of such reforms is to reduce the average payout among filed claims. Because such changes reduce the value of claims to the plaintiffs' attorney, they should also, according to conventional economic theories of litigation, reduce the amount of tort litigation, as fewer cases will meet the threshold necessary for the case to be a "good bet" for the plaintiffs' attorney.

Though the empirical evidence is mixed, tort reforms implemented over the past three decades may well have reduced the volume and cost of litigation. The steady pressure to make suing and winning more difficult has helped make plaintiffs' attorneys a hardy lot; they have strong incentives to make careful judgments about which cases they will carry forward and which they will turn away or drop in the early stages of litigation. It is hard to see why a plaintiffs' attorney who was following a rational economic path would bring meritless, or "frivolous," claims.

Yet, an emphasis on the vices of frivolous litigation is precisely what has driven much of the political enthusiasm for tort reform in recent years. There is some research to support the prevalence of unfounded malpractice litigation. Epidemiologic studies of medical injury and malpractice claims in New York in the 1980s and Utah and Colorado in the 1990s suggested that litigation was profoundly imprecise and that that imprecision involved commission of both type one and type two errors. Type one errors were those in which negligently injured patients did not claim. As noted previously, comparison of estimates of total negligent injuries with total claims suggests that the "shortfall" in the latter is massive and could increase at least sevenfold without compromising (indeed, perhaps improving) the legitimacy of the claims being litigated. Type two errors, on the other hand, are those in which the claim is brought in the absence of actual injury, negligence, or both.

Our previous data had suggested that there are many such inappropriate claims.[10] Other studies had drawn similar conclusions. Although many of these questionable claims appear to get weeded out – either dropped after initial discovery shows them to be unfounded or defended vigorously until eventually closure without payment – the medico-legal analyses in New York had suggested that a nontrivial proportion of them attracted payment.[11] The

[9] P. Baker 2005.
[10] Weiler et al. 1993.
[11] Brennan, Sox, and Burstin 1996.

prevalence of type two errors today is not known, although preliminary findings in ongoing research by our group suggests that they may be less frequent than is popularly thought among tort critics. It is certainly possible that the accumulated impact of tort reforms through the 1970s, 1980s, and 1990s, particularly the pressure placed on the plaintiffs' attorneys' calculus, may have whittled down the number of frivolous cases, forcing the plaintiffs' attorneys to be much more exacting about which cases they bring.

The process of "toughening" the caseload in medical malpractice litigation through tort reform may be continuing today. We note with great interest both the prospects for a federal tort reform package and a potent series of reforms enacted or in the process of being enacted by state legislatures. In Georgia, for example, the legislature recently instituted a one-way shift in attorneys' fees when the plaintiffs' attorney fails to gain as much at the conclusion of litigation as was offered earlier in the process.[12] This seemingly benign intervention to encourage early settlement looks set to significantly decrease the amount of tort litigation; the plaintiffs' attorney, who may be offered only a trivial settlement, faces the prospect of paying the entire defense costs if the trial is lost. In Florida, the legislature has restricted contingency fees radically, raising questions about whether medical malpractice will be a viable line of work for the average plaintiffs' attorney.[13] Clearly, these moves respond to the perception that there is too much tort litigation and that the reasonableness of many claims is highly questionable.

Disclosure

The restrictions on plaintiffs' attorneys are odd in light of new reform directions inspired by the patient safety movement. The patient safety movement, spawned by the IOM's report, which in turn drew heavily on the empirical insights from the malpractice studies in New York and Utah/Colorado, is pushing hard for transparency. Physicians and hospitals are being encouraged to disclose injuries due to error to patients. In addition, doctors and hospitals in about half the states are now required to report injuries to a state-operated adverse event reporting system, which may be housed within newly established patient safety units. The overarching objective for reporting systems is to have the reports analyzed and feed findings back to reporting facilities to enable them to design and implement interventions to reduce error. Federal reporting laws that contemplate the same goals are currently being debated in Congress.[14]

Most states have laws that protect reported data from use in legal proceedings; however, these protections appear to be weaker in some states

---

[12] National Conference of State Legislatures 2005.
[13] Ibid.
[14] Patient Safety and Quality Improvement Act.

than others.[15] Reporting systems offer a potential goldmine for plaintiffs' attorneys. A plaintiffs' attorney could decrease litigation costs significantly by asking a patient to report the case to a public reporting system, have the public system's staff undertake the initial investigation, and use the findings to inform the decision about whether to take the case. If the necessary identifiers are available and accessible, reporting systems could also help plaintiffs' attorneys to identify new cases. These possible uses of reported data raise the specter of more litigation. Concerns about this prospect are driving physician groups and their insurers to try to ensure that strong confidentiality laws are in place.

The same type of tension surrounds disclosures to patients. Some pundits believe that disclosure could reduce litigation. The argument proceeds as follows: The litigation system has one currency – money. Yet, what many (perhaps most) injured patients really want are nonmonetary remedies, such as an explanation of what happened, an apology, or an assurance that steps will be taken to ensure that other patients do not suffer the same plight. If such open and honest responses to patient injury are forthcoming, therefore, patients will be less likely to sue their doctors. Although this scenario is alluring and certainly a very happy one, we believe that it is unlikely to reflect the harsh realities of patient injury. Moreover, there is scant empirical evidence to support the deterrant impact of disclosure on litigation, although a single report from a Veterans Administration Hospital is often cited.[16]

Consider the following scenario: I am involved in an automobile accident. I was driving in a negligent fashion and hit one of my neighbors, destroying her car. I am reasonably insured for vehicle damage. Instead of going through the usual approach of exchanging information on insurance, letting my insurance company pay for the cost of the accident, and incurring the hike on my experience rating, I apologize profusely to the person I hit. It is unlikely that the reaction of my neighbor is going to be, "Fine, thanks so much for the apology. No need for any compensation." We suspect that if apologies and complete disclosures are consistently made, liability costs may increase. This is especially true when one considers the huge reservoir of potential claims.

How large is that potential reservoir? No one really knows for sure. The estimates from the New York and Utah/Colorado studies suggest that there are five to seven times as many medical negligent injuries as litigated cases. Eye-popping as those ratios might seem, they actually represent quite conservative estimates. Studies from Australia, the United Kingdom, and New Zealand predict that rates of injury are 50 percent to 100 percent higher than those found in Utah/Colorado. Reliability analyses of the original

---

[15] Hanscom et al. 2003.
[16] Kraman and Hamm 1999.

Utah/Colorado data demonstrate that the chart-based studies may have underestimated the level of medical injury by a factor of two.[17] Methods used by other researchers, in particular direct observation,[18] also suggest considerably higher rates are detectable when estimates are not tethered to documentation in medical records. Finally, almost all of the comprehensive studies of injury rates have been performed in the inpatient setting, but most care today is delivered in the outpatient setting. Thus, huge numbers of injuries due to ambulatory care are omitted from existing estimates.[19]

Medical Injury Policy at the Crossroads

The different directions of reforms being pursued in the tort and patient safety realms place state policy makers at a crossroads. Some states may decide that litigation costs are too high and that problems associated with defensive medicine will become unbearable if they do not protect physicians. These states will institute tort reform, for example, the comprehensive MICRA-type approach of which President Bush is a strong advocate, or even more radical reforms such as those undertaken by Georgia and Florida.

Other states may decide that the medical injury problem is the primary issue and prioritize patient safety initiatives over policies related to litigation. Their approach will be to use a combination of incentives and penalties to encourage disclosure of medical injuries to patients and ensure injury reporting to public health agencies, and face the consequences with regard to increased liability costs. Again, we believe that the only logical consequence of policies that seek honest disclosure and complete reporting about medical injuries is that the scale and cost of compensation will increase, notwithstanding the fact that some subset of disclosed to patients may be assuaged and decide not to seek compensation when they otherwise would have.

These two impulses, tort reform and disclosure/reporting, are the key policy options for addressing concerns about medical injury. States may offer significant tort reform or no tort reform, and high degrees of disclosure or no disclosure. Depending on their choices, states will fall into one of the four cells shown in Figure 6.1.

In the first cell (upper left) are states that disclose but also institute tort reform. They will make it more difficult for people to sue, but they will encourage doctors to disclose injuries to patients. This seems to be an inconsistent policy and will lead to many stories of known-to-be-injured patients who cannot obtain compensation.

---

[17] Thomas et al. 2002.
[18] Andrews et al. 1997; Petersen et al. 1994; Landrigan et al. 2004.
[19] Gandhi et al. 2003.

	Strong disclosure/reporting laws	Weak or no disclosure/ reporting laws
Aggressive tort reform	**Many recognized negligent injuries, little compensation**	**Reduction in claims**
Limited or no tort reform	**Increase in injury recognition and claiming**	**Status quo**

FIGURE 6.1. Liability/Safety Policy Options.

The second cell (lower left) situates states that do not undertake tort reform but do encourage disclosure and reporting. These are places where liability costs should increase, perhaps as much as fourfold. In these states, we should expect considerable pressure on physicians with respect to liability premiums, and our research on defensive medicine, which we summarize later, suggests how this pressure may bring changes to some aspects of physicians' clinical practice styles.

The third cell (upper right) captures states that undertake tort reform but do not encourage disclosure. Although they may well control the volume and cost of litigation they experience, these states are clearly prioritizing stability in medical malpractice climate above interests of injured patients. It is certainly true that stable liability environments can redound to the benefit of patients. For example, less defensive medicine may benefit patients if the practices in questions (e.g., biopsy) pose a risk of harm to patients. Similarly, if liability markets are extremely volatile, physicians may leave practice and create problems for patients in accessing care (although there is little evidence that this risk has materialized in any significant way during previous malpractice crises). Nonetheless, setting aside the potential for some such indirect gains to patients, states that pressed forward with major tort reform initiatives and deemphasized patient safety reforms would not be serving the interests of injured patients – and might well harm them. The final cell depicts states in which there is no effort to promote disclosure and no (further) tort reform. These states would be maintaining the status quo.

The menu of choices that states confront provides the context for this chapter and our empirical work on the effects of the malpractice crisis in Pennsylvania. We were interested in exactly how physicians reacted to liability increases in their state: Were they changing the nature of the services they provided or the mix of patients they served? Were they willing to relocate from high liability cost areas to lower ones? In the simplified policy framework we have sketched, states will, to some degree, "choose" their future liability costs in the tradeoffs they make between tort reform and disclosure/reporting policies. Variations in these choices across states will heighten the disparities between states in terms of liability costs, amplify pressures that stem from defensive medicine, and potentially encourage mobility. With this set of tensions and tradeoffs as background, we turn to the data we gathered on the responses of specialist physicians to the malpractice crisis in Pennsylvania.

DEFENSIVE MEDICINE IN PENNSYLVANIA IN 2003

Surveying the "Leading Edge" of Defensive Medicine: Strengths and Weaknesses

Measurement of defensive medicine poses several daunting challenges for researchers. Distinctions between inappropriate and appropriate clinical practice are unclear in many clinical situations.[20] Moreover, it can be difficult to disentangle liability motivations from the manifold factors that influence clinical decision making. (Where, for instance, does concern about good patient–physician relations end and fear of lawsuits begin?[21]) Previous efforts to isolate defensive practice have used one of two approaches: surveys of clinicians about their behavior and linkage of variation observed in practice patterns to variation in liability exposure. Each of these approaches has methodological strengths and weaknesses, which have been reviewed exhaustively in previous literature.[22]

We pursued a survey approach. This approach has the advantage of being able to sidestep the trickiest methodological challenges, namely, the dual questions of what constitutes and what motivates inappropriate care. Respondents themselves are called upon to make these determinations by reflecting on their own clinical decision making.

We sought to improve and build on previous survey work in three main ways. First, many previous surveys have centered on physicians subject to relatively low levels of litigation, placid malpractice environments, or both.[23] Some have also focused on single specialties, such as obstetrics.[24] We selected a cluster of specialties at the high end of the liability risk spectrum in a state that has been significantly impacted by the latest medical malpractice crisis.

However, the main limitation of all survey research in this area also confronted our study: socially acceptable response bias. Our findings are

---

[20] Eddy 1998.
[21] Veldhuis 1994; Bradley 1992.
[22] Klingman et al. 1996; U.S. Congress 1994.
[23] Cook and Neff 1994; Charles et al. 1985; Goold et al. 1994; Weisman et al. 1989.
[24] Vimercati et al. 2000; Griffin et al. 1999; Tussing and Wojtoycz 1992; Localio et al. 1993; Baldwin et al. 1995; Ennis, Clark, and Grudzinskas 1991; Sloan et al. 1995.

based on what physicians told us. Physicians and other health care professionals would, of course, like to pay less for malpractice premiums, and they realize that if they suggest that malpractice causes inefficiencies or has negative repercussions on health care, then they will be building a case for reduction in such premiums. Hence, the central problem with survey research on defensive medicine: Physicians have incentives to report that malpractice litigation leads them to practice clinically inappropriate medicine.

Our study was designed to combat this bias in three ways. First, we asked not just whether physicians practiced defensively but precisely what those practices were. Second, some of the defensive practices we asked about, such as unnecessary biopsies, pose risks for patients and are clearly indicative of poor care. Mixing questions about these practices in with questions about unnecessary and costly, but not obviously dangerous, care blurred preconceptions about what type of response really was socially desirable. Third, because our survey was completed in the midst of extreme volatility in the Pennsylvania's medical liability environment, we were interested not just in the absolute levels of defensive practice but in how these levels compared with previous surveys (which presumably would have been subject to the same biases).

The Concepts of Assurance and Avoidance Behaviors

William Sage has conceived of defensive medicine as involving both "assurance" and "avoidance" behaviors. Assurance behaviors involve the ordering of unnecessary tests or the performance of inappropriate procedures. They are intended to decrease the probability of litigation by eliminating remote risks of harm and providing evidence that the physician is adhering to the standard of care. The extreme end of the assurance behavior spectrum is better quality care, consistent with a deterrent effect from tort law, but additional care can also be clinically inappropriate. Assurance behaviors therefore represent "overdeterrence," practices that consume health care resources without providing higher quality care.

Avoidance behaviors involve constraints on practice, again for purposes of guarding against the prospect of litigation. The constraints may involve not caring for patients who are high-risk by virtue of their condition (e.g., elderly, pediatric, multiple comorbid illnesses) or personal characteristics (e.g., combative, a practicing lawyer); they may also involve decisions not to perform procedures that are high risk in the sense that the probability of unsuccessful outcomes is high. The significant policy issue associated with avoidance behaviors is reduction in access to care: orthopedic surgeons refusing to take care of trauma patients, neurosurgeons refusing to practice in community hospitals, obstetrician-gynecologists refusing to deliver babies or practice in rural areas, and so on. Assurance behaviors increase health care costs unnecessarily, whereas avoidance behaviors reduce the availability of care.

Sample, Survey Administration, and Analysis

Our survey was developed and fielded in association with Harris Interactive, Inc. We drew a stratified random sample of 1,333 physicians in six specialties (emergency medicine, general surgery, neurosurgery, obstetrics/gynecology, orthopedic surgery, and radiology) from the American Medical Association Physician Masterfile. These were the specialists who paid the most for liability insurance in the 2001–3 period; they also saw the most dramatic hikes in premiums. The strata were based on geographic location, divided into high-risk and low-risk regions of the state, with high-risk being the five counties in southeast Pennsylvania that key informants identified as most affected by the crisis. Sampling was proportionate by specialty except that neurosurgeons were oversampled to ensure adequate representation.

The survey instrument was a six-page questionnaire using topics and response categories suggested by the key informant interviews. The questionnaire was pretested on ten Pennsylvania physicians in the targeted specialties who were debriefed in cognitive interviews focusing on comprehension and appropriateness of question topics, wording, response options, and layout. After revision, the questionnaire contained forty-one questions.

The survey was mailed in May 2003 along with a $75 honorarium. The adjusted response rate after exclusion of sixty-five noneligible physicians was sixty-five percent, which is considered very good in a survey of physicians. The data were analyzed using the STATA 7.0 statistical software package with appropriate corrections for the survey design. Subgroup comparisons were made using adjusted Wald Tests for trend and design-corrected Pearson chi square analysis.

Respondents

Table 6.1 summarizes the study sample. Respondents were quite experienced clinicians; 96 percent had been in practice for more than ten years. Eighty percent of the sample had a strong personal connection to Pennsylvania, having either grown up, attended medical school, or done residency training in the state. Approximately two thirds of the sample practiced in the five "high-risk" counties around Philadelphia. One in eight respondents (13%) practiced in less populated parts of Pennsylvania not within a Metropolitan Statistical Area (MSA).

Of particular interest was the fact that 88 percent of responding physicians had been previously sued, and nearly half had been sued in the previous

TABLE 6.1. *Characteristics of Study Sample (n = 824)**

Specialty			Source of liability insurance		
Emergency medicine	148	18%	coverage		
General surgery	155	19%	Hospital	302	37%
Orthopedic surgery	127	15%	Commercial carrier	516	63%
Neurosurgery	52	6%	**Practice location**		
OB/GYN	187	23%	High-risk region	534	65%
Radiology	155	19%	Lower-risk region	290	35%
Gender			In MSA	718	87%
Male	717	87%	Outside MSA	106	13%
Female	107	13%	**Claims experience**		
Years in practice			Sued < 3 years ago	399	48%
1–10	29	4%	Sued > 3 years ago	322	39%
11–19	217	26%	Never sued	100	12%
20–29	291	35%	**Dropped by insurer**		
30+	287	35%	1995–2000	228	28%
Ties to Pennsylvania			2000–2003	328	40%
Grew up in PA	454	55	**Attitude to liability**		
Medical school in PA	437	53	**insurance premiums**		
Residency/fellowship in PA	541	66	Not a burden	19	2%
Began practice in PA after	230	28	Minor burden	89	11%
training out of state			Major burden	369	45%
Moved from practice out	141	17	Extreme burden	339	41%
of state			**Confidence that**		
Practice type			**current insurance**		
Solo	161	20%	**provides adequate**		
Group	322	39%	**coverage**		
Hospital clinic	227	28%	Very confident	62	8%
Other	111	14%	Somewhat confident	350	42%
Primary hospital affiliation			Not very	263	32%
Not-for-profit	694	84%	Not at all	146	18%
For-profit	93	11%			
Government	14	2%			

* Unweighted data. Subcategories may not sum to 824 because of rounding error or refusals to answer.

three years. In addition, nearly 70 percent had been dropped by a liability insurer since 1995. The rate of suit is impressive; even more impressive is the evidence of hectic change within the malpractice insurance industry. This signals tremendous instability in the liability insurance markets to which these physicians turn for coverage.

Consequently, it was not surprising that 86 percent of the physicians felt that the liability insurance premiums they paid were a major or extreme burden in their practice. More than half also lacked confidence that their current insurance would provide adequate coverage in the event they were sued (again).

Frequency of Assurance and Avoidance Behaviors

Table 6.2 outlines the assurance behaviors undertaken by the physicians in each of the various specialties (excluding radiology). Overall, 59 percent reported "often" ordering more tests than were medically indicated. Fifty-two percent reported that they often referred patients to other specialists in unnecessary circumstances; this was a particularly common practice among obstetrician-gynecologists (59%). One third of specialist physicians reported often prescribing more medications than were medically indicated, and the same proportion reported often suggesting invasive procedures in clinically inappropriate circumstances. General surgeons were especially likely to say that they often suggested invasive procedures (44%).

These findings suggest that liability concerns are increasing the cost of health care substantially and unnecessarily. Of course, it is very easy for physicians to answer these questions in a socially responsive fashion, but the recent spectacular increases in medical imaging across the country suggest exactly how much elasticity there is in physician decision making.

Table 6.2 also shows that avoidance behaviors were common, with 32 percent of physicians forgoing certain kinds of procedures and interventions and 39 percent avoiding high-risk patients. Avoidance behavior appeared to be especially prevalent when specialists involved were in a position to exert control over relatively elective procedures. For example, 57 percent of orthopedic surgeons said they avoided caring for high-risk patients and 42 percent reported that they often avoided certain high-risk procedures. Obstetrician-gynecologists were also likely to avoid high-risk interventions. The presumption is that these kinds of inhibitions would increase with liability premiums and volatility in the liability insurance markets.

In addition to questioning physicians about the frequency of their defensive practice in selected fixed categories, we asked them to provide details of their most recent defensive act. Table 6.3 presents selected verbatim responses.

Overall, imaging studies were the most prevalent recent act. More than half of the emergency physicians, orthopedic surgeons, and neurosurgeons who reported an act described a CT, MRI, or X-ray that was not clinically necessary. More radical avoidance behaviors such as leaving practice or modifying practice were also in evidence among our respondents. About 4 percent of specialists reported that they would definitely relocate out of Pennsylvania within the next two years because of the cost of professional liability insurance and 7 percent definitely planned to retire early (Table 6.4). As well, 43 percent had already personally reduced or eliminated high-risk aspects of their practice and 50 percent said

TABLE 6.2. *Frequency of Assurance and Avoidance Behaviors, by Specialty**

	All Specialties†				Emergency Physicians (n = 148)		General Surgeons (n = 155)		Orthopedic Surgeons (n = 127)		Neuro-surgeons (n = 52)		Obstetricians (n = 187)	
	Often		Never/Rarely		Often	Never/Rarely	Often	Never/Rarely	Often	Never/Rarely	Often	Never/Rarely	Often	Never/Rarely
	n	%	n	%	%	%	%	%	%	%	%	%	%	%
Assurance behaviors														
Order more tests than medically indicated	405	59	52	8	70§	4	55	9	62	7	50	22	54	8
Prescribe more medications (e.g., antibiotics) than medically indicated	223	33	207	31	30	29	35	30	43§	30	19‡	55	28	32
Refer to other specialists in unnecessary circumstances	349	52	78	11	52	11	50	13	48	13	29§	32	59‡	7
Suggest invasive procedures (e.g., biopsies) to confirm diagnoses	221	32	199	29	19§	32	44§	22	28	35	21	61	38	25
Avoidance behaviors														
Avoid conducting certain procedures or interventions	216	32	189	29	21§	43	25	28	42§	19	39	33	38‡	25
Avoid caring for high-risk patients§	268	39	236	35	13§	54	43	35	57§	22	38	43	46	28

* Weighted data. Adjusted Pearson χ^2 tests were used to test for significant differences between the proportion who reported often conducting the behavior within each specialty and the corresponding proportion for all other specialties combined.

† Radiologists were excluded because of the high proportion of their responses indicating that the defensive practice was in applicable to them (e.g., 54% reported overprescription was inapplicable; 37% reported that referral to other specialists was inapplicable).

‡ $P < 0.01$ compared with frequency of "often" responses for the other specialties combined.

§ $P < 0.05$ compared with frequency of "often" responses for the other specialties combined.

¶ The survey question asked whether respondents believed their practice or hospital would avoid caring for high-risk patients in the next two years. Response options ranged from "definitely will/already decided to" to "definitely will not." The column headed "Often" reports the "definitely will/already decided to" responses; the column headed "Never/rarely" reports "definitely will not" and "not likely" responses combined.

TABLE 6.3. *Selected Verbatim Descriptions of Defensive Medical Practice*

General Concerns

Radiologist: "I now often suggest CT because of a recent malpractice case. I never practiced 'defensive medicine' except for the last 4 yrs. This is my 43rd year in radiology."

Emergency physician: "I admit all 'young' patients with 'atypical' chest pain because if I'm wrong even at a 1/1000 batting average, I will likely be personally bankrupted by a wrongful death verdict."

Radiologist: "Every day [I practice defensive medicine]. One mistake and I will not be insured. Job satisfaction & quality of life does not exist."

Cost Effects

Emergency physician: "Almost every chest pain – even very unlikely pathology gets a $1,000 workup."

Orthopedist: "A woman called saying that her son was coming from college with an injured knee and she requested an MRI before he was even seen. It was easier to order the MRI, than to explain to her that a h+p would diagnose > 90% of knee problems; why risk refusing and have her upset if I then decided an MRI not necessary."

Neurosurgeon: "If a patient requests an MRI, I order it, no questions asked – if it pertains to the spine or cranium."

Access Effects

Orthopedist: "Patient with complex infected non-union; options are salvage attempt (high risk) or amputation (low risk) or defer treatment. Did not accept case due to sense of litigious nature. Not worth providing 'cutting edge' care or efforts to salvage in this environment."

General surgeon: "A new patient's family expressed concern about the outlook for his ischemic leg. They looked like litiginous people to me. I refused to care for him."

General surgeon: "I referred patient with bile duct obstruction to a university hospital provider that I could have performed myself and have done many times in the past. Patient could not get an appointment for over a month and her surgery was delayed and cancer had metastasized."

Technical Quality Effects

Emergency physician: "I now refer all facial lacerations to a plastic surgeon – no matter how simple."

Ob-Gyn: "Referring patients to breast surgeon for benign changes on mammogram. 'Can you promise me I don't have cancer, doctor?' was patient's question. Answer: no, but perhaps a bilateral mastectomy will get you a 99% guarantee."

General surgeon: "I routinely perform breast biopsies on obviously benign nodules because I do not win anything by being wrong."

Interpersonal Quality Effects

Ob-Gyn: "I performed a pregnancy test on a patient who averred she could not be pregnant. I 'knew' she would lie if there was a bad outcome involving a diagnosis of pregnancy."

Ob-Gyn: "Random drug checking in pregnancy – transfer patients who are non-compliant or high risk."

Neurosurgeon: "I now routinely will not assume the elective care for patients that I regard as personally difficult, contentious, or perceived by me as litigious."

General surgeon: "Every day [I practice defensive medicine], something but usually small – today I've obtained an extra chest X-ray on a patient I know to be actively suing another doctor."

TABLE 6.4. *Physician Decisions to Leave or Modify Practice, by Practice Setting**

	Overall (n = 824)	Solo Practitioners (n = 161)	Group Practitioners (n = 322)	Hospital Based (n = 227)
			%	
Likelihood of relocating practice time out of state in next 2 years because of liability costs				
Definitely will (already decided to)	4	6†	3	3
Very likely	12	22	12	6
Somewhat likely	17	17	21	13
Not likely/definitely will not	68	54	64	77
Likelihood of retiring early or ceasing direct patient care in next 2 years because of liability costs				
Definitely will (already decided to)	7	10‡	5	4
Very likely	13	27	12	9
Somewhat likely	19	24	20	17
Not likely/definitely will not	61	39	64	70
Have personally reduced or eliminated high-risk aspects of practice in last 3 years because of liability costs				
Yes	43	62§	42	32
No	57	38	58	68
Likelihood of personally reducing or eliminating high-risk aspects of practice in next 2 years because of liability costs				
Definitely will (already decided to)	12	16|	10	10
Very likely	19	28	22	13
Somewhat likely	19	21	24	15
Not likely/definitely will not	50	35	45	62

* Weighted proportion of completed responses. Percentages may not sum to 100 because of rounding. Subgroup analysis omits "Other" category (n = 111).
† $P < 0.0004$ in adjusted Wald Test for trend.
‡ $P < 0.0001$ in adjusted Wald Test for trend.
§ $P < 0.0001$ in design-corrected Pearson chi-square analysis.
| $P < 0.0001$ in adjusted Wald Test for trend.

they would likely (continue to) do so over the next two years. In light of such numbers, and when one considers the relative mobility of a high-risk and highly compensated specialty like neurosurgery or orthopedic surgery, it would appear that current liability costs in Pennsylvania are high enough to make physicians consider very radical avoidance behavior.

The important policy point is that if states like Pennsylvania create the conditions for high liability costs by requiring reporting and disclosure and not instituting significant tort reform, then it seems likely that there will be some migration of physicians and reduction of availability of certain kinds of procedures. Physicians are also recognizing that if they cannot avoid certain kinds of risks, and if assurance behaviors do not really decrease the amount of litigation, then they will need to increase their income in order to compensate for increased overhead costs. As Table 6.5 makes clear, many physician practices are already strategizing to increase compensation by decreasing charity work, increasing the volume of patients seen, and seeking patients whose insurance provides relatively high reimbursement.

Finally, Table 6.6 reveals a rather extraordinary level of dissatisfaction among specialist physicians in Pennsylvania. Pennsylvania specialists were more than twice as likely to be dissatisfied as national samples of specialists surveyed in 2001 and 1999.[25] Overall, 39 percent of Pennsylvania physicians were somewhat or very dissatisfied, compared to 18 percent in the 2001 national sample. Given this level of discontent, it is hard to believe that physicians with some mobility would not seek to move to states that have instituted tort reform and have not imposed significant new requirements around disclosure.

THE PHYSICIANS' VIEW

Physicians typically invest a great deal of emotion in the malpractice issue, usually to a degree that is out of proportion to the actual risk. It is hard to understand why this is the case at times, but two explanations present. First, malpractice litigation is the one form of regulation that cannot be captured by the profession. Plaintiffs' attorneys lie beyond the broad reach of the medical lobby. The right to jury trial is a hardy commitment in most jurisdictions, and so it is as if the medical profession can do little but rail. Tort reform has made inroads, but the fact remains that negligent physicians will often be sued.

The second explanation lies in the adversarial process. Physicians believe, in most cases rightfully so, that their devotion to patients runs deep. It draws them out of the commercial world and into a dyad of trust and intimacy. Thus it is particularly shocking for physicians when they are brought crashing back

---

[25] Landon et al. 2003. The CTS and Pennsylvania samples of specialists were not identical; see Table 6.6 for details.

TABLE 6.5. *Physician Reports of Steps Likely to Be Taken by Hospitals and Physician Practices in Response to Liability Costs**

Likelihood of *Practice or Hospital* Where Physician Sees Most Patients Taking the Following Steps Within Next 2 Years Because of Liability Costs	%			
	Overall (*n* = 824)	Solo Practitioners (*n* = 161)	Group Practitioners (*n* = 322)	Hospital Based (*n* = 227)
Increasing the number of patients whose health insurance has relatively high reimbursement rates				
Definitely will (already decided to)	6	3	7	5
Very likely	21	19	26	19
Somewhat likely	28	32	25	28
Not likely/definitely will not	45	46	42	48
Not accepting new patients whose health insurance has relatively low reimbursement rates				
Definitely will (already decided to)	9	11†	11	5
Very likely	21	18	27	17
Somewhat likely	23	32	20	21
Not likely/definitely will not	47	39	42	58
Decreasing the amount of charity work				
Definitely will (already decided to)	10	13‡	1	5
Very likely	17	19	20	13
Somewhat likely	26	28	21	28
Not likely/definitely will not	48	41	47	53

* Weighted proportion of completed responses. Percentages may not sum to 100 because of rounding. Subgroup analysis omits "Other" category (*n* = 111).
† *P* = 0.001 in adjusted Wald Test for trend.
‡ *P* = 0.007 in adjusted Wald Test for trend.

into market liberalism through the vehicle of a lawsuit. It is felt as a betrayal and can be an extremely stressful experience for the physician-defendant. The blame usually does not fall on the patient (perhaps paternalistically, the physician cannot blame him or her) but rather on the lawyer. The charge of negligence is felt as an unwarranted criminal accusation, and the doctor immediately becomes the victim. In this way, malpractice litigation excites the basest emotions.

But the world of medicine is changing. Fewer and fewer doctors work alone in practice. More and more are members of large medical groups with leadership trained in business. Alert to the health services research, they realize that errors occur and should be prevented. They also realize that errors cause injury and that society takes steps to provide compensation for injury. Thus, malpractice insurance is, for these administrators, another part of the costs of doing business; malpractice lawsuits are a time-consuming part of that overhead.

TABLE 6.6. *Pennsylvania Specialist Physician Satisfaction Compared to National Benchmark*[†]

Satisfaction with Overall Career in Medicine	%		
	Pennsylvania Sample, 2003[‡]	National Sample, 2001[□]	National Sample, 1999
All specialists			
n	824	4,723	5,040
Very satisfied	24[*¥]	42	41
Somewhat satisfied	36	39	38
Neither satisfied nor dissatisfied	2	1	1
Somewhat dissatisfied	24	14	15
Very dissatisfied	15	4	4
Surgical specialties[§]			
n	330	1,407	1,578
Very satisfied	28[¥]	40	43
Somewhat satisfied	30	39	36
Neither satisfied nor dissatisfied	2	1	1
Somewhat dissatisfied	23	15	15
Very dissatisfied	17	5	4
Obstetrician/gynecologists			
n	186	446	466
Very satisfied	15[¥]	34	35
Somewhat satisfied	33	38	38
Neither satisfied nor dissatisfied	3	1	< 1
Somewhat dissatisfied	29	20	17
Very dissatisfied	20	6	9

[†] Weighted proportions of completed responses. Percentages may not sum to 100 because of rounding.

[‡] Pennsylvania sample is from the present study and includes emergency medicine physicians, general surgeons, neurosurgeons, obstetrician/gynecologists, orthopedists, and radiologists.

[□] National samples are from the Community Tracking Study Physician Survey and include all specialists except radiologists, anesthesiologists, and pathologists. Data sources: Landon et al. 2003, 442–9; Center for Studying Health System Change, Community Tracking Study Physician Survey, 2000–2001 (Washington, DC: Center for Studying Health System Change [producer], 2003; Ann Arbor, MI: Inter–university Consortium for Political and Social Research, 2003); Center for Studying Health System Change, Community Tracking Study Physician Survey, 1998–1999 (Washington, DC: Center for Studying Health System Change [producer], 2001; Ann Arbor, MI: Inter–university Consortium for Political and Social Research, 2002).

[§] Pennsylvania surgical specialties sample includes general surgeons, neurosurgeons, and orthopedists; CTS national sample includes all surgical specialties.

[*] Significantly different ($p < 0.01$) from 2001 national sample in M^2 test for trend in ordinal data. See: Agresti 1996, ch. 2.

[¥] Significantly different ($p < 0.01$) from 1999 national sample in M^2 test for trend.

In medicine practiced as a business, defensive medicine is understood and may even be profitable. In a fee-for-service environment, increased use of services that a medical group controls, or that a hospital offers, will create revenue. Thus, overutilization is acceptable in that it may allay legal concerns while simultaneously increasing reimbursements. This will be the case unless there are cost-control features in place such as capitation – something more prevalent eight years ago than today – or pay-for-performance contracts – something we expect to see more of in the near future. In these situations, there is a financial imperative to eliminate unnecessary care and so defensive medicine will be scrutinized closely.

Another important point is that the extent to which the average physician, hospital, or medical group feels the costs of our present, inefficient system of medical justice will likely increase as time wears on. As medical care inflation increases over the next decade and the country ages, the cost issue will become grinding. Sooner or later even a societal fixture like malpractice law must come under scrutiny and the waste of adjudicating individual cases in the courts recognized. At that point, all parties (providers, insurers, and payers) will realize that they cannot afford to provide a good living for a small group of attorneys (both defense and plaintiff) and will have to turn to a more efficient if less "corrective" approach.

These points become ever more salient as the pressure grows to disclose errors and the injuries they cause. Today, advocates of disclosure simply want the patient to know he or she was injured. They expect that this knowledge, plus a carefully worded apology, will be sufficient. However, where in the rest of tort law do we find that claiming is extinguished by good manners and honesty? In fact, one could argue that an ethical physician would be driven to inform the patient of the possibility of compensation, as the doctor is committed to the good of the patient.

Ultimately, disclosure will likely bring more litigation. In so doing, it will bring more concerns about defensive medicine and overhead costs. Most physicians cannot see it now, but increased disclosure with no counterbalancing constraints in the tort environment will represent a significant wealth shift from doctors to patients, just as cost control becomes more stringent.

The average practicing physician only sees the emotional impact for now and is not in a much different position than his or her predecessors a generation ago. But the business aspect of medicine is taking over, and with the projected future growth in malpractice costs must come greater awareness that the malpractice system and the defensive care it provokes constitute unaffordable overhead in an era of decreasing income.

POLICY IMPLICATIONS

Overall, our results are sobering. They reveal, in a conventional liability crisis, very dissatisfied physician populations. These physicians appear to be much more prepared than physicians in previous surveys to pursue both assurance and avoidance behaviors. Assurance behavior should have a significant impact on cost, although one could imagine situations in which insurance companies and other payers could move to counteract that effect. For example, it might not be possible for a practicing physician to order an unnecessary MRI in the future if reimbursement is contingent to adherence to specific indications for imaging. But if that cost central program is seen as increasing risk for malpractice costs, it will lead to greater dissatisfaction and likely more avoidance behavior.

Avoidance behavior is the more salient issue. If some states do choose radically different approaches to patient safety and malpractice – that is, some states engage in tort reform with no disclosure and other states forgo tort reform but insist on disclosure – it follows that the variation in "physician friendliness" of state liability regimes will widen. Our findings suggest a much more motivated physician population than have previous surveys evaluating defensive medicine. We expect that physicians will be much more likely to vote with their feet to find low liability states.

One set of changes we have not discussed is avoidance behaviors in which physicians seek other payers for their liability. This can be done particularly through hospitals. A neurosurgeon or orthopedist faced with significant new liability costs might try to gain employment from the hospital and then have the hospital pay the physician a salary and cover liability costs. The Office of Inspector General of the Department of Health and Human Services has agreed that in most circumstances this form of appointment, even the up-front payment for liability costs, is not a form of fraud and abuse.[26] We could see it grow dramatically over the next decade.

Another important issue is that of specialty pooling. The burden of liability costs falls most heavily on particular subspecialties, such as neurosurgery and high-risk obstetrics. Smaller subspecialties could see dramatic increases in their liability premiums in the future, which may lead physicians to consider how to undertake greater pooling by aggregating into multispecialty groups. Our research indicates that many physicians are interested in such changes, and this will no doubt lead to decreases in solo practice.

SUMMARY

Our analysis of current trends in safety enhancement and liability reform suggests that states could choose radically different approaches to deal with the compensation and deterrence of injuries due to errors and negligence. Perhaps the most rational approach – one that seems to be an outgrowth of

[26] Office of Inspector General 2004.

the safety movement – is to increase reporting of adverse events to public authorities and disclosure to patients. The insights into the causes of patient injury that such transparency allows for may, in the long term, mean fewer injuries and possibly also fewer claims; but for the foreseeable future, we believe the likely result will be more claims. The result of higher rates of claiming will be higher premiums for physician and hospital liability insurance. Some states may act to blunt this effect by implementing tort reforms that lead to significantly smaller returns on lawsuits for patients and their lawyers. All else equal, however, a disclosed case should for the plaintiffs' attorney be an easier and cheaper case to bring and win.

What would the effect of such a scenario be on physicians? Our research suggests that as liability costs grow, so does physician dissatisfaction with the practice of medicine. To reduce their risk and costs, they will pursue assurance responses, but the impact of that general response on exposure to litigation is somewhat doubtful. Avoidance responses are a surer bet, and these provoke significant policy concern because of their potential to constrain access to care. If mobile subspecialty surgeons leave states to avoid liability costs, it would appear there is a possibility of real physician shortages in some geographic areas. More likely, those physicians will stay, but cease to provide necessary but potentially high-exposure practices, such as caring for patients injured through trauma. Policy makers will have to consider this daunting prospect as they experiment with changes in the liability environment.

7

Medical Liability and the Culture of Technology

Peter D. Jacobson

During the past thirty years, the United States has witnessed three separate medical liability crises. One common theme has been the outcry for reform and the concomitant failure to effectuate meaningful change. Each crisis has led to incremental reforms, but fundamental changes in how medical professional liability is determined have remained elusive.

Despite all the attention accompanying these crises, one aspect, medical technology, has not featured prominently in the liability debate. This chapter explores the central but often unappreciated role medical technology plays in the recurring malpractice crises. The analysis will attempt to demonstrate several premises. First, culture is the most important factor driving technology development and use. Second, technology is the principal driver of health policy through its impact on cost, access, and quality. Third, technology is the primary driver of negligence law. Fourth, the history of medical malpractice liability is synonymous with the development of medical technology.

In short, the culture of technology drives medical liability. For any malpractice reform effort to be effective, it must take account of how technology influences malpractice liability. Tort reform that fails to deal with the historical and cultural determinants of technology use is unlikely to alter the basic dynamic of the recent malpractice crises.

The chapter adopts the Institute of Medicine's (IOM's) broad definition of technology as "techniques, drugs, equipment and procedures used by health care professionals in delivering medical care to individuals and the systems within which such care is delivered."[1] This definition excludes diagnoses and interventions that rely mainly on physician observation and deduction as well as errors or misdiagnoses based on provider misjudgment (e.g., adverse drug interactions). There are at least two kinds of medical technology that affect physicians: technology that directly shapes patient care (such as new diagnostic tools or medical devices), and information technology (such as

---

[1] Institute of Medicine 2000, 53.

online medical databases or telemedicine). A further distinction could be made between low-technology equipment (e.g., hospital beds) and high-technology equipment (e.g., CT scans), but malpractice litigation almost always involves high-technology equipment.

In a sense, technology is both savior and culprit: Savior in extending length and improving quality of life; culprit in causing rapid increases in health care expenditures and, for physicians, considerably more exposure to liability. Because there is no single dominant technology, there is no single appropriate legal or health policy response. What might be effective for one technology might not work for another. For a novel direct technology, such as a full body scan, a technology assessment process might be the most effective policy approach. For an application of information technology, such as telemedicine, the key issue might be defining the standard of care.

TECHNOLOGY AND HEALTH LAW

Technology has been the central component in shaping the contours of legal doctrine concerning negligence generally and medical liability specifically.[2] For instance, the emergence of railroads in the nineteenth century and the attendant social consequences (i.e., increased injuries to workers and bystanders) drove the development of modern negligence principles (the concept of fault-based liability). Likewise, the development of mass-produced goods in the twentieth century led to strict product liability principles (the concept of liability without regard to fault) in the 1960s.[3]

The development of malpractice liability standards is no different. The history of medical professional liability is a struggle between technological advances and injuries suffered when those advances fail. As a medical historian put it, "the development and implementation of new technologies and procedures have played a consistent and central role throughout the history of malpractice litigation."[4] The first wave of medical malpractice lawsuits, between 1820 and 1850, was fueled by rapid technological advances in treating bone fractures. This pattern of technology stimulating malpractice litigation would consistently replicate itself over the succeeding years.[5] By the late 1800s, it was apparent that rapid technological change enhanced physicians' stature but exposed them to litigation.

Although technical advances in medical care would seem to increase positive patient outcomes and satisfaction, they actually added to the problem. The public's demand for perfect health helped to drive these advances in medicine, but with advances came added risk. New techniques and medical advances allowed better physicians to take on more difficult cases, whereas

[2] Grady 1988, 293.
[3] Jacobson and Pomfret 1999.
[4] De Ville 1998, 197.
[5] De Ville 1990, 217; Mohr 1993.

a less qualified practitioner might decline altogether to treat the case. In the case of a compound fracture, an educated physician would attempt to save the limb rather than amputate. Often, the result was a shorter limb with some loss of functioning. Patients unhappy with this outcome looked to the courts for compensation. In large part, medical advances came to delineate the standards of care for the "better" practitioners and became the basis of a lawsuit when the result was not what the patient anticipated.[6]

Innovative, sometimes radical techniques raised expectations of a cure, while the general public did not often understand the attendant risks. Innovations in radiography and orthopedics were particularly susceptible to lawsuits, as the spread of X-ray technology in the first part of the twentieth century illustrates. Radiography undoubtedly advanced patient care, but it soon became the largest source of malpractice liability (in both claim frequency and award severity) for excess radiation and failure to interpret the films properly. "Radiographic tests also opened to exposure other sorts of medical mistakes that were previously difficult to demonstrate in court."[7] This pattern of new technology exposing or creating new types of medical mistakes accelerated in the latter part of the twentieth century.

At the same time, there is a life cycle to technology. Initially, the technological advance leads to inflated expectations, then litigation when the expectations are not met. Subsequent technological improvements then limit risk and reduce injuries.[8]

THE EFFECTS OF TECHNOLOGICAL CHANGE ON MEDICAL LIABILITY

As we enter the twenty-first century, technology develops faster and plays an even greater role in medical practice and medical liability exposure than in prior eras. During the past thirty years, unprecedented innovations have had great clinical and economic importance for U.S. medicine. Millions of people have been able to live longer, better quality lives because of new treatments, new surgical procedures, new drugs, and vastly improved diagnostic techniques. Medical technology has played a major role in conquering many dreadful and once incurable disease conditions. But it has also created new challenges for health care administrators and policy makers, including a propensity for litigation.

The General Liability Propensity

Technological advances create opportunities for error in both diagnosis and treatment, and those errors may result in more visible and more severe injuries. Diagnostic technology in common use may not always improve

[6] Mohr 1993.
[7] Mohr 2000, 1734. See also De Ville 1998; Howell 1995.
[8] De Ville 1998, 201–2.

medical outcomes, but paradoxically contributes to a higher legal standard of care. In obstetric and gynecologic practice, the failure to employ genetic testing, electronic fetal monitors, ultrasonography, and new information technologies can create liability, as can improperly interpreting the results. Absent a viable diagnostic test, for instance, the failure to detect prostate cancer through a biopsy might not result in litigation. Just as important, physicians and institutions are vulnerable to claims that they failed to adopt cutting-edge technological innovations, though these claims are likely to be less frequent than claims regarding misuse and failure to use when technology is available.

Technology also helps create unrealistic patient expectations that every newborn child will be perfect or can become so. The ability to save a severely injured, low birth-weight infant, when that same infant would not have survived twenty years ago, carries with it the potential for litigation that seeks to blame the obstetrician for any permanent disability.[9] Even noteworthy technological advances that generally improve health outcomes are not immune from exposing physicians to liability.

Perhaps most significantly, medical innovations are increasingly complex. The precision of new technologies means that momentary lapses or minor mistakes can have serious consequences, even if the probability of harm is low. "The cost of momentary lapses of concentration is typically greater in the new technology, because the promise of benefit is greater, but also because the procedure itself is sometimes more dangerous."[10] The more advanced the technology, the greater the skill needed to use it appropriately and successfully. Although that complexity allows physicians to undertake procedures previously unavailable, the potential costs of errors are that much greater.[11]

General advances in surgery are particularly liability-inducing. Danzon (1987) found that the number of surgical procedures per capita was a statistically significant explanation of claim frequency and award severity. Minimally invasive surgery, for example, reduces recovery time but requires careful training and monitoring for error. Laparoscopic cholecystectomy (for gallstone disease) replaced an open surgical procedure that had low complication rates. When patients availed themselves of the minimally invasive alternative, however, some suffered major injuries to the common bile duct or the liver, resulting in a wave of unwelcome litigation. Consider the following description of an older surgeon's first use of laparoscopic cholecystectomy, when he mistakenly cut into the patient's liver (apparently without lasting harm): "This was new terrain, requiring new tricks to compensate for not

---

[9] See, e.g., *Brownsville Pediatric Association v. Reyes*, 68 S.W.3d 184 (Tex.App. 2002), for a graphic depiction of how the failure to use technology can result in permanent harm to a neonate and a large jury verdict against the physician.

[10] De Ville 1998, 203.

[11] Mohr 2000, 1734.

being able to touch what he was cutting, for not being able to plainly see where his instruments were."[12]

Recently, the overall safety of American health care has come under attack, with the IOM attributing between 44,000 and 98,000 deaths annually to medical error.[13] Technology contributes significantly to the problem, as evidenced by high error rates in technical specialties such as vascular surgery, cardiac surgery, and neurosurgery.[14] The IOM report highlights how advances in technology contribute to medical error. On one level, technology prevents error by replacing fallible humans with automated systems. But learning to implement new technologies is hazardous; the IOM report observes that "all technology introduces new errors, even when its sole purpose is to prevent errors."[15] Thus, as with the laparoscopic cholecystectomy example, technology can make medical procedures "opaque" to operators, who may be overwhelmed by complexity and therefore unable to assess the situation and make corrections.

Advanced technology may also have indirect effects on litigation.[16] By driving up life expectancy, new technology increases the number of encounters with physicians and therefore opportunities for error. Because physicians are more willing to intervene if potentially life-saving technology is available, frail patients may suffer serious harm that would otherwise not be attributable to medical care. Further complicating matters is that there is no one trajectory for how technology might lead to litigation, especially with regard to determining the standard of care. Compare, for example, high-dose chemotherapy with autologous bone marrow transplant (ABMT) and "whole body scans." In the ABMT cases, the dominant legal issue was whether the procedure's widespread use among community oncologists overrode the absence of scientific evidence that it was effective. In contrast, the new body scan diagnostic technology, equally unproven, primarily raises issues of unnecessary surgery resulting from false positive findings.

Specific Technologies

Aside from the general liability propensity, it is instructive to consider how specific technologies raise liability concerns. For this project, I attempted to obtain information from malpractice insurance carriers regarding technology-related claims to address two key issues. First, do a few technologies account for a significant portion of liability risk in any given year? Second, what is the overall contribution of technology to claim frequency

[12] Gaster 1993, 1280.
[13] Institute of Medicine 2000.
[14] Leape et al. 1993; Kacmar 1997.
[15] Institute of Medicine 2000, 151.
[16] I am indebted to Phil Peters for suggesting this approach.

TABLE 7.1. *PIAA Data*

	Claim	Frequency of Claim	Mean Award	% of Claims Paid[17]
Laparoscopic cholecystectomy	Error in use; Improperly performed surgery	1990–4: 331 1995–9: 869	$136,000 $236,384	54% 50%
Neurologically impaired infants	Failure to interpret diagnostic technology	1985–97: 3,466	$568,283	47%
Breast cancer	Failure to detect or diagnose	1985–2001: 3,437	$217,500 (1995) $438,047 (2002)	41%
Anesthesia monitoring	Anesthesia-related injury and substandard care	1988: 1,004 Substantial declines after guidelines used	$10,000– $6 million	62%

and award severity? The answers to these questions are important because they would illuminate what types of technology policy responses might be effective to relieve pressure on the malpractice system, perhaps by developing special liability arrangements for particularly risky technologies. Unfortunately, very little data are available in the form needed to address these questions. Studies conducted by the Physician Insurers Association of America (PIAA) reveal some interesting trends but fall short of providing clear policy direction (Table 7.1).

PIAA studied three specific procedures at different points in time: neurological impairment in newborns, laparoscopic injury, and breast cancer. Each represents a different type of technology claim. For breast cancer, the issue is failure to screen for and detect disease. For laparoscopic surgery, the issue is error using therapeutic technology. And, for neurological impairment, the issue is failure to properly interpret new monitoring devices available during routine procedures. Although PIAA has not published a synthesis of these studies, a PIAA analyst suggested that technology claims are on the rise and are consuming a greater portion of insurance claim payments.[18] In her view, new technology makes errors more obvious and causation of injury more likely. This is consistent with the view that claims increase upon the introduction of a new technology but then level off over time, in part

---

[17] Physician Insurers Association of America 1998, 2000, 1994, 2002, 1995.

[18] Personal communication with Robin Traywick, PIAA, December 2002.

because "a new procedure is typically more complex and exacting than previous treatment" methods.[19]

The PIAA data have several limitations. First, PIAA reports only paid claims, so the averages tend to overstate indemnity. Second, the data are self-reports from PIAA member companies. Not all members submit data on each of the surveys, so it is difficult to make any broad generalizations about the findings. Nevertheless, the data help identify the likely influence of technology on medical liability.

In addition to the PIAA data, this section discusses mechanisms, such as clinical practice guidelines, that have been effective in protecting against liability for using new technologies. The section concludes with an exploratory analysis of litigation in three states currently designated "in crisis" by the American Medical Association (AMA).

Laparoscopic Cholecystectomy. Before minimally invasive surgical techniques were developed, removing the gallbladder required painful and disfiguring abdominal surgery with a lengthy recovery period and was done only when absolutely necessary. The new procedure reduces all of these effects, which results in much greater frequency of use. However, less visibility and unfamiliar instruments occasionally lead surgeons to injure the common bile duct, perforate the bowel, lacerate the liver, or cut the iliac artery. These risks result in more malpractice claims and larger damage awards than in the era before laparoscopic cholecystectomy was available.[20]

From 1990 to 1994, before minimally invasive techniques entered widespread use, PIAA received 750 claims relating to gallstone surgery and made indemnity payments of approximately $42 million. In 1995–9, the number of claims rose to 1,426, with indemnity payments of around $104 million. In the latter period, 60 percent of claims involved allegations of improperly performed cholecystectomies, which PIAA attributes to both higher numbers of cholecystectomies being performed and a greater risk of complications from the laparoscopic technique. Tellingly, the rate of paid claims involving cholecystectomy (50%) vastly exceeds PIAA's overall rate of paid claims (31%), and the average indemnity payment is 26 percent higher.

Breast Cancer. In PIAA's three breast cancer surveys, the dominant claim was failure to diagnose, which implicates two different effects of technology. Improved diagnostic technology creates liability if used improperly, while improved therapeutic technology increases liability for delay. Diagnostic technologies also allow mass screening, which is otherwise impractical.

PIAA identified certain trends across the studies. Radiologists were named in 33 percent of the 2002 study claims, up from 24 percent in 1995. By

[19] De Ville 1998, 202.
[20] See, e.g., *Dunning v. Barnes*, 2002 Del. Super. LEXIS 487, and *Lucas v. Collins*, 743 N.E.2d 847 (Mass. App. Ct. 2001).

contrast, ob/gyn claims declined from 38.6 percent in 1990 to 23 percent in 1995 and 2002. Between 1995 and 2002, the median paid indemnity claims rose a robust 45.3 percent (from $301,460 to $438,047). PIAA suggests two reasons for the increase. One is that the average delay in diagnosis (the longer the delay, the more severe the patient's condition) rose from 12.7 months in 1990 and 14 months in 1995 to 16.3 months in 2002. The other is the rise in negative or equivocal first mammograms from 68 percent in 1990 to 80 percent in both 1995 and 2002. According to PIAA, "This result is rather surprising as it would seem that diagnostic accuracy should be improving given the advances in technology of mammography equipment."[21]

Perhaps. But it may also indicate that technological advances create more opportunities for missed diagnoses than less sophisticated diagnostic technologies that could never detect certain lesions. Thus, of the 1,077 individual physician claims in the 2002 survey, 703 (or 65%) were for a negative mammogram report, misreading a mammogram, or physical findings that failed to impress. Most important, the percentage of misread mammograms rose from 22.7 percent in 1995 to 37.8 percent in 2002 (resulting in more than $57 million in indemnity payments). Because there is no reason to believe that radiologists are any less capable of interpreting films now than they were in the past, it seems reasonable to assume that improved technology exposed them to expectations of higher, more precise readings than is perhaps justified.

Neurologically Impaired Infants. The claims data for neurologically impaired infants present a more complex picture than the other two areas. One reason is that causal attribution for negligence is notoriously difficult in these cases. Indeed, physicians argue strenuously that most adverse birth outcomes result from unknown etiologic factors as opposed to negligence. Another interpretive problem is that the comparison data across the 1987 and 1997 studies are less complete than the two studies already discussed. But because these claims, as of 1997, represented PIAA's largest single area of claim frequency and award severity, it is worth attempting to understand technology's role. That role occurs at two points – antepartum tests and labor.

According to the PIAA data, interpretation of any antepartum test or procedure was a factor in 16.7 percent of all cases. The failure to perform a test or procedure occurred in an additional 19.8 percent of all cases. In both instances, diagnostic ultrasonography was the primary technology involved. During labor, the use and interpretation of electronic fetal monitors (EFMs) seem to be the driving litigation factors, but PIAA's analysis is difficult to interpret. Still, PIAA concludes that "[a]bnormalities detected through electronic fetal monitoring resulted in a case payment value 71% higher than when no abnormality was detected."[22]

---

[21] Physician Insurers Association of America 2002, 6.
[22] Physician Insurers Association of America 1997, 5.

Two comparisons between the 1997 and 1987 studies are particularly relevant to the role of technology. In the 1997 survey, fetal distress appeared in 88 percent of cases, up from 41 percent in 1987. PIAA suggests that this resulted from the substantially increased use of EFMs. There was also a marked increase in the use of diagnostic ultrasound (88% in 1997, compared to 32% in 1987). PIAA makes no attempt to attribute the rise in average indemnity payments to these two issues, yet it seems reasonable to conclude that advances in technology have actually exposed physicians to higher liability claims.

One reason may be that this type of technology will not be able to prevent adverse fetal events. A report just released by the American College of Obstetrician Gynecologists (ACOG) indicates that many instances of hypoxic-ischemic encephalopathy (HIE) in newborns (a form of cerebral palsy [CP]) result from factors that cannot be detected intrapartum. HIE was thought to be largely caused by events during labor, but clearly technology utilized during labor may be too late to correct or prevent much of the damage done to the fetus during pregnancy. As a result, it might not be the fault of technology but rather the failure to utilize technology at the appropriate time during pregnancy that contributes to the inability to predict or prevent conditions such as HIE or CP.

Anesthesia Monitoring. The use of clinical practice guidelines is a very tempting means of establishing a standard of care and, concomitantly, to advancing the patient safety movement. Physicians who follow the guidelines can use that as a defense. Of course, the failure to follow recognized guidelines can correspondingly result in liability. But, as several observers have argued, it is unlikely that courts will rely solely on guidelines to set the standard of care. Instead, the trend appears to be that judges will allow the jury to weigh them as one piece of evidence in determining liability. Given the physician judgment inherent in any clinical situation, the potential multiplicity of competing and conflicting guidelines, the usual lack of certainty in the guidelines development process, and direct physician testimony, it is improbable that any guideline will suffice to set the standard of care. In any event, technology may diffuse faster than professional societies can develop appropriate guidelines.

Nevertheless, one technology, anesthesia monitoring, demonstrates the potential for such guidelines to reduce liability exposure.[23] During the 1970s, liability claims against anesthesiologists resulted in higher claims frequency and award severity than any other category. In response, anesthesiologists developed the Harvard Anesthesiology Practice Guidelines.[24] Following their widespread adoption, both claims frequency and award severity against

---

[23] Indeed, Hyams et al. (1996) found that following guidelines deterred the initiation of litigation.

[24] Eichhorn et al. 1986.

anesthesiologists declined dramatically.[25] For example, one study found that "anesthesiology monitoring guidelines reduced losses at Harvard facilities from $5.24 per anesthetic in the period from 1976 to 1985 to somewhere between $.78 and $2.00 per anesthetic."[26] Another noted that one Massachusetts insurer closed 27 claims between 1976 and 1986 but faced no claims in 1988, after the anesthesia guidelines were implemented.[27] Several insurers also lowered their insurance rate classifications based on the guidelines' overall success in reducing claims. Especially during surgical delivery, pulse oximetry reduces injury by alerting the anesthesiologist to poor oxygenation. By providing an evidentiary trail, it shifts legal liability for any hypoxic birth injury to the obstetrician and away from the anesthesiologist. In this sense, the technology is both protective (for the anesthesiologist) and deflective (onto the obstetrician).[28] Once again, technology is both savior and culprit.[29]

Studies of pulse oximetry used during sedation indicate a dramatic difference in injuries resulting when pulse oximetry is utilized compared to its absence. A study by the American Academy of Pediatrics looked at injury to children sedated in hospital as compared to nonhospital settings. "When a serious adverse sedation event occurred in a non-hospital-based facility, 93% of children suffered death or permanent neurologic injury as the outcome, a 2.5-fold increase compared with children sedated in a hospital-based venue."[30] Similarly, in a hospital facility, 30.2 percent of complications resulted in death and 30.2 percent resulted in prolonged hospitalization without injury, whereas 82.1 percent of those in a nonhospital setting resulted in death and only 7.1 percent led to prolonged hospitalization without injury. The results of the study indicated that much of the injury in nonhospital settings could have been prevented with proper monitoring. "The rank order of severity of adverse outcome and the incidence of death and permanent neurologic injury were significantly less in children monitored with pulse oximetry compared with those not monitored at all."[31]

Thus, pulse oximetry is an excellent example of a procedure that provides for protection against liability. Physicians who use pulse oximetry dramatically reduce the likelihood of adverse outcomes. Unlike legislative or legal protections, this is a self-implemented protection or one that can easily be endorsed through practice guidelines.

[25] Cheney et al. 1989.
[26] Holzer 1990.
[27] Pierce 1990.
[28] I am indebted to Bill Sage for the phrase "both protective and deflective."
[29] See, e.g., *Suttle v. Lake Forest Hospital*, 733 N.E.2d 726 (Ill. App. 2002), upholding a $10.9 million jury verdict for failing to monitor maternal and fetal blood pressure rates.
[30] Cote et al. 2000.
[31] Ibid.

TABLE 7.2. *Three-State Analysis*

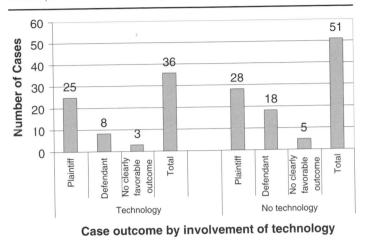

Case outcome by involvement of technology

Recent Cases in Three States. One question we might ask is whether cases involving technology (as defined earlier) have different outcomes than cases involving errors of judgment or mistakes having nothing to do with the use or misuse of technology. To do so, I analyzed cases in three states noted by the AMA as medical liability crisis states – West Virginia, New Jersey, and Pennsylvania (as shown in Table 7.2). I divided all medical liability cases from 2001–3 into technology/no technology (eliminating a large number of cases involving only procedural matters). These cases reveal a picture generally consistent with the PIAA studies.

Several findings are worth noting. To begin with, there is a notable increase in plaintiffs' victories in technology cases. When technology is involved, plaintiffs win 69.4 percent of the time, as opposed to 54.9 percent in non-technology cases. Curiously, that figure is almost reversed in Pennsylvania, where plaintiffs won 58.3 percent of the technology cases and 71.4 percent of the nontechnology cases.[32]

Second, technology cases represent 43 percent of the total. At first glance, this is contrary to my thesis that technology is driving medical liability. But for three reasons, that conclusion might not be warranted. To determine whether technology cases are increasing as a percentage of total liability claims, we would need to assess data in the years prior to 2001. Beyond that, it is likely that technology cases result in higher damage awards (especially for noneconomic damages, i.e., pain and suffering), which would amplify their

[32] Because of the relatively small *n*, it is difficult to determine whether the Pennsylvania cases differ systematically from the other two states. One possible explanation is that coding errors shifted some cases from the technology to the nontechnology column.

importance relative to the more frequent nontechnology cases. As such, the technology verdicts may well overwhelm the more numerous but smaller nontechnology verdicts. In addition, data from the other sources discussed previously support the basic thesis.

Third, plaintiffs are winning more than 50 percent of the time in technology-based cases. Historically, plaintiffs have won 20 to 50 percent of litigated cases. A steady increase in plaintiffs' victories, setting aside the damage award trends, would certainly add to the perception of a malpractice crisis. Why plaintiffs might be winning more cases is beyond the scope of this chapter.

For several reasons, this analysis should be considered both tentative and preliminary. First, the time frame is arbitrary, selected to make the analysis manageable. A longer time horizon might show different results. Second, it is not always easy to determine whether the case actually involves the definition of technology used here. In some instances, the court deals with subsidiary issues even though the case arose because of technology. Third, I selected only a few states to undertake a preliminary analysis. Fourth, although the denominator was all reported cases available on Lexis-Nexis, it is likely that there are numerous additional cases that were not available. Finally, there needs to be a comparison to noncrisis states to determine whether technology is actually driving the malpractice crisis.

EXPLANATORY FACTORS: THE CULTURE OF TECHNOLOGY

In view of technology's crucial role in liability trends, it is worthwhile to examine the factors driving the development and use of technology. Observers of the U.S. health care system frequently remark on the nation's culture of technology. Americans expect, indeed demand, both continued innovation and widespread (though not universal) availability. As one observer notes, "Technology has become the symbol of our culture and the symbol of progress."[33] Not surprisingly, the public wants it both ways – quick access to the latest technology but also a mechanism for compensating the inevitable failures.

Cultural Explanations

The national culture of technology underlies the relationship between law and medicine. No other factor plays such a powerful explanatory role in litigation trends or overall health policy. Liability and health care reform

[33] Hoffman 2002, 681. See also G. Smith 2001, 286; Howell 1995, 249.

arc unlikely to succeed without taking into account the cultural aspects of technology.

Historian Kenneth De Ville has been a leading proponent of the relationship between technology and medical liability. One important feature of De Ville's work is its focus on the cultural determinants of the technological imperative as they influence liability trends. His explanatory framework for recurrent medical malpractice crises invokes both long-term cultural factors and short-term topical influences and is a useful starting point for understanding litigation trends and for adopting appropriate policy responses.[34]

Under long-term cultural trends, De Ville notes several factors: (1) an upward-sloping baseline proclivity to sue, (2) breakdown of community solidarity that discouraged litigation, (3) a rising secular belief that humans can improve their lives, (4) a growing preoccupation with physical well-being, and (5) increased demand that there be a remedy for every wrong. Topical influences include (1) attitudes toward the medical profession, (2) more sophisticated plaintiffs' attorneys, (3) increasing media coverage, (4) changes in legal doctrine, and (5) the absence of national health insurance. The inadequacy of health insurance deserves special attention as an incentive for litigation. When technology-laden medical care is needed following iatrogenic injury, the expense to an uninsured patient can be devastating.

Three aspects of the cultural dimension particularly influence liability. One is the oft-noted phenomenon of success breeding unrealistic expectations that all medical interventions, particularly those relying on innovative technology, will be successful. As De Ville notes, "Inflated public expectations are common following periods of dramatic medical advancement."[35] These expectations not only lead more patients to litigation, but they also encourage juries to award ever higher damages when the technology is perceived to have failed.

A second aspect is the pressure that cultural expectations put on manufacturers and physicians to use the latest technology without adequately assessing its value. We are in the midst of a technology-driven cycle in which early adapters push reluctant physicians to adopt new technology before diffusion is appropriate. The cycle is reinforced by professional competition: "Having the latest technology offers substantial professional status to a physician group."[36] The examples of electronic fetal monitors and high-dose chemotherapy with autologous bone marrow transplant (HDC-ABMT) for metastatic breast cancer patients show the dangers of premature technology diffusion. EFMs led to litigation over the failure to use the technology or

[34] De Ville 1998.
[35] Ibid., 202.
[36] Chernew et al. 2004.

properly interpret the results; the latter led to litigation over the need to provide insurance coverage.

The third aspect is overconfidence in the scientific basis of technological innovation, which reinforces the lack of assessment by not putting pressure on the system to justify new technologies. As part of a project looking at the history of HDC-ABMT, one interview respondent noted that "[t]he greatest failure of the last half of the 20th century has been the uncritical acceptance of medical innovation as *a priori* effective."[37] All of this no doubt leads to remarkable medical advances, but at a high cost.

The Demand for Technology

From the industrial revolution to modern computing and telecommunications, the advance of technology has been a major determinant of our social and economic well-being. Health care delivery is so manifestly a product of technology that it seems entirely appropriate to speak of a technological imperative in health care – "the lure of always pushing toward the greatest feat of technological performance or complexity which is currently available."[38] The seemingly inexhaustible demand for high-technology medical interventions has shaped the course of American health care for at least a century. In many communities, civic pride, patient demand, and competition for physician allegiance has created a technology arms race, in which each hospital rushes to acquire the latest equipment. Of course, this leads to considerable duplication and waste.

Americans have high expectations for medicine and show great resistance to cost or other constraints on medical technology. These expectations will continue to rise dramatically as new technologies are introduced, many claiming unique effectiveness. Recent advances in genomics and proteomics, to give two prominent examples, fuel such hopes today.[39]

Individual patient preferences bolster the general cultural propensity to favor technological solutions to medical problems. Patients often want the newest drug or the most cutting-edge surgical procedure when they fall ill or are injured, even if they lack enthusiasm for the increased premiums and out-of-pocket payments needed to pay for such innovations.[40] Patients' tendency to equate more tests and procedures with higher quality care puts pressure on physicians to adopt the latest technology.[41] All of this, combined with the cultural factors noted previously, helps explain why direct-to-consumer advertising has become so important for the pharmaceutical industry.

[37] Interview conducted by Richard A. Rettig, June 30, 2003.
[38] Pacey 1983, 79.
[39] Heffler et al. 2001.
[40] Ibid.; see also Danzon and Pauly 2001.
[41] Barger-Lux and Heaney 1986.

A key aspect of technology diffusion is physicians' eagerness about using the latest innovations. Studies trying to understand physician adoption of new technologies repeatedly mention the reimbursement environment, concerns about quality of care, and patient preferences as the predominant factors. Even when the overall clinical benefits are marginal and the incremental cost substantial, physicians will opt for new technology if there is a perceived advantage in patient comfort or safety.[42]

Physician specialization reinforces physician demand for increasingly sophisticated technology. Technology makes subspecialization possible, such as microsurgery on different parts of the body. An IOM report on medical errors indicates that specialization accounts for a great many of the errors studied: "The contribution of complexity and technology to such error rates is highlighted by the highly technical surgical specialties of vascular surgery, cardiac surgery, and neurosurgery."[43]

The Supply of Technology

Demand alone, needless to say, does not explain technology trends. The pressure to develop and market innovative technologies is equally relentless. Rapid technological advances transform the way health care is organized, delivered, and financed. Improved diagnostic, surgical, and anesthetic techniques are resulting in better outcomes and speedier recoveries, which enable more care to be provided in lower-acuity settings.[44] New medical technology is no longer the exclusive domain of academic medical centers but is disseminated to a broader set of hospitals and physician practices. Not only does this accelerate the pace of practice change, but it also perpetuates fragmentation in health care delivery.

Manufacturers, patient advocates, and political figures can also be fervent advocates for expanding the supply of new technologies. Product manufacturers have especially strong economic incentives to encourage technology adoption and diffusion. For example, the goal of direct-to-consumer advertising is to exploit cultural attitudes predisposed toward technology and encourage patients to pressure physicians to prescribe or use the latest innovations. All the while, manufacturers bombard physicians with free samples, seminars, and deals to encourage the technology arms race.

Americans' heightened interest in new medical discoveries and higher expectations for medicine are likely to translate into pressure on policy makers and health plans to spend more on new medical technologies, drugs, and medical research.[45] The National Institutes of Health (NIH), the National

---

[42] Jacobson and Rosenquist 1996.
[43] Institute of Medicine 2002, 30.
[44] Myers and Burchill 2002.
[45] Kim, Blendon, and Benson 2001.

Science Foundation (NSF), and other federal agencies spend billions of dollars annually on biomedical research. If past is prologue, the preference for ever more technology will trump rising costs at almost every turn, even in a slower economy. Most Americans believe that the frontier of medical miracles is endless, and thus far they have been willing to pay for progress.[46]

Many industries contribute to and benefit from the commercialization and production of medical technology. Even in its infancy, the biotechnology industry is important because of its promise for developing useful medical technologies (especially drugs for diseases that currently have no available treatment), its powerful hold on the public's imagination, and the ethical and moral challenges it raises.

Collectively, the biotech products currently on the market or in late-stage clinical trials for use in cardiovascular or neurological care represent incremental and additive rather than breakthrough or disruptive technologies. But over the next decade, developments such as gene testing, gene therapy, and stem cell therapy will affect the health care industry in far more profound ways. For example, gene chips will render diagnosis faster and more accurate, and more health care may move to ambulatory settings as biotech therapies (typically drugs and injections) replace surgeries and other invasive procedures.[47]

Health care institutions, especially hospitals, have always played an important role in driving technology. A facility's use of the latest technology attracts both physicians and patients, giving rise to a medical arms race.[48] With the advent of managed care in the late 1980s, many policy makers anticipated that managed care organizations (MCOs) would restrict the use of technology to control cost, either through utilization review or medical necessity determinations. In the mid-1990s, managed care was reasonably successful in controlling the increase in health care utilization, but there is no indication that the industry's cost-containment policies altered either the use or culture of technology.

Policy Controls

One explanation for rapid diffusion is that available policy levers to restrain its use have not worked. For example, technology assessment has been inadequate, and insurers have not insisted on cost-effectiveness as a criterion for reimbursement. In principle, coverage and reimbursement policies could act as a barrier to the premature dissemination of technology. In reality, these control mechanisms have rarely been effective. One reason is that courts do not always support coverage denials, even those based on scientific evidence.

[46] Iglehart 2001.
[47] Myers and Ehrlich 2001.
[48] Luft et al. 1986.

Another reason is that legislatures (both state and federal) often succumb to pressure from patient advocacy groups, making new therapies rapidly available through public programs and mandating coverage of controversial techniques by private insurers. Even managed care has had only limited ability to "stand in the way of the innovation 'steamroller.'"[49] In response to patient demand and physician resistance, MCOs have retreated from stringent coverage policies that were both unpopular and prone to litigation.

POLICY RECOMMENDATIONS

Advances in technology will continue to influence legal doctrine, public policy, and health care delivery. Because of our collective cultural belief in technology as the guarantor of continued medical progress, the supply and distribution of technology are inextricably linked to liability policy. Indeed, a more deliberate connection between technology policy and liability policy is desirable. Liability and innovation are not mutually exclusive concepts. Thoughtful reforms are needed to provide greater stability to the medical liability system while encouraging the broad and safe diffusion of new technologies. But there is no clear set of legal and policy changes that would clearly support innovation without undermining the tort system's compensation and deterrence functions. If that set existed, the changes would have been implemented long ago.

Conventional tort reforms may well be appropriate policy responses. Incremental reforms, such as caps on damages, might reduce malpractice insurance premiums but will not appreciably reduce health care costs.[50] Systemic reforms, including a no-fault system based on enterprise liability, focus appropriately on patient safety and a rigorous technology assessment program. Any enduring solution to recurrent medical malpractice crises, however, must include sustained engagement with the underlying culture of technology.

The Culture of Technology

Regardless of how society resolves the dilemma, we need a much more forthright debate about the cultural aspects of technology. It may well be that we have simply become too devoted as a society to the technological imperative to have a meaningful dialogue about it right now. Indeed, there are powerful arguments in its favor. There is no question that technology permits physicians to attack conditions that would otherwise cause suffering and even death. Technology has clearly contributed to higher quality of life and perhaps longevity as well.

49 Chernew et al. 2004.
50 Congressional Budget Office 2004.

Still, I am afraid that without some way to limit public expectations, physicians will never escape the quandary technology imposes. Too much pressure exists throughout the medical system to adopt innovative technologies without adequate time to determine their appropriateness and effectiveness. The current fragmentation in the health care system, with profitable specialty facilities advertising the latest in technological advances, forces competitors to match the technology. So a technology spiral is evident: Patients want the latest technology (especially when they do not absorb the full costs), physicians are forced to provide it at the risk of losing patients, and manufacturers happily oblige with new products.

Even if some type of legal change is necessary, it is not sufficient – witness the past two decades of attempted reforms. What is needed is a concomitant set of cultural changes. In this sense, changes in culture are an important manifestation of what the community wants from the tort system, though certainly this is not explicitly recognized in measurable or tangible ways. As long as people value technological advances, there is no reason to expect the public either to support major limitations on technology's availability or to abjure the option of litigation when technology fails.

At best, cultural change will not occur quickly and will be difficult to achieve. To begin the process of altering the culture of technology, physicians can play a significant role by communicating the limits of technological solutions to medical problems. This needs to occur at both the individual patient encounter and at the professional society level. During the physician–patient encounter, patients need to understand that technology is not a magical solution. Yet, as the experience with ABMT suggests, patients whose only hope lies with the latest technology, even if unproven, have little incentive to listen to the caveats. At the professional society level, medical leaders should begin a dialogue with the public based on more realistic expectations about medical care's limits. The dialogue should focus on reducing the public's reliance on technology and properly depicting technology as only one aspect of medical care.

Second, a respected institution, such as the IOM, should convene a committee to address the culture of technology in medicine and ways of informing the public about technology's limits. Recent IOM reports on patient safety and quality of care have been widely publicized and have led to broad public discussions and incipient policy changes.

Third, the media have a responsibility for explaining the limits of the latest technological breakthrough. This is not to suggest that the media should avoid covering technological advances. But it is far easier to report on innovation than to dampen expectations. The tendency to herald new innovations is understandable; the challenge is to offer more realistic information about the limitations.

As a caveat to this discussion, there are serious issues of ethics and values that must be examined when placing limits on technology. When dealing with "last hope" interventions, it is understandable that individuals will want not just aggressive therapy but the latest technology available (even if it has not been shown to be effective in clinical trials). In the dialogue about limits to technology, we must at least keep individual patient needs and legitimate demands in mind. Perhaps the best we can do is to manage conflicting values and develop institutions to mediate the competing interests.[51]

Legal and Policy Changes

Numerous legal and policy changes have been proposed during each of the recent malpractice crises, and some have been implemented. Most have had little impact. Although most of the policy attention has been focused on tort reform, such as no-fault or enterprise liability systems, caps on noneconomic damages, and so on, I remain skeptical that even full implementation of these systems will make a fundamental difference. For example, enterprise liability – shifting liability responsibility to the relevant health care institution – will not solve the problem of technology-induced liability; it only determines who pays for the error.

To be sure, aspects of both enterprise and no-fault liability systems are very attractive. In particular, no-fault liability for cases involving indeterminate causation, such as neurologically impaired babies, would respond to legitimate physician complaints that they are being held responsible for adverse outcomes from the natural course of disease rather than any manifest physician error. Likewise, enterprise liability offers the potential for imposing more stringent quality of care and accountability measures. Pay for performance would also provide incentives for reducing clinical error.

Technology Assessment. Developing a more robust technology assessment (TA) process has been a key policy objective for many years. TA can restrain the cultural imperative by relieving pressure on physicians to use the latest technology. First, TA can form the basis for determining whether an insurer will cover (i.e., reimburse) a particular technology. Second, TA can inform individual clinical decisions based on medical necessity determinations. Using rigorous TA will place insurers in a better position to avoid litigation for denying procedures that have not been shown to be effective.

Certainly, TA is not a panacea and is less useful for determining whether and how to provide the technology to a particular patient. Clear answers for controversial technologies may not be available even with rigorous clinical trials. Many high-profile issues, such as the efficacy of PSA tests for men and mammography screens for women younger than age 50, are likely to be in an ambiguous category, dominated by conflicting opinions and political

---

[51] Rettig et al. 2005.

considerations. And rapidly evolving technology places a heavy burden on any systematic approach to evaluating medical interventions.

Even so, federal legislation to address the problem would be appropriate. At a minimum, Congress should either reconstitute the federal Office of Technology Assessment (OTA) or otherwise enhance the government's technology assessment portfolio (i.e., at the Agency for Health Care Research and Quality). In addition, Congress should reinforce Medicare's process for assessing technology before reimbursing for it and also encourage HHS to include cost-effectiveness analyses in the TA process. Congress should also consider whether procedures should be subject to the same kinds of premarketing approval as FDA regulations require for drugs and medical devices.

CONCLUSION

The various malpractice crises have generated an enormous amount of commentary, empirical study, and reform proposals, but we seem no closer to a solution than we were thirty years ago. Time after time, the technological imperative has trumped science, legal doctrine, and even the inevitability of disease and death. Unrealistic public expectations, often encouraged by physicians and exacerbated by industry marketing practices, make it all but impossible for policy makers to slow the adoption and use of new technologies. As long as society demands technological innovation, physicians' liability exposure is an inevitable consequence.

In the end, the malpractice cycle will continue, in part because Americans refuse to accept resource limits. The insatiable demand for more and better technology has brought incredible innovation and exciting medical advances. So far, the public is effectively saying that the cost, including the liability cost, is worth it.

THREE

MALPRACTICE REFORMS THAT SOLVE THE RIGHT PROBLEMS

8

Promoting Fairness in the Medical Malpractice System

Maxwell J. Mehlman

Fairness is a key social value. It is important instrumentally: People are more likely to support public policies that seem fair. It is also valued intrinsically. Fairness is a basic element of justice, embodying reciprocity, proportionality, and impartiality that are central to conceptions of just behavior. Sensitivity to fairness may even be instinctive. As philosopher D. D. Raphael pointed out, "Fairness is a notion that is acquired at an early stage of life: young children are quick to complain that action which discriminates in favor of one child or one group is unfair, and they do not confine this complaint to thought of their own advantage but are ready to speak up for the claim of others."[1]

Medical malpractice is one public realm that has undergone a great deal of reassessment lately. Much of the rhetoric concerns fairness. In urging major malpractice reform, President Bush stated, for example: "If you get hurt, you ought to be able to go to your court, the courthouse and be treated; you ought to get fair compensation for your economic damages. But we cannot have unlimited, non-economic damages and punitive damages drive health care away from the people. So I strongly support, and I urge Congress to have reasonable federal limits on non-economic damages – $250,000 is reasonable." But the president does not tell us why he thinks $250,000 is fair compensation. The head of the Association of Trial Lawyers of America takes the opposite view of limits on compensation – so-called caps: "Are malpractice damage caps unfair to patients? Yes. Caps on damages set absolute, arbitrary limits on what medical malpractice victims may receive for injuries suffered. They make no distinction between a patient whose facelift left unexpected scarring and one left brain dead because of an overdose of anesthesia."[2] Boyle tells us that the reason caps are unfair is that they are absolute and arbitrary, but that is not necessarily true. The amount of caps can be based on average jury awards for comparable losses, for example,

---

[1] Raphael 2001, 240.
[2] White House 2002, 6; Boyle 2002, 1.

and not be "arbitrary," and caps need not be absolute; they can be adjusted, for example, for the degree of injury, as in Ohio.[3] A report of the Institute of Medicine (IOM) calling for reform gives as one of its goals to "make compensation for injury more predictable, timely, and fair."[4] But are predictability and timeliness not elements of fairness? Would it not feel unfair to malpractice victims[5] if it was difficult to tell in advance whether they had a good malpractice case or not, or if they had to wait an unreasonable amount of time to receive due compensation? If so, then apart from timeliness and predictability, what does the IOM mean by "fair"?

Despite the importance of fairness, it has not been closely examined by scholars or jurists.[6] As a result, it has not been possible to determine if the current malpractice system, or specific reforms that have been enacted or proposed, are fair. This chapter attempts to understand and explain fairness, and then apply this understanding to the existing system and to potential changes.

WHAT FAIRNESS MEANS

The meaning of fairness depends on the context; a "fair" game of tennis is not the same thing as a "fair" malpractice system, although the two have some elements of fairness in common. Moreover, there are two kinds of fairness:

[3] In Ohio, noneconomic ("pain and suffering") damages are capped at $250,000 or three times economic loss to a maximum of $350,000 per plaintiff or $500,000 per occurrence, except in the case of permanent and substantial physical deformity, loss of limb or bodily function, or permanent physical functional injury limiting activities of daily living, when award limits increase up to $500,000 per plaintiff and $1 million per occurrence. O.R.C. §2323.43 (2004).

[4] Institute of Medicine 2002, 85.

[5] The term "victim" is used throughout this chapter rather than "plaintiff" or "patient." "Patients" would not be accurate because by far most patients are not victims of medical malpractice. The term "victim" is meant to imply also that the individual has suffered losses as a consequence of a genuine compensable event. The term includes the victim's family, who seek compensation for their own losses (including their loss of a loved one) as well as for any losses that the patient is unable to collect by virtue of being deceased.

[6] Bovbjerg and Sloan referred to "fairness to individual participants, that is, to claimants and implicated medical providers" (Bovbjerg and Sloan 1998) and noted the importance of two kinds of "equity": "horizontal" and "vertical" (Bovbjerg, Sloan, and Blumstein 1989). In an article entitled "Linking Tort Reform to Fairness and Moral Values," Kathleen Payne asserted that "caps on non-economic damages in medical malpractice actions are most unfair because ... [r]isks in medical malpractice actions are non-reciprocal; the risk of harm runs only to the patient and not to the health care provider." She also pointed out that caps especially affect the seriously injured, the young, and the poor, and states that "[l]imiting or eliminating non-economic damages in less serious cases and uncapping recoveries for devastating injury is a more just approach to tort reform" (Payne 1995). Yet, nowhere does she define what she means by fairness. As noted in the text, the IOM declares fairness to be one of its reform goals but also does not explain what the term means. In its major study of medical malpractice in 1987, the U.S. Department of Health and Human Services lists "Prompt Resolution and Fair Compensation" as one of eight policy objectives, but its only amplification of what constitutes "fair compensation" is that it should be "in amounts proportional to the injury" (U.S. Department of Health and Human Services 1987).

substantive and procedural. Substantive fairness concerns the nature of the governing rules and the outcomes they produce; procedural fairness concerns how the rules are applied.

For the public policy realm in which medical malpractice is located, a substantively fair system is one that pursues appropriate goals. As is the case with any tort-based scheme, the goals of the malpractice system ostensibly are to compensate victims, deter malpractice, and punish wrongdoers. Taken separately, each of these goals is appropriate in theory. But the devil, as they say, is in the details. There is arguably a consensus that compensation should be awarded only for truly compensable events (i.e., that the system does not fail to compensate when it should or award compensation when it should not), that the amount of compensation should be proportional to the injury (i.e., that victims with minor injuries should not receive greater compensation that victims with more serious injuries), that it should be adequate (i.e., the right amount given the seriousness of the injury and the degree of fault), and that clinicians should know in advance what behavior will and will not result in liability. But there is considerable disagreement about what should count as a compensable event (e.g., whether victims should be compensated whenever they were injured as the result of medical care, or only when the injury was avoidable, or only when the care was rendered negligently); whether victims should be compensated for non-economic as well as economic losses; whether they should recover for losses for which they are reimbursed by insurers or employers (so-called collateral sources); and how to decide what amount of compensation the victim should receive.

Controversy also exists over whether those who actually cause the victim's injury should bear the costs or whether the costs should be passed on to others, such as to other patients, in the form of higher fees, and no one is quite sure how far up the causal chain liability should reach (e.g., should the hospitals where surgeons operate be accountable for surgical errors, or just the surgeons?). There is also disagreement over whether the malpractice system is the proper mechanism for punishing wrongdoers, as opposed to, say, state medical boards, and even a dispute over whether malpractice should be regarded as a "wrong" at all, rather than, as devotees of continuous quality improvement might deem it, an opportunity to improve the quality of medical care. Finally, although everyone agrees that compensating victims and deterring practitioners from making medical errors are laudable objectives, they disagree over how to balance the goal of error-free medicine against cost and accessibility. What if it would cost so much to compensate all victims fairly that there would not be enough money left to pay for health care? One way to improve quality might be to limit those who are allowed to perform tricky procedures to clinicians with exceptional training, experience, and skill, but this would come at the price of availability and affordability. Is it better that one patient gets first-rate health care and three others in equal need get none, or that all four get mediocre treatment?

Fortunately, procedural fairness is much more straightforward. Thanks to the evolution of the concept of due process, there is little disagreement about most of what it entails: rules acceptable to all parties that produce substantively fair outcomes, meaningful opportunity for the parties to be heard, adequate representation, proceedings on the record and not based on *ex parte* communications, decisions reasoned and in writing, neutral and impartial decision makers, participants treated with dignity and respect, and accountable decision makers. But there is uncertainty about whether the decision-making process should be adversarial, inquisitorial, or cooperative. Some free-market advocates urge that the parties should be able to design a custom process that does not include some of the foregoing practices, but their views have largely been discredited by the realization that the resulting procedures would tend to favor the stronger party, namely clinicians, who might use their superior bargaining power to impose biased rules on patients.[7] Finally, it is unclear how much procedural fairness is worth, both in terms of outright value and the opportunity costs to the victims of having their recoveries delayed while procedural fairness is provided.

HOW FAIR IS THE ORIGINAL MALPRACTICE SYSTEM?

Despite our limited understanding of fairness, we can run the original malpractice system past what we do know and see how it measures up. By "original" system, I mean the common law as it stood in the absence of state legislative reforms that have been adopted beginning in 1975.

The original system seeks to achieve the appropriate goals of a malpractice system, but it does so in such a such a way that the punishment goal conflicts with the deterrence goal. The system is highly punitive; it not only makes wrongdoers pay damages but also makes the process of being found liable for malpractice an extremely negative punishing experience. The experience is so unpleasant that it gives clinicians no incentive to admit their mistakes. The resulting culture of silence makes it very difficult for the system to carry out its deterrence function because it produces little information about why mistakes occur or how they can be prevented in the future. Moreover, the punishment is imposed wastefully; defendants who are subsequently exonerated as well as those ultimately held liable are forced to endure most of the negative aspects of the process. Finally, the system carries out its deterrence function too inaccurately. On the one hand, clinicians complain of "defensive medicine" or overdeterrence – being forced to be more careful than they should be, such as doing unnecessary tests, just to ward off the risk of being sued. On the other hand, the IOM estimates that approximately 98,000 persons nationwide die every year from medical

---

[7] *Tunkl v. Board of Regents of the University of California*, 1963.

negligence, suggesting that the system does not do enough to prevent medical mistakes.[8]

The original system falls short in other respects as well. Most of those likely to find themselves defendants feel that the rules are unfair. The system often appears invalid, having trouble distinguishing between what is and is not medical negligence, a key prerequisite for identifying compensable events. Subsequent case reviews have found a large number of false positives and negatives – instances in which victims receive damages when it appears that they should not have and vice versa. A particular target of criticism is the primary device for identifying negligence: expert medical testimony evaluated by a lay judge and jury. The system also has difficulty estimating the degree of fault, which affects the amount of damages to which the victim may be entitled, and calculating the proper amount of damages. Here, the ire of reformers is directed at awards for pain and suffering, which appear to them to be purely arbitrary. In short, the system appears to many to be inconsistent, disproportionate, and inscrutable.

Questions are also raised about how well judges and attorneys do their jobs in giving the parties an adequate opportunity to be heard. Many claims, namely those that are settled, are resolved without a record being made and without the decision makers being held accountable for perceived unfairness. There are reports that the steep rise in malpractice insurance premiums is forcing clinicians to abandon risky specialties like obstetrics and to stop serving insufficiently remunerative patient populations, like those in rural areas. Some of these reports are false or exaggerated,[9] but they are such powerful trumps in the fight to modify the malpractice system and clinician antipathy toward the system is so great that the stories nonetheless are widely repeated. Finally, there is little doubt that the system does not always treat the participants with dignity and respect.

This evaluation raises two immediate questions: How did the system get so unfair, and why has this unfairness by and large been allowed to persist? The answers to both questions are complex and reflect the interplay of many factors. The system became more unfair in part because patient expectations rose, yet medicine was unable to deliver on all of its promises; this provoked patients disappointed with their outcomes to blame clinicians rather than to accept the limitations of medical science. Attorneys are partly responsible: The ranks of plaintiffs' attorneys include numbers of aggressive lawyers. Managed care and clinician avarice play a role, making the delivery of care an assembly-line process, for example, and speeding the line up to the point that clinicians made stupid mistakes, like removing the wrong arm or leg. At the same time, clinicians who make mistakes are too frightened to admit them. The hassle of managed care enrages patients. Finally, the financial mechanism

[8] Institute of Medicine 2000.
[9] U.S. General Accounting Office 2003b.

for the malpractice system relies largely on inadequately regulated private insurers, who respond to market fluctuations by abruptly raising and lowering premiums. All of this combines to create an atmosphere of dissatisfaction and distrust, perfect conditions for unfairness.

Why has this been allowed to persist? In part because of the power of the trial lawyers' lobby, but also because, despite all of its unfairness, the system works well enough sufficiently often that, apart from the clinicians themselves, there is little popular support for change. It is noteworthy, for example, that no consumer group has promoted any of the reforms favored by organized medicine.

But reforms nevertheless were adopted, and others have been proposed but not yet implemented. How fair are they?

HOW FAIR ARE THE REFORMS?

Having identified some main prerequisites of a fair system and seen some of the major deficiencies in the original system, we can perform the same analysis on actual and proposed reforms to determine if they offend one or more criteria for substantial or procedural fairness. An additional element of fairness now enters into the equation, however. This time, we are evaluating a dynamic phenomenon: moving from the original to a modified system. As a result, fairness depends not only on how differently the new system functions substantively and procedurally from the old, but also how the differences in function affect the welfare of the participants – in economic terms, the marginal cost or benefit to them of the shift. Moreover, although there are a number of participants in the malpractice system whose welfare might be affected by reforms, a fairness approach dictates that we focus at least at first, if not primarily, on those who are made worst off by medical malpractice, namely, patients who are most seriously injured. If they do well by the change, that is a good indication that the reform is fair. On the other hand, if they become worse off still, or worse off than they would be under the original system, then we must ask: to whose benefit? And if the answer is "to the benefit of those better off," then, according to the widely accepted Rawlsian theory of justice, the reform is per se unfair. If the worse off do better or at least maintain the status quo, then the reform is presumptively fair, although we would still want to know what goals it intended to achieve and how well it achieved them.

On this basis, a number of reforms are transparently unfair.[10] One of these is caps on damages, as they have a disproportionately negative effect on those victims who stand to gain the most compensation under the original system,

---

[10] A full discussion of the fairness and unfairness of malpractice reforms can be found in Mehlman, "Resolving the Medical Malpractice Crisis: Fairness Considerations" (2003), http://medliabilitypa.org/research/mehlman0603.

who tend to be those who are the most seriously injured by malpractice. A recently published study by the Rand Institute for Civil Justice found just this result from examining California's experience with the caps it enacted in 1975, part of a medical malpractice reform program called "MICRA" (Medical Injury Compensation Reform Act of 1975). To quote its findings:

Plaintiffs with the severest injuries (brain damage, paralysis, or a variety of catastrophic losses) had their non-economic damage awards capped far more often than all plaintiffs with injury claims and had median reductions of more than one million dollars (compared with a median reduction of $286,000 for all injury cases).

- Plaintiffs who lost the highest percentage of their total awards were often those with injuries that led to relatively modest economic damage awards (about $100,000 or less) but that caused a great loss to their quality of life (as suggested by juries' million-dollar-plus awards for pain, suffering, anguish, distress, and the like). These plaintiffs sometimes received final judgments that were cut by two-thirds or more from the jury's original decision.
- Death cases are capped more frequently than injury cases (58 percent versus 41 percent), and when they are capped, death cases have much higher percentage reductions in total awards than injury cases, with a median drop of 49 percent versus a 28 percent drop for injury cases.[11]

Some data show that, in exchange, caps lower malpractice insurance premiums, but there is contradictory data as well.[12] Even if premiums were lowered, redounding to the benefit of all patients, including the worst off, this would still be unfair because it would come disproportionately at the expense of those claimants who would now have to accept the smaller, capped amounts of compensation – that is, claimants who were worst off. In other words, if we ask who benefits, the answer may be "everybody," but if we ask whose ox is gored, the answer is those who are most seriously injured. This thus violates two of the cardinal rules of distributive justice: first, the Kantian principle that people must not be treated as means to increase the welfare of others but as ends in themselves, and, as Rawls observed about transferring welfare, it must not be taken from the worst off and given to the better off.[13]

A number of reforms designed to make it harder for deserving claimants to recover at all raise similar objections. One of these is abolishing joint and several liability. This doctrine holds that once a plaintiff who sues multiple defendants establishes wrongdoing and resulting injury, the burden shifts to the defendants to avoid liability even though the plaintiff cannot pinpoint exactly who did what during the episode of care. An illustration of this

---

[11] Pace, Golinelli, and Zakaras 2004, 47.
[12] Compare U.S. Congress, Office of Technology Assessment 1993 and Weiss Ratings, Inc. 2003.
[13] Kant 1785; Rawls 1971.

doctrine occurs in the 1944 case *Ybarra v. Spangard*.[14] The plaintiff underwent surgery for appendicitis and woke up with an injured shoulder. The plaintiff had been unconscious at the time the alleged negligence took place, so he could not prove which of the many individuals in the operating room or involved in transferring him to the ward had caused his harm. Because proving who committed negligence is normally a prerequisite for recovery, the plaintiff would not have received compensation except for the intervention of the doctrine of joint and several liability. Faced with the choice of favoring innocent victims or wrongdoers, the doctrine operates fairly to shift the cost of uncertainty to the latter. Abolishing it, as a number of states have, makes it harder for deserving victims to recover, which is unfair.

Joint and several liability has another effect as well: It maximizes the chances that deserving plaintiffs will actually receive compensation. It does this by enabling a victorious plaintiff to apportion responsibility for the payment of the damages awarded by the court among the defendants, including, if the plaintiff chooses, collecting everything from a single individual – presumably the one with the deepest pockets. In theory, defendants who were made to pay a disproportionately large amount of the damage award can rectify this by seeking payments – called "contribution" – from the other defendants who were found liable. But in practice, the other defendants may be so poor that the payer is left holding all or most of the bag. This may seem unfair, but it is certainly fairer than the alternative – leaving the innocent victim holding the bag. This is another reason why abolishing joint and several liability is unfair.

The same arguments apply to another reform – abolishing *res ipsa loquitor*. This is Latin for "the thing speaks for itself," and, like joint and several liability, is a device that shifts the loss to the wrongdoer when the only other option is to assign it to the victim. *Res ipsa* does this by waiving the normal requirement that the plaintiff prove exactly what went wrong in order to establish that the defendant was negligent. Again, the *Ybarra* case furnishes a good illustration. Because the victim was unconscious, he could not tell what exactly went wrong. Did the surgeon accidentally nick something he should not have? Did the anesthesiologist rest an elbow on the patient's shoulder for too long? Was the patient dropped on his shoulder before waking up in bed? Under the original approach, the plaintiff would have lost his case, but the doctrine of *res ipsa* says that if the plaintiff can prove that whatever happened would not have occurred but for the fact that one or more defendants were negligent, the plaintiff can recover even though, through no fault of his own, he could not pinpoint the exact cause of his injury.

Surprisingly, perhaps, there is only one reform that is unequivocally fair – that is, that seeks to accomplish an appropriate objective and does not transfer wealth from more to less deserving individuals. This is the suggestion to

---

[14] 154 P.2d 687 (Cal. 1944).

more carefully regulate malpractice insurers so that they do not have to increase premiums so suddenly or steeply. Greater moderation in the fluctuation of premiums would be accomplished, for example, by giving state insurance regulators the power to set not only the maximum but also the minimum premium rate; this would prevent insurers from reducing rates in order to attract more business or enter a new market when the economy was flush, only to have to increase rates precipitously when the general economy went sour but the frequency and severity[15] of claims continued to rise.

The rest of the reforms, by far the largest number, may or may not be fair depending on how they are implemented. Deterring frivolous lawsuits is laudable in theory, for example, but could be accomplished unfairly by defining "frivolous" too loosely, so that deserving victims were denied redress, or by punishing victims who do not know any better, rather than the lawyers who do, for bringing frivolous cases.

Similarly, it is not necessarily unfair to impose limits on attorneys' contingent fees as attorneys generally possess greater bargaining power than malpractice victims. But the attorneys' reward must be large enough that victims continue to be able to obtain adequate representation.

Expert screening panels and medical courts would only be fair if the decision makers were unbiased. This would not be true of reform proposals that call for the decision makers to comprise at least a majority of clinicians, such as most proposals for "medical courts." The composition of the panel would be fairer if it was more neutrally composed, having, for example, a majority of nonclinicians and an equal number of experts chosen by each party and by a consensus of those experts.

Practice guidelines also run the risk of bias as invariably they are established by clinicians. This raises the suspicion that their primary purpose is to prevent malpractice recoveries rather than to prevent medical errors or reduce costs. A notorious example is legislation enacted by the Maine legislature in 1991, which permits certain practice guidelines created by Maine specialty societies to serve as conclusive evidence of the appropriate standard of care, but only when introduced by malpractice defendants.[16] In other words, although physicians can introduce the fact that they complied with the guidelines as conclusive evidence that they were *not* negligent, plaintiffs in Maine cannot introduce the fact that the physician deviated from the guidelines to raise an inference that the physician was negligent. Even if the guidelines were redistributively neutral – that is, not likely or calculated to transfer an unreasonable amount of wealth from patients to clinicians – they can be misused. At one point, for example, the organization that represents rheumatologists promulgated a practice guideline aimed at arthritis patients; it advised them to obtain treatment from a board-certified rheumatologist.

---

[15] Frequency refers to the rate at which malpractice claims are asserted; severity to the size of awards.

[16] Maine 1994.

The organization that represents primary care physicians responded with its own guideline saying that primary care physicians were perfectly competent to treat arthritis. Although the rheumatologists were legitimately concerned about whether nonrheumatologists could render quality care for arthritis, their guideline looked too much like a turf grab, which was how it was interpreted by the generalists.

One reform that looks at first blush like it would be fairer to victims than the original system is no-fault, which aims at reducing the costs of dispute resolution by eliminating the requirement that the plaintiff prove negligence. No-fault seems fairer because it would permit many more patients who were injured as the result of medical care to receive compensation. By itself, this would be laudable. The problem comes in figuring out how to pay for it, because the unavoidable result of a greater number of successful claimants would either be to spend a lot more money to fund the system or, as is typically proposed, to reduce significantly the amounts of recovery. The latter will be familiar – it is none other than caps – and unfair for the reasons already given. The only way to avoid this would be to save so much in dispute resolution costs to furnish the financial resources needed to pay claims fairly. According to Bovbjerg and colleagues, the two existing examples of capped, no-fault medical malpractice systems – the Virginia and Florida birth-related injury programs – pay victims the same amount of compensation that the victims would have received under the original system, largely due to much lower attorneys' fees (Bovbjerg et al. 1997). But it is doubtful that these results could be achieved if no-fault were extended beyond the narrow range of events compensable under these programs, given the expected increase in the costs of resolving claims.

Another reform that has mixed potential in terms of fairness is the use of nontraditional techniques such as arbitration and mediation to resolve malpractice disputes. These might appear fair in theory. The decision makers usually are chosen fairly (using the each-side-picks-one-and-then-these-two-agree-on-the-third technique recommended earlier for screening panels and medical courts). Although the amount of compensation may be somewhat less than what the victim would receive under the original system, the victim gets the money more quickly. The problem is that victims who pursue claims using alternative dispute resolution may not have been given the choice of whether or not to employ the original system instead. There have been too many instances in which patients have been forced either to agree to use alternate methods of resolving malpractice disputes or forego needed health care altogether. (See, for example, *Wheeler v. St. Joseph Hospital.*[17])

Another reform the fairness of which depends on the details is periodic payment, whereby instead of receiving a lump sum, the victim receives a

[17] 63 Cal.App.3d 345 (1976).

series of payments over time. This is supposed to save the defendant money at the same time that it fully compensates the victim, but it is hard to see how this would happen unless the victim received less overall compensation than under the original system, as presumably the value of the lump sum payment under the original approach is discounted to present value. One version of periodic payment reform would have the amount of each payment subject to judicial or administrative review so that it could be adjusted upward or downward depending on changes in the victim's circumstances. This might save money if the health problems the victim suffered as a result of the malpractice unexpectedly improved, but there is no reason to believe that that would happen more frequently than the opposite: that the victim's health problems unexpectedly worsened. Moreover, procedural costs would rise substantially because of the costs of the periodic reexaminations.

One of the hardest reforms to understand in terms of fairness is abolishing the collateral source rule. This reform seeks to reduce transactions costs by shifting the burden of paying a certain set of claims from defendants and their malpractice insurers to the plaintiff's health insurers, in effect creating a first-party rather than a third-party insurance scheme. The rule under the original tort system is that the fact that the plaintiff is entitled to recover losses from collateral sources, such as health or disability insurance or gratuitous salary payments by an employer, is not to be taken into account in calculating the damages owed by the defendant. One rationale is that the defendant should not be relieved of having to pay for injury because the plaintiff had the foresight to arrange for first-party insurance or because the plaintiff's employer generously paid wages even when the plaintiff was laid up. Another theory is that the plaintiff actually paid for these first-party benefits, in the form of premiums for the insurance and higher productivity or lower wages in return for the employer's largesse, so that being compensated by the defendant was not really a windfall. In the case of insurance, moreover, the money that the plaintiff recovered from the defendant usually had to be repaid to the insurers under a subrogation agreement. Nevertheless, many states have abolished the so-called collateral source rule, allowing juries and judges to consider these collateral payments in calculating the amount of damages. The intent of this reform may not necessarily be to reduce the victim's compensation, but care must be taken that this does not happen inadvertently. To prevent this, some jurisdictions that have repealed the collateral source rule require defendants to pay a proportion of the plaintiffs' premiums for their first-party health and disability insurance, on the theory that otherwise the defendants would be getting a windfall at the plaintiffs' expense.[18]

By this point it becomes apparent how reformers have been able to persuade the public to adopt measures that, although not inherently unfair, are

---

[18] See, e.g., N.Y. CPLR §4545(c).

applied unfairly. The reformers speak in generalities. Instead of specifying what counts as a frivolous lawsuit and how frivolous lawsuits will be detected, they merely call for "stopping frivolous lawsuits." They ask for limits on attorneys' fees without considering how this will affect victims' ability to obtain adequate representation. They applaud no-fault, without disclosing the likely reduction in awards for the worst off. And so on. The only way to prevent unfairness is for the public and its legislators to be on their guard. Sadly, too often legislators are swayed by pressure from interest groups determined to reform the malpractice system one way or the other.

But there is hope. One of the conclusions of this research is that scheduled damages may be fair. This may seem unanticipated as they are typically proposed along with caps, which as demonstrated earlier, are unfair. But scheduling damages does not necessarily mean capping them; it only means assigning monetary values, or ranges of values, to specific compensable events. A damage schedule could include an unlimited upper amount of awards for the most egregious cases.[19] In this fashion, the use of schedules as part of a worker-compensation-like system, one that attempted to reduce transaction costs by employing an administrative rather than judicial process, could be made fairer.

THE FAIRNESS OF THE REFORM PROCESS ITSELF

Reforming a system not only changes the rules of the system but also the status quo. Determining if a change in the status quo is substantively fair is quite different than assessing the fairness of a given system because it requires that the prereform welfare of those affected be compared with their welfare postreform. But there is also a different question about procedural fairness: Not only are we interested in whether the resulting procedures are fair, but we are also interested in whether the procedures used to adopt the reforms are fair. And this procedural fairness differs markedly from the type of procedural fairness discussed earlier, which applies to the rules of a static rather than a dynamic system.

What makes the process of adopting a reform fair? The obvious answer is that afterward everyone agrees that it produces fair outcomes. But that amounts to trial and error. To achieve trial and success, we need to be able to predict what adoption methods are most likely to yield these desirable results.

It clearly is not the legislative process currently in use. This process is dominated by interest groups that do not necessarily represent the interests of the most important stakeholders: victims and patients. Some groups that claim to, like the American Medical Association (AMA) and the Association of Trial Lawyers of America (ATLA), have their own institutional axes to

---

[19] As proposed in the 2004 Rand report (Pace, Golinelli, and Zakaras 2004, 50).

grind. Public interest groups like Public Citizen, Families USA, and Consumers Union probably come closest to truly representing victims, but none of them are governed exclusively by victims; there simply is no "American Patients" or "American Medical Victims" organization to rival the AMA and ATLA. The result is a distortion of democracy best described by Larry Yackel in 1989:

The representative process tends to degenerate into a bewildering political marketplace dominated by factions about which Madison warned the nation in her crib. Effective political accountability is owed primarily to the diligent, the organized, the historically dominant, and the well-heeled.[20]

Nor is the current judicial process a fair way of making reforms, at least not in most states, where state judges are elected by a largely oblivious electorate.

In an ideal world, the process of reform would be what Rawls described in *A Theory of Justice* (1971). It would be conducted behind a veil of ignorance in which no one knew his or her place in the society that the rules would govern. This is obviously impossible in the real world because legislators, judges, and lobbyists all know where they stand. The closest we can come is to imagine what people behind the veil of ignorance would do. But in order to do this fairly, we need to know what all relevant constituencies think is fair. That is why it is so striking that in the current debate over medical malpractice reform, almost no one is asking the primary stakeholders: victims and patients. One of the few exceptions is a survey released in October 2002 by the Project on Medical Liability in Pennsylvania of The Pew Charitable Trusts.[21]

Another critical step in making a reform process fair is to be on the lookout in case a reform is a mistake. Medical malpractice reform is a social experiment; we are trying things out to see how well they work. Therefore, the experiment needs to be designed so that it has the best chance of yielding useful information. There need to be appropriate, clearly identified measures of success and failure, including measuring the impact of the reforms not only on malpractice premiums but also on the welfare of the victims and patients. Valid techniques for evaluation must be employed. Moreover, experimentation must not be a subterfuge for more permanent reform. The experiments should be constructed with automatic termination dates far enough in the future that the reforms can have their intended effect but not be so lengthy that the experiment becomes an excuse to impose long-term policy. Finally, and most important, because we are talking about studies on human subjects, if any significant risk of harm is imposed on the experimental subjects, the subjects must be allowed to refuse to participate in the experiment and to opt out at any time.

[20] Yackle 1989, 274.
[21] Pew Project on Medical Liability in Pennsylvania 2002.

TESTING THE THEORY: THE IOM PROPOSAL

The initial objective of this chapter was to create a set of criteria that would enable us to tell whether a medical malpractice system was fair. In order to help determine if the criteria were valid, the previous section analyzed a number of malpractice reforms. One final validity test will be to consider the fairness of a proposal put forth by a panel of the IOM.[22] This proposal is bold: It would schedule damages and employ administrative rather than judicial procedures. It is not so much a set of new ideas as a synthesis of several other approaches, but that is one of its strengths: it concentrates on how to stitch existing ideas together into a functional system rather than reinventing the wheel. More important, it explicitly declares fairness to be one of its goals.

It is an "early-offer" approach. Pioneeered by Jeffrey O'Connell, the idea is to reward victims for agreeing to settle a case before trial. Rather than give them a premium, O'Connell proposed to permit them to escape punishment: The plaintiff would forfeit a portion of the recovery if a jury later awarded less than the amount offered earlier by the defendant. This was unfair, because the scheme was one-sided; defendants suffered no reciprocal consequences if they refused to settle for an amount proposed by the plaintiff and a jury later awarded the plaintiff a larger sum.[23]

The IOM's version of early offer is quite different. The hospital – initially, the idea would only be applied through hospitals; office-based clinician liability would come later – would make an early offer to a patient who had suffered a compensable event. Once the offer was made, the victim would have no choice but to accept it. By itself, this would seem even more unfair to victims than O'Connell's approach, but it would be accompanied by a number of quid pro quos. The hospital would have a strong incentive to make early offers because otherwise it would be defaulted to the tort system, where it would be subjected to all of the vagaries and injustices about which hospitals complain. Consequently, it would notify patients voluntarily when they had suffered a compensable event. This would make it far more likely that victims would receive compensation; one study estimates that only about one out of fifteen actual cases of negligence occurring in hospitals results in a paid claim (Localio et al. 1991). This stems from a combination of the victims' inability to realize as a result of their lack of medical sophistication that they have suffered malpractice, and the culture of silence that the medical community has adopted in self-defense.

Another important potential benefit to victims would be far lower transactions costs. Currently, a substantial percentage of the jury's award goes to pay attorneys' fees. Presumably the jury is aware of this and adjusts

---

[22] Institute of Medicine 2002.
[23] See, e.g., J. O'Connell 1982.

the amount of award accordingly, but there is no evidence that this always happens. Moreover, to the extent that patients pay for increased malpractice insurance premiums through higher charges driven up by transaction costs, the lowering of premiums that would be expected to result from the IOM approach would reduce health care costs to all patients, including victims.

The flaw in this position is that nothing says that hospitals or attendant physicians who would pay lower malpractice insurance premiums would pass the savings on to patients, rather than pocket them themselves. To fix this, a birth-related injury compensation system proposed in the New York legislature in 1993 mandated that health care providers pass the savings on.[24] This proposal faltered after it was pointed out to the providers that, added to the annual fee that they would have to pay to buy into the new system, having to disgorge the savings would end up costing them more money than they paid under the original system.[25] A better solution might be to assess providers a larger participation fee but let them keep premium savings; this also has the virtue of rewarding any providers whose premiums decline because they make fewer errors. The IOM report made no specific mention of this problem, but it would certainly become an issue if the IOM proposal were tried.

Victims would get one other thing under the IOM proposal: an apology. Currently clinicians and hospital personnel are discouraged from apologizing to patients for their mistakes by the fact that this would make victims aware of claims they did not know they had, which could result in more malpractice cases. In addition, in all but approximately fifteen states (Arizona, California, Colorado, Georgia, Illinois, Maryland, Massachusetts, Missouri, Ohio, Oklahoma, Texas, Virginia, Washington, West Virginia, and Wyoming), an apology is admissible as an admission of liability in a court case. The IOM proposal would eliminate both these impediments: In order to bring a claim within the early-apology program and eliminate the risk that victims will discover the error and pursue a claim in the original system, the provider has to admit the mistake. And because the dispute would never come before the courts, it would not matter if courts continued to regard apologies as admissions by the defendants.

Apologies reduce the likelihood that a victim will assert a claim.[26] One reason may be that most apologies are accompanied by an offer of compensation – at least, an offer to pay the necessary medical expenses and not charge for the botched episode of care. This may be enough to satisfy the victim. Another reason may be that an apology reduces anger, decreasing

[24] New York Assembly Bill 8097, 1993.
[25] Mehlman 1994.
[26] Witman et al. 1996.

the motivation to assert a claim. Furthermore, an apology arguably makes the victim feel better, in effect reducing the extent of the victim's suffering.

Another key feature of the IOM proposal is that it is expected to reduce clinician error, perhaps significantly. It would do this by collecting and analyzing all the errors that providers admitted to victims. This would create a vast database that researchers could mine to discover why errors happen and how they could be prevented. This information would be passed on to the providers so that that they could adjust their practices.

As the IOM recognizes, however, its proposal must fulfill several further conditions in order to be fair. One is that the amount of compensation must be fair to victims. The IOM proposal would create a list of compensable events ahead of time, accompanied by a capped schedule of damages, as under the workers' compensation system. Fairness requires that the list of events be sufficiently robust so that compensation is proportional to injury. Several malpractice scholars have created scheduling systems, which have yet to be tested.[27] An interesting question is whether they should factor in the degree of provider blameworthiness, on the basis that the victim, say, of a surgical procedure that was botched by an assistant because the real surgeon wanted to play golf deserves more than the victim of a more innocent mistake.

Fairness also requires that the amount of compensation be adequate. The IOM proposal merely speaks in terms of scheduling the amounts and capping damages "at reasonable levels." The notion of a cap on damages is highly suspect; as noted earlier, caps could be unfair if they left victims worse off than they would be in their absence. Clearly, the $250,000 limit adopted by California's MICRA program in 1975 is inadequate today, which is one reason why the damage cap supported by organized medicine and the Bush Administration – $250,000 – is nothing short of shameful. A better stab at fairness would create a compensation schedule based on average jury awards in states without caps.

Another requirement of fairness results from the fact that the IOM proposal would be an experiment on human subjects. Therefore, the subjects must give their informed consent to participate. This means not only explaining to them what would happen if they agreed to participate in the experiment (e.g., they would lose the right to sue in return for more assured but perhaps smaller payments), but also enabling them to still obtain access to needed health care if they declined. These conditions are not fulfilled, for example, by the Florida and Virginia birth-related injury compensation systems described earlier. These systems allow for choice, but principally on the part of health care providers, who can decide whether or not to participate. The enabling statutes require that patients be given the opportunity to choose a

---

[27] See, e.g., Bovbjerg, Sloan, and Blumstein 1989.

nonparticipating provider by being notified in advance whether the provider is participating or not, but adequate notice may not always be provided, and because virtually all eligible providers have chosen to participate, the patient is unlikely to have any practical alternative.[28]

CONCLUSION: IS FAIRNESS ATTAINABLE?

This is a deliberately ambiguous question. In the first place, it asks whether we have the vision and political will to create a fair malpractice system, which would require warring constituencies to stop fighting and start collaborating. Despite the acrimony of the current debate, it may be hoped that the time for such cooperation has not come and gone.

Another aspect of the question concerns the affordability of fairness. Fairness is not without its cost. Fair procedures like due process, for example, are likely to take longer to implement than star chambers. If the IOM proposal resulted in many more victims being adequately compensated than is presently the case, the money required to pay awards could swamp malpractice insurers, and in turn patients and third-party payers who ultimately bear the expense. This could cause marginal practitioners to abandon practice, decreasing patient access to needed health care.

The chief adversary of procedural fairness might seem to be efficiency. Consistency and proportionality, for example, require consideration of the specific facts of a case, but case-by-case determinations demand more time and effort. The relationship between fairness and efficiency is a balancing act.

It is beyond the scope of this chapter to determine how this balance should be achieved. What is important is to acknowledge the vital relevance of fairness, identify the mechanisms that allow it to be gained and lost, and recognize the need to place a value on fairness so that it can be weighed against other values, like efficiency. Only in this way will we be inclined to adopt reforms that are as fair as possible and be able to gauge whether objectives achieved at the expense of fairness are worth the price.

A final consideration is the fairness of focusing exclusively on medical malpractice rather than on the tort system more generally. On the one hand, it seems unfair to limit the recoveries of one class of victims – those injured by malpractice – while permitting other tort claimants to recover more fully. Why should someone whose leg is mistakenly amputated, for example, get less than someone who loses a leg when they are run over by a negligent, insured motorist? On the other hand, health, and access to the services that sustain it, are such critical needs that they can be said to merit special attention. In paying this attention, however, we must strive to make the malpractice system as fair as it can be.

---

[28] Bovbjerg and Sloan 1998.

9

Caps and the Construction of Damages in Medical Malpractice Cases

Catherine M. Sharkey

The perceived need for tort reform, and particularly medical malpractice damages caps, is among the most salient political issues of our time. President Bush himself has advocated a uniform federal cap on noneconomic damages in medical malpractice cases as the centerpiece of a tort reform agenda aimed at reining in a "judicial system [that] is out of control." The 2004 election, moreover, spawned a resurgence of state legislative reform efforts.[1]

This chapter explores the politically divisive issue of damages caps and takes a closer look at the assumptions that inhere in the arguments for them and against them. I conclude that the most prevalent form of damages caps, those that cap only the noneconomic portion of medical malpractice awards, are hardly the surefire limits on damages awards that their advocates hope – and their detractors fear – them to be.

BACKGROUND: DISAGGREGATING MEDICAL MALPRACTICE DAMAGES

Medical malpractice damages, like tort awards in general, are comprised of compensatory damages and punitive damages. Compensatory medical malpractice damages, in turn, consist of economic damages, often referred to as "special" or "pecuniary" damages, and noneconomic damages, also known as "general" or "nonpecuniary" damages.

Economic damages aim to compensate an injured party for past and future monetary damages, such as lost wages, medical expenses (past and future), rehabilitation expenses, and other financial costs. For the most part, these

For an elaboration, and empirical exploration, of the ideas presented in this chapter, see Sharkey 2005.
[1] Bush 2005; Dao 2005.

damages attract little attention. They tend to be viewed as predictable and easily quantifiable, even by juries.[2]

In stark contrast are noneconomic compensatory damages, which aim to rectify a plaintiff's more "subjective" harms: pain and suffering, physical impairment, disfigurement, marital losses, anguish, and inconvenience.[3] Legal academics, legislators, and politicians alike have devoted much attention to these damages in medical malpractice cases, which are generally perceived as inherently imprecise and unpredictable. The theoretical critique of noneconomic damages awards stems from their relationship to the primary objectives of tort law: deterrence and compensation (or insurance). Certain economists argue that, in quasi-contractual tort realms such as products liability and medical malpractice, tort liability is not necessary to regulate care because customers know the quality (and inherent risks) of the goods and producers can create signals through prices.[4] Damages, then, serve mainly to insure against injuries. And, the critique continues, there is little justification for compensating noneconomic losses because people facing a risk of serious permanent injury or death will insure against economic losses but not noneconomic ones.[5] Even those economists who adhere to the view that tort liability plays an important deterrent role in the medical malpractice realm must concede that it is not "optimal" to compensate victims fully for noneconomic losses, because victims necessarily pay for this type of "insurance" up front, in the form of higher prices. Put differently, even when deterrence requires some compensation for nonpecuniary losses, a balance must be struck between the deterrence and insurance goals of tort law.[6]

Noneconomic damages face institutional and practical criticism as well. Critics in these camps focus upon the lack of objective criteria for valuing pain and suffering and other noneconomic losses.[7] They argue that, consequently, courts cannot appreciably guide juries as to how to measure such

---

[2] Bovbjerg et al. 1989, 910; Baldus et al. 1994, 1125–6. See also *Barlow v. N. Okaloosa Med. Ctr.*, 877 So. 2d 655, 658 (Fla. 2004) (finding that Florida medical malpractice reform provisions limiting noneconomic damages only "were enacted to address soaring noneconomic damage awards, rather than the more predictable economic damage awards"). Kelso and Kelso found, contrary to conventional wisdom about the predictable nature of economic damages, that there is actually greater variation in economic damages than in noneconomic damages (Kelso and Kelso 1999, 18). Interpreting their results, they concluded that "juries are not making erratic assessments of noneconomic losses in medical malpractice cases" (ibid., 19).

[3] Vidmar and Brown 2002, 9.

[4] G. Priest 1992, 252; Epstein 1984, 490–1, 506. But see Spence 1977, 563–71; Geistfeld 1995b, 786; Arlen and MacLeod 2003, 1979; Arlen and MacLeod 2005, 22–3.

[5] Schwartz 1988, 408; G. Priest 1992, 254. But see Arlen 2000, 705; Croley and Hanson 1995, 1791.

[6] Geistfeld 1995b, 800.

[7] Leebron 1989, 313; Sharkey 2003, 401–4.

damages, which, in turn, leads to erratic, often extremely inflated awards that bear no logical relationship to the injuries at issue.

Against this backdrop, it should come as no surprise that, to date, the thrust of tort reform efforts in the medical malpractice realm has been to rein in noneconomic compensatory damages. Thus, most proposed or already-enacted damages caps specifically target this component of medical malpractice awards and leave economic compensatory damages unfettered. This chapter explores the efficacy, and some unintended consequences, of this piecemeal approach to tort reform.

TARGET: PROBLEMS THAT DAMAGE-RELATED REFORMS AIM TO SOLVE

Advocates of damages caps contend that the tort system, dependent as it is on jury-determined awards, has systematically resulted in overcompensated plaintiffs and overdeterred defendants. In these advocates' view, juries' out-sized noneconomic damages awards have pernicious effects that reverberate far beyond the confines of the courtroom. These take the form of exorbitant malpractice insurance premiums and, in turn, the availability of adequate and affordable health care.

Insurance Industry

There is no dispute that this country has experienced staggering increases in medical malpractice insurance premiums and that those increases have been episodic. According to many observers, we are now in the midst of a "third wave" of a medical malpractice insurance crisis that began in the early 2000s, the first and second waves having transpired in the mid-1970s and the mid-1980s. According to the American Medical Association, twenty states are experiencing "full-blown medical liability crises," due to sharply increasing premiums.[8]

Many states enacted damages caps in response to alleged liability insurance crises. California was one of the first states to do so in response to the medical malpractice insurance crisis of the mid-1970s. Its response took the form of the Medical Injury Compensation Reform Act of 1975 (MICRA). That statute, which has never been modified since its enactment in 1975, imposes a $250,000 cap on medical malpractice noneconomic damages.[9] As reported in an August 2003 study by the General Accounting Office (GAO), "since the periods of increasing [insurance] premium rates during the mid-1970s and mid-1980s, all states have passed at least some laws designed to

---

[8] American Medical Association 2004.
[9] Cal. Civ. Code § 3333.2 (West 1997).

reduce medical malpractice premium rates."[10] Five states specifically profiled in the GAO study – Florida, Mississippi, Nevada, Pennsylvania, and West Virginia – enacted damages caps, of one form or another, specifically aimed at lowering medical malpractice premiums.[11]

Health Care Industry

A separate, but closely related, argument often articulated by proponents of damages caps is that the escalating premium rates for malpractice insurance, caused by runaway jury verdicts in malpractice cases, translate into a smaller supply of physicians, as the cost of doing business drives many out of the profession.[12] Highly visible examples are Florida, New Jersey, Mississippi, and West Virginia, where doctors have recently gone on strike to show their support for proposed noneconomic damages caps legislation.[13]

It has hardly been proven that rising malpractice insurance rates are threatening physician supply in any real way. The August 2003 GAO report determined that problems with physician supply, at least in the areas of emergency surgery and baby deliveries, were limited to rural locations and, furthermore, often attributable to factors other than malpractice pressures.[14]

Furthermore, malpractice premiums are not experience rated, meaning they are not based on past malpractice claims.[15] As a result, negligent and nonnegligent physicians pay similar premiums, and they will face the same incentives to restrict services or, at the extreme, to shut down. This raises the question whether the underlying problem is the level of damages themselves or, alternatively, some aspect of the insurance system that is preventing the appropriate experience rating to ensure that physicians pay premiums more appropriately gauged to their risk level.

Still another problem that damages caps purport to address is that form of overdeterrence in the medical profession known as "defensive medicine." Defensive medicine commonly refers to those situations in which physicians decline to provide necessary services or to even take on high-risk patients for fear of unmanageable malpractice liability (termed "negative" defensiveness or "avoidance behavior"), as well as to those situations in which physicians employ costly precautionary treatments despite the lack of medical necessity,

---

[10] U.S. General Accounting Office 2003b, 10–11.

[11] Ibid., 38, 44. Each of these states has some form of damages cap. Florida, Mississippi, and Nevada each cap both noneconomic compensatory damages in medical malpractice cases and punitive damages in general tort cases. West Virginia caps noneconomic compensatory medical malpractice damages, and Pennsylvania caps punitive damages in medical malpractice cases (Sharkey 2005, App. 1).

[12] Hellinger and Encinosa 2003b; Klick and Stratmann 2003.

[13] Sage 2003b, 21.

[14] U.S. General Accounting Office 2003b, 13.

[15] Geistfeld 2005b, 444; Sloan 1990, 128, 132.

also for fear of facing large medical malpractice awards (termed "positive" defensiveness or "assurance behavior").[16]

Certain empiricists, as well as the GAO in its August 2003 report, however, have determined that there is hardly a clear link between the threat of high malpractice awards and the incidence of defensive medicine and, furthermore, have explained that there is no clear way to estimate the societal cost of the practice of defensive medicine.[17]

In this chapter, I do not purport to determine whether large malpractice damages awards are in fact to blame for escalating premiums, threats to physician supply, or trends in defensive medicine. But what is key, at least for present purposes, is that there is an assumption shared by those who subscribe to this view and those who do not: that caps on the noneconomic components of medical malpractice awards – that is, those components generally understood to be most susceptible to overstatement – will indeed limit jury verdicts in malpractice cases and consequently lower insurers' costs and the premiums they impose on doctors. The remainder of this chapter challenges that assumption. But, first, it is necessary to explore the variety of state approaches to damages limitations in medical malpractice cases.

DAMAGES CAPS IN ACTION

Variations on a Theme: Damages Caps Around the Country

Proceeding on the assumption that damages caps will indeed lower total medical malpractice awards and, in turn, insurers' costs and premium rates, states have imposed various forms of damages caps. Although certain states impose caps on total compensatory damages awards, the large majority have enacted caps that specifically target noneconomic damages.

Since the 1970s, twenty-five states have imposed limits on compensatory damages in medical malpractice awards. An additional ten states have enacted more general limitations on compensatory damages awards applicable to all civil cases, including medical malpractice cases. Of these thirty-five states' caps, twenty-eight remain in effect today.[18]

The most common form of caps restricts noneconomic damages only. Sixteen states currently have laws originally enacted to cap noneconomic damages in medical malpractice cases. An additional six states – Colorado

---

[16] Bovbjerg and Raymond 2003, 11; Kessler and McClellan 1996, 354.

[17] Sloan and Bovbjerg 1989, 27–9; U.S. General Accounting Office 2003b, 26–30.

[18] Sharkey 2005, 412, App. 1. Since the publication of Sharkey 2005, the Wisconsin Supreme Court held that the $350,000 legislative cap on noneconomic damages in medical malpractice cases violated the equal protection guarantees of the Wisconsin Constitution. See *Ferdon ex rel Petrucelli v. Wis. Patients Compensation Fund*, 701 N.W.2d 440 (Wis. 2005). Thus, the number of compensatory damages caps presently in effect is 28 (as opposed to 29, reported in Sharkey 2005).

(which also has a noneconomic damages cap), Indiana, Louisiana, Nebraska, New Mexico, and Virginia – have imposed caps on *total* compensatory damages in medical malpractice cases. The capped limits in these states range from $500,000 to $1.75 million.[19] Every one of these six states that has imposed total compensatory damages caps has also created some form of Patient Compensation Fund, which further limits physicians' liability in medical malpractice cases but provides additional compensation to the plaintiff up to the amount of the cap.

The caps that apply across the board to noneconomic damages in all civil cases typify the caps imposed in the 1980s, whereas those enacted in the 1970s and 2000s tend to be those that apply only to medical malpractice cases.[20] Still, the caps imposed since the year 2000 are more sophisticated than their 1970s counterparts. They are more likely to include categories of exceptions to the caps and/or sliding damages scales, with higher ceilings for more serious injuries.[21]

Texas is an interesting case of its own. There, the state legislature proposed a constitutional amendment expressly to authorize damages caps. Proposition 12, which was passed by public referendum in 2003, allows the legislature to impose liability limits for all damages and losses, "however characterized, other than economic damages."[22]

Only a small number of states have addressed punitive damages limitations on medical malpractice awards, most likely because medical malpractice cases rarely result in punitive liability.[23] Various scholars have opined as to why punitive damages are so rare in this realm. For instance, Neil Vidmar, who has conducted interviews with jurors who have participated in medical malpractice trials, has found that most jurors believe that doctors, as a general matter, aim to do good work and should not be punished for human errors.[24] Jennifer Arlen and Bentley MacLeod suggested a related reason: that the errors at issue in malpractice cases are almost always accidental, caused by inadequate "expertise," such as inadequate investment in the capacity to diagnose or in systems designed to prevent error. By contrast, Kip Viscusi

---

[19] More specifically, the cap amounts are as follows: $500,000 (Louisiana); $600,000 (New Mexico); $1 million (Colorado); $1.25 million (Indiana); $1.5 million (Virginia); and $1.75 million (Nebraska) (see La. Rev. Stat. Ann. § 40:1299.42 (West 2001); N.M. Stat. Ann. §§ 41-5-6, 41-5-7 (Michie 1996 & Supp. 2003); Colo. Rev. Stat. § 13-64-302 (2003); Ind. Code § 34-18-14-3 (2003); Va. Code Ann. § 8.01-581.15 (Michie Supp. 2004); Neb. Rev. Stat. § 44-2825(1) (Supp. 2003)).

[20] Bovbjerg 1989, 543; Sharkey 2005, 413.

[21] Sharkey 2005, App. I, 498–500 ("Recent substantive tort reform legislation") (detailing cap legislation enacted since 2000 in Florida, Georgia, Mississippi, Nevada, Ohio, Oklahoma, Texas, and West Virginia).

[22] Tex. Const., art. III, §66.

[23] T. Cohen 2004.

[24] Vidmar 1995, 169–71; Pace, Golinelli, and Zakaras 2004, 59–60.

and Patricia Born suggested that the current low levels of punitive awards may be a direct result of the enactment of reforms in the mid-1980s.[25]

Report Card: Evaluating the Effectiveness of Caps

How effective have these measures been in achieving their goal, that is, the reduction of malpractice damages awards and, in turn, the maintenance of reasonable malpractice insurance premium levels?

Effects on Plaintiffs' Total Recovery. Over the past twenty years, several researchers have explored the relationship between damages caps and plaintiffs' total recovery in medical malpractice cases. For instance, Patricia Danzon conducted a study in the 1980s in which she employed data from the 1970s and 1980s to conclude that damages caps reduced the average value of paid medical malpractice claims by 23 percent.[26] Frank Sloan, Paula Mergenhagen, and Randall Bovbjerg studied malpractice cases from 1975 to 1978, and 1984. In their study, which was based on cross-sectional data that both pre- and postdated damages reforms of the 1970s, they, like Danzon, concluded that damages caps do reduce plaintiffs' total recovery. Unlike Danzon, they reported – without exploring further – significant differences between the effect of total compensatory damages caps and noneconomic damages caps, finding that the former reduced payments to plaintiffs by 38 percent and the latter reduced payments to plaintiffs by 31 percent.[27] In a more recent study, Kip Viscusi and Patricia Born analyzed insurance data from 1984–91 and found that incurred losses in states with noneconomic damages caps are 16 to 17 percent lower than such losses in noncap states.[28]

A few case studies are also worthy of note. Albert Yoon examined the effects of damages caps in Alabama relative to its neighboring states that had not imposed caps – Arkansas, Mississippi, and Tennessee. Although Alabama had enacted three different types of damages caps in 1987, they were stricken in 1991, 1993, and 1995 on the grounds of unconstitutionality. Yoon's study concluded that the average relative recovery by Alabama plaintiffs decreased by $23,000 (relative to the control states) after the Alabama legislature implemented damages caps, and plaintiffs' recoveries increased by approximately double that amount (relative to the control states) after the caps were deemed unconstitutional and no longer enforced. Yoon, however, does not differentiate the individual effects of the three different types of caps.[29]

---

[25] Arlen and MacLeod 2003, 1950; Viscusi and Born 2005, 24.
[26] Danzon 1986, 59, 76.
[27] Sloan et al. 1989, 678.
[28] Viscusi and Born 2005, 32.
[29] Yoon 2001, 205–7, 203.

The effects of California's MICRA cap on noneconomic damages was the subject of a 2004 study by RAND. Evaluating 257 medical malpractice trial verdicts issued by juries from 1995 to 1999, the study calculated posttrial reductions according to MICRA's rules to the 45 percent of verdicts that exceeded MICRA's $250,000 cap. The study concluded that, as a result of MICRA, final judgments were reduced by 30 percent from original jury verdicts; broken down further, MICRA translated into a 25 percent reduction in those cases involving injuries and a 51 percent reduction in those cases involving death.[30]

A study by William Gronfein and Eleanor Kinney concluded that damages caps actually *increase* plaintiffs' recovery. They explored the disposition of what they term "large" malpractice claims (those exceeding $100,000) in Indiana to that in Ohio and Michigan. For the time period covered by their study, 1977–88, Indiana (as mentioned previously) had a cap on total compensatory damages, economic and noneconomic, of $500,000. Michigan and Ohio had no caps at all, at least according to the authors.[31] They determined that although maximum claims in Michigan and Ohio did exceed the amount of Indiana's cap, the average malpractice claim in Indiana was 39.6 percent greater than the average Michigan claim and 33.5 percent higher than the average Ohio claim. They reached the surprising conclusion that Indiana's mean payment for large malpractice claims, in turn, was substantially higher than the mean payment for similar claims in Michigan or Ohio. They ascribed their results to the existence of Indiana's Patient Compensation Fund – neither Michigan nor Ohio had such a fund – and also speculated that the existence of the damages caps actually worked as a floor in malpractice trials, rather than as the ceiling on damages that it was meant to be.[32] (This anchoring effect is discussed in more detail later.)

While providing invaluable contributions to the field of damages research, each of these studies is limited in certain material respects. They have usually relied on data from previous decades and have yet to be updated. In the case of the Danzon, Yoon, and Gronfein and Kinney studies, no effort was made to distinguish the effects of caps aimed at noneconomic damages only versus caps aimed at overall medical malpractice damages. Even Sloan et al., whose analysis did report the different impact of each type of cap on plaintiffs' recovery, did not pursue the issue further or consider the resultant policy implications. And the RAND study did not employ regression analysis,

---

[30] Pace, Golinelli, and Zakaras 2004, 12, 20–1. An analysis of California verdicts, using multivariate regression technique, by David Studdert, Tony Yang, and Michelle Mello reported a similar 34% reduction in total plaintiff recoveries as a result of the imposition of the MICRA cap (Studdert, Yang, and Mello 2004, 54, 58).

[31] Although neither state had a cap on total compensatory damages, Michigan has capped noneconomic damages since 1986 (albeit with a host of exceptions), and Ohio capped noneconomic damages from 1975 to 1991 (Sharkey 2005, 428).

[32] Gronfein and Kinney 1991, 447, 458–9.

thereby failing to control adequately for various independent factors that may have affected the results, such as severity of the plaintiff's injury.

To help address this gap in the literature, I designed and performed an empirical study of my own, employing regression methodology, premised on current jury verdict data and aimed at assessing the distinct impact, if any, of noneconomic damages caps in the medical malpractice realm.

That test and accompanying research produced a surprising result that furnishes one possible explanation for why noneconomic damages caps are not particularly effective measures of limiting medical malpractice plaintiffs' total recovery: They may very well contribute to an *increase* in the economic component of a compensatory damages award in medical malpractice cases.

INCREASED ECONOMIC DAMAGES. There is no question that, even as more and more states have enacted caps on noneconomic damages, total compensatory damages have been on the rise in medical malpractice cases. According to a U.S. Department of Justice report, "[a]fter remaining stable in 1992 and 1996, the median amount awarded in [medical malpractice] jury trials to plaintiff winners increased from \$287,000 in 1996 to \$431,000 in 2001." Moreover, some research suggests that, in the context of medical malpractice damages, "the economic component . . . generally dominates over the noneconomic component."[33]

Researchers have developed various explanations for the increases in economic damages over time, which include increases in plaintiffs' average life and working-life expectancy, real wages, and medical costs. For one, humans live longer now than ever before. In 1970, the average life expectancy for males and females was 70.8 years. By 1980, this figure had increased to 73.7 years, and to 75.4 by 1990. The preliminary figure for 2001 sets average life expectancy at 77.2 years.[34] This total increase, of nearly seven years, could have a dramatic effect on economic damages awards. For instance, in determining the value of support that a decedent would have provided to his or her survivors, jurors are asked to consider, among other factors, the age, health, and working-life expectancy of the decedent at the time of death. At the same time, this increase in average life expectancy might be offset by a decrease in the average retirement age, which has dropped in recent years, at least for men.[35]

Another key component of economic damages is probable future earnings. As more and more women have entered the workforce, and as a wider sector of the population generally has begun to attain higher-level jobs, amounts awarded in connection with this factor have likely increased over time, in keeping with societal shifts.[36]

---

[33] T. Cohen 2004; Kelso and Kelso 1999, 18.

[34] See National Center for Health Statistics, U.S. Department of Health and Human Services, 143, tbl. 27 (2004) at http://www.cdc.gov/nchs/data/hus/hus04trend.pdf (last viewed Oct. 11, 2005).

[35] Gendell 2001, 12.

[36] Lawrence 2004, 43.

Still another explanation lies in rapidly increasing medical costs. A recent RAND study found that "[r]ising claimed medical costs appear to be one of the most important factors driving increases in jury verdicts." The study analyzes plaintiffs' verdicts from 1960 to 1999 in San Francisco County, California, and Cook County, Illinois, and finds that "claimed medical losses account for approximately 58% of the observed growth in tort awards from 1960–1999." Moreover, "[a]verage medical losses stayed flat until the late 1980s and early 1990s when they began to increase sharply."[37]

Rising medical costs may in turn be driven by great advances that have been made in medical technology over the past decades. As a result of these advances, malpractice victims' lives may be spared, when previously they would have died. Moreover, it is increasingly possible to keep even severely injured victims alive for many years after the injury-causing event from which their lawsuit arises. The medical costs associated with both increasing survival rates and improving quality of life are extremely high. Thus, Clark and Kari Kelso have determined that injuries to newborns or very young children produce the largest damages awards and have further found that, of these, economic damages are usually substantially larger than noneconomic damages. But, as the RAND study authors argued, increased medical costs do not, in and of themselves, provide a sufficient explanation for increased payments for medical losses.[38]

Researchers who have compared trends in economic damages to noneconomic damages in medical malpractice cases have made some surprising discoveries. One such study was performed by Kelso and Kelso in 1999. They reported that the mean economic damages award is greater than the mean noneconomic damages award, whereas the median for noneconomic damages is four times larger than for economic damages. They determined, in other words, that noneconomic damages are higher than economic damages in more cases, but the total amount awarded for economic damages across the board is larger than the total amount awarded for noneconomic damages.[39]

An apparent trend of increasing economic damages finds a modicum of statistical support in various analyses of insurance data. Relying on data collected by the Missouri Department of Insurance, Kenneth Thorpe reported that "[r]ising economic costs (future medical expenses, lost wages) appear to be rising slightly faster than overall indemnity payments (the sum of noneconomic and economic awards." Data collected by the Texas Department of Insurance on closed cases from 1988 to 2000 likewise has been used to demonstrate that economic damages have increased steadily over the period while noneconomic damages have, surprisingly, remained constant. In a press release in March of 2003, Public Citizen, analyzing the Texas data,

---

[37] Seabury et al. 2004, 3, 19, 14.
[38] Kelso and Kelso 1999, 22; Seabury et al. 2004, 15–16.
[39] Kelso and Kelso 1999, 18–19.

claimed: "By separating malpractice payouts into their components – economic damages (for lost income and medical care), noneconomic damages (for pain and suffering) and exemplary damages (punitive) – and charting the rise and fall of each, it is clear that the rising value of payouts has been caused by an increase in economic damages, not awards for pain and suffering."[40]

A rising trend of economic damages in medical malpractice cases is significant in ways that have not been fully recognized. Such a trend poses a challenge to the traditional view that it is the *noneconomic* component of medical malpractice damages that needs to be reined in – a view that has, more times than not, dictated the nature of damages caps enacted by state legislatures.[41]

THE CROSSOVER EFFECT. My own research provocatively suggests that the increases in economic damages may in fact be amplified by the enactment of noneconomic damages caps.

My research was inspired by medical malpractice cases, arising out of states with noneconomic damages caps, where very large jury verdicts were sustained after both posttrial motions and appellate review.[42] My sense was that juries were compensating for noneconomic damages caps by pouring more damages into the economic damages category. The large verdicts in the face of partial caps, in other words, were quite possibly the product of noneconomic damages "crossing over" into the economic damages category.

My research suggests that plaintiffs' attorneys, the experts they hire, juries, and courts all play a role in enabling this crossover effect. Plaintiffs' attorneys, confronted with caps on noneconomic damages (which are usually not disclosed to the jury), have learned new ways to pitch their clients' cases to the jury. Whenever possible, they will characterize clients' damages as economic damages in the hopes that juries will do the same, and that their verdicts will remain unchanged even in the face of noneconomic damages caps (generally imposed postverdict).

An early example of the crossover effect is found in wrongful death cases. Wrongful death claims are statutory, as opposed to common law, claims, and traditional wrongful death statutes protected only the pecuniary interests of dependent survivors. They allowed only for the recovery of economic damages and barred recovery for such losses as grief or mental anguish. This led to particularly harsh results when the decedent was a minor, retired

[40] Thorpe 2004, W4–23; Press Release, Consumers Union, March 17, 2003, at http://www.consumersunion.org/health/malprac303-2.htm (last viewed Oct. 11, 2005). According to Charles Silver, however, this is a "contestable story" (Silver 2004). Silver discovered that Public Citizen assigned the entire settlement payment to economic damages when insurers failed to provide breakdowns by category of damages, as they did a majority of the time. And when Silver reanalyzed the data (eliminating the undifferentiated cases), noneconomic damages emerged as more significant than economic (ibid.).

[41] See supra note 3 and accompanying text.

[42] Sharkey 2005, 429.

person, or otherwise "unproductive" family member, whose death did not readily translate into economic loss.[43]

To mitigate the effects of these restrictive wrongful death statutes, attorneys, jurors, and judges developed methods to "transform" the pain of a lost loved one into a dollar amount that reflected the value of services once provided by the deceased to the survivor-plaintiff. Thus, courts would exaggerate the pecuniary value of household and other services that the decedents had allegedly provided. This approach became known as the "services solution." A more sweeping solution developed later, by which courts assigned monetary value to intangible aspects of relationships. Lost companionship and society, love, and advice and guidance (often referred to, collectively, as "consortium") were deemed to have reimbursable, monetary value. Ultimately, several state legislatures rewrote their wrongful death statutes to allow plaintiffs expressly to recover for grief and mental anguish or, in those states where the statutes were ambiguous in this regard, courts construed them to allow for the recovery of grief and mental anguish. Thus, the crossover effect, in the realm of wrongful death cases, eventually triggered dramatic changes in the relevant statutes and in the manner in which courts interpreted them.[44]

Returning to the realm of general medical malpractice cases, there is evidence that courts are at least cognizant, if not supportive, of the crossover effect. This is apparent in cases discussing whether or not damages caps are affirmative defenses, susceptible of waiver by a defendant who fails to invoke them. In *Ingraham v. United States*,[45] the Fifth Circuit held that Texas's noneconomic damages cap was an affirmative defense and the defendant, having failed to invoke it at the time of trial, could not benefit from the cap via its posttrial imposition on the award that had already been determined by the jury. In so holding, the court explained that plaintiffs would be prejudiced by such an after-the-fact imposition of the cap and, as proof, pointed to the plaintiffs' own comment that "[h]ad [we] known the statute [cap] would be applied, [we] would have made greater efforts to prove medical damages which were not subject to the statutory limit."[46]

The Seventh Circuit similarly recognized the prevalence of the crossover effect, and in a similar context. Commenting on the potentially prejudicial effect on a plaintiff that a posttrial imposition of a noneconomic damages cap would have, Judge Richard Posner, in *Carter v. United States*,[47] wrote:

There might be harm in a case such as this if for example a plaintiff had some leeway in classifying damages as economic rather than noneconomic, or if knowledge that

---

[43] Witt 2000, 742; Zelizer 1985.
[44] Dobbs 1993, § 8.3(5), 440–2; cf. Leebron 1989, 305–6.
[45] 808 F.2d 1075 (5th Cir. 1987).
[46] Ibid., 1079.
[47] 333 F.3d 791, 796 (7th Cir. 2003).

noneconomic damages were unavailable would have induced her to devote less effort to proving up such damages and more to proving her economic damages.[48]

One court has used the crossover effect as grounds to prohibit the disclosure of the MICRA noneconomic damages cap to the jury. In *Green v. Franklin*,[49] the court explained that "an instruction based on the terms of the statute would only serve to increase the possibility that a jury may simply label damages that otherwise would have been denominated noneconomic as economic losses."[50] An interesting counterexample lies in *Guzman v. St. Francis Hospital*,[51] in which the Wisconsin Court of Appeals *advocated* disclosure of the noneconomic damages cap in certain situations, so as to counteract evidence that *defendants* "would seek to have the jury load up on noneconomic damages with the hope that this would bleed money from its award of economic damages."[52]

Expert testimony, which is heavily relied on in medical malpractice cases to establish past and future lost earnings and medical costs – that is, the classic components of economic damages – is a key tool in the implementation of the crossover effect. Experts can be used not only to speak about the value of these economic damages but also to assign dollar values to such concepts as loss of services or loss of consortium. By turning aspects of damages traditionally thought of as noneconomic into a quantifiable category of damages, they may, over time, enable these noneconomic losses to be transformed into economic damages.[53]

Plaintiffs' lawyers, in turn, can maximize the potential benefits of the crossover effect for their clients by retaining experts to testify about the monetary value of an ever-increasing category of so-called economic damages. In other words, the more creative they can be in terms of sweeping into the definition of economic damages categories of loss traditionally deemed noneconomic, the more plaintiffs' attorneys stand to gain. A smaller component of their clients' awards will be capped, and they will, as a consequence, reap higher awards in the form of their contingency fees.

Hedonic damages are a good example. These controversial damages, which aim to compensate a victim for "loss of enjoyment of life," are, more and more, the subject of expert testimony and the subject of separate jury instructions.[54] As one commentator, Dr. Thomas Ireland, has noted, a "new industry of expert witnesses has arisen ready to testify to the pecuniary

[48] Ibid.
[49] 235 Cal. Rptr. 312 (Cal. Ct. App. 1987) (unpublished opinion).
[50] Ibid., 322–3.
[51] 623 N.W.2d 776 (Wis. Ct. App. 2000).
[52] Ibid., 787.
[53] Sharkey 2005, 438–41.
[54] V. Schwartz and Silverman 2004, 1041–6.

value of hedonic or whole life values on behalf of plaintiffs."[55] The more persuasively experts and the plaintiffs' attorneys who retain them can argue that hedonic damages can be valued at an amount certain, a precise "value of life" or of activities foregone, the greater the chances that these damages – traditionally deemed part and parcel of pain and suffering damages (at least in those jurisdictions where they are not altogether dismissed as a noncognizable category of damages) – may be "transformed" into economic damages.

My empirical research is consistent with the theory of the crossover effect. I performed multivariate linear regression analyses on roughly 550 "plaintiff winner" medical malpractice jury verdicts collected at three points in time (1992, 1996, and 2001) from state courts of general jurisdiction from 46 of the 75 most populous counties in the United States as part of a project of the National Center for State Courts. Analyzing these data, I found that caps on noneconomic damages – when controlling for the independent effects of severity of plaintiff's injury and for a variety of litigant characteristics, state law, and county demographic variables – had no statistically significant effect on the size of overall compensatory damages verdicts or judgments.[56]

Effects on Insurance Premiums. From a public policy perspective, the causal relationship of interest is not that between caps and jury verdicts (or settlements) per se, but between the effect of caps and insurance premiums. Several empirical studies have specifically explored the relationship between insurance premiums and noneconomic damages caps. These studies, viewed as a group, reach qualified results as to whether caps translate into lower premium rates. Although studies by such empirical scholars as W. Kip Viscusi, Patricia Born, and Frank Sloan find that caps do decrease malpractice premiums, their studies, for the most part, rely on data from the 1970s and 1980s.[57] While encouraging, these studies are hardly conclusive proof that caps are fulfilling their intended objective.

The GAO performed a study in August 2003, which also seemed to show that states with caps on medical malpractice damages tend to have lower insurance premiums for doctors.[58] The study further found that the presence of caps appears to slow the growth rate of premium levels. From 2001 to 2002, states with caps experienced an average percentage growth in premium

---

[55] Ireland et al. 1992, 49.

[56] Sharkey 2005, 446–7, 450, 469, 472–80. Of course, it is critical to interpret empirical results cautiously. For a discussion of the methodological limitations of my study as well as alternative explanations for my results, see ibid., 464–8, 483–92.

[57] See Sloan 1985, 637; Viscusi and Born 1995, 474; Viscusi and Born 2005, 23; Zuckerman et al. 1990, 167. More recent data were analyzed in two unpublished reports: see Danzon et al. 2003; Thorpe 2004.

[58] U.S. General Accounting Office 2003b, 32.

rates of only slightly below 10 percent, as compared to a premium rate growth of 29 percent in states without caps.[59]

Despite these findings, however, the GAO report specifically cautioned its readers not to draw the conclusion that the presence of caps necessarily means lower insurance premiums. In so doing, it noted that there are a host of potential intervening factors, as opposed to a direct causal link, that would have yielded the results described in the report. Among these are unrelated tort reforms in the states with caps, or laws in those states that directly regulate premium rates.[60]

Indeed, the view that insurers have had no choice but to raise malpractice premium rates in order to offset large noneconomic medical malpractice awards is a vigorously contested one. Alternative explanations abound. Many blame the insurance companies themselves, asserting that their poor business decisions over the years have, because of the vagaries of the stock market, devalued their investments, leaving them no choice but to pass the costs of these bad decisions onto their physician-insureds.[61] Alternatively, as Kip Viscusi and Patricia Born have cautioned, "Premium effects are often difficult to predict because they capture a variety of influences other than simply the riskiness of the state's legal arenas."[62]

One salient example of the tenuous link between caps and insurance premiums has recently come to light. Medical Protective Company, one of the nation's largest medical malpractice insurance companies, caused quite a stir when it told regulators that noneconomic damages caps, recently enacted in Texas, would lower payouts by a mere 1 percent. This disclosure was made in a filing to the Texas Department of Insurance, in which the company sought authorization to raise its premium rates by 19 percent.[63] Moreover, among the reasons posited by the insurance company disputing a direct link between caps on noneconomic damages and lower rates was that "[w]ith big dollars at stake, plaintiff attorneys will find ways to shift costs from non-economic to economic damages"[64] – in other words, the threat of a "crossover effect."

Problems That Caps Inadvertently Exacerbate

Increased economic damages are not the only potential byproduct of noneconomic damages caps. There are at least two other unintended results of damages caps: anchoring and screening by plaintiffs' attorneys.

---

[59] Ibid., 31.
[60] Ibid., 34, 37.
[61] Bovbjerg and Raymond 2003, 24.
[62] Viscusi and Born 2005, 38.
[63] Hallinan and Zimmerman 2004, A6.
[64] Memorandum from Melissa Cokar, regulatory specialist, Medical Protective Company, to Jose O. Montemayor, insurance commissioner, Texas Department of Insurance 2 (Oct. 30, 2003a) at http://www.aisrc.com/caps.pdf (last viewed Oct. 11, 2005).

Anchoring. Anchoring is "the judgmental process of selecting an initial value, or 'anchor,' as a starting point from which to arrive at an award by a process of adjustment."[65] This process, which scholars recognize takes place in most cases in which litigants are permitted to suggest damages amounts to the jury,[66] means that jurors, if apprised of the applicable caps, are likely to view the cap amount as a floor rather than as a ceiling in assessing plaintiffs' damages and, in so doing, severely undercut the caps' very purpose.

In a study designed to examine the effects of various forms of "jury guidance" on pain and suffering awards in personal injury cases, Michael Saks and collaborators included a "cap condition" in their experiments whereby jurors were informed of a $250,000 cap on total damages. Mock jurors were exposed to three different scenarios, one involving a plaintiff who had experienced low injury, one who had experienced medium injury, and one who had experienced high injury.[67] Surprisingly, these scholars found that disclosure of the caps to the mock jurors *increased* the size of the awards in the low-injury and medium-injury scenarios. They ascribed their findings to the anchoring effects of disclosure of the caps.[68] Although most states prohibit disclosure of caps to jurors, some academics have noted that this does not mean that jurors are unaware of those caps. They may know about them from newspaper reports or previous experiences as jurors or litigants, or conversations with others, leaving the threat of anchoring intact.[69]

Attorneys in Massachusetts seem to take the anchoring effect as a given. There, unlike in most states, disclosure of medical malpractice caps to the jury is permitted.[70] Massachusetts caps medical malpractice noneconomic damages at $500,000 but makes an exception for cases involving a substantial or permanent loss of function, substantial disfigurement, or other "special circumstances."[71] However, a defendant must specifically request the judge to instruct the jury about the caps or else waive entitlement to the caps altogether.

Despite the high stakes of nondisclosure, studies show that most Massachusetts defense attorneys deliberately decide not to request disclosure to the jury of the damages cap, for fear of anchoring. This practice was commented on by the Massachusetts federal district court in *Primus v. Galgano:*[72]

[T]he failure of defendants . . . to request a charge on the cap is consistent with the practice in the defense bar to avoid any mention of the cap because that would give the plaintiff's attorney an opportunity to argue a figure, $500,000, which otherwise

---

[65] Sharkey 2003, 408.
[66] Sunstein et al. 2002, 62–76.
[67] Saks et al. 1997, 246–9.
[68] Ibid., 253–4. See also Gronfein and Kinney 1991, 458–9 (discussing anchoring effect).
[69] Greene et al. 2001, 224; Babcock and Pogarsky 1999, 352.
[70] Mass. Gen. Laws Ann. ch. 231, § 60H (West 2000).
[71] Ibid.
[72] 187 F. Supp. 2d 1 (D. Mass. 2002), *aff'd*, 329 F.3d 236 (1st Cir. 2003).

would not be permissible under Massachusetts practice and procedure with regard to permissible jury argument on general damages.[73]

However, at least one study has questioned whether disclosure of the caps will lead necessarily to anchoring or, instead, will have the desired effect of prompting the jury to "self-limit" its award. In its study of MICRA and its effects, RAND concluded that the results of disclosure of MICRA's caps to the jury are unclear.[74]

Screening by Plaintiffs' Attorneys. Noneconomic damages caps may very well be affecting, and limiting, the kinds of cases that are going to trial. More specifically, plaintiffs' attorneys may be turning down potential clients who have incurred few or little economic damages and whose cases, therefore, offer few avenues to evade, or at least mitigate, the effects of caps on noneconomic damages caps on total potential recovery (and, in turn, on the attorneys' contingency fees).

For instance, imagine two potential clients who seek to retain the same personal injury lawyer. The first is a young lawyer disabled by medical malpractice, the other a middle-aged housewife who has incurred malpractice-related injuries of equal severity. The young lawyer is a far more attractive client from the personal injury lawyer's perspective, as his case offers the potential for large foregone future earnings, that is, economic damages. The housewife, in contrast, has no lost market earnings, at least in a technical sense, and her case will require some creative lawyering (that is, longer hours that will erode the value of the contingency fee) if her noneconomic damages are to be transformed into uncapped economic damages. In a state where there are no caps, the personal injury lawyer is likely eager to take on both clients (assuming large enough noneconomic damages). But in a state that has imposed noneconomic damages caps on medical malpractice awards, he will think twice before taking on the housewife's case and, if he has room for only one more client at the time, may turn down her case altogether in favor of the young lawyer's.

LOOKING AHEAD: NEW DIRECTIONS FOR REFORMS

This chapter suggests the complexity of damages caps. Contrary to conventional wisdom, caps vary significantly, as may their efficacy as a result.

If true, the crossover effect might point in two polar opposite directions. On the one hand, acknowledgment of crossover could mean that caps on *total* compensatory damages might be more effective than caps on noneconomic damages only in limiting plaintiffs' total recoveries and preventing

[73] Ibid., 2–3.
[74] Pace, Golinelli, and Zakaras 2004, 13, 66, 67.

unmanageable escalation in insurance premium rates. This does not mean, however, that the appropriate tort reform solution is the implementation of total compensatory damages caps across the board. Such caps may not withstand constitutional challenge. Indeed, many courts that have ruled on the constitutionality of noneconomic damages caps have upheld their constitutionality precisely because they were *not* caps on total compensatory damages. Thus, in *Fein v. Permanente Med. Group*,[75] the California Supreme Court, in upholding MICRA, emphasized that, in enacting it, the Legislature had "placed no limits whatsoever on a plaintiff's right to recover for all of the economic, pecuniary damages – such as medical expenses or lost earnings – resulting from the injury."[76] The court specifically distinguished MICRA from caps on total compensatory damages, which had recently been deemed unconstitutional by other state courts.

Constitutionality is only one potential barrier to total compensatory damages caps. Fairness concerns are another. And here is where the opposite route presents itself. Many oppose such caps on the ground that they "seem intuitively unfair to plaintiffs with large claims; they impose a limit on compensation which bears no relation to the damages the plaintiff actually sustained."[77] Others have pointed out that noneconomic damages caps may disproportionately affect certain disadvantaged sectors of the population, such as minorities, women, and the young, who do not work or else receive lower wages.[78]

Furthermore, it is as yet unclear how, if at all, caps affect some of the key problems facing our health care system, some of which were described previously, including physician supply, overall quality of health care, and incidence of malpractice.

Alternative reforms have been proposed in recent years. These range from minor modifications to more comprehensive no-fault systems. One interesting reform is based on a system of scheduled damages, reflective of past payment patterns. Randall Bovbjerg, Frank Sloan, and James Blumstein have outlined various models by which noneconomic damages can be scheduled.[79] One model creates a matrix of values that would award fixed damages according to the severity of injury and age of the plaintiff.[80] Another gives systematic information on appropriate awards based on past experience. Rather than binding, however, this information would be suggested to the jury as helpful guidelines and benchmarks in evaluating the damages of the plaintiff before it.[81] A third model involves the establishment of flexible

[75] 695 P. 2d 665 (Cal. 1985).
[76] Ibid., 680.
[77] Gronfein and Kinney 1991, 442.
[78] Rustad 1996; Rustad and Koenig 2002; Finley 2005.
[79] Bovbjerg et al. 1989, 909.
[80] Ibid., 938–45.
[81] Ibid., 953–6.

monetary ranges, with floors and ceilings, depending on the age of the plaintiff and severity of injury.[82]

The systems described by Bovbjerg et al. are appealing on many levels. They address many of the fairness problems associated with caps while, at the same time, satisfying the predictability concerns of defendants and insurers. Moving away from fixed, specific numerical caps on particular components of damages may be a step in the right direction. As Kip Viscusi has recognized, "the character of the reforms that have been proposed to date often are not ideal. Past proposals have been designed strictly with respect to the narrow objective of reducing insurance costs, which is not necessarily equivalent to fostering sound insurance market performance."[83] Furthermore, scheduling proposals would also seem to address the problems created by the "crossover" effect that I have discussed here – that is, at least as long as the schedules are applied to *both* economic and noneconomic compensatory damages.[84]

It is difficult to know what the future holds for medical malpractice reform. But, at a minimum, it is time to treat damages more holistically and recognize that rigidly imposed selective caps on noneconomic damages may be an exercise in futility.

[82] Ibid., 959–60; Blumstein et al. 1991, 178–85.
[83] Viscusi 2004, 10.
[84] Abraham 1992, 188; Danzon 1988, 122. But see Bovbjerg et al. 1989, 930; Baldus et al. 1994, 1254–7; Schuck 1991, 218; Geistfeld 1995b, 792.

10

Expertise and the Legal Process

Catherine T. Struve

As other contributions to this volume demonstrate, some approaches to the malpractice crisis would remove medical liability claims from the civil justice system – for instance, by employing alternative dispute resolution or by instituting an administrative claims system. When considering such measures, it is important to assess whether the present litigation system could be improved. Arguably, if enhancements are feasible, then it is the enhanced system against which alternative possibilities should be measured.

Each stage of litigation provides opportunities for reform. Certificate-of-merit requirements could alter the choices made by some plaintiffs' lawyers when deciding whether to assert a claim. Judicial training could improve judges' supervision of the pretrial process and their resolution of cases prior to trial on motions for summary judgment. Jury reforms could refine the jury's ability to assess liability and determine damages. And a heightened remittitur standard could empower judges to decrease the variability of jury awards, particularly in the area of noneconomic damages.

PLAINTIFFS' LAWYERS AND THE DECISION TO SUE

Though many valid medical liability claims are never brought, some claims that are asserted turn out to be weak.[1] Specialist medical malpractice attorneys are relatively unlikely to bring weak suits, but nonspecialist plaintiffs' lawyers may sometimes do so. Certificate-of-merit requirements, which require the plaintiff's lawyer to consult a medical expert at the outset, may help filter out insubstantial claims.

Thanks to Bill Sage and Rogan Kersh for comments; thanks also to The Pew Charitable Trusts for research support.

[1] Weiler et al. 1993, 69–71. Roughly half the malpractice suits that end before trial do so with no payment to the plaintiff. U.S. General Accounting Office 1987, 37, 82.

To bring a claim, the plaintiff must obtain representation. (Self-representation is grueling and often fruitless; thus, if no lawyer is willing to bring the claim, it generally will not be brought.) Few claimants can pay an hourly rate; plaintiffs' lawyers typically use contingent fee agreements, under which the lawyer recovers fees only if the plaintiff obtains money through a judgment or settlement. This arrangement gives the lawyer an incentive not to bring meritless claims.[2]

That incentive operates properly only if the lawyer accurately assesses the claim. Lawyers who specialize in bringing medical malpractice claims routinely obtain an expert evaluation before suing and will avoid claims that are likely to lose. Nonspecialist plaintiffs' lawyers, however, may lack the skill necessary to assess the claim[3] and may not obtain an expert's opinion prior to suing.

Responding to this concern, at least seventeen states have adopted certificate-of-merit provisions. These measures typically require the plaintiff's lawyer to certify, at or near the outset of the suit, that a qualified expert has reviewed the claim and has found some basis for it. The provision should be carefully designed to deter flimsy claims without imposing undue burdens on valid ones. Prior to suing, the plaintiff may lack information necessary to assess the claim; thus, the expert should be required to certify not that the claim definitely should succeed but rather that, based upon the available information, there is a reasonable likelihood that the claim has merit. There should be no certification requirement in cases in which the defendant fails to comply readily with the plaintiff's request for relevant records. If the plaintiff chooses to use the same expert to provide the certification at the start of suit and to provide medical testimony later in the suit, the defendant should not be permitted to argue that the expert's initial certification evidenced a rush to judgment.

With these safeguards, a certificate-of-merit requirement could prove beneficial by deterring nonspecialist lawyers from bringing weak claims.[4]

---

[2] Theoretically, a lawyer could bring a claim seeking a "nuisance settlement" – i.e., a settlement in which the defense pays simply to make the claim go away. But as the costs of initiating suit rise – due, for example, to the certificate-of-merit provisions discussed below – nuisance claims become less likely.

[3] Peeples, Harris, and Metzloff 2002, 885, found that claims brought by malpractice specialists are more likely to be perceived (by an insurer's outside reviewers) as strong claims.

[4] Empirical data on the effects of certificate-of-merit requirements are scarce. One study of 1980s legislation in Maryland examined malpractice filings before and after the adoption of reforms that included a certificate-of-merit requirement. Morlock and Malitz 1993, 5, 10. Postadoption, Medicaid recipients, and the uninsured formed a smaller percentage of claimants – leading the authors to raise concerns "that reforms have depressed claim filings by restricting access to the legal system." Id. at 15, 25. However, the study's sample size and controls were insufficient to provide firm conclusions, and any effect on low-income plaintiffs may have arisen from other roughly contemporaneous reforms, such as a cap on noneconomic damages. Id. at 23, 26.

JUDGES, PRETRIAL CASE MANAGEMENT, AND MOTIONS FOR SUMMARY JUDGMENT

Nine-tenths of malpractice suits never reach trial. They are settled for payment, dropped without payment, or dismissed by the court.[5] The critical role of the pretrial process highlights the importance of reforms that could help the judge to manage pretrial discovery and settlement talks and to address motions for summary judgment.

The discovery process enables the plaintiff to seek information to support his claims and permits the defendant to seek information with which to rebut those claims. Some jurisdictions direct the judge to take an active role in managing pretrial discovery. In these jurisdictions, the judge will confer with the parties early on and issue pretrial scheduling orders that establish deadlines for the completion of discovery and for pretrial motion practice. The judge may also try to encourage settlement. Active case management requires judicial dexterity, but the relevant skills are not unique to medical liability cases.

Summary judgment motions are more likely to present challenges that are specific to medical malpractice. Ordinarily, questions concerning liability and damages are reserved for the jury, but if no reasonable jury could find the defendant liable, the defendant can obtain summary judgment dismissing the claim prior to trial. To prove liability for medical malpractice, the plaintiff must establish the standard of care, must show that the defendant breached that standard, and must show that the breach caused the plaintiff's injury. Because the plaintiff will almost always need expert testimony to prove these elements, the defendant might try to obtain summary judgment by arguing that the plaintiff's proposed expert witnesses are not qualified to testify.

Expert testimony will vary depending on the requirements for proving standard of care and causation. In non-medical-malpractice cases, tort law sets a standard of "reasonable care": Would a reasonable person have taken a particular precaution to avoid a risk of harm? Medical malpractice law, however, has traditionally employed a different standard: Did the physician comply with "medical custom" (i.e., what doctors in the relevant community usually do)?

In theory, to give content to this standard, one could present survey data or an analysis of health care databases to show that a particular treatment approach either does or does not comport with medical custom.[6] No jurisdiction has yet imposed such a requirement, however. Experts who testify about the standard of care frequently draw on their own views of appropriate

---

[5] U.S. General Accounting Office 1987, 37, 82.
[6] Meadow and Sunstein 2001, 641; Cramm, Hartz, and Green 2002, 700; Hall et al. 2002, 819–20.

treatment rather than on a systematic analysis of what physicians, as a group, tend to do.[7]

Correlatively, courts generally permit the plaintiff to establish the standard of care using the opinion of a physician who testifies on the basis of her professional experience and judgment. Some jurisdictions require that the expert be certified in the relevant medical specialty and/or that the expert have recent practice or teaching experience. Such requirements, however, although they narrow the field of possible experts, do not change the nature of the court's inquiry: The court need only decide whether the expert has the requisite credentials. By contrast, if a court were to adopt a standard that required a statistical inquiry – either an inquiry into what doctors actually do or an inquiry into the risks and benefits of alternative treatment options – then the court would have to assess whether the expert possessed the necessary statistical (as well as medical) expertise.

In at least some medical malpractice cases, the court's consideration of expert testimony on causation will require such an assessment. Sometimes causation will be straightforward: Where a surgeon mistakenly performed the wrong operation, it is simple to determine that the surgeon's action caused the plaintiff's injury. In other cases, the question of causation may be subtler. The plaintiff might need to present a statistical analysis of many similar cases to establish how often similar injuries occur in the absence of negligence.[8] If the plaintiff proffers testimony concerning such statistical analysis, the court must assess whether that testimony is admissible.

Opinion is split on the appropriate test to employ in assessing technical or scientific expert testimony. Under the older *Frye* test,[9] an expert is qualified to testify if the expert's methods of research and analysis are generally accepted in the relevant scientific community. Under the more recent *Daubert* test, the judge performs his own assessment of the scientific validity of the expert's proffered testimony, by considering such factors as falsifiability, peer review, standards, probability of error, and acceptance in the relevant scientific community.[10] The *Daubert* test demands that the judge understand the basic concepts of scientific evidence; at least one study suggests that judges need more training in those concepts.[11]

Some have suggested that judicial expertise could be increased by creating specialized courts that would hear only medical malpractice cases. A specialized court, however, would risk a substantial increase in the politicization

[7] Hall 1991, 127.
[8] Meadow 2002, 680–1.
[9] *Frye v. United States*, 293 F. 1013 (D.C. Circuit 1923).
[10] *Daubert v. Merrell Dow Pharmaceuticals*, 509 U.S. 579, 593–4 (1993).
[11] Gatowski et al. 2001, 444–7.

of the selection and retention of judges. Medical liability litigation involves repeat players on both sides: physicians and insurers on the one hand, and plaintiffs' lawyers on the other. In a special-courts regime, all medical liability claims would be heard by a small number of judges, and both sets of interest groups would have an incentive to press for the selection of sympathetic judges. Such pressures arise even with respect to generalist courts, but the pressures would be much more intensely focused in the case of a specialized court.

Specialized divisions within a state's trial court of general jurisdiction would be a better option. Judges on the general trial court could rotate into a specialized division for a number of years. While serving within the division, judges could receive special training and would gain concentrated exposure to medical liability cases. Because the judges would be elected within the general pool of trial judges, political pressures would be reduced. Admittedly, this solution will be more practicable in populous areas (where there are large numbers of trial judges) than it is in rural areas (where there may be only a handful).

Whether or not a state adopts specialized divisions, it should adopt a "continuing judicial education" program that trains judges in case management skills and equips judges to assess the qualifications of medical, statistical, and economic experts. Such a training program should also improve judges' ability to implement the jury reforms discussed in the next section and to engage in more stringent review of jury awards, as described in the final section of this chapter.

JURY PERFORMANCE AND TRIAL REFORMS

As we have seen, pretrial motions can require a judge to consider the admissibility of expert testimony. For claims that reach trial, the judge serves a similar gatekeeping function.[12] But the task of weighing the expert and other evidence, and resolving liability and damages, falls to the jury. Thus, reforms at the trial stage should focus on improving the jury's decision making.

Determining liability requires jurors to assess medical testimony on standard of care and causation. Juries do fairly well at this task: In studies comparing expert reviewers' assessments of liability with actual jury verdicts, the verdicts generally correlated with the reviewers' assessments of liability,[13] except when juries tended to exonerate defendants whom the reviewers

---

[12] In addition to deciding the admissibility of evidence, the judge must also resolve (either during or after the trial) any motions for judgment as a matter of law. Such a motion typically would be made by a defendant and would require the same general type of analysis as a pretrial motion for summary judgment.

[13] Sloan, Githens, and Hickson 1993, 166–8; Farber and White 1994, 786–7, 802.

found negligent.[14] However, studies indicating that jurors have difficulty processing complex technical evidence – particularly statistical evidence – do suggest the need for reforms that enhance juror understanding.[15]

Assessing damages obliges juries to weigh both medical and economic testimony. Though past medical expenses and lost wages can readily be determined, future harm presents a tougher problem. The question of future economic harm can require medical testimony (on the likely degree of impairment the plaintiff will suffer in future years), actuarial calculations (to determine the plaintiff's life expectancy), and economic testimony (to establish the likely future cost of medical and other care, the amount of future wages the plaintiff will lose as a result of the injury, and the present value of those future costs). Each of these issues can generate vigorous dispute between the parties' experts.[16]

Generally, plaintiffs also seek compensation for the physical and emotional pain that resulted from the injury. Medical and actuarial testimony will be relevant here, too, because the jury will need to project the plaintiff's future condition and life expectancy. But expert testimony will not tell the jury how to quantify the plaintiff's suffering. In many jurisdictions, juries perform that task with little or no guidance. Unsurprisingly, awards of noneconomic damages tend to be more variable than economic damages awards.[17]

Liability and damages issues in medical malpractice cases can be challenging. This section discusses ways in which the trial process could be altered to assist the jury.

Preliminary Instructions on Substantive Law

In the traditional order of trial, the judge provides only a brief set of largely procedural instructions to the jury at the outset of the case; not until the end of trial does the judge instruct the jury in any detail on the substantive law. This places the jury in the awkward position of hearing evidence without knowing what the plaintiff must prove in order to win. Jurors may better assess and recall the trial evidence if they are instructed beforehand regarding the relevant claims and defenses; such instruction can provide a framework into which jurors can fit the evidence presented during trial.[18] However, skeptics warn that pre-instruction might bias jurors in favor of plaintiffs and suggest that it would be difficult to draft the substantive instructions before the evidence has been heard. Studies provide some support for the claim that pre-instruction can improve jury performance, but the effects of

[14] Liang 1997, 125–9, 158–60 tbls. 2A–2F.
[15] Cecil, Hans, and Wiggins 1991, 756–60.
[16] Greene and Bornstein 2000, 745.
[17] Diamond, Saks, and Landsman 1998, 317; Bovbjerg, Sloan, and Blumstein 1989, 937 tbl. 3.
[18] Dann 1993, 1249–50.

pre-instruction may be subtle and may vary depending on factors such as the complexity of the evidence.

Pre-instructed jurors may be better able to recall relevant facts and to apply the law to those facts. For example, ForsterLee et al. conducted a jury experiment using an audiotaped, simulated toxic tort trial. They used two different sets of substantive instructions – a simple overview of the substantive law and a more detailed exposition. Some jurors received the simple overview prior to hearing the relevant evidence (and the detailed exposition after hearing the evidence); other jurors heard the detailed exposition prior to hearing the relevant evidence. Researchers tested each juror's knowledge of facts from the trial; jurors given the detailed pre-instructions were significantly more likely to correctly identify trial facts (among a set of actual trial facts and "lures") and to independently recall probative facts from the trial.[19] An early study by Elwork et al. found a similar effect: In an experiment using a videotaped simulation of a tort trial concerning a car accident, jurors pre-instructed on negligence law were significantly more likely than post-instructed jurors to recall that the plaintiff had not looked to see whether there was oncoming traffic.[20] Smith, in a jury experiment using a videotaped reenactment of a murder trial, found that instruction timing had no significant effect on jurors' recall of facts, abstract understanding of the law, or verdict preferences. However, she found that jurors who were given substantive instructions "both before and after the evidence" did significantly better than other jurors in answering questions that required the juror to apply the law to the facts of the case.[21]

Providing pre-instruction (or providing both pre- and post-instruction) may improve jurors' decisions on liability. In an early jury experiment, Kassin and Wrightsman used a videotaped criminal trial simulation. Jurors who were pre-instructed on the reasonable doubt standard were less likely than post-instructed jurors to find the defendant guilty; as the authors concluded, "most preinstructed subjects 'presumed innocent,' whereas the others 'presumed guilty.'"[22] An experiment by Cruse and Brown suggests that providing both pre- and post-instruction on the elements of a crime can improve jurors' liability determinations; the pre- and post-instructed jurors were less

---

[19] ForsterLee et al. 1993, 16–19.

[20] Elwork et al. 1977, 177. The authors do not explicitly state that this conclusion demonstrated a more accurate recollection of the testimony, but their discussion indicates that it did: They argue that "this finding supports our hypothesis that" pre-instructions will help jurors "to distinguish the relevant evidence as it is being presented and to later remember it." Id.

[21] V. Smith 1991, 223–5. Smith also found that pre-instructed jurors "were significantly more likely to defer their verdict decisions," id. at 225, rather than making up their minds early in the trial. To the extent that pre-instruction helps jurors to keep an open mind until they have heard from both sides, pre-instruction may improve the quality of jurors' decisions. See id. at 226.

[22] Kassin and Wrightsman 1979, 1885.

likely to find the defendant guilty of larceny and were more likely to note and apply a key legal issue (whether the defendant intended to return the property). This improvement, however, occurred only when jurors received instructions both before and after the evidence; the researchers concluded from this that the difference stemmed not from the timing of the instructions but merely from the fact that the pre- and post-instructed jurors encountered the instructions twice.[23]

A field study in Wisconsin also provides some support for the notion that pre-instruction may improve jury determinations. Heuer and Penrod surveyed judges, lawyers, and jurors from civil and criminal trials in state court; pre-instructions (on burden of proof, and sometimes on other substantive issues) were given in roughly half the trials, and post-instructions were given in all trials.[24] Though jurors liked the idea of pre-instruction, juror responses (after the trial) to multiple-choice questions concerning the judge's instructions showed little or no benefit from pre-instruction: Pre-instruction produced no significant change in accuracy in civil cases and only a "marginally significant improvement" in criminal cases.[25] However, judges were significantly "less surprised" by, and "more satisfied" with, the verdicts in cases in which the jury had been pre-instructed.[26]

One experimental study, however, suggests that pre-instruction does not always improve jurors' performance in determining liability. Bourgeois et al. employed two audiotaped versions of a simulated medical malpractice trial; some jurors heard a tape that used highly technical language, while others heard a tape that conveyed the same substance but used less technical language. For each level of technicality, some jurors heard the instructions before the evidence, and others heard the evidence before the instructions. The evidence favored the defendant. "Preinstruction increased verdicts for the defendant when the evidence was low in technicality, whereas it increased verdicts for the plaintiff when the evidence was high in technicality." In the authors' view, this result "suggest[s] that preinstruction, when presented in a less complex trial, will generally aid systematic processing but when presented in the context of more complex evidence will augment a proplaintiff bias."[27] No single jury reform occurs in a vacuum: To reap the benefits (and avoid the possible downside) of pre-instruction, it is necessary to ensure that

[23] Cruse and Browne 1987, 131–2. This experiment lacked verisimilitude, in that the subjects read booklets containing the trial instructions and evidence rather than listening to or watching tapes.

[24] Heuer and Penrod 1989, 416–18. All pre-instructions included instructions on the burden of proof: "the [pre-instructing] judges were encouraged to include any other [instructions] (e.g., case specific substantive instructions) that they believed would help," id. at 417, but it is not clear how many did so.

[25] Ibid., 424–5.

[26] Ibid., 425–6 and tbl. 10.

[27] Bourgeois et al. 1995, 64–5.

testimony – particularly expert testimony – is presented in understandable terms rather than impenetrable jargon.[28] Methods of improving the comprehensibility of expert testimony are discussed later.

Some (but not all) of the experimental evidence suggests that preinstruction can increase the accuracy of jurors' damages determinations. The audiotaped toxic tort trial employed by ForsterLee et al. involved four plaintiffs with varying levels of injury; the researchers varied the technical complexity of the evidence ("either high or moderate") and gave detailed substantive instructions either before or after the evidence. Both preinstruction and technicality of evidence affected the jurors' performance in awarding damages: "Jurors more clearly differentiated among the plaintiffs [as to damages level] when preinstructed than when postinstructed," and jurors who received the "moderately technical" version distinguished among plaintiffs, whereas jurors who received the "highly technical" version did not.[29]

Using the highly technical version of this toxic tort trial, Bourgeois et al. also tested the effects of pre-instruction on damages. Most jurors were told they would be deliberating, but others were told beforehand that they would have to decide the issues by themselves (the "lone jurors"). Among both lone and deliberating jurors, instruction timing varied. All jurors filled out questionnaires (deliberating jurors filled out two sets, pre- and post-deliberation). Because the plaintiffs' evidence was strong, the researchers expected better-functioning jurors to award higher damages; they found that pre-instructed jurors awarded higher damages and that this held true for deliberating jurors' award preferences after deliberation as well.[30] However, deliberating jurors showed no greater ability to distinguish among the plaintiffs' injury levels when pre-instructed. Lone jurors who were pre-instructed were the only group to differentiate among the plaintiffs, awarding higher damages to the more severely injured. A "social loafing" theory may explain why pre-instruction failed to produce as much benefit among deliberating jurors as among lone jurors: "Interactive jurors may have failed to pay full attention to the evidence, with the expectation that any memory deficiencies would be compensated by other individuals during group discussion."[31]

---

[28] The example given by Bourgeois et al. illustrates this point: Where the highly technical testimony stated that "[a] diagnosis of infiltrating ductal carcinoma was made on the basis of the results of an incisional biopsy," the less technical (but still accurate) version of the testimony explained that "[c]ancer of the breast was diagnosed by surgically removing part of the lesion and analyzing it." Bourgeois et al. 1995, 65.

[29] ForsterLee et al. 1993, 17–18.

[30] Bourgeois et al. 1995, 60–1, 64. The authors cautioned that though this finding could indicate a benefit of pre-instruction, an alternative explanation could be that pre-instruction might "lead to a confirmatory evidence search strategy, [such that] the instructions may also engage proplaintiff bias, simply because the plaintiffs present their case first." Id. at 64.

[31] Ibid., 62–3.

Pre-instruction may improve jurors' liability determinations so long as the evidence is not unduly technical, and may improve jurors' sensitivity to information (such as the severity of injury) that bears on the question of damages. But the data suggest the need for caution and for further research:[32] Pre-instruction may lead to a pro-plaintiff bias in cases where scientific evidence is incomprehensible to jurors, and the benefits of pre-instruction may be lost if jurors (knowing they will deliberate as a group) pay less attention because they believe they can free-ride on other jurors' knowledge. Nonetheless, there are reasons to think that pre-instruction holds promise. Real jurors may be much less likely to "loaf" than mock jurors. And even if the precise mechanisms are not yet clearly understood, field evidence showing a higher rate of judge–jury agreement in cases with pre-instruction provides some real-world support for the asserted benefits of the practice.

Interim Arguments During Trial

When a particular line of testimony is presented during trial, the jurors may have difficulty understanding how that testimony connects to the key issues in the case. Lawyers attempt to draw those connections during opening and closing arguments, but interim statements may prove helpful, especially in long trials. The court could permit the lawyers to make such statements either before or after a particular portion of the testimony; the lawyer presenting the testimony could briefly point out what she wanted to establish through the testimony, and the opposing lawyer could briefly respond.

Data on the effects of interim statements are scarce. In a recent pilot project in Tennessee state court, when counsel were told they could make interim statements, few lawyers took that opportunity, and when they did so, their statements were typically brief. Overall, judges tended to consider the interim statements useful, though some mentioned instances when lawyers had "[gone] off on tangents."[33]

Courts should be given discretion to allow interim statements in lengthy or complex cases. Judges who permit such statements should consider imposing time limits; for example, each side's counsel could be given an hour of interim statement time and could be permitted to choose how to divide it.[34]

Note-Taking by Jurors

Another proposed reform would permit jurors to take notes during trial; this practice is gaining popularity, but some judges still reject it. Proponents of

---

[32] Because many of the extant studies focused on individual mock jurors, it would be particularly useful to amass data concerning the interaction of pre-instruction and jury deliberations.

[33] Cohen and Cohen 2003, 32.

[34] Committee on Federal Courts of the New York State Bar Association 1988, 557.

note-taking assert that the practice will help jurors pay attention to and recall relevant evidence. Skeptics caution that note-taking might distract jurors from the testimony, might produce an inaccurate record, might give better-educated jurors an inappropriate advantage, and might favor the plaintiff if jurors took notes assiduously during the first part of trial but became tired of taking notes by the time of the defense case.[35] Existing data provide both mild support for the asserted advantages of note-taking and a strong rebuttal of its putative disadvantages.

An experiment by Rosenhan et al. suggests that note-taking can improve juror performance. Students serving as mock jurors viewed a videotape of the judge's opening remarks and counsel's opening statements in a civil case. Roughly half were allowed to take notes. Each juror then answered a questionnaire. The researchers found that "notetaking increased recall of trial information and enriched the subjective experience of jurors" but that note-taking did not significantly affect the jurors' likelihood of favoring a particular outcome.[36]

By contrast, field studies have failed to detect an improvement in jury performance, but the design of those studies may have made it unlikely that they would detect such improvements. Heuer and Penrod conducted one field experiment in civil and criminal trials in Wisconsin state courts[37] and another in civil and criminal trials in state and federal courts in thirty-three states.[38] Synthesizing the information from these two studies, Penrod and Heuer reported no evidence for the potential benefits of note-taking; but their method would not necessarily detect "benefits such as increased juror comprehension, better recalled evidence, and better reasoned decisions." In any event, note-taking does not produce the effects feared by some critics. Penrod and Heuer found that jurors' notes are accurate and "do not produce a distorted view of the case," that note-takers do not wield inappropriate influence, that note-taking is not distracting, and that note-taking "does not favor either the prosecution or the defense."[39]

Because the field studies found no downsides, courts should permit juror note-taking. At the outset of trial, the judge should tell the jurors that they can take notes but should caution them not to let the note-taking distract them from listening to the testimony and not to be swayed during deliberations by the mere fact that one juror took notes while another did not. With these precautions, note-taking may be helpful and should not, at any rate, be harmful.

---

[35] Flango 1980, 437.
[36] Rosenhan et al. 1994, 59.
[37] Heuer and Penrod 1988, 244–51.
[38] Heuer and Penrod 1994a, 135–40.
[39] Penrod and Heuer 1997, 271, 281.

Juror Questions for Witnesses

Pre-instruction, interim statements, and note-taking all may assist jurors in processing the information presented to them during trial. A more controversial reform would permit jurors actively to shape the content of that information by submitting questions to witnesses. Traditionally, questioning witnesses was seen as a task for the lawyers, though the judge might occasionally pose additional questions. Some commentators have argued that jurors should be permitted to submit questions; the responses to such questions might clear up a juror's confusion and might occasionally supply a piece of information that otherwise would have been overlooked. Also, jurors who are permitted to submit questions might listen more attentively. Skeptics have warned, however, that a juror might ask an inappropriate question and might penalize a party for objecting to the question; partisan jurors might also submit questions designed to argue with a witness.

Studies of actual trials provide some support for the benefits of juror questions – particularly in complex cases – and show little or no evidence of the projected disadvantages. In Heuer and Penrod's Wisconsin and national field studies, jurors' self-reports indicated that they felt "better informed" in trials in which juror questions were allowed than in other trials.[40] In the national field study, Heuer and Penrod found that this benefit was especially noticeable in cases "where the evidence or the law were particularly complicated."[41] Jurors' survey responses tended to disprove the fears that a juror whose question was disallowed would feel antagonistic toward the objecting lawyer, and judges' and lawyers' survey responses generally countered the concern that juror questions would harm one side or the other.[42] Likewise, in a Tennessee pilot project, judges' survey responses indicated that juror questions were relatively rare and usually unproblematic.[43] Jurors appreciate the opportunity to ask questions,[44] and judges who have permitted juror questions generally (though not always) view the practice positively.[45] Lawyers seem more divided on the advisability of permitting juror questions;[46] one

[40] Ibid., 274–5. By contrast, judges and lawyers in cases where juror questions were permitted did not believe that those questions had promoted truth-seeking or had revealed points on which jurors were confused. Id. at 275.

[41] Heuer and Penrod 1994b, 49. A similar benefit did not appear "for the [type of] complexity associated with large quantities of information." Id.

[42] Penrod and Heuer 1997, 277–9.

[43] Cohen and Cohen 2003, 42–3.

[44] Cohen and Cohen 2003, 43–4, found that 90% of jurors who had been permitted to ask questions found the practice useful.

[45] Sand and Reiss 1985, 444–5, found that "[t]he participating judges generally were in favor of" allowing juror questions, but that one judge feared that question-asking jurors were "likely to have preconceptions" and another judge "found the procedure...disruptive."

[46] Cohen and Cohen 2003, 44.

early (and numerically limited) study found that prosecutors and plaintiffs' lawyers were more likely than defendants' lawyers to take a favorable view of the practice.[47]

Judges should be given discretion to permit juror questioning of witnesses. Juror questioning will likely be most useful in cases that involve technical testimony or complex legal concepts. When a judge permits juror questions, the judge should discuss the practice during the preliminary instructions to the jury at the start of trial. The judge should tell the jurors they can pose factual or clarifying questions by submitting the questions to the court, in writing, before the witness is excused. The jury should be told in advance that the judge will discuss each question with counsel, outside the hearing of the jury, before deciding whether to pose it, and that jurors should not draw any conclusions from the judge's refusal to ask a particular question.[48]

Permitting Jury Discussions Prior to Deliberations

In the traditional view, not only should jurors not participate in shaping the trial evidence, but they also should not discuss that evidence among themselves until all the evidence is in and jury deliberations formally begin. The ban on jury discussions during trial is intended to minimize the risks that jurors will make up their minds prematurely and that they may do so on the basis of discussions that take place when not all the jurors are present.[49] Some suggest the ban is counterproductive: Because jurors do not wait until deliberations to begin thinking about the significance of the evidence, allowing early discussions among the jurors could enable jurors to benefit from group deliberation.

Arizona's recent decision to permit early discussions in civil trials has permitted researchers to study the practice. Their findings suggest that early discussions may improve jurors' ability to recall and process information, but that they also carry some risks that warrant further study. In 1995, Arizona adopted (in Civil Rule 39(f)) a presumption in favor of telling juries that they may "discuss the evidence among themselves in the jury room during recesses from trial when all are present, as long as they reserve judgment about the outcome of the case until deliberations commence."[50]

An early study used judge, juror, lawyer, and litigant questionnaires to examine the effects of Arizona's new rule; the researchers compared survey

---

[47] Sand and Reiss 1985, 445.

[48] Cappello and Strenio 2000 provide a useful discussion of proposed cautionary instructions.

[49] In criminal cases, courts have taken the view that early discussions could endanger the defendant's constitutional right to a fair trial. See, e.g., *United States v. Resko*, 3 F.3d 684, 689–90 (3d Cir. 1993).

[50] Arizona Rule of Civil Procedure 39(f). Juror discussions "may be limited or prohibited by the court for good cause." Id.

responses from jurors in trials where Rule 39(f) instructions were given to survey responses from jurors in trials where the judge told the jury not to discuss the case prior to deliberations. Roughly 80 percent of jurors who had discussed the case during trial felt "that trial discussions improve the jury's understanding of the trial evidence," but the presence or absence of early discussion did not significantly affect judge/jury agreement on the verdict. Jurors' responses provided no support for the prejudgment concern: Early discussion did not significantly affect the points in time when jurors (according to self-reports) started to favor one side or settled on a preferred outcome. On the other hand, those responses did give some support to the concern that early discussions might take place when not all jurors were present. Jurors in trials in which discussions were permitted "were more likely than the No Discussions jurors to say that they had spoken informally with other jurors."[51] Overall, most judge and juror respondents favored early discussions, but "attorneys and litigants [we]re divided in their views of this reform."[52]

A somewhat smaller but richly detailed study analyzed videotapes of trials, juror discussions, and jury deliberations in fifty civil cases in Arizona's state court. The trials were divided between "Discuss" cases – meaning that the court gave the instruction permitting juror discussions prior to deliberations – and "No Discuss" cases – meaning that the court told the jurors not to engage in predeliberation discussions. The researchers quantified how often jurors in each type of case engaged in early discussions; in addition, the researchers performed an in-depth qualitative review of the discussions in certain complex cases by comparing the videotaped juror discussions with the relevant trial testimony. Jurors in Discuss cases had extensive early discussions, whereas jurors in No Discuss cases rarely talked about the case and any discussions that did occur were typically short. In the complex cases, "when factual questions arose about the evidence, discussion tended to improve the accuracy of recall." Although no significant differences emerged in jurors' responses concerning understandability of legal instructions or the evidence in general, "jurors reported significantly greater ease in understanding the expert testimony" in Discuss cases. Because the judges "rated the Discuss and No Discuss cases similarly on all three measures" of difficulty, the difference between juror responses in Discuss and No Discuss cases indicates that early discussion may help jurors to make sense of expert testimony.[53]

The videotape study, like the earlier study, found support for the concern that jurors might violate the terms under which early discussions were permitted. Jurors had "many substantive discussions ... when a sizeable number

[51] Hannaford et al. 2000, 365, 369, 371 tbl. 3, 372, 374, 376.
[52] Hans et al. 1999, 349.
[53] Diamond et al. 2003, 20–1, 43–4, 70–1 and tbl. 7.5, 75.

of the jurors were not present." Likewise, though jurors were warned "not to take a final position during discussions on what the outcome of the case should be," certain jurors on a number of the Discuss juries did take such a position. On the other hand, those jurors sometimes changed their position by the time of deliberations, and "cases with early verdict statements did not disproportionately favor the plaintiff." Thus, the researchers discerned "no clear indication that [early verdict statements] were responsible for altering case outcomes."[54]

The Arizona studies indicate that early discussions may help jurors process trial evidence, particularly in cases involving challenging expert testimony. Jurisdictions that are not yet ready to adopt this innovation should periodically review the evidence emerging from Arizona, in order to update their assessment as more data become available. A judge who permits early discussions should provide oral and written instructions at the outset of the case to warn jurors not to discuss the case unless all jurors are present and not to state views, prior to deliberations, on who should win the case; the judge could reiterate that admonition during trial and also post a reminder in the jury room.[55]

Improving Expert Testimony

Judges who do not authorize early discussions among jurors can use other methods to improve jurors' comprehension of expert testimony. In the standard order of proof at trial, the plaintiff presents all of her initial witnesses before the defendant puts on any of his witnesses; the plaintiff then may present rebuttal evidence. In a long trial, the testimony of plaintiff and defense experts may be separated by days of unrelated testimony, making it harder for the jury to assess differences between the experts' views. Some suggest reordering the presentation of evidence so that the two experts on a given issue can testify back-to-back. In that way, points of disagreement between the experts can be highlighted.

Reordering the expert testimony should improve comprehensibility; but some cases may present such complex issues, and such a sharp disagreement between the parties' experts, that the jury may find it challenging to resolve the relevant issues unassisted. In such cases, the court may consider appointing a third expert – selected by the court, after consultation with the parties – to comment on the testimony of the parties' experts and to provide the jury with a framework for assessing that testimony. A court-appointed expert should supplement rather than supplant the parties' expert evidence. On many questions, there may be room for reasonable specialists to disagree, and if a court-appointed expert were the sole authority

[54] Ibid., 75.
[55] Ibid., 76–8.

presented to the jury, the jury might not be alerted to the existence of that disagreement.[56]

Providing Guidance on Damages

The court and the lawyers can take additional steps to give the jury better guidance concerning damages. Because damages determinations will require expert medical and economic testimony, reforms that improve jurors' ability to process such testimony should help, particularly with respect to economic damages. Defendants' lawyers sometimes fail to present evidence or argument concerning damages, out of concern that such a presentation might appear to concede the issue of liability.[57] This concern is likely misplaced; presenting such evidence could assist the jury in reaching a balanced damages assessment. In addition, judges could provide more detailed instructions concerning the factors that should be considered in awarding noneconomic damages.

Making Jury Instructions More Comprehensible

Many jurisdictions could improve jury performance by providing clearer jury instructions. Jurors often misunderstand traditional jury instructions. Good drafting practices – avoiding jargon and double negatives, for example – can help make instructions more understandable. Ideally, the rewritten instructions should be tested on a representative group of jury-eligible subjects in order to gauge their effectiveness. Such tests are costly; states should coordinate their research agendas so as to share the expense and maximize the benefits.[58]

The judge's manner of presenting the instructions is also key. Judges traditionally read the instructions aloud to the jury; providing each juror, in addition, with a written copy of the instructions should improve juror comprehension. Three studies attempted to measure the effect of written copies, but each study appears flawed: Apparently, each tested jurors' comprehension by means of questionnaires administered after trial, at points when there was no assurance that the jurors would still have the written copy of the instructions with them. Not surprisingly, two studies found that jurors who had been given written copies did no better than jurors who had not;[59]

---

[56] Deason 1998, 63, 84, 116.
[57] Vidmar 1995, 197–8, 247.
[58] Elwork et al. 1982, 25, 77–8.
[59] Heuer and Penrod 1989, 417, 420 (Wisconsin field study; questionnaires were handed out at end of trial and respondents mailed them back); Reifman et al. 1992, 545, 551 (Michigan state court field study; jurors received questionnaire in the mail after their jury service ended).

interestingly, the third study found that the jurors who had previously been given written copies scored significantly better.[60] In any event, jurors like having written copies of the instructions[61] and they tend to consult those copies several times during deliberations.[62] Because written instructions seem likely to improve jurors' understanding, and because studies have disclosed no real downside,[63] the court should provide each juror with a copy of the instructions.[64]

It may also be helpful for the judge to ask the jurors whether they have any questions on the instructions.[65] When the jury does ask for clarification of an instruction, it is critical that the judge respond in a helpful fashion. Some judges merely reread the relevant instruction to the jury (or direct the jury to reread it, if written copies have been provided). Although this may insulate the judge from reversal on appeal, it is unlikely to assist the jury. Instead, the judge should consult with counsel and then try to provide a direct answer to the jury's question.[66]

THE JUDGE'S ROLE AFTER THE VERDICT

The trial reforms considered previously should enhance jurors' understanding of the evidence and issues and should thus improve determinations of liability and damages. An additional means of reducing the variability of damages awards is to provide for more stringent posttrial judicial review. The mechanism of remittitur in effect permits the trial judge to reduce the verdict: The judge offers the plaintiff a choice between accepting a reduced award or facing a new trial. Traditionally, remittitur was granted only if the award was so far outside the range of reasonable awards as to "shock the conscience" of the judge – a difficult standard to meet. Some jurisdictions now mandate remittitur if the award "deviates materially" from reasonable compensation – which should result in more frequent reductions.[67] This mechanism can usefully decrease award variability, so long as judges are given sufficient guidance and training on how to apply the standard (for example, by comparing the award to those approved in prior, similar cases).

---

[60] Kramer and Koenig 1990, 406, 409, 428 (Michigan state court field study; questionnaire was given to jurors right after end of trial; jurors apparently filled the questionnaire out at the courthouse, but it is not clear whether they still had copies of the jury instructions).

[61] Heuer and Penrod 1989, 419.

[62] Cohen and Cohen 2003, 58.

[63] Heuer and Penrod 1989, 423–4 tbls. 7 and 8.

[64] Lieberman and Sales 1997, 628.

[65] Dann 1993, 1260.

[66] Dumas 2000, 702.

[67] N.Y. CPLR 5501(c); Pa. R. Civ. P. 1042.72. New York also mandates the converse – additur – if the award is unreasonably low, but additur is granted more rarely.

CONCLUSION

No single reform discussed in this chapter will provide a quick fix for the malpractice crisis. Some measures – such as pre-instructions and early jury discussions – require additional study. But reforms at each stage of litigation hold the promise of improving the performance of plaintiffs' lawyers, judges, and juries in malpractice cases.

11

Disclosure and Fair Resolution of Adverse Events

Carol B. Liebman and Chris Stern Hyman

The health care system in the United States is in turmoil. Patients are being harmed by too many, often fatal, mistakes.[1] At the same time, physicians and hospitals are trying to cope with a costly medical malpractice crisis. These two crises create a vicious cycle. When something goes wrong in patient care, physicians and hospitals withhold apologies and offer as little information as possible for fear that anything they say may be used against them should patients or family members sue. Family members, in many cases, sue not only to receive compensation for injuries, but also in search of answers and explanations and because no one has said, "I'm sorry." Each new suit reinforces providers' fears and inhibits the sort of conversation and exchange of information with patients and colleagues that might restore trust and prevent errors being repeated, thereby decreasing lawsuits. This chapter explores ideas developed as part of the Pew Demonstration Mediation and ADR Project ("ADR Project") to help break the cycle.

Between 2002 and 2004, the ADR Project conducted a participant observer study that examined how mediation and conflict resolution skills might be helpful in disclosing adverse medical events and, when appropriate, reaching fair resolution of resulting claims for compensation. We focused on how those skills could be used to repair ruptured relationships between patients and physicians, to turn conversations about what went wrong into opportunities for learning about ways to improve patient safety, to include patients and their families in discussions about safety, and, when appropriate, to provide patients fair and timely compensation for their injuries. We also considered how mediation and conflict resolution skills could address the mismatch between what research has shown patients want after a medical error and the way physicians typically respond. We offered mediation services and conflict resolution training at no cost to four Pennsylvania hospitals

---

[1] Institute of Medicine 2000; Miller and Zahn 2004.

and ultimately provided mediation services for one and training for three of the four.[2]

As the ADR Project was beginning, the Pennsylvania legislature passed a tort reform act, the Medical Care Availability and Reduction of Error Act (often referred to as "MCARE" or "Act 13"), which took effect in March 2002. The new law requires hospitals to notify the patient or the patient's family in writing within seven days of a "serious event" and imposes penalties for failure to do so. This legislative mandate to disclose was a national first. Florida, Nevada, New Jersey, Oregon, and Washington have followed Pennsylvania's lead and passed laws requiring disclosure. Florida and Nevada require in-person disclosure by the medical facility. New Jersey's disclosure law does not specify the form the notice must take. The definitions of what must be disclosed to the patient or family member and the time frame for disclosure vary from state to state. All four statutes make the disclosure inadmissible in any subsequent litigation. We anticipate that other states will enact laws requiring disclosure to patients and their families.[3]

Although Pennsylvania was the first state to require disclosure as a matter of law, both the Joint Commission on Accreditation of Healthcare Organizations (JCAHO) regulations and American Medical Association (AMA) ethical standards have, for many years, required disclosure. JCAHO's Standard RI. 1.2.2 requires that "[p]atients and, when appropriate, their families are informed about the outcomes of care, including unanticipated outcomes."[4] The AMA Council on Ethical and Judicial Affairs in its Code of Medical Ethics articulates a standard of conduct for physicians that, if followed, would obviate the need for elaborate statutory measures to ensure full disclosure. The standard, E-8.12, states:

It is a fundamental ethical requirement that a physician should at all times deal honestly and openly with patients. Patients have a right to know their past and present medical status and to be free of any mistaken beliefs concerning their conditions. Situations occasionally occur in which a patient suffers significant medical complications that may have resulted from the physician's mistake or judgment. In these situations, the physician is ethically required to inform the patient of all the facts necessary to ensure understanding of what has occurred. . . . Ethical responsibility includes informing patients of changes in their diagnoses resulting from retrospective review of test results or any other information. This obligation holds even though the patient's medical treatment or therapeutic options may not be altered by the new

---

[2] A more detailed account of the Pew Demonstration Mediation and ADR Project is available at www.medliabilitypa.org.
[3] Many states have laws requiring that adverse events be reported to state agencies. Those reporting laws do not require disclosure to patients or families.
[4] Joint Commission on Accreditation of Healthcare Organizations 2003.

information. Concern regarding legal liability which might result following truthful disclosure should not affect the physician's honesty with a patient.[5]

Despite this unambiguous ethical directive, full disclosure occurs only sporadically. Physicians fail to tell their patients about adverse events,[6] even though research shows disclosure may benefit the physician by decreasing the likelihood of being sued[7] and by increasing the strength of the physician's relationship with the patient and family.[8] Hospitals throughout the United States underdisclose the most serious adverse events at an alarming rate.[9] The new laws add penalties for failure to disclose, clear statements about who must disclose, and, in some cases, specific time frames within which disclosure must occur. What remains to be seen is whether the statutes increase disclosures to patients and their families, whether disclosure results in more or fewer lawsuits, and whether states actually impose penalties for failure to disclose.

RECOMMENDATIONS

This chapter discusses three measures that hospitals and physicians should consider to help manage the fallout from an adverse event, medical error, or mistake:[10]

1. Create a consult service of communication experts whose members can help plan and conduct a disclosure conversation with patients and families after an adverse event and provide debriefing and emotional support to the health care providers.
2. Apologize when appropriate and attend to the form of apology most likely to be helpful in restoring trust between the patient and physician.
3. Use mediation to resolve claims promptly, possibly before a claim is filed.

---

[5] American Medical Association, Code of Medical Ethics, 1994.
[6] Wu et al. 1997; Gallagher et al. 2003.
[7] Wu et al. 1997; Gallagher et al. 2003.
[8] Wu et al. 1997; Mazor, Simon, Yood, et al. 2004.
[9] Lamb et al. 2003. The national survey showed that an adjusted rate for only the most serious adverse events resulted in an estimate of 44–66 medical injuries per 10,000 admissions that should have been disclosed. Only 2 of the 245 respondent hospitals in the survey were in that range and fewer than 10% were making 20 disclosures a year.
[10] We use "adverse event" to refer to "an unintentional, definable injury that was the result of medical management and not a disease process" (Pierluissi et al. 2003, 2839, citing Reason 1990). A "medical error" is "defined as the failure of a planned action to be completed as intended or the use of a wrong plan to achieve an aim." (See Pierluissi et al. 2003, 2839, citing Reason 1990.) Often, "medical error" is used to refer to a preventable systemic problem rather than a problem resulting from poor performance by a health care provider (Barach 2003). Depending on the facts involved, a serious event could be a medical error or an adverse event. "Mistake" refers to individual physician errors, resulting from deficiencies in knowledge, skill, or attentiveness, that cause significant harm (Wu et al. 1997).

These recommendations are designed to create a culture that supports candor, free exchange of information, fair outcomes for patients and physicians, and improved patient safety.

WHAT PATIENTS AND FAMILIES WANT AFTER AN ERROR

Before discussing each of the recommendations, it is useful to review research showing a mismatch between patients and families' needs after an error or adverse event and the way that physicians tend to respond. What patients and families experience as unresponsive communication causes anger. Researchers have found that after an error the factors that put physicians at risk of being sued are not the quality of medical care,[11] not their chart documentation,[12] not negligent treatment,[13] but ineffective communication with patients.[14] What the physician says often is less important than the process and tone of the conversation.[15]

Hickson's important study of the reasons parents sued after a perinatal injury documents examples of ineffective physician communication. He found that 33 percent sued because they were advised to do so by a third party, often a health care provider; 24 percent sued because they felt the doctor was not completely honest or lied to them; another 24 percent needed money for the child's future care; 20 percent could not get anyone to tell them what had happened; and 19 percent were seeking revenge or to protect others from harm.[16] Those suing felt their physician would not listen (13%), would not talk openly (32%), attempted to mislead them (48%), or did not warn them of the long-term neurodevelopmental problems of their child (70%).[17]

In another major study on physician–patient communication, Gallagher looked at the attitudes of patients and physicians after a medical error and identified what patients want in a disclosure conversation, how physicians are likely to talk to patients, and how both groups feel in the aftermath of an error. What he and his colleagues found is that patients want "basic information" – meaning an explanation of what happened and why, the health implications of the error, and how the problem will be corrected so future errors can be prevented. For reasons that are intuitively understandable, physicians after an error tend to chose their words carefully, are likely to mention the adverse event but not that an error has occurred, and

---

[11] Levinson et al. 1997, citing Entman et al. 1994.
[12] Ibid.
[13] Harvard Medical Practice Study 1990.
[14] Lester and Smith 1993; Levinson et al. 1997.
[15] Levinson et al. 1997.
[16] Hickson et al. 1992.
[17] Ibid.

are unlikely to tell the patient what caused the error and how it might be prevented.[18]

Both patients and physicians experience powerful emotions after an error and want emotional support. Patients want an apology; many physicians would like to apologize but are worried about legal liability. Both need a process that allows those feelings to be expressed in order to restore the patient–physician bond.

ESTABLISH A COMMUNICATIONS PROCESS CONSULT SERVICE

Physicians are trained to be expert in a set of skills that enable them to diagnose medical problems and provide appropriate treatment. Their ability to help patients depends on being able to elicit information, explain diagnoses and treatment plans, and communicate with other members of the caregiving team. The communication skills physicians use while caring for patients are helpful when disclosing a medical error or explaining an adverse event, but the communication task in such situations is more difficult, complex, and demanding than in ordinary exchanges. After an adverse event, physicians may be so caught up in the struggle to manage their own emotions of shame, self-doubt, disappointment, guilt, and grief about their failure to meet their own and the profession's standards[19] that they are, understandably, unable to access those skills.[20]

Physicians are used to giving help but not receiving it, and to providing care but not being cared for. Like most people enmeshed in emotionally divisive conversations, however, they are likely to benefit from the assistance of a skilled expert to help them communicate about and manage the consequence of the error. Even those who have been trained to use effective communication skills or who are naturally empathic listeners may have difficulty drawing on those skills when they have made an error that has caused grave harm to a patient. Moreover, in the midst of trying to manage their own reactions while delivering what may be devastating information to patients or their families, physicians are unlikely to be accurate judges of whether the disclosure conversation has gone well or badly. Both the patients and physicians will benefit from the services of an expert skilled in facilitating highly charged and emotional discussions.

Patient and family narratives of medical error contain many examples of poor physician communication skills.[21] Examples include the physician who repeatedly insists that the surgery was a success even though the patient has died or the physician who tells the patient she has "failed" chemotherapy.

[18] Gallagher et al. 2003.
[19] Newman 1996; Christenson et al. 1992.
[20] Redinbaugh et al. 2001.
[21] Berlinger 2005.

These inept comments cause pain to family members and are often cited to prove that physicians are terrible communicators. Such an interpretation of those statements is too judgmental and lacks compassion for the physician. Those inept and insensitive comments can also be read as distorted expressions of pain from the physician confronted with her own inadequacies and the knowledge that she has failed to carry out the foundational precept of medicine, to first do no harm.

Consider the case of Mr. B.[22]

Mr. B, a retired husband and father with end-stage chronic obstructive pulmonary disease, was admitted to the hospital's Intensive Care Unit. A medical student supervised by a surgical resident attempted to insert a subclavican central line (an IV placed in a vein under the collarbone). As the line was being placed, the lung was nicked and collapsed. Mr. B went into cardiac arrest and died.

The resident called Mrs. B at home and urged her to come to the hospital immediately. When she arrived the attending physician informed her of her husband's death. She was then left standing alone in the hall outside her husband's room. No one explained what had happened then or in the days and weeks that followed. She filed a lawsuit partly in search of an explanation. She had no communication with the physician or hospital representative between the time that she was informed of her husband's death and the beginning of a mediation where the case was settled.

In Mr. B's case, both the attending physician who delivered the bad news to Mrs. B and the resident could have benefited from a communications consultation to help them, in the brief time before Mrs. B arrived at the hospital, to think through how to deliver the bad news and support her at that moment. Both she and they would have been helped had there been a structure in place to plan and conduct a follow-up discussion with the family. As is all too common, the attending physician and the resident took what at the moment may have seemed the easy and least painful way out and avoided further communication with the family. Although it is impossible to know whether additional, skilled, and empathetic conversations would have avoided the lawsuit, such conversations would not have made things worse.

We recognize that calling in a member of a communications process consult service may be perceived by many physicians as unnecessary and

---

[22] Much of the information about this case – and Mr. L and Mr. D's cases, which appear later – is available in the pleadings, which are public documents. Participants in the mediations agreed in advance that descriptions of the mediation process without identifying information could be included in reports about the project provided that nothing that anyone said during the mediation would be revealed. They were also informed that if they had any hesitation about having their mediation included in final project reports, they could still have the services of the mediators. Copies of a longer version of Mr. B and Mr. D's descriptions were also provided to the parties via their counsel, so that they could indicate whether they had confidentiality concerns about anything in the case descriptions. None did.

time-consuming, and that the shift of the physician's role from authoritative decision maker to collaborative participant may be threatening. In a study of attitudes toward litigation among physicians, hospital leaders, and nurses, only one-quarter believed that physicians are likely to discuss adverse events. Only 5 percent thought that physicians are comfortable discussing medical errors.[23] Fear of litigation is the primary reason for not having discussions with colleagues, even though two-thirds of those surveyed found that being able to discuss adverse events and errors with colleagues was helpful in avoiding similar mistakes.

As a result of our work on the ADR Project, we have concluded that, although some basic communication skills training for all physicians is desirable and can have an impact on physician behavior, its major benefit is to help sensitize physicians to the complexity of disclosure conversations after an adverse event and to normalize the use of a communications consultant, especially when a serious error has occurred. After Mr. B's death, it is conceivable that a medical explanation of what happened, an opportunity for his family to ask questions about his care, and an appropriate apology might have reassured them and even avoided litigation. In addition, such a conversation would have alerted the hospital to, first, the discrepancy between the hospital's policy of how grieving family members were to be treated and what this widow needed, and second, the possibility that the hospital might need to reconsider (even if not change) protocols for deciding where to place a central line and how to supervise medical trainees. But the physicians were, understandably, so distressed by his death that they were unable, on their own, to communicate with the family.

The skills that are vital to a successful disclosure conversation – one where information is provided, apologies are offered if appropriate, feelings are expressed, questions answered, and the patient and family become part of the problem-solving effort – take time to master and can be maintained only with repeated use. Basic mediation or conflict resolution training typically runs from three to five days and is followed by an apprenticeship. In hospitals, where time is a scarce resource and most providers will be involved in relatively few disclosure conversations during their careers, it is not practicable to train all physicians, nurses, and other caregivers to be first-rate managers of disclosure conversations. Instead, a core group should be formed and provided with extensive training in conflict resolution and communication skills.[24] Candidates for this group include the chief of medicine and the

---

[23] AEI–Brookings Joint Center for Regulatory Studies, April 2002.

[24] Only twelve United States medical schools require a course on physician–patient communication (Association of American Medical Colleges 2001). And a survey of graduate medical education programs found that residency programs and fellowships typically devoted only ten to twelve hours to physician–patient communication. Lefevre, Waters, and Budetti 2000.

chiefs of other services, the chief of nursing, the risk manager, the patient safety officer, and those within the institution, regardless of title, who have exhibited skills as natural problem solvers and conflict resolvers.[25] A consult service composed of people with natural skills, extensive training, and status within the institution will be a resource that health care providers who understand the complexity of conducting a disclosure conversation will learn to utilize. Consultation will also increase the likelihood that the conversation serves the interests and needs of the patient, the physician, and the hospital.

Planning Disclosure Conversations

The disclosure process is complex and requires careful planning. No matter how much or how little time is available, those who will be participating in the conversation should consider the following:

- Who has the best-established relationship with the patient or family?
- Who has the best information about the event?
- What are the best words to use in explaining the event?
- Who is emotionally able to participate in the conversation?
- Who will have the answers to patients' questions about their treatment and prognosis?
- Who will have the answers about payment for additional treatment?
- What is known about the event and what further investigation will be conducted?
- Who should lead the discussion?
- What questions are the patient and family likely to have?
- Who will be the follow-up contact person?

Using these questions as organizing principles helps assuage the turmoil of an adverse event. It is necessary to find time for careful consideration of these points and to recognize that spending time early on preparing for the disclosure conversation will ultimately save time. It is equally important to understand that disclosure is not an isolated event but part of an ongoing process that may require a series of meetings between the health care providers and the patient or family, and a series of planning sessions to prepare for those meetings.

Having the person with the best available information at the disclosure conversation is important for three reasons. First, patients expect to hear from the physician most involved and may become suspicious should that person not attend the meeting. Second, having the person with the best information present avoids having others succumb to the temptation to fill in

---

[25] Kressel et al. 2002.

the blanks by speculating about what happened. Finally, receiving information and explanations can change the way those involved in the event view each other's motives. If the physician most involved in the adverse event or error is unable to participate in the disclosure conversation, it is essential that the reason for nonattendance be made clear. In most cases, an opportunity for a future conversation with the physician should be offered. Even though it is difficult for a professional to admit that he or she does not have answers to significant questions, speculations often prove wrong. The subsequent provision of correct information that is inconsistent with the initial speculation may be seen as "changing the story" or "covering up."

Finally, when patients and their family members receive information about what happened and why after a patient has been harmed by an event or error, they may react with less anger and blame. Attribution theory research examines both how people arrive at conclusions about the causes of behavior and the resulting implications on their emotions and reactions.[26] Most people tend to attribute other people's negative behavior to the other's innate disposition, while defending their own behavior as resulting from circumstances beyond their control. The person harmed attributes the negative behavior to causes under the control of the other and responds with anger. At the same time, the person who has caused injury attributes his or her behavior to circumstances beyond his or her control. Receiving information about what happened can change the negative motivations that the patient attributes to the health care providers and avoid the anger and blame. In addition, providing information about what happened can help resolve the patient's cognitive dissonance when the physician she has trusted to provide her with care has harmed her.

Conducting Disclosure Conversations

In a disclosure conversation, the focus of the health care providers will be on explaining the adverse event, but they will also have to respond to the patient and family. Physicians have experience delivering bad news to patients and discussing treatment options. Much of this expertise is relevant to disclosure conversations, but there are other skills, often referred to as active listening skills, used by mediators and conflict resolvers that are less familiar to physicians. Developing skill as an active listener allows the physician to show attentiveness to the patient and family, acknowledge the patient's or family member's feelings, and encourage their participation in the conversation. Having a member of the consult service present allows that person to assess whether the physician is accurately gauging the patient's or family member's

---

[26] Allred 2000.

concerns and to take corrective action during the conversation. The techniques of an effective active listener include

- maintaining appropriate body language;
- keeping eye contact;
- asking the patient or family member clarifying questions rather than assuming what they intend by a statement or demand;
- identifying and responding to the patient's interests, not just to their stated positions;
- using summaries to let the patient or family member know that their concerns have been heard;
- acknowledging the patient's or family member's feelings.

The first two techniques are nonverbal responses by the listener, which may seem minor but can significantly change the patient's perception about the level of concern of the health care provider who is speaking. Research has shown that physicians who enter a room and sit down to talk with patients are perceived as spending considerably more time with the patient than physicians who are actually present for longer but stand during the conversation.[27]

Even physicians who are committed to full disclosure and are comfortable participating in difficult conversations, showing concern, sharing information, and remaining nondefensive are nonetheless often ineffective listeners. They make assumptions about the meaning of statements or questions, do not use a summary of what the patient or family member said to show that they have been listening, and fail to acknowledge the feelings that have been expressed. Nor do they explain plans for gathering additional information, ask the patient and family members what they think about the plans, or ask for suggestions. Even basic questions (e.g., "What would be helpful to you?") and basic information (e.g., a telephone number and name of a hospital staff member who can answer follow-up questions) are often omitted.

During the disclosure conversation, it may fall to the expert disclosure consultant to draw out frightened, confused, or disempowered patients or family members. Families who feel that their views are valued may reveal information such as a failure of a provider to listen when the patient questioned an action, poor communication between providers, consequences of staffing shortages, and other ignored patient or family observations, complaints, or suggestions. This sort of information may be key to selecting measures to improve patient safety. Inviting patient and family input also may reveal concerns about how they were treated, which, although not material to health outcomes, may be critical to how families interpret and respond to adverse events.

[27] Strasser et al. 2003.

Goals Differ for Participants

The goals and motivations of the physician and other health care professionals during a disclosure conversation may be different from those of department heads or hospital administrators, a fact which further complicates planning and conducting the conversation. The health care professional may be anxious to get the conversation over with as quickly and painlessly as possible, with minimal damage to the relationship with the patient and to the provider's reputation and self-image. The hospital, on the other hand, may be interested in additional goals such as gathering information – for example, about system failure, communication problems among caregivers, or failure to listen to the patient's or family's attempts to question what was going on. Being aware of participants' diverse goals and motivations allows disclosure conversation planning to be responsive to the interests of each.

It will most likely be the expert consultant who will be aware that three conversations tend to occur simultaneously in any "difficult conversation." Stone, Patton, and Heen explained that each difficult conversation is really a conversation about what happened; a conversation about the feelings being experienced by the participants; and an identity conversation, which is the internal conversation we have with ourselves about what a situation means to us.[28] The consultant will be equipped to address the issues raised by these three simultaneous conversations.

Debriefing After Disclosure Conversations

Not only are communication skills of the core group of consultants vital to planning and conducting the disclosure conversation, but also the empathy and experience of these experts are essential in debriefing health care providers after an adverse event. In training sessions, physicians have told us they wish the hospital's culture supported discussions with colleagues after an adverse event. Without the opportunity to process their own emotions, the health care provider is much less able to focus on the needs of the patient or family and will be unable to learn from the event in order to improve patient care. If senior staff members responded to news of an adverse event by discussing their own past mistakes, such openness would be a powerful source of support for other physicians.[29]

An adverse event often brings into sharp focus the fact that grief is an occupational reality for health care professionals. Although less commonly acknowledged than feelings of shame, guilt, and failure, research shows that grief-related job stress can be activated by witnessing a patient suffering, by failure of a treatment, or by a treatment error. The research also shows that health care professionals develop a variety of coping strategies for dealing

[28] Stone, Patton, and Heen 1999, 7–8.
[29] Vincent 2003, 1051–6.

with stress and suggests that a hospital can meet the emotional needs of its staff by understanding and supporting these coping strategies.[30]

A consult service can guide the planning process before a disclosure conversation and help conduct the actual conversation. After an adverse event, it should be just as routine to seek communication process expertise as to request a psychiatric or palliative care consult. The consultant can make certain that the patient and family are clear about the next steps the hospital will be taking and whom to contact with questions and concerns. Clarity about future communication confirms the hospital's commitment to openness and sharing of information.

Consider again the case of Mr. B. The physicians might have benefited from a consultation with a communications expert who could have helped them deal with their own emotions, plan a follow-up conversation with the widow, consider what type of apology might be appropriate, and tell the widow that they too were grieving. A follow-up conversation would have provided a setting where the physicians could answer the family's questions about what happened to their loved one, including, in this case, why a medical student rather than a senior physician was performing the procedure.

APOLOGIZE WHEN APPROPRIATE

Traditionally, advice to physicians from lawyers and risk managers has been: Say as little as possible after an adverse event and do not apologize, or if you do be sure you do not admit fault.[31] This advice flies in the face of what research tells us patients are looking for after an adverse event[32] and of recent empirical studies by Robbennolt and Mazor that demonstrate the value of an appropriate apology and disclosure of information.[33]

The doctor–patient relationship is built on trust. Patients trust their doctors to diagnose their problems and design appropriate treatment plans – plans that may involve difficult and uncomfortable interventions. When an error occurs, this trust is violated. When the physician fails to acknowledge the error and to apologize, the injury is compounded. We expect that someone worthy of our trust will do the right thing and will behave ethically by taking responsibility for harming us.

Apologies usually take one of two forms. Apologies of responsibility – "I'm sorry I did this to you" – are also referred to as full apologies. Apologies

---

[30] Redinbaugh et al. 2001.

[31] See, e.g., Fiesta 1994. The author recognizes that what often most upsets patients and family members is poor communication on the part of physicians, but nonetheless buys into the traditional fear of apology mindset cautioning health care providers never to admit fault. In contrast see J. Cohen 1999; Levi 1997.

[32] Gallagher et al. 2003; Levinson et al. 1997; Hickson et al. 1992.

[33] Robbennolt 2004; Mazor, Simon, Yood, et al. 2004.

of sympathy – "I'm sorry this happened to you" – are also called partial apologies. Until recently, many people thought that a partial apology would always be preferable to saying nothing. But research by Jennifer Robbennolt (2004), in the context of a nonmedical tort, suggests that where fault is clear a partial apology may have a worse effect than saying nothing. When an individual who was clearly responsible for an injury fails to take responsibility, the injured party is less likely to accept a settlement. In that situation, no apology may be preferable to a partial apology.[34]

Robbennolt's findings regarding the impact of a full apology show that the person making the apology "was seen as having offered a more sufficient apology, as experiencing more regret, as being more moral, as being more likely to be careful in the future, as believing that he or she was more responsible for the incident, and as having behaved less badly. In addition, participants who received a full apology expressed greater sympathy, less anger, and more willingness to forgive the offender," and were more positive about the future relationship with the offender and the adequacy of settlement offers.[35] Research by Mazor and colleagues (2004) reports similar findings in the medical context. They found that after full disclosure and an apology, respondents were more trusting, satisfied, and less likely to change physicians than when they received incomplete and evasive explanations.[36] The Mazor study did not find that the form of disclosure affected the likelihood that the patient would consult a lawyer, at least in the case of serious harm. But where harm is serious, seeking legal expertise is appropriate and need not inevitably lead to adversarial litigation.

If further studies support these findings – and we anticipate that they will – physicians and hospitals will need to think carefully about the words they use when disclosing an error and apologizing. Situations in which a mistake has been made but the health care provider was not negligent, or in which the patient suffers from an adverse event after being warned that the event might occur, provide special challenges. For example, what is the appropriate response when a mistake has been made but the physician was not negligent? When a surgeon nicks the bowel during surgery, a mistake has been made but the physician's conduct may have been well within acceptable standards of care and not be grounds for a legal claim of negligence. What is the appropriate response when the appropriate treatment is correctly selected and provided, but the consequence of the treatment happens to be harm to the patient? The physician may feel he or she has nothing to apologize for because the patient and family were warned of the risks of the treatment. But the patient, despite being advised in advance of the risks of treatment, may have been emotionally unable to hear the warnings and instead believe that

[34] Robbennolt 2003.
[35] Robbennolt 2004, 3.
[36] Mazor, Simon, Yood, et al. 2004, 409–18.

someone must have done something wrong. If the communication is seen as evasive, the already damaged relationship between the medical professionals and the family is likely to be further harmed, and the likelihood of litigation and the cost of settlement will go up.

More research is needed on the complex topics of the impact of disclosure and apology. But our advice is always to disclose when harm has occurred, for several reasons. First, it is the right thing to do. Patients have the right – legal and moral – to know what has happened to them and why. In addition, they need details in order to make informed decisions about further treatment. Full disclosure invites the kind of conversation with the patient and family members that might be critical to avoiding reoccurrence of the harm.

Furthermore, if the hospital and health care provider have enough information to know that they caused the adverse event, medical error, or mistake, an apology is warranted from both a pragmatic and ethical standpoint. If fault is clear, an apology of responsibility should be offered. A clear explanation, one that adjusts the content and pace of discussion to the ability of the patient or family to absorb what is being said, allows time and opportunity for questions, and honors cultural norms, is the best course of action.

Although it is important to match the content and type of apology to the nature of the event, it is also important that whatever is said is authentic. In our work as mediators in nonmedical malpractice cases, we have observed the damaging effect of grudging or hollow apologies, or what Lazare refers to as a "botched apology."[37] What this means is that insincere apologies offered only for strategic advantage may do more harm than good.[38]

Twenty-four states have passed statutes protecting apologies from being used against the apologizer at trial.[39] Only Arizona, Colorado, Connecticut, Georgia, and Oregon give protection to full apologies or apologies of responsibility – and only in the health care setting.[40] Ironically, the laws that protect only partial apologies discourage the most desirable form of apology, both from a moral and pragmatic perspective, while encouraging a type of apology that may be counterproductive. As Daniel Serviansky pointed out (2004), laws that protect only apologies of sympathy are likely to be the result of legislative compromise between advocates of protection for full

---

[37] Lazare 1995; Oregon Revised Statutes § 677.082.

[38] See Partners for Patient Safety (2004) video, for vivid examples of nonapology, inauthentic, partial apology, and full apology. See Berlinger 2003 for discussion of what beyond apology is required to achieve "true grace."

[39] The states that provide protection for apologies of sympathy / partial apologies are California, Florida, Massachusetts, New Hampshire, and Texas. Arizona, Colorado, Connecticut, Georgia, Illinois, Louisiana, Maine, Maryland, Missouri, Montana, North Carolina, Ohio, Oklahoma, Oregon, South Dakota, Virginia, Washington, West Virginia, and Wyoming protect apologies of sympathies / partial apologies by health care providers.

[40] See J. Cohen 2002 for a comprehensive discussion of arguments for and against laws barring admissibility of apologies.

apology and those who want to maintain admissibility. Although compromise is vital to the legislative process, it may have produced undesirable results in the apology statutes.

We are not advocating apologies simply as a tactic to avoid litigation and adequate compensation when a patient is injured by a health care provider's error. We do think that appropriate apologies accompanied, when warranted, by a fair offer of compensation can reduce litigation and its unnecessary costs – both emotional and financial; begin to repair the physician–patient relationship; and set a tone that allows patients and their families to be part of the discussion about how to avoid future errors.

USE MEDIATION TO RESOLVE CLAIMS PROMPTLY

Mediation is a confidential, voluntary process in which an impartial third party – the mediator or, at times, comediators – works with parties in a dispute to help them negotiate a resolution to their conflict. It is based on three core values: autonomy, informed decision making, and confidentiality. Mediation has a number of advantages over other dispute resolution processes.

- The parties make decisions about the resolution rather than having it imposed on them by a judge or arbitrator.
- Participants can discuss all issues that are important to them, not just those that provide the basis for a legal claim.
- Because it is a confidential process, apologies made during the mediation will not be admissible in subsequent litigation should the parties fail to reach agreement.
- The mediation process helps the parties overcome some of the barriers that prevent agreement in negotiations.
- When used soon after an injury, it can allow the parties to resolve claims promptly, thereby allowing both patients and physicians to avoid the added emotional and economic costs incurred during the discovery process.
- Where appropriate, injured patients can receive compensation sooner.
- In mediation, participants have the opportunity to exchange information that may be critical both to repairing the relationship between the physician and the patient and to making changes that will improve patient safety.

Participants Make the Decisions

Unlike arbitration, in which the arbitrator decides who is right or wrong and imposes a resolution, in mediation the parties are the decision makers. Participants retain control over the outcome, are not required to settle, and are free to end the process at any point and return to litigation. Mediators work with the parties to help them identify interests, exchange information, and explore and evaluate options. They guide the process and facilitate the conversation but do not make legal findings. At least three hospital systems have patients in nonemergent cases sign an agreement to use mediation before filing a medical malpractice lawsuit.[41] Because participants are free to end participation in mediation if they do not find the process useful, agreements to mediate do not raise the due process concerns raised by agreements for binding arbitration.

Participants Can Discuss All Issues Which Are Important to Them

Mediation can provide maximum value when parties are encouraged to resolve not just the legal and financial issues but all of their concerns. In mediation, participants can bring up issues that are important to them even if those issues do not provide the basis of a legal claim. A challenge for mediators in medical malpractice cases is to expand the discussion beyond the traditional focus of settlement discussions: money alone.

Consider the case of Mr. L.

Mr. L, an unmarried man in his early 30s with a long history of sickle cell anemia who lived with his mother, went to the emergency room of a city hospital with what turned out to be chronic hepatitis. The initial diagnosis included partial bowel obstruction. It was the day before a national holiday. There were no attending physicians present in the emergency room and the staff on duty could not answer the family's questions about laboratory results for tests that had been performed several days before, nor could they discuss Mr. L's case knowledgeably.

Mr. L was admitted to the hospital and died there several days later. The family remained convinced that the staff shortage on the day of admission contributed to his death. The plaintiff's and defense lawyers disagreed about the medical explanation of the cause of death but in the mediation agreed to put aside these differences and concentrate on the issues that could lead to resolution.

The mother's strong feelings were viewed as such a liability that both she and her lawyer agreed before the mediation that she would not speak for fear of destroying the negotiation. In the first caucus the plaintiff's lawyer explained the rationale for her not speaking in the joint session. With reassurances and coaching from the mediators, they ultimately recognized that the anger expressed in a caucus could be safely expressed to the hospital's lawyer and channeled into a constructive proposal that would identify for the hospital how staffing affected patient safety.

The settlement agreement included both a monetary amount and a provision that a letter to be written by the plaintiff and her attorney describing the staff shortages on that holiday weekend and raising concerns about understaffing at such times would be delivered by defense counsel to the chief executive officer of the hospital. The

---

[41] McGoldrick 2004; Oxholm 2004; Kidwell 2004.

agreement about the letter allowed the family to hope that their loss might prevent another family's suffering. At the end of the mediation, plaintiff's counsel said Mr. L's mother's eyes were shining at the prospect of writing the letter.

Mediation Styles Differ

Mediators vary in their styles – that is, in their philosophy, the techniques they use, what they see as the goals of the process, how they deal with feelings, and whether or not they evaluate cases.[42] It is important for hospitals and physicians to consider which approach is appropriate and select a mediator accordingly. We generally advocate using mediation soon after an injury has occurred or a claim has been filed and selecting mediators who are trained to deal with a broad range of issues, not just those relevant to the legal claim; who are comfortable helping all participants express their often quite strong feelings; who recognize the value of noneconomic agreements; and who are skilled at facilitating a learning conversation that can lead to an exchange of information critical to preventing an adverse event's reoccurrence. Mediators describe this approach as "facilitative" mediation.

Some well-known medical malpractice mediation programs use retired judges or active medical malpractice defense and plaintiffs' lawyers to mediate cases when the trial date is near.[43] In those programs, the focus is on finding a dollar amount that will settle the case. The plaintiffs, although usually present, are not active participants, and apologies are offered only after an agreement.[44] The mediators use an "evaluative" style. They frequently offer their opinion of the value of the case and their prediction of the outcome if the case were to proceed to trial. These mediations often feel familiar to the attorneys because they resemble judges' settlement conferences. In our opinion, it is risky for mediators to predict a judicial outcome, as it is unlikely that after a few hours or even days of mediation the mediator will acquire necessary information to make an accurate prediction of outcome. Counsel or parties may keep in reserve information that might be valuable at trial should mediation be unsuccessful, or they may withhold unfavorable information from the mediator. In addition, the information presented at mediation is substantially different from what would be permitted at trial. Even more important, evaluative mediators, because of their focus on the money, too often fail to help the patient realize the broader, often healing, benefits of mediation.

The lines drawn between these two styles are not absolute. In a particular case, a facilitative mediator may respond to a party's request for an opinion of the case's value or, after some hours of work, make a mediator's proposal. It is less likely that an evaluative mediator will be able to

---

[42] See Riskin 2003 for discussion of mediator styles.
[43] Brown 1998.
[44] Brown 2003.

expand her style to include areas of inquiry used by a facilitative media-tor. It is important for physicians, hospital leaders, and their lawyers to be aware of the benefits of different mediator approaches, to resist the tempta-tion to select the evaluative approach because it seems familiar, and, instead, to choose mediators with the skills to match the needs of the parties and of the case. In addition, because evaluative mediation tends to occur much later in the litigation process, any information about practices that may have led to the harm can be so dated as to have little use in improving patient safety.[45]

Apologies Offered During Mediation, a Confidential Process, Are Likely Protected From Admissibility in Court

As discussed previously, physicians are often afraid to offer apologies after an adverse event out of fear that the apology will be used against them should the case go to trial. More states have statutes protecting confidentiality of mediation communications than apologies. Well over half of the states have enacted laws protecting mediation communications, and six have adopted the sophisticated and well-thought-out Uniform Mediation Act. In jurisdic-tions where statutory protection is lacking, parties sign written mediation agreements in which all participants contract to keep mediation communi-cations confidential and agree that what is said in mediation will not be used by any of them in subsequent adjudicatory proceedings. Evidentiary rules barring admission of settlement discussions are likely to give additional pro-tection against use of mediation communications in subsequent litigation. It is more difficult, however, to predict how courts will treat attempts by nonparties to the mediation to discover what was said in a mediation. The strong public interest in encouraging settlement and promoting the use of mediation is likely to lead to courts granting broad, if not total, confiden-tiality for mediation communications.

Mediation Helps the Parties Overcome Barriers That Prevent Negotiated Agreements

Many factors keep cases from settling until the parties are on the "courthouse steps" – if then. Imperfect information, personality clashes between lawyers, and psychological phenomena such as reactive devaluation (devaluing pro-posals made by an adversary) and loss aversion (rejecting or accepting an option depending on whether it is seen as a gain or a loss) all set up barri-ers to settlement.[46] Mediators use a number of techniques to counter these

---

[45] Sage 2004b.
[46] Arrow et al. 1995; Mnookin, Peppet, and Tulumello 2000, 156–72.

phenomena[47] and to encourage the exchange of information that can change the participants' perceptions of each other, help them refine their own goals and preferences, help them understand the medical facts, and evaluate the legal claim. Mediators meet with the parties to explore not just their legal positions but also the underlying interests represented by those positions and to explore monetary as well as nonmonetary options.

Mediation Used Soon After an Injury Can Help Parties to Resolve Claims Promptly

We recommend that hospitals and plaintiffs consider using mediation to settle claims as soon as both sides have had time to evaluate the merits of a claim, rather than waiting until the often brutal discovery process has increased the emotional and economic costs for all parties. It is important that both sides are equipped to make informed judgments about the merits and value of a case and that patients have time, if they choose, to consult lawyers. It is also important to realize that the information needed to make an assessment of the value of a case is different and much more limited than that needed to prove or defend a case at trial. It costs an estimated $60,000 to defend a standard medical malpractice case[48] and as much as $100,000 to present a wrongful death claim.[49] At a minimum, early mediation will save a good deal of these transaction costs for both sides and at the same time avoid having physicians, hospital administrators, and other health care providers spend days preparing for and tied up in depositions. In addition, settling a case early allows the plaintiff to receive funds needed to deal with the aftermath of an injury when they may be most needed.

Hospitals, physicians, and insurers share in the decisions shaping a disclosure policy. We know of one hospital and two hospital systems that make offers of compensation before a claim has been filed: the Veterans Affairs Medical Center in Lexington, Kentucky ("Lexington VA"); Catholic Healthcare West ("CHW"), a forty-eight-hospital, nonprofit health care system in the western United States; and the University of Michigan Health System.

The Lexington VA in 1987 instituted a radical policy of apologizing to patients as soon as possible after the occurrence of a medical error, and when appropriate offering a fair settlement.[50] It makes the disclosure even if the patient has been discharged and must be tracked down. During the disclosure conversation, the chief of staff acknowledges the error or event, apologizes,

---

47 See Dubler and Liebman 2004 for a discussion of mediation techniques especially useful in resolving health care disputes.
48 Lee 2004.
49 Zimmerman 2004.
50 Kraman and Hamm 1999.

and gives a full explanation of the harm caused and the steps the hospital has taken to correct the problem and prevent future harm. The patient and family have the opportunity to ask questions and are advised to retain a lawyer to help them in the resolution process. Options are reviewed and settlement discussions are initiated. As a result of this policy, the Lexington VA has experienced moderate liability payments, with the payments negotiated based on calculations of actual loss. In 2000, the mean malpractice settlement with the VA system was $98,000 while the average settlement for the Lexington VA was $15,000.[51] Although the federal hospital system and its employees have a limited exposure to liability, unlike physicians and hospitals in the private sector, the ethical and practical rationale for disclosure would seem to apply in both settings.

CHW also incorporates fair compensation into its disclosure process.[52] After an adverse event, patients and their families are given a copy of the medical record and all relevant information about the event, the extent and the cause of the harm, and the right to fair compensation. Unlike the federal system, CHW has had to negotiate with its own insurers as well as its voluntary physicians to gain their acceptance of the disclosure policy and to overcome resistance based on fear of increased malpractice premiums or other negative consequences of settlement. A risk manager initiates the discussion of fair compensation and focuses, as does the VA, on actual losses: out-of-pocket expenses, lost wages, reduction in income, disability, and other relevant factors.[53] CHW is aware that families trying to cope with serious injury or loss of a loved one may need a lawyer to provide a frame of reference for deciding whether an offer of compensation is fair. CHW includes the obligation to advise patients and family members to consult a lawyer to represent them in their statement of principles for managing error.[54] As Carol Bayley, CHW's ethicist, put it, "We think we can work things out between us [and patients or their families] and we certainly don't want to be adversarial, but neither do we want them to wonder down the line whether they really were treated fairly. We suggest that a lawyer can help them be at peace with whatever we work out."[55]

The University of Michigan Health System in 2002 began a program in which physicians report errors and, after review by risk management, disclose the error to patients and families and apologize. The impact on the health system's rate of litigation has been dramatic. In June 2001 the average number of claims against the system was 250–260, and it took an average of 1,100 days to dispose of cases. By December 2004, the number of open

---

[51] Hamm and Kraman 2001.
[52] Berlinger 2004.
[53] Ibid.; Bayley 2001.
[54] Bayley 2001.
[55] Bayley 2004.

claims had fallen to 130 and claims were being resolved in 320 days.[56] The cost of handling claims has also declined from approximately $3 million to $1 million for attorneys' fees.[57]

Several insurance companies have taken more limited steps toward payment to patients and their families for expenses and lost earnings after a medical error or adverse event without directly addressing the issue of fair compensation. A leading example is COPIC Insurance Company ("COPIC"), a medical professional liability insurer in Colorado. In 2000, COPIC started a postincident risk management program called the 3 Rs Program. Within forty-eight to seventy-two hours of a complication or injury to the patient, this program seeks to have the physician and patient engage in an open, honest, empathic conversation in which the physician explains what happened, any additional treatment, steps that will be taken to minimize recurrence, and answers questions. If the patient has a medical disability as a result of the injury or complication, the program, within seventy-two hours of the injury, can offer to pay $100 a day for up to fifty days. Any additional out-of-pocket expenses of the patient related to the injury, such as home care costs, child care, or flying a relative in from out of town, or additional hospital expenses, can also be paid. The total maximum benefit payable to a patient is $30,000. The patient is not asked to sign a waiver or general release and therefore is able to file a liability claim despite having received the payment, but few patients have done so.[58] It is too soon to know whether these tangible acknowledgments of responsibility and caring will have an impact on the rate of litigation, but initial experience in the COPIC program suggests that the volume of litigation is being reduced.[59]

Based on research findings, clear ethical directives, and the experiences of these institutions, we endorse a disclosure process that offers prompt compensation for immediate needs without requiring patients to waive their legal rights. We also encourage an early attempt to settle claims before lawsuits have been filed but after patients and their families have consulted lawyers. We recognize in some cases – for example, when the long-term impact of the error is uncertain or other information needed to evaluate the worth of the claim is unavailable – that early settlement may not be appropriate.

When an early settlement program has credibility, it will often be possible for health care providers, hospital representatives, their lawyers, insurers, patients, their families, and usually legal counsel to resolve issues of compensation themselves. In other instances, it will be necessary for a neutral third party to be involved in these negotiations. We recommend mediation as the process best able to assist in these negotiations.

[56] Boothman 2004.
[57] Berg 2004.
[58] COPIC 2000; Taylor 2003.
[59] Taylor 2003.

Repairing the Physician–Patient Relationship and Improving Patient Safety

Mediation enables patients and families, who have brought lawsuits because they could not get information, to be heard and have their questions answered. It is also a setting in which both legally relevant claims and concerns that could not presented in court can be discussed and resolved. Consequently, the hospital and physicians can acquire information about failures of health care providers to follow hospital practices and about ways patients and families are treated – in a nonmedical sense – which may have contributed to a decision to sue.

Consider the case of Mr. D:

Mr. D, an elderly man on Coumidin, arrived in the *ER* the morning after a fall. He was accompanied by his wife. Mr. D was initially misdiagnosed as having an infection rather than internal bleeding. After a second reading of the *CT* scan later in the day the correct diagnosis was made, but he died before remedial steps could be taken. Contrary to hospital policy, Mrs. D was not allowed to be with her husband during his final hours of life spent in the emergency room. As soon as the hospital leaders learned of the error, they talked to the attending physician, who met with the widow to disclose what had happened.

At the mediation, the chief of medicine was able to listen empathically to the anger of the widow and respond with an apology of responsibility, acknowledging the hospital's complete responsibility for the misdiagnosis and explaining exactly what the treatment had been. He became the embodiment of the hospital for the plaintiff, which gave her the opportunity to express fully her rage and sadness and then her gratitude in response to his apology, his patience, and his clarifications. The presence of the chief of medicine and his participation was healing for the widow and probably could not have been accomplished as successfully by their attorney or risk manager. His stature as chief of medicine and his commitment of time to the mediation eloquently conveyed the hospital's determination to accept responsibility and learn from their mistakes.

The mediation process allowed both the hospital and the widow to benefit in ways that would not have been possible in litigation. The hospital learned of a correctable gap between policy and practice regarding family access to patients in the emergency room and agreed to provide additional training for ER staff. The widow was reassured that the outcome for her husband would not have changed had she been able to persuade him to go to the emergency room earlier. The exchange of information was possible for several reasons:

1. The informality of mediation encourages discussion without the hindrance of rules of evidence.
2. The people with information about the event and the ability to explain it authoritatively were present.

3. The mediators were interested in having the parties tell their stories fully, rather than confining the focus to the amount of money that would settle the case.

In this case not only was the lawsuit settled in the mediation for monetary and nonmonetary remedies, including an annual memorial lecture in honor of the deceased and additional training for the ER staff, but significant progress toward repairing the relationship between the hospital and the deceased patient's family was also made, and the hospital learned ways it could improve.

Barriers to Use of Mediation

In our experience, the resistance to using mediation to resolve medical malpractice lawsuits is in part the fear of the unknown or slightly known. Many plaintiff and defense counsel do not regularly participate in mediations or are more familiar with evaluative mediation ordered by a court when a case is close to trial. In both these contexts, the full benefits of mediation are not available. Either the litigation has been protracted, the parties' positions have hardened and money is the only issue of interest to them, or the mediator's limited perspective leads him to focus on money and use an approach that is often described by lawyers as "beating up on both sides" until they settle. Familiarity with facilitative mediation and its use earlier in the litigation process would increase attorneys' understanding and convince them, through personal experience, of the utility of the process.

Deciding to mediate a case after a decision has been made about exposure and liability requires a leap of faith for attorneys who are trained to equate extensive discovery with diligence. Voluntarily limiting discovery is uncomfortable for many litigators and decreases defense counsel's billable hours. These negatives can be countered by experiencing the benefits for their clients and developing expertise in identifying cases best suited to mediation and determining when to engage in the process.

Physicians can be resistant to mediation because they believe litigation provides them an opportunity for a "win" and for personal vindication. What is not well understood by physicians is that a small percentage of cases go to trial and an even smaller number go to verdict. In state courts, where most medical malpractice cases are heard, only 15.8 percent of all cases filed go to trial[60] and in federal courts the trial rate has dropped to 1.8 percent.[61] The vast majority of cases are settled before a verdict, so the question is whether to settle earlier or later.

---

[60] Lande 2004, 20.
[61] Galanter 2004, 3.

Medical liability insurance companies are reluctant to start a mediation program for fear that it would encourage smaller claims, ones not currently pursued by plaintiffs' attorneys because of high out-of-pocket expenses that might not be recouped.[62] The initiative to start such a mediation program will likely come from clients – that is, physicians and hospitals – when they have experienced its benefits.

Time pressures of modern medical practice make physicians and hospital personnel reluctant to attend mediations, especially when they are dubious about the benefits of being at the table. When physicians participate in a medical malpractice mediation, focus is broadened to include discussion of the medical care provided as well as claims for monetary damages. Physicians are better able than attorneys or risk managers to explain treatment choices and their consequence, and to provide the patient and family members with more complete understanding of what occurred. The physician either personally or on behalf of the institution is able to experience the relief of having eased some of the pain for family members or the patient, and may receive a measure of forgiveness from the patient or family members.

CONCLUSION

Medical errors and adverse events are unavoidable, but the number of errors is more likely to be reduced if physicians and other health care providers are able to speak freely with each other and with patients about what has happened. When conducted with skill, disclosure conversations provide the opportunity to answer the questions of patients and families, reassure them about the competence and good intentions of their caregivers, and help them deal with the consequences of the harm. Poorly done disclosure conversations create anger, mistrust, and an increased risk of being sued. We need to study disclosure conversations to better anticipate questions from patients and families, to understand what content is most effective,[63] and to measure the impact, if any, on patient safety.

Communication with someone whom you have harmed is difficult. Physicians and other health care providers should be supported by communication experts as they plan and conduct disclosure conversations. It will be important to track the impact on the rate of disclosure and the rate of malpractice litigation of the new laws requiring health care facilities to disclose medical errors and adverse events to patients and families. It will also be important to learn from the experience of five states protecting full apologies by health care professionals whether that protection leads to improved communication between physicians and patients and whether apologies result in less malpractice litigation.

---

[62] Dauer, Marcus, and Payne 2000.
[63] See Mazor, Simon, and Gurwitz 2004 for a survey of research on disclosure conversations.

Unlike many of the recommendations being made to cure the ills of the health care system that require new laws or regulations, all of the proposals in this chapter can be undertaken by hospitals and physicians now. All that is needed is the courage to question conventional wisdom; the imagination to see the benefits to patients and physicians of full disclosure after an error, apology, fair offers of compensation, and the use of mediation when needed; and the will to adopt new policies and procedures and to invest the relatively limited resources needed to implement them.

FOUR

IN SEARCH OF A "NEW PARADIGM"

12

Enterprise Liability in the Twenty-First Century

Randall R. Bovbjerg and Robert Berenson

For decades health policy advocacy and analysis have tried to solve two apparently separate and seemingly intractable problems. First, physicians and other providers can face extreme difficulties in obtaining and financing malpractice insurance – and periodic insurance crises demand policy makers' attention. Second, preventable injuries to patients occur all too frequently in the course of health care. This continuing reality received new prominence from the Institute of Medicine's (IOM's) landmark 2000 book *To Err Is Human*, which also described new methods of systematically promoting patient safety.[1] Reformers have long proposed a shift from individual to enterprise liability, both to improve the efficiency and operations of liability insurance and to enhance patients' safety. This chapter examines the theory of and the prospects for institutional liability, given recent evolution of tort law and of medical service delivery.

TODAY'S POLICY CONTEXT

The malpractice insurance crisis proclaimed in the early 2000s is the third in thirty years. For several years, many practitioners in many states had to scramble for coverage or struggle to afford what they find.[2] Physicians typically must have insurance coverage to practice; coverage is normally required by hospitals as a condition of privileges, by managed care organizations as a condition for inclusion in provider networks, and occasionally even by states as a condition of licensure, as in Pennsylvania.[3] Like the past two, this crisis has been more severe and longer lasting for medical liability than for other types of property-casualty insurance. Medical risks are harder to predict and reserve against than others because medical claims are relatively infrequent

---

[1] Institute of Medicine 2000.
[2] Mello, Studdert, and Brennan 2003; Sage 2003a, 2004b.
[3] Bovbjerg and Bartow 2003.

but very large, and both the rate of claims and the size of payout are highly variable. Moreover, most claims are slow to resolve. This long "tail" of disputation prolongs uncertainty and increases fiscal disruption for insurers if claims trends have been inaccurately projected.[4] As of early 2005, the most recent crisis may be abating. Medical liability insurance markets are once again returning to a kind of "normalcy," although not in all localities.

Yet for physicians and hospitals, each postcrisis return to normalcy has meant higher premiums than before as well as reduced choice of insurance carrier or less coverage.[5] From the mid-crisis year of 1975 to that of 2002, total medical liability premiums grew more than five times faster than the consumer price index and almost two-thirds faster even than other, rapidly rising, health care spending.[6] Distributional issues may also affect access to medical care. For example, high-risk specialists in high-risk locales bear a high share of overall cost, and physicians nearing retirement face disincentives to gradually phasing out their services, especially obstetricians, who face a very long tail of liability for delivering babies.[7] Even after providers have weathered the storm, a climate of inefficiency remains in liability insurance markets.

Unlike insurance crisis, high levels of avoidable injury are not a periodic, acute problem but rather a nagging chronic condition. Medicine and the greater health care system have made remarkable progress in extending lives and reducing disability and suffering, albeit at high cost and with uneven quality.[8] In terms of avoiding new injury to patients, however, progress seems elusive. Detailed studies continue to find a troubling incidence of preventable injury: Some 2 percent of hospitalizations seem to incur avoidable injuries. About half of those, or 1 percent of the total, are due to negligence in that they do not meet a defined professional standard of care.[9] Nonhospital care is less studied, but preventable injuries exist throughout health care.[10]

These recurrent insurance crisis and continuing injury problems have renewed concerns about the performance of today's liability system – personal injury law and process as funded and staffed by liability insurance policies bought by each medical provider. The most important legal rationale for imposing liability on physicians and other medical providers is that doing

---

[4] Insurers surprised by a rise in claims payouts must not only raise future premiums but also increase claims-reserve funding for many years of past claims in the "pipeline" awaiting resolution. See generally Sloan et al. 1991; Bovbjerg 2005a.

[5] Bovbjerg 2005a.

[6] Calculations by authors from Sutter 2003; CMS 2005b; and Federal Reserve Bank 2005.

[7] Sage 2004b; Bovbjerg 2005a.

[8] See, e.g., Peterson et al. 1956 (60% of directly observed therapy below acceptable standards); Institute of Medicine 2001 (large share of medical encounters feature overuse, underuse, or misuse of medical care).

[9] Mills et al. 1977; Brennan et al. 1991; Thomas et al. 2000; see also sources given in Institute of Medicine 2000; Wachter and Shojania 2004.

[10] See sources cited in Institute of Medicine 2000; Miller and Bovbjerg 2002; Lapetina and Armstrong 2002.

so deters substandard practice.[11] Beyond legal theory, however, the evidence that deterrence works in practice is not strong.[12] Moreover, despite whatever positive effect liability may now have, it has left patients exposed to the high levels of error and avoidable injury documented in so many studies.[13]

Providers naturally want a stable liability insurance market so that they can buy coverage to protect their assets. The key social rationale for maintaining access to such protection is that it allows providers to undertake risky activities, namely treating sick and injured patients, especially fragile patients. Given the seriousness of injury that can occur, such risks are manageable only where spread across many insureds. Liability insurance also assures compensation for successful claimants, up to the level of defendants' policy limits. Insurance supplies the financing without which today's high-award cases would usually be infeasible to pursue or pay out.

Insurance makes today's liability system feasible, but it also dilutes the risk-reduction incentives that liability law ostensibly creates for defendants. Insurers defend and pay claims, so "tortfeasors" themselves avoid the law's intended economic incentives except where insurers can impose new controls or incentives on insureds' behavior. (Insurance is recognized to conflict with deterrence in that state law often bans coverage of punitive damages, which are meant only to deter and not to compensate.) Moreover, inefficiencies arise because medical practitioners and institutions are sued and insured separately: The presence of multiple defendants makes litigation more complex and, according to conventional wisdom, easier for claimants to win. Furthermore, variation in liability outcomes for different defendants even within a single incident confuses deterrent signals to caregivers. Separate risk bearing and claims resolution also increases total system expense well above the cost of the payouts that benefit claimants. Every party needs their own expert consultants and witnesses, for example.

To improve insurance risk-bearing as well as patient safety, many analysts have long proposed that hospitals or other institutions should assume some or all of the liability for medical injuries now borne by individual practitioners. We turn next to the history of institutional liability under existing law and the parallel history of reform proposals.

THE RISE OF INSTITUTIONS – AND OF THEIR LEGAL RESPONSIBILITIES

Hospitals have long been the health care system's main medical institution, but they traditionally had almost no role in medical liability. Early tort law looked almost exclusively to physicians if a patient was injured in the course of care because physicians in that era made and implemented almost all

---

[11] Bovbjerg 1986; Mello and Brennan 2002.
[12] Bovbjerg and Sloan 1998; Mello and Brennan 2002.
[13] See citations in notes 9 and 10 supra.

decisions about diagnosis and treatment. Hospitals were perceived as merely a "doctor's workshop" rather than as providers of patient care in their own right.[14] Legal doctrine also shielded hospitals from liability – for non-profit hospitals by charitable immunity and for public facilities by sovereign immunity.[15]

Physicians were often held responsible even for the acts of hospital personnel. The "captain of the ship" doctrine deemed surgeons, for example, to be in command of hospital staff in the operating room.[16] (This doctrine also allowed courts to compensate some injured patients despite hospitals' immunity.) Traditional health insurers also had little or no liability for patient injuries, as they were far removed from clinical control, mere "third parties" expected to pay for services without active involvement in care.[17]

From the late 1950s, as institutional services and funding grew rapidly, the law increasingly curtailed traditional hospital immunities and imposed new duties.[18] Hospitals and other institutions thus became liable for their own negligence, initially with regard to nonclinical responsibilities, such as maintaining safe premises to protect against slips and falls. Over time, hospital obligations grew to include procuring and maintaining up-to-date medical equipment, having adequate staffing levels, and following safety rules. Having lost traditional immunities, hospitals as employers also became responsible for any negligence of their employees, including nurses and others involved in clinical care.[19]

Still, until the mid-1960s, community hospitals were not held liable for the negligence of physicians, even though community physicians practiced extensively in hospitals. Physicians other than house staff in large teaching hospitals typically were (and are) not hospital employees but rather "independent contractors" and hence not seen as under hospital control. Over time, in a major legal extension of their responsibilities, hospitals have also been found liable for substandard physician care where their credentialing of a physician for staff privileges was negligent or where they failed to meet recognized standards for monitoring in-hospital physician services.[20] Standards may be set by a hospital's internal rules or by external regulations.[21] A hospital can be also be found liable for the torts of a nonemployed physician who appears to be an employee or agent of the hospital.[22] Such "ostensible agency" is most obvious in emergency rooms, where patients

[14] Pauly and Redisch 1973; Starr 1982; Stevens 1989.
[15] Furrow et al. 2000, 378–80; Boumil et al. 2003.
[16] Furrow et al. 2000, 381.
[17] Califano 1986, 36–57 (chap. 3); Zelman and Berenson 1998.
[18] Southwick 1988, chap. 13; Furrow et al. 2000, 379–80.
[19] Id., 380–86.
[20] Id., 386–98.
[21] *Darling v. Charleston Community Memorial Hospital*, 33 Ill.2d 326, 211 N.E.2d 253 (1965), certiorari denied, 383 U.S. 946 (1966).
[22] Southwick 1983, 1988.

Year	Liability costs ($ millions)		Shares of total		Total liability costs		Nat'l health care spending	
	Hospitals	Physicians	Hospitals	Physcians	(nominal)	(1975$)	(nominal)	liabil. share
1975	$426.1	$526.3	41.0%	50.7%	$1,182.8	$1,182.8	$129,841.0	0.91%
2002	$6,574.6	$12,574.2	30.2%	57.7%	$24,598.0	$7,364.7	$1,553,009.0	1.58%

FIGURE 12.1. Medical Malpractice Tort Costs
Source: Authors' tabulations from sources in note 27.
Notes: Dollars are in millions; for liability costs, include losses and loss adjustment expenses; deflation to 1975 dollars by CPI.

choose the hospital rather than the physician. The ER doctors may be employed by an outside contractor, but from the patient perspective they come with the hospital and look like hospital employees or agents. Courts have also held hospitals liable for advertising or other "holding out" of physicians as their apparent employees.[23] Meanwhile, unlike conventional insurers, staff-model HMOs also began to be held liable for care provided by their affiliated physicians and hospitals.[24] Later, as "managed care" expanded from those early roots into mainstream financing, even more loosely organized health plans sometimes also faced liability.[25]

The practical result of all these changes in legal doctrine is that by the 1970s, medical tort law had become much more "institutional" than it traditionally was. Injured patients could often sue both their physician(s) and the hospital. Each practitioner or institution is normally insured separately and mounts a separate legal defense, but "joint and several" liability allows a successful claimant to collect all damages from any or all negligent defendants, regardless of their relative contributions to the injury. Institutional defendants often say that their "deep pockets" make them disproportionate targets.[26]

To what extent did these legal changes alter liability risk-bearing as measured by actual malpractice premiums? Malpractice costs can only be tracked starting in 1975 (see Figure 12.1[27]). In that year, the first major malpractice insurance crisis prompted insurers and regulators to recognize malpractice as a separate line of insurance. In 1975, hospitals indeed accounted for 41 percent of malpractice premiums, including self-insured retentions and other analogues of premiums. Physicians' share was 51 percent. This balance presumably reflected two decades of growth in hospitals' liabilities relative to doctors'.

However, the hospital share of premiums has not risen further since then. Until 1988, the hospital share hovered near 40 percent (not presented). From 1989 through 2002, it dropped to 30 percent, while that of physicians rose

[23] Furrow et al. 2000, 381–6.
[24] Bovbjerg 1975; Curran and Moseley 1975.
[25] Furrow et al. 2000, 401–22.
[26] Bovbjerg 1989.
[27] Sources: Sutter 2003; Federal Reserve Bank 2005; Centers for Medicare and Medicaid Services 2005b.

to 58 percent. Given how significantly legal doctrines seem to have increased hospital responsibilities, it is surprising that malpractice liability in practice remains so noninstitutional.[28]

HOSPITAL ENTERPRISE LIABILITY AS A MEDICAL LIABILITY REFORM

Many liability theorists have long sought to incorporate the costs of accidents into the costs of an enterprise's business, especially for larger institutions.[29] Workers' compensation effectuated the first and most thoroughgoing of such shifts a century ago. Casual jurisprudence suggests that this philosophy's rise reflected the increasing role of large corporations in industry and commerce as well as the emergence of a property and casualty insurance industry capable of large-scale funding.[30] Rationales for imposing most risks on institutions included not only that they can best manage risk by preventing injuries, as corporations have done under workers' compensation,[31] but also that enterprises can spread the risk through insurance and include the costs of compensating injury in the price of their products.[32]

Such thinking applied to health care led 1960s academics to propose increases in hospitals' legal responsibilities. One proposal was to compensate medical injuries through hospital accident insurance.[33] Another was for states to license only institutions, rather than also the physicians and others who work within them; the theory was that hospitals could better oversee physicians and other caregivers.[34] The mid-1970s brought a spate of reform proposals in response to the first nationally recognized malpractice crisis. Most proposals sought to trim back tort remedies or create publicly "backstopped" insurance pools to insure physicians.[35] An unusual, creative 1975 proposal from Myron Steves urged that hospitals insure physician liability along with hospitals' liability.

[28] The summary statistics presented in Fig. 12.1 likely reflect some imprecision in estimates of percentage shares. Hospital self-insurance in the form of high deductibles could be undercounted or hospital premiums may be overcounted where hospitals such as medical school centers insure doctors together with hospital liabilities. The Sutter report (2003) says that it adjusts for such phenomena, but the adjustments are not documented.

[29] See, e.g., Harper and James 1956 ("best and most efficient way to deal with accident loss ... is to assure accident victims of substantial compensation, and to distribute the losses involved over society as a whole or some very large segment of it"); see generally Priest 1985.

[30] Keeton et al. 1984, 584–96; see generally Sugarman 1992 (discussing different jurisprudential approaches).

[31] Bovbjerg and Sloan 1998.

[32] Keeton et al. 1984, 573 (the successful political slogan for workers' compensation was "the cost of the product should bear the blood of the Workman").

[33] Ehrenzweig 1964.

[34] Hershey 1969.

[35] Feagles et al. 1975 (legislative proposals as of 1974); Bovbjerg 1989 (enactments through the mid-1980s crisis).

Steves recommended moving from traditional liability coverage of individual practitioners to hospital-based coverage for all in-hospital care.[36] The proposal responded to physicians' need for coverage after many commercial insurers exited the market in the 1970s. Pooling claims losses at the hospital level would make them more predictable, and hence more insurable, than the disparate experience of individual physicians.[37] Other expected advantages included reduced claims-handing costs from joint investigation and defense and diminished insurance overhead from larger scale, lower sales and underwriting costs, and the like. Moreover, insurance costs would constitute a lower share of hospital revenues than of physician practice revenue, Steves argued, which would facilitate liability insurance financing. Similarly, hospital-based coverage would be more stable because hospitals provide continuity of operations over time. Such stability seemed more obvious in the 1970s than it is today, after industry downsizing and fiscal stress. Many hospitals have struggled in the current crisis to fund even their own coverage, much less that of physicians as well.[38]

The 1975 proposal also addressed medical quality. For one thing, hospital-based coverage would increase medical providers' incentives to improve outcomes, because they could thereby reduce their insurance costs.[39] Steves and others since have often noted that premiums for traditionally insured individual physicians are unaffected by their loss experience, leaving them less motivated to improve. However, hospitals are large enough to be experience rated, and they can achieve 100 percent experience rating by self-insuring.[40] Another advantage is that hospitals have more capability to take constructive action to prevent injuries that occur within them, whereas physicians "organized in small economic units" simply "cannot support proper quality control with information feedback."[41] The importance of such feedback as an improvement tool became one of the centerpieces of "patient safety" reform two decades later.[42]

Steves framed his proposal for hospital-based physician coverage as a voluntary alternative that would "improve the cost to benefit" ratio of liability insurance, not as a broad social reform demanding mandatory implementation. He also suggested that residual physician coverage for care outside hospitals be provided through national specialty societies or another

[36] Steves 1975.
[37] See Roddis and Stewart 1975, 1290–7 (companion article to Steves, describing actuarial difficulties of predicting individual physician losses, especially under "occurrence" policies that insure against claims that may be made many years after the policy year).
[38] But see Mello, Studdert, DesRoches, et al. 2004 (despite hospitals' recent struggles in Pennsylvania, some reaching out to cover physicians).
[39] Steves 1975, 1329, n. 104 (joint defense); 1325, n. 91 (continuity); and 1327–8 (quality).
[40] See Steves 1975, 1322 (on individuals) and 1326, nn. 92 and 93 (on hospitals); Danzon 1985; Sloan 1990.
[41] Steves 1975, 1331; cf. Danzon 1985 (reasons for lack of deductibles in physician policies).
[42] See later discussion of patient safety.

mechanism for pooling risk. The existence of this residual physician risk does somewhat undercut Steves's argument on insurance efficiency: If most physician liability were shifted from individual coverage to hospital coverage, the truncated insurance markets for outpatient care would lose predictive power and ability to spread risk.[43] New inefficiencies would also arise, as some litigation would arise at the boundary between ambulatory and inpatient care, necessitating a separate defense by each set of insurers.

In practice, physicians and hospitals in the late 1970s did create new mechanisms for bearing all risks, whether in or out of hospitals – by forming their own mutual and other single-line insurance enterprises.[44] Initially derided as "bedpan mutuals," these new insurers grew to dominate the physician liability insurance market and insure many hospitals as well.[45]

Steves's concept of insuring physicians under (or in coordination with) hospital coverage was later effectuated in some places in the form of voluntary hospital–physician "channeling" programs. Especially after the mid-1980s crisis, some observers promoted channeling as a reliable source of physician coverage and a potential way of getting physicians and hospitals to work together on risk management and defense of claims.[46] Two oft-cited examples were the programs of the Risk Management Foundation of the Harvard Medical Institutions, in Boston, and the Federation of Jewish Philanthropies Service Corporation, in New York City.[47] Such programs have not become widespread, in part owing to physician resistance.[48] Academic medical institutions appear most likely to have such arrangements. They build on a natural community of interest between the medical staff and the hospital, and they are large enough to self-insure or create a "captive" insurer, which facilitates innovation in coverage.[49]

AN EARLY 1990S PROPOSAL FOR MANDATORY, EXCLUSIVE HOSPITAL LIABILITY

The late 1980s brought new proposals to make hospitals responsible for physician liability, again as a way to improve both liability insurance and

---

[43] This point assumes that currently non-hospital-affiliated physicians would remain so. Less adequate community-based liability coverage might encourage more to affiliate more closely with hospitals, although market incentives are likely to be more important. See discussion of recent market developments after note 79.

[44] Sloan et al. 1991.

[45] Physician Insurers Association of America 2005.

[46] Holzer 1987; Jones and O'Hare 1989.

[47] Studdert and Brennan 2001a; Bovbjerg 1989 (New York in 1985 mandated that hospitals provide coverage for physician liability above $1 million per claim).

[48] Cf. New York State Insurance Department 2004 (only one channeling program in New York state); Todd 1993 (in channeling, "physicians felt unduly controlled" and "were required to provide some of the funds for insurance, neither of which they thought was appropriate").

[49] Mello and Brennan 2002; Crawford and Co. 2004.

medical quality incentives. The proposals first came from Paul Weiler, Kenneth Abraham, and others associated with an American Law Institute (ALI) study of personal injury law in general.[50] They argued that traditional personal injury law does not work well in general and that focusing tort liability on enterprises in many different spheres would improve incentives to reduce costs and enhance quality. For medicine, their subsequent more detailed analysis addressed the same problems as Steves – inefficient liability insurance for physicians and weak deterrence/quality incentives from individual physician liability.[51]

Their proposed solution also included hospital-based liability insurance, but unlike Steves' plan, their proposal would have created it by changing the underlying law of liability. They urged that hospitals should have exclusive "organizational" or "enterprise" liability for all inpatient care, including services provided by independent physicians.[52] Most liability claims arise in hospitals, they noted, even those targeting physicians.[53] Furthermore, they argued, "Precisely because" hospitals' function is "to deliver health care, they are in the best position to make decisions about how to optimize the mix of potential risks and benefits associated with treatment of any particular patient's medical condition."[54] On the insurance front, having a single insured defendant would allow efficient risk-bearing, combined defense in litigation, and reduced claims-adjustment costs. Simpler litigation would speed resolutions; reduced transaction costs could increase claimants' share of recoveries.[55] Experience rating and self-insurance would reward improved risk management.[56]

Exclusive hospital liability was designed to tie physicians more tightly to hospitals and hence to help create a community of interest. This would encourage not only better claims investigation and resolution but also more efforts to prevent claims by improving quality. The reformers recognized that removing individual liability would reduce that avenue of legal accountability, but argued that insurance dilutes that accountability anyway.[57] They also asserted that hospitals' oversight would be better: The entire treatment team could collaborate to improve care, and hospitals could encourage high physician standards and refuse privileges to those

[50] The ALI team produced a "reporters' study" as a report "to" the Institute, rather than "of" the Institute's recommendations. American Law Institute 1991a, 1991b; Weiler 1991; Sugarman 1992; Abraham and Weiler 1994a, 1994b.
[51] Weiler 1991, 123–7 (insurance advantages) and 129–32 (deterrence/quality).
[52] See, e.g., Weiler 1991, 126–7; Abraham and Weiler 1994b.
[53] Abraham and Weiler 1994b; U. S. General Accounting Office 1987.
[54] Abraham and Weiler 1994a.
[55] Abraham and Weiler 1994b.
[56] Weiler 1991, 130.
[57] Abraham and Weiler 1994b, 408 ("diluting").

not cooperating.[58] The reformers appreciated that the prospect of greater hospital control "raises the hackles of physicians and their associations," but saw this only as an obstacle to voluntary reform and another argument for making the change mandatory.[59]

In a later version of the proposal, Abraham and Weiler proposed to include even nonhospital care within hospital liability. This change would have required assigning physicians to a hospital with which they had some affiliation or simply to a nearby institution.[60] No model of hospital-based enterprise liability was ever enacted,[61] although the concept continues to attract interest.[62] These authors and, later, others also proposed enterprise responsibility under a "no-fault" administrative compensation system.[63] This article focuses upon enterprise liability under current tort law, but very similar issues about enterprise and individual responsibility arise under an alternative, nonfault system.

THE HEALTH SECURITY ACT AND ENTERPRISE LIABILITY
FOR HEALTH PLANS

The next major proposal for institutional liability in health care came from the Clinton Administration's Task Force on National Health Reform in 1993. It also proposed to create "enterprise" liability focused not on hospitals but rather on broader-based enterprises – the managed care health plans that qualified as "accountable health plans," or AHPs, under the administration's proposed Health Security Act.[64] The Task Force proposal assigned liability to AHPs as part of its larger overhaul of the entire health care system. The particular vision of managed competition adopted in the Health Security Act called for regional health insurance purchasing cooperatives to offer enrollees a choice of prepaid care from among competing AHPs, all constrained under a budget cap.

AHPs were to manage many responsibilities – employing or contracting with medical providers managing the ensuing provider networks, assuring access to and quality of care, and controlling costs. They were to be held

---

[58] Weiler 1991, 130–1.
[59] Id., 131.
[60] Abraham and Weiler 1994a;
[61] Kessler 2004.
[62] American College of Physicians 1995, 2003.
[63] American Law Institute 1991a; W. Johnson et al. 1992; Abraham and Weiler 1994b; Studdert et al. 1997; Studdert and Brennan 2001a, 2001b; see also Havighurst and Tancredi 1974 (different "no-fault" approach).
[64] Starr and Zelman 1993; Priest 1993; Anders et al. 1993. The acronym AHP today can also mean "association health plan," a different concept now promoted by the Bush Administration, but we use it in the Health Security Act meaning (Centers for Medicare and Medicaid Services 2005a).

accountable in numerous ways – by having to compete with other AHPs for enrollees, by measurement of quality and outcomes, and by having to live within their capitated budgets.[65] As senior members of the Task Force explained, the approach sought "to encourage the integration of health insurance and health care provision into the same organizations (the health plans). The more integrated the plans, the better able they will be to control cost and quality. Thus, the new system will tend to alter the organization of services, not just the flow of funds."[66]

In this new context, it was logical to make AHPs integrated enterprises accountable for enrollees' personal injuries caused by their health care as well. By design, AHPs were to deliver as well as to finance care, and they were expected to select and control their participating medical providers, or, in AHPs organized as looser provider networks, at least to heavily influence them through various AHP policies and procedures.

The Clinton Task Force's enterprise liability proposal also had political objectives. It addressed public fears that AHPs would cut corners and endanger patients in their zeal to control costs, despite the reform's quality controls and AHPs' need to attract enrollees. Health reform planners saw making the AHPs bear full and direct liability for negligent outcomes as an additional way to reassure the public. This mechanism sought to "internalize" the cost of any harm done to patients by AHP-affiliated providers within each AHP's finances. Liability was to be a cost just like paying a fee of A for service B. Thus, AHPs would be motivated, in their cost–benefit analysis of alternative ways to deliver and oversee care, to achieve efficiencies in safety as well as in financing services.[67]

Institutional liability was also meant to win support from physician groups not disposed to favor insurer-managed care or a larger federal role in health care. There was no malpractice crisis in 1993, but malpractice reform was as usual still a leading issue for organized medicine, and some Task Force leaders expected physicians to embrace a reform that fully exempted physicians from direct liability for professional negligence.

The architects of the enterprise liability proposal preferred to make AHPs liable, rather than hospitals, for several reasons: Many errors occur outside hospitals, often in physicians' offices, and in the early 1990s the proportion of ambulatory claims (e.g., for "failure to diagnose" cancer) seemed to be rising.[68] Holding hospitals liable for ambulatory activities that they could not control or even influence seemed unsatisfactory. That approach might achieve some of the insurance efficiencies sought by institutional liability but certainly did not improve patient safety. AHPs could reach further than

---

[65] See, e.g., Bovbjerg 1994.
[66] Starr and Zelman 1993, 11.
[67] See Sage et al. 1994.
[68] Preston 1998.

hospitals, as broad-based enterprises that assured access to and quality of virtually all of the health care covered under insurance – ambulatory, inpatient, postacute care, and so on. Thus, AHPs would have some control over all aspects of care. In short, reform architects thought that AHPs required to finance and deliver a full range of health services could adapt to changing patterns of health care better than hospitals could.

It quickly became clear that physicians, in fact, wanted no part of enterprise liability, especially not when lodged in health plans.[69] Physicians knew nothing about planned-for "accountable health plans," but they knew a lot about rapidly expanding managed care organizations, especially health maintenance organizations. In narrow financial terms, physicians understood that any savings from decreased personal liability insurance premiums would likely be offset in reduced payments for professional services, as health plans absorbed the shifted liability costs. Liability relief might provide some psychic comfort but probably not meaningful fiscal benefit. Furthermore, the physician mutual liability companies, started and nurtured by state medical societies, could expect a greatly diminished role in a world of enterprise liability and had reason to oppose it.[70]

By far the most important reason for resistance was that this liability reform ratified precisely what physicians fought against in managed care, that is, the loss of professional autonomy. (Legislation for exclusive hospital liability, had it been similarly promoted, likely would have faced similar opposition.) Physicians were also concerned that another party would be empowered to settle cases of physician liability without the concurrence of affected physicians, thereby potentially harming their reputations. The vehemence of opposition was epitomized by one physician's challenge to the author (R.A.B.)'s advocacy of enterprise liability on behalf of the Clinton Task Force: "I have a constitutional right to be sued, and you can't take it away from me."[71]

Nor did health plans support liability for their contracted provider networks. Although the Clinton proposal envisioned health plans as merging financing with delivery, evolving toward the tightly integrated, closed-panel HMO model like the Kaiser Health Plan, most health plans still maintained their distance from providers. They were certainly willing to determine plan benefits, a traditional insurer function. Yet, plans were reluctant to intervene in clinical practice decisions and typically stipulated in network-provider contracts that they would not interfere with provider control of clinical quality and patient safety. Such provisions appear designed to soothe providers and deflect malpractice claims against plans.[72]

[69] *New York Times*, May 14, 1993.
[70] D. Rogers 1993.
[71] This occurred at a 1993 public meeting of the Physician Insurers Association of America.
[72] U.S. General Accounting Office (1997) called these "anti-gag clauses."

Health plans also articulated a specific concern that proponents of hospital-based enterprise liability would have to confront: the possibility that an impersonal, corporate enterprise, substituting as the defendant for a personal physician, would be viewed by potential litigants as a "deep pocket" target of opportunity.[73] Given that only a small percentage of negligently injured patients actually file suit,[74] the potential for many new lawsuits became a significant concern. Proponents of hospital-based enterprise liability also argued that health plans were much less capable than hospitals of preventing injury in the clinical context, as even with heightened accountability, plans would remain more a financing than a delivery vehicle.[75]

Even before the Clinton health reform proposal collapsed, enterprise liability was reduced to a demonstration project: Reformers could not force a marriage that neither party wanted to enter into. That is, neither existing health plans nor physicians and hospitals favored remaking accountability in general and certainly not malpractice liability in particular.

Subsequently, proponents of the two different approaches debated the alternative merits of hospitals and health plans as the appropriate locus of institutional liability.[76] The two approaches had striking similarities. Both sought to create better, more organized oversight of medical care. In one, health plans would build on their credentialing of participating providers and monitoring of resource use. The other emphasized hospitals' traditional credentialing and oversight of physician activities within the hospital.

Both proposals held out hope that physicians would appreciate no longer having to fight liability claims on their own or face sudden upsurges in liability premiums. Both expected that the fiscal incentives of experience rating would create positive incentives for improvement. Both recognized that relying on individual caregivers to improve safety was insufficient and that litigation with multiple individual defendants was needlessly costly. And both held that institutions would be better positioned than individual professionals to craft contractual alternatives to malpractice litigation, for example, arbitration and "early offers" of settlement.[77]

Moreover, each camp made provision for the other's perspective in designing implementation procedures. The Clinton proposal permitted health plans to contract out of their liability by shifting it through indemnification agreements to hospitals and large group practices where the latter were deemed better able to prevent injuries. The hospital liability proposal recognized

---

[73] See, e.g., Hammitt et al. 1985.
[74] Meyers 1987; Localio et al. 1991.
[75] Abraham and Weiler 1994a.
[76] Compare Sage et al. 1994 (accountable health plans as enterprises) with Abraham and Weiler 1994a (hospitals).
[77] Sage 2004b, 18.

that in some circumstances other enterprises, such as integrated health plans, "would be a superior risk-bearer and risk-avoider" and, accordingly, would be permitted to bear the liability, also by contract.[78] The important difference was mainly in the "default" rule that assigned initial responsibility to different enterprises. Both proposals made the default modifiable by subsequent contract negotiations, and in practice actual risk-bearing and risk-reduction activities (i.e., injury prevention) could occur at various levels of enterprise.[79]

MANAGED CARE'S RISE AND RETRENCHMENT

Despite the demise of the Clinton reform, the health system continued for several years to evolve toward greater integration both among medical providers and across health insurers, a trend that could facilitate the development of either model of enterprise liability. A decade ago, vertically integrated health systems seemed the future of health care delivery. Managed care was rapidly moving from a fringe form of health coverage to the dominant mode of health insurance. Commercial health insurers were consolidating, and not-for-profit Blues plans reorganized as mutual companies or for-profit firms to raise capital to better compete; many also merged to compete with commercial enterprises. Both for-profit and nonprofit hospital chains similarly expanded, while other hospitals and physicians sought market power through affiliations and consolidations. And hospitals began buying physician practices to assure patient referrals. "Integrated delivery systems" seemed likely to dominate many markets across the country.[80] Their advocates promised all manner of new management capabilities[81] as well as the scale to buy liability coverage on favorable terms or to operate as their own liability insurers.

Indeed, for a brief time it appeared that the debate over the relative merits of alternative models of enterprise liability might become moot. With fully vertically integrated units responsible for both financing and delivery of care, the distinction between health plans and hospitals becomes murky. But that period was short-lived, as managed care and health care integration have not proceeded as many envisioned.

A well-publicized managed care backlash set in.[82] The buying public resisted managed care interventions into medical care. State and federal

---

[78] Abraham and Weiler 1994a, 1994b.

[79] This decision about which entity would be a better locus for responsibility under various circumstances echoes the seminal thinking of Guido Calabresi (1970). He held that liability should be assigned to the lowest-cost cost avoider, that is, the entity that can best minimize the combined cost of injury and of risk-reduction activities.

[80] See Higgins and Meyers 1987; Shortell et al. 1994; but see J. Robinson 1994 (noting that increased delivery-system integration was not the only possible future).

[81] Howe 1994.

[82] M. Peterson 1999.

"patient protection" enactments curbed some practices and threatened liability for denials of service. Some courts found plans liable for patient injuries tied to health plan economizing.[83] In response, health plans eased a host of techniques for managing costs. Changes affected gatekeepers previously imposed between patients and specialty care, rules on prior authorization of medical services, disallowances for consumer-initiated emergency visits, and second-guessing of practitioner prescribing patterns.[84] In short, health insurers have continued to consolidate but no longer under the banner of managed care. Their ability to manage care – and to assume responsibility for medical injuries – is diminished. This drawing in of the horns reduced insurers' legal risks, but hospitals cannot follow in exactly the same footsteps. Regulation of hospitals and their own structures call for them to supervise physicians at least to the extent of deciding on staff privileges.[85]

Consistent with the retrenchment in health plans' management of care, vertical integration that merges the financing and delivery functions of health care has also waned. Two leading practitioners of integrated care recently concluded that full vertical integration is unlikely to occur in U.S. health care and that the success of Kaiser plans is a historical anomaly.[86] Preferred provider health plans are ascendant, using contractual reimbursement methods akin to traditional fee for service.[87] The latest innovation in insurance provision is "consumer-directed health care," which relies for its success on patient/enrollee incentives to shop prudently for care, not on organized control over caregivers' practices.[88]

Consumer shopping for medical care is nearly the antithesis of enterprise-managed care, although insurers' rules and practitioners' advice will surely remain influential. Society has moved far from entrusting responsibility for care to health plans. If anything, health plan–based enterprise responsibility today looks harder to impose than it was even at the height of opposition to the Health Security Act. Given how the backlash has changed the behavior of managed care and health plans generally, key assumptions about plans' responsibility for quality and safety seem dated, if not obsolete.

---

[83] The seminal case is *Fox v. HealthNet*, an unreported decision that received much attention in the media and from opponents of managed care, e.g., at http://www.harp.org/contr.htm. The plaintiff won a $89 million jury verdict because of a plan's refusal to cover autologous bone marrow transplant for advanced breast cancer, *Fox v. HealthNet*, Civ. No. 219692, 1993 WL 794305 (Riverside County Super. Ct./Central Cal. Dec. 23, 1993).

[84] J. Robinson 2001; Mays et al. 2003. The Supreme Court has also set limits on lawsuits against managed care plans (see Jost 2004).

[85] We are indebted to Bill Sage for this point.

[86] Halvorson and Isham 2003.

[87] J. Robinson 2001; Hurley et al. 2004.

[88] J. Robinson 2004; Herzlinger 2004; Porter and Teisberg 2004.

In an ironic echo of the Clinton proposal, the brief heyday of managed care plans in the mid-1990s prompted strong calls to increase the liability of health plans through "patient protection" legislation.[89] However, the goal was not to make plans responsible for physician conduct and thereby to promote joint plan–provider efforts to improve safety in delivery of care. Indeed, physicians seeking to maintain their professional autonomy vis-à-vis health plans were among the strongest supporters of allowing enrollees to sue their plans. The stated objective was to prevent health plans in their role as financers of care from corner-cutting in benefit determinations, also a concern of the Clinton reformers.

Physicians' political objective was to undercut plans' limitations on traditional physician prerogatives to determine the medical appropriateness of care and hence eligibility for plan payment. "Patients' rights" to sue their plans was a rallying cry for using legislation to resist the growing power of managed care. Again, as in the Clinton-era physician's plaint about the right to be sued, legal accountability was conjoined with professional autonomy. Reforms were sought initially through state legislation; after the Employee Retirement and Income Security Act of 1974 (ERISA) blocked most litigation in state court, advocates promoted a federal solution.[90]

Some academic proposals seized on this movement to suggest more health plan responsibility for quality and errors in physician care.[91] These never attracted serious political support. Indeed, the political drive to reform managed care liability was part of the backlash, in no way supportive of enterprise liability. In 2001 different versions of federal patient protection passed the House of Representatives and the Senate, but the bills languished amid only tepid support from the Bush White House and then the press of more urgent business after the atrocities of September 11th.[92]

THE RECEDING OF PROVIDER INTEGRATION

Provider integration has similarly receded in recent years. During the early to mid-1990s, hospitals and physicians used a variety of mechanisms to affiliate more closely with one another, but these efforts mostly failed. Many hospitals that purchased primary care physician practices have seen productivity drop and have sold these acquisitions.[93] For all the expectations that solo and small group physician practices could not survive, their dominance in the market for physician services is undiminished.[94] On occasion, physicians

[89] Bovbjerg 2003.
[90] Mariner 2000.
[91] Havighurst 1997, 2000; Sage 1997; Jacobi and Huberfeld 2001.
[92] See generally Bovbjerg 2003.
[93] J. Robinson 2001; Lake et al. 2003.
[94] Casalino et al. 2003.

actively resist hospital-salaried practice.[95] At the same time, hospitalists are increasingly taking responsibility for inpatient care, and many primary care physicians rarely even set foot in the hospital.[96] They do not regard the hospital as having any particular authority over their office-based practices.

As managed care growth has waned, hospitals are shifting their focus away from employing primary care physicians and from building physician hospital organizations and independent practice associations that acquire and manage capitated health plan contracts. Instead, they seek to build stronger relationships with specialists in order to benefit from high-margin specialized services and to avert potential competition in delivering outpatient services.[97]

Indeed, the trend in many markets toward the development of single-specialty medical groups threatens the hospital's traditional role as the natural ally of specialists. Hospitals do benefit from the improved revenue streams from consolidated specialty groups able to negotiate better payment rates from health plans. For their part, however, many of the specialty groups see themselves as independent of hospitals – and sometimes as competitors with the very hospitals to which they continue to admit patients. Increasingly, specialists are generating income as passive investors in various kinds of enterprises, including ambulatory surgical centers, imaging centers, and specialty hospitals, which serve patients who otherwise would go to a general community hospital.[98]

Entrepreneurial activities aside, specialty groups of sufficient size and market standing can participate on multiple hospital staffs and use their control over patient flows to gain leverage with hospitals over everything from favorable operating room scheduling to better parking spaces in the physicians' lot.[99] Furthermore, for some specialties like neurological surgery there may not be enough volume at any individual hospital or hospital system to assure exclusive admitting.[100] When actively admitting patients to multiple hospitals, these physicians are less likely to feel an affinity with any single one. In contrast, institutional liability's safety objectives are greatly enhanced if physicians feel closely affiliated with the responsible hospital.

These various trends make the hospital-based enterprise liability model as problematic as the health plan–based one has proved to be. Improving delivery of services through broader integration strategies now appears unlikely. Moreover, many physicians now are engaging in vigorous business

[95] See, e.g., Ostrom 2004.

[96] Pham et al. 2005.

[97] Lake et al. 2003; Pham et al. 2004. Hospitals also combine horizontally to build market power in local markets (Cuellar and Gertler 2003), though such combinations also fail (Hoadley et al. 2003).

[98] Medicare Payment Advisory Commission 2005; U.S. General Accounting Office 2003.

[99] Herzlinger 2004; Porter and Teisberg 2004.

[100] Berenson et al. 2003.

competition with hospitals. Finally, physicians' manifest and continuing desire for professional autonomy makes deference to any enterprise, including a hospital, undesirable for many physicians.[101]

Thus, the 1990s quasi-debate over hospitals and accountable health plans as competing loci for institutional liability[102] was "won" by hospitals only by default. Nothing like AHPs was ever legislated, and market-driven health plans' management of care has receded rather than increased. The case for hospital liability has weakened as well, owing to new forces keeping physicians and hospitals apart. The persistence of ambulatory practice continues to confound the logic of covering all medical injuries exclusively through hospital liability. The rapidity and extent of recent change also undercut any assertion that any particular institution(s) will best promote safety in the future. This uncertainty militates against using legal fiat to enshrine exclusive liability for hospitals – or any other currently prominent institution.[103]

INSTITUTIONAL PATIENT SAFETY AND ENTERPRISE LIABILITY

The Patient Safety Movement

Enterprise liability reform proposals have recurred over time for a good reason: Systems can do more to promote safety than can individuals acting alone. Individual incentives may be helpful, but are insufficient. Systems add value in airline safety, for instance, even though pilots face the strongest possible individual incentive to be careful – the prospect of arriving first at the scene of any crash.[104] Such insights came new to health care in the 1990s. They originated in quality and safety methodologies developed for workplace safety and in continuous quality improvement for industry as well as in catastrophic accident avoidance in industry and government.[105]

Outside health care, organizations and industries adopting these methods have achieved stunning reductions in accident rates.[106] The approach seems beneficial in health care as well: By 2000, IOM's *To Err Is Human* could not only publicize earlier findings on the extent of injury[107] but could also cite

---

[101] Berenson et al. forthcoming; Hargraves and Pham 2003; Stoddard et al. 2001.

[102] Compare Abraham and Weiler 1994a (hospitals) with Sage et al. 1994 (accountable health plans).

[103] Additional changes beyond the rise of hospitalists and others just noted include the potential emergence of what Paul Batalden and colleagues call "microsystems" of care, in which key clinical and safety groupings could cut across traditional lines. See, e.g., Nelson et al. 2002.

[104] Bovbjerg et al. 2001.

[105] See generally Reason 1990 (general theory and evidence); Berwick 1989; Bogner 1994 (heath care applications).

[106] See, e.g., Reason 2000; Institute of Medicine 2000.

[107] Institute of Medicine 2000; earlier work included, e.g., DHEW 1973; Mills et al. 1977; Brennan et al. 1991. Much work in the late 1980s and 1990s arose from Robert Wood Johnson Foundation projects; see Cantor et al. 1997.

early successes of new safety approaches to reducing injury, mainly in hospitals.[108] Subsequent case reports show further progress.[109] Safety and liability are overlapping concerns, and patient-safety paradigms constitute the first major practical alternative to the dominant medical–legal paradigm. That traditional approach relies on individual responsibility enforced not only through lawsuits but also through private peer review and public discipline against careless or incompetent practitioners.[110]

Patient safety has a sharply different worldview: Most mistakes occur not because people are careless but because they are human. Any set of processes has an innate propensity to generate a certain level of errors, no matter what people are involved. The best solution is not to affix blame but to fix the problem. System participants should not be personally cited for errors but rather encouraged to share information on mistakes, even inconsequential ones. Information and analysis can then make production processes more resistant to error, build in appropriate levels of redundancy and backup, and rely more on teamwork to catch any errors before harm occurs or to promptly remediate injuries that nonetheless occur.[111]

Liability incentives apply differently outside of medicine, for the corporate structure of non–health care enterprises shields individual employees from fiscal liability. Still, the traditional internal response of enterprises was to blame and sanction workers for perceived shortcomings, just as under personal liability. Systems safety approaches instead hold that errors are golden – because they teach enterprises how to improve their processes. What is blameworthy is not the normal human propensity to slips and lapses but the refusal to cooperate with systematic efforts at improvement, which requires disclosure and learning from problems. In practice, moving away from fault-finding for most problems has helped to greatly reduce the number of problems.

Patient Safety and Liability

The relevance of patient safety for enterprise liability is that safety concerns and capabilities might serve as a new driver for focusing liability on hospitals or other medical enterprises, much as they are in other industries. Medical institutions that promote patient safety – mainly hospitals – are showing that they can enhance safety beyond what individual physicians have accomplished, whether motivated by professionalism, market forces, or liability.

---

[108] See, e.g., Institute of Medicine 2000 (mainly hospitals); Lapetina and Armstrong 2002 (outpatient care).
[109] See, e.g., Wachter and Shojania 2004 (book-length treatment drawing on personal experience and numerous case reports from others); Wachter et al. 2002; Agency for Healthcare Research and Quality 2005; National Patient Safety Foundation 2005.
[110] Bovbjerg et al. 2001 (explicating dichotomy of worldviews).
[111] Institute of Medicine 2000; Wachter and Shojania 2004.

Regulators are now mainly looking to hospitals to promote patient safety precepts like disclosure of injuries and "root cause" analyses of problems or "sentinel" events.[112] Such regulatory assignment of safety responsibilities to institutions is essentially the logic of enterprise liability.[113] And patient-safety theory's rejection of individual blaming also supports legal change, as fear of personal liability is said to keep physicians from acknowledging injuries, which suppresses valuable information about problems.[114] Exclusive hospital liability would shield doctors from such direct liability, and hospitals' more targeted liability insurance incentives would arguably promote safety efforts and reward success with lower liability premiums, as argued by earlier reformers.

Even without liability reform, patient-safety efforts can achieve some of the progress sought by enterprise-liability theorists. After all, the reason that systematic approaches are known to work in health care is that some are working already. The main motivation for safety to date has been hospitals' need to satisfy the quasi-regulatory requirements of the Joint Commission on Accreditation of Healthcare Organizations.[115] Some market-based initiatives, such as the Leapfrog Group's patient-safety standards, are also winning attention from hospitals, though their impact has been modest to date.[116] Liability motivations for hospital safety may also increase over time. Hospitals may lack exclusive enterprise liability but they do have corporate liability, and more hospitals seem to be self-insuring because of the current malpractice insurance crisis.[117]

As hospital regulatory obligations become clearer and as hospitals respond to the need to reduce corporate litigation exposure, more physicians might be swept into patient safety efforts, even without formal business integration of hospitals and physician practices or channeling or other integration of liability insurance. Under this scenario, a hospital's corporate responsibilities and liability might spur the safety objectives that enterprise liability strives for, at least for hospitalized patients. To succeed, hospitals will have to involve physicians. As a practical matter, community physicians' services to inpatients often cannot be separated from hospital operations. For example, in responding to the recently promulgated JCAHO accreditation standard that hospitals disclose errors to patients, hospitals can and do require physicians on staff to participate in the disclosure, whether or not the physician otherwise would choose to disclose.[118] Such a change will not come

---

[112] See, e.g., Joint Commission on Accreditation of Healthcare Organizations 2003.
[113] Cf. Calabresi 1970.
[114] Berwick 2000.
[115] Devers et al. 2004.
[116] Id.
[117] Insurance Information Institute 2005; Mello, Studdert, Thomas, et al. 2004.
[118] Bovbjerg 2005b.

easily. Physicians do not believe medical errors are as significant a problem as the IOM report suggests, and most lack a sense of urgency about addressing safety issues.[119] Voluntary medical staff also face barriers to cooperation and participation in patient-safety activities.[120] Such attitudes help explain the halting safety progress to date, especially given the high expectations created by the IOM book.[121] In sum, an alignment of physician and hospital interests directed at errors and safety has not occurred, and market trends suggest that these interests will continue to diverge. Yet, achieving more systematic approaches to safety remains important because so many patients are injured in health care, as is increasingly recognized by the general public as well as experts.[122]

The Law as the Instrument of Systems Change?

In this situation, it is tempting to use the law – in this case, the imposition of a regime of exclusive enterprise liability – as an external force to accomplish a realignment toward systems and systems safety that the market and safety regulation seemingly cannot. Some safety researchers and advocates argue for enterprise liability on this ground.[123] However, just mandating exclusive institutional tort liability cannot fully achieve the safety objectives desired by policy makers, for several reasons:

First, supporters of exclusive institutional liability rightly note that physicians must be intimately involved in any truly serious attempt to reduce medical errors. Outsiders can and should exhort doctors to join hospitals in such efforts,[124] but it seems implausible that a single-issue legal ukase could join together what manifold professional and market forces have kept asunder. Nor would ending personal physician liability alone make physicians eager to cooperate in disclosing and preventing medical errors. It may be true that "[c]linicians' fear of malpractice litigation is the most significant obstacle to the open reporting of medical mistakes,"[125] but a culture of silence long predates the modern American legal system – and exists throughout the non-American world today.[126]

Second, systems safety requires a system. Imposing institutional liability would presumably create a joint insurance enterprise, but it would not create a fully functional business and clinical enterprise with a joint community of interest and the capabilities that make enterprise liability work in other commercial spheres. Some physician-including system must precede system

---

[119] J. Robinson et al. 2002; Blendon et al. 2002.
[120] Berenson et al. forthcoming.
[121] Wachter 2004; Leape and Berwick 2005; Millenson 2003.
[122] See, e.g., Blendon et al. 2002.
[123] See, e.g., Berwick 2005. See also notes 39 and 40 supra (Steves).
[124] Schoenbaum and Bovbjerg 2004; Institute for Healthcare Improvement 2004.
[125] Aulisio 2001; see also Weissman et al. 2005.
[126] Gibson and Singh 2003.

safety. There can be no comprehensive system when Americans want to select each health care provider individually and to pay them all separately. Hospitals cannot take charge of physician aspects of safety when patients mainly want their own doctors and rely on those doctors to select which hospitals to use. If and when American patients, medical providers, and voters decide that they want a more coordinated approach to financing and delivery of care – dare we say better management of care?[127] – more capable medical systems will emerge to combine or coordinate operations of physicians, hospitals, and other providers. There will then be a business case for creating managerial capabilities to meet everyday operational needs, not merely to worry about liability premiums. Health payers and patients also need to be willing to fund those capabilities, either by increasing payments or by accepting changed practices that achieve economies.

Once capable systems exist, they should be held accountable for their care, including liability for patient injuries. The key to "systemness" in health care is an ongoing community of interest between professionals and institutions, rather than formal legal affiliation. We suspect that such community of interest needs to evolve naturally and to begin integrating various managerial spheres before it can actually develop the desirable capabilities that the institutional theorists simply posit.

Third, even within a system, liability incentives alone are not a strong enough motivator to create systems management of medical injuries. Individuals and institutions have innumerable nonliability goals and concerns. Within institutions, safety efforts must compete with all other demands for managerial attention and resources – ever more constrained resources, at present. Many factors influence institutional policies on medical injury. One study of large, heavily capitated physician groups found that the groups paid for their physicians' liability coverage as a matter of course, but that such responsibility alone did not lead the groups to seek to control injuries so as to control costs. Liability concerns were only one factor affecting progress in injury management. The most important determinant was the group's leadership and managerial capabilities, which were honed by the pressures of capitation payment, not of liability (see Figure 12.2).[128]

Fourth, injuries are not independent of other quality problems, nor are safety improvements completely different from other improvements. A few interventions may be relatively straightforward technological fixes readily achievable, even on a nationwide basis. These include using pulse oximeters to quickly and easily measure blood oxygen levels under anesthesia or bar-coding drug labels to avoid inadvertent mixups in dispensing.[129] Very often, however, safety interventions necessitate changes among people and processes not even involved in a liability case, deep within the "production"

[127] Zelman and Berenson 1998.
[128] Bovbjerg and Miller 2000; project fully described in Miller and Bovbjerg 2002.
[129] See, e.g., Tinker et al. 1989; Oren et al. 2003.

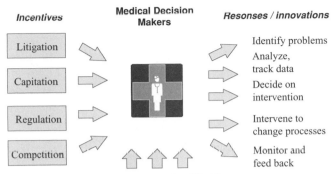

Incentives	Medical Decision Makers	Resonses / innovations

FIGURE 12.2. Factors Influencing Safety Policy.

or support processes of medicine.[130] The best solution for a surgical prob-lem may be to change how personnel interrelate in the operating theater, as was done earlier in airline cockpits.[131] Even fixing a quintessentially liability problem rather than a quality one – like lawsuits from patients who are less injured than angry about bad communication – is apt to require a thorough-going shift in operations. It also probably calls for improving communication across the board – for example, by paying attention to nonliability patient complaints.[132]

In sum, thoroughgoing safety management reform involves many parts of institutions, affects a complex web of interrelationships with separately organized physicians, and requires high-level management attention and sub-stantial resources.[133] We therefore believe that any shift to a true enterprise approach will come only with very significant changes in health care delivery and financing that merge physician and institutional interests. Big changes in regulation akin to institutional licensure, a return to capitationlike payment for bundles of services by payers demanding better safety, a shift out of the traditional tort system into a workers' compensationlike administrative sys-tem of paying for injuries – such broad shifts seem far more likely to leverage change than mandated enterprise liability superimposed atop existing indi-vidual licensure, reimbursement, and liability law.

UNINTENDED SIDE EFFECTS OF ENTERPRISE LIABILITY

This chapter has thus far compared institutional with individual capaci-ties for managing safety and liability risks. We now need to recognize that

[130] Wachter and Shojania 2004.
[131] Nance 2005; Sexton and Helmreich 2003.
[132] Hickson et al. 2002.
[133] Wachter 2004; Leape and Berwick 2005.

shifting to an exclusively institutional focus while retaining the fault basis of traditional tort could *change* liability risks as well as *manage* them better. As health plans complained to the Clinton reformers, people are generally more likely to bring claims against larger institutions, and juries are likely to award higher sums against "deep pocket" defendants, although the extent of these impacts is unclear.[134] One proposal for institutional liability (of health plans, not hospitals) sought to counter this effect by making plans only vicariously responsible for the individual negligence of a participating physician, not liable in their own right.[135] One wonders how long judges and juries would apply such a limitation literally.

More subtly, given the evolutionary nature of tort doctrine, institutional liability could well create expansive new duties of care, new standards for what constitutes negligence, and new entitlements for claimant discovery of information about injury. Such changes are important for liability and insurance given the large pool of potentially litigable cases that are not brought forward as claims.[136] Once hospitals are seen as responsible for all negligent injuries during childbirth, for example, one can imagine claimants' attorneys seeking to obtain and review not merely the medical records on Mrs. Smith's childbirth, but also on all similar deliveries within the statute of limitations – with a view to showing systemic hospital failures. Class actions might be brought for an alleged pattern of neglecting to enforce any plausibly applicable hospital rule, and punitive awards seem more likely if such cases are proven against an institutional defendant.

Such changes may represent nightmare scenarios from a hospital perspective, but hospitals are already facing new demands to disclose the results of internal patient-safety investigations.[137] It seems to us that social expectations for medical practice and oversight of care should in fact be raised higher, but we feel considerable disquiet about setting them accurately or consistently through the current judicial process or enforcing them through threats of high jury awards of damages.

Shifts in the incidence or extent of litigable injury are possible because a medical injury is not an objectively verifiable event like a car or airplane crash but rather a subjective judgment about causality. Determinations of negligence are also subjective. And, especially where negligence consists of failing to ameliorate the natural course of an injury or disease, rather than actively causing new harm akin to a car crash, negligence is measured against perceived medical capabilities and according to claimant/juror expectations. An additional conceptual complication applies, well beyond the issue of individual versus institutional responsibilities: Society now vaguely recognizes

---

[134] Bovbjerg et al. 1991.
[135] Havighurst 1997, 2000.
[136] Danzon 1985; Meyers 1987; Localio et al. 1991.
[137] Lamb et al. 2003; Weissman et al. 2005.

different types of quality standards but has created no clear cut rules on what these mean for courtroom determinations of negligence: To what quality standards should medicine aspire? What constitutes good care for which patients should prefer one provider over another? What constitutes substandard care that should be sanctioned through liability and if common enough through discipline as well?

Full discussion of such broader issues goes beyond our scope here, but we cannot resist three parting comments: (1) Legal indeterminacy helps explain why doctors on the front lines, who are producing medical advances and improved patient outcomes, understandably perceive that no good deed goes unpunished. They confront increasing liability risks, partly resulting from these very advances. Preventing injury and avoiding medical–legal risks is not like running the hurdles but rather like the pole vault: Every time you have done well, they raise the bar. The bar can also be raised by others' improvements, social standards or expectations, or a hospital's own written aspirations embodied in policies or procedures. (2) These uncertainties, like others, caution against imposing exclusive institutional liability as a tool to promote more systematic safety management. (3) In liability, as in seeking to promote quality generally, society would be well served by relying more on evidence-based practice and less on implicit standards and battling experts.

CONCLUSION

A series of proposals for enterprise liability starting in the 1960s sought to make hospitals or health plans responsible for injuries attributable to physicians and other caregivers associated with them. The proposals' two key goals are to encourage more prevention of medical injuries and more efficient insurance against the risk of such injuries. Society would benefit from achieving such goals, and systems-based approaches to patient safety have shown that they have considerable potential to make improvements.

A key policy issue is whether any shift to conjoin institutional and individual legal responsibilities should lead or follow market and regulatory patterns of health care organization. A decade ago, proponents of enterprise liability believed that markets were moving toward greater integration between physicians and hospitals[138] and between medical providers and managed health care plans.[139] Such trends have now reversed,[140] and these more recent market developments suggest that public policy should not now mandate integration of liability in hopes of integrating safety efforts.

If markets were today poised at a tipping point, mandating joint tort liability for hospitals and physicians or for medical providers and health

---

[138] Abraham and Weiler 1994a, 1994b.
[139] Sage et al. 1994.
[140] See Nichols et al. 2004; see also sources cited in notes 81–100 supra (vertical integration).

plans could succeed. However, medical markets are farther from tipping into any form of vertical integration today than a decade ago. Accordingly, policy makers for now should instead seek better injury prevention in different ways. Government can improve safety by acting as a demanding purchaser, an effective promulgator of performance standards, a funder of research and development, and a communicator of information to patients and health plan enrollees. Assuming that medical institutions and individual practitioners later join together to respond effectively in their own newly aligned interests, thereafter it will be time for liability law to evolve as well. Enabling legislation may then be helpful to help structure enterprise liability and reduce deleterious side effects.

13

Private Contractual Alternatives to Malpractice Liability

Jennifer Arlen

Patients currently face a substantial risk of being injured by the medical care they receive. These injuries often are the result of medical error that could be reduced by increased investment in care.[1] Tort liability has the potential to reduce unnecessary error. Medical providers can be induced to invest in cost-effective measures to improve medical quality if tort liability ensures that negligent providers pay for the costs they impose on their patients when they fail to provide adequate care.

In practice, the current malpractice liability system has not been effective at reducing error because it is plagued with problems. Effective malpractice reform has proven elusive. Proposals that would improve the system rarely obtain political support. All too often, legislatures focus on reforms that would exacerbate existing problems.

Leading law and economics scholars claim that the best way to achieve malpractice liability reform is to end government control over malpractice liability and permit patients and medical providers to determine the scope of malpractice liability by contract. Contractual liability proposals vary. Some would permit patients to contract over liability directly with

I benefited from the helpful comments of Barry Adler, James Blumstein, Richard Epstein, Alejandro Fernandez, Mark Geistfeld, Clark Havighurst, Keith Hylton, Marcel Kahan, Rogan Kersh, Sylvia Law, Bentley MacLeod, Geoffrey Miller, William Sage, Catherine Sharkey, and participants at the Columbia Law and Economics Colloquium and the Vanderbilt University Law and Economics Colloquium. I also would like to thank my research assistant, William Bunting. Finally, I would like to thank The Pew Charitable Trusts and the New York University School of Law for their financial support.

[1] See, e.g., Weiler et al. 1993, 42–4, 137–9 (one in twenty-five hospitalized patients was injured by the medical care they received; one-quarter of these were the result of medical negligence); Andrews et al. 1997, 311 (on-site observation of surgical error found that almost 18% of the patients were the victims of at least one serious error, and most of these errors were not recorded in writing); McGlynn et al. 2003 (20% of patients with chronic diseases received care that is contraindicated).

their physicians.[2] Others would shift all malpractice liability to large medical care entities (such as hospitals or managed care organizations [MCOs]) and then allow these entities to contract with patients over the scope of malpractice liability for both their own negligence and that of affiliated medical providers.[3]

Despite their differences, these contractual liability proposals share a common economic foundation. The central economic argument for contractual liability is simple and intuitively attractive. Patients and medical providers should be permitted to contract over liability because they are in the best position to know what liability rules best serve their interests. Contractual liability, moreover, allows liability rules to be tailored to an individual patient's preferences. Individual contracting over liability is beneficial because patients differ in their willingness to pay for liability. Accordingly, it is argued that individual contracting is superior to even the best malpractice liability system because it allows those patients who are not well served by standard malpractice liability to contract for the liability regime they prefer. The right to contract over liability cannot hurt patients who would have benefited from standard malpractice liability, it is claimed, because these patients can (and will) simply replicate malpractice liability by contract.[4]

The conclusion that patients are not hurt by contracting leads many contractual liability proponents to argue that contractual liability is superior to even the best malpractice liability system. The only potential problems for contractual liability that they consider arise from information problems, which leading contractual liability proponents generally do not believe are serious.[5] Moreover, information problems can be remedied by ensuring that patients are informed, not by placing limitations on contracting, it is argued.

This chapter examines the claim that patients are always better off when they are free to choose the liability rules that govern them.[6] This claim rests on two central premises. The first premise is that patients (or those contracting for them) are sufficiently well-informed to contract in their own best interests. The second is that all patients who would have benefited from malpractice liability can, and will, obtain that same benefit by contracting into liability, if they are informed. This chapter shows that neither premise holds for many patients.

---

[2] Epstein 1976.

[3] For example, Abraham and Weiler 1994b; Sage, Hastings, and Berenson 1994; Havighurst 1995; see also Danzon 2000 (contractual enterprise liability for MCOs).

[4] Economic arguments favoring contractual liability include Epstein 1976; Abraham and Weiler 1994b; Danzon 2000; Epstein and Sykes 2001. For a more pragmatic argument for contracting over liability, see Havighurst 1995, 2000.

[5] For example, Epstein and Sykes 2001.

[6] This chapter only considers proposals to permit patients to contract over liability. It does not examine contracts that require arbitration of malpractice claims. It also does not examine proposals to allow contracting over the standard of care used to determine actual treatment.

Proponents of contractual liability assume that patients who benefit from tort liability will replicate it by contract because they assume that liability obtained by contract affords patients the same benefits as liability imposed by tort. This is not the case. Patients often cannot obtain the same benefits from contracted-for liability as they can from tort liability. As a result, contractual liability may hurt those patients who would be willing to pay for tort liability in order to obtain higher quality care.

Patients may benefit less from contractual liability than from tort liability because patients governed by malpractice liability do not benefit simply from liability imposed for their own injuries. They also benefit from the threat of liability for harms to other patients as well as the threat of liability for harms to themselves occurring in the future. Collective and multiperiod liability is important because liability benefits patients through the incentives it provides medical caregivers to invest in reducing medical error. These investments include investments in expertise and health information technologies that benefit all of a provider's patients (now and in future periods) by improving his capacity to diagnose patients, assess treatments, and deliver care with less error.[7] Tort liability is potentially able to induce optimal investment in expertise (and other forms of durable, collective care) because tort liability is a collective and durable (e.g., multiperiod) form of liability. Patients thus benefit not only from the liability imposed for their own injuries, but also from the threat of liability for negligence to others (as well as from the commitment to impose tort liability on future providers).

Patients cannot necessarily replicate these incentive benefits by contract because contractual liability does not offer patients the option to impose collective, multiperiod liability to govern all patients and providers, both now and in the future. In other words, contractual liability does not offer patients the option to impose tort liability. Instead, it offers patients the option to impose an entirely different, and more limited, form of liability: specifically, liability on each patient's current providers, for his own injuries, for the duration of the contract.[8] This more restricted form of liability potentially confers lower benefits on those patients who benefit from the collective, multiperiod incentives offered by tort liability. Accordingly, patients who would have benefited from tort liability may not elect to impose contractual liability because the lower benefits of contracted-for liability may not exceed the costs. These patients are worse off under contractual liability because contracting eliminates their preferred choice (tort liability) and replaces it with a less valuable option.

In addition, contracting may make patients worse off if they are not sufficiently well-informed to contract over liability in their own best interests

---

[7] See Arlen and MacLeod 2003.

[8] Even contracting that occurs through entities still is limited in scope to current providers (e.g., current MCOs) and may not include all of a physician's patients.

because they underestimate the benefit of malpractice liability. If so, patients may waive the right to sue negligent providers even when doing so leaves them worse off. Channeling contracting through employers does not necessarily remedy this problem.

Accordingly, this chapter concludes that the argument for contractual liability cannot rest on the claim that contractual liability always makes patients better off. Contracting is likely to benefit some patients, but it will hurt others. This does not imply that contractual liability is necessarily inferior to tort liability. But legislatures should not rush to adopt contractual liability unless it can be shown that, on aggregate, the benefits of this reform would exceed the costs. At present, there is no guarantee that this is the case.

This chapter is structured as follows: The first section presents the economic justification for malpractice liability and discusses problems with the existing system. The second section discusses the standard economic argument favoring contractual liability. A third section discusses the evolution of contractual liability proposals toward those that channel contracting through large entities, such as MCOs. Finally, a concluding section shows that even the best contractual liability proposals may hurt many patients, even when patients are sufficiently well-informed to contract in their own best interests.

THE ECONOMIC PURPOSES OF MALPRACTICE LIABILITY

To understand the current debate about contracting over malpractice liability, it is useful to summarize the economic justifications for imposing malpractice liability on negligent medical providers and identify some of the problems with the existing system.[9]

The Potential Benefits of Liability

The primary economic purpose of medical malpractice liability is to give physicians, MCOs, and other medical providers financial incentives to deliver optimal medical care (defined as the quality of care that informed patients would be willing to pay for).[10]

Both patients and providers benefit when medical caregivers can be relied on to provide optimal care. Patients obtain the greatest value from contracting for medical care when they receive the maximum quality of medical care that they are willing to pay for.[11] Medical providers benefit because patients

---

[9] This section only briefly presents the economic arguments for malpractice liability. For a more in-depth discussion of the economic role of malpractice liability, see Arlen and MacLeod 2003; see also Arlen and MacLeod 2005 (providing a formal model).

[10] See generally Shavell 1980 (discussing optimal care by producers).

[11] Patients thus want providers to deliver optimal care, not care that maximizes patient health without regard to cost.

arc willing to pay more for medical care when they expect to receive optimal quality care.[12]

Patients will not be willing to pay more in order to obtain optimal quality care unless they are confident that medical providers will in fact deliver this level of care. This implies either that patients must be able to observe (or contract over) the quality of care delivered or that mechanisms must exist to ensure that medical providers want to deliver optimal care (even when patients cannot observe the quality of care delivered). Malpractice liability is just such a mechanism for giving medical providers incentives to deliver optimal care when quality is unobservable.[13]

Absent malpractice liability, patients will not be willing to pay the high cost of optimal medical care (even when it is offered to them) because they cannot determine whether in fact they are being offered optimal quality care. Patients do not have sufficient information about provider quality to be able to determine expected patient outcomes for any given physician or hospital at the moment of contracting. At best, patients have anecdotal information on quality from fellow patients and professional reputation. Moreover, many patients may be unable to act on (and thus may have little incentive to obtain) information on provider quality because health insurers often give patients strong financial pressures to select providers from a predetermined list. Patients may select an inferior network provider because they are unable to pay the additional costs of using a nonnetwork provider. Finally, patients cannot determine the quality of care they will receive because medical quality is not fixed at the moment of contracting but depends on actions (and afflictions) that occur postcontract. Thus, patients cannot base their willingness to pay on actual quality because the quality of care depends on actions taken after the patient has selected the provider and agreed to a fee schedule.[14]

Because patients cannot observe quality, they will not expect to receive optimal care (and thus will be unwilling to pay prices as if care is optimal) unless medical providers benefit from delivering optimal care even when

[12] Id. By definition, a patient's willingness to pay to receive efficient care instead of substandard care exceeds the additional cost to the medical provider of efficient care. See Arlen and MacLeod 2003.

[13] In theory, quality regulation might be able to induce optimal quality, but it has not done so to date. See Arlen and MacLeod 2003 (discussing the limits of continuing education, licensing, and state regulation of medical professionals).

[14] A patient thus may stay with an inferior network provider, instead of a superior off-network provider, even when it is inefficient because if he uses the superior provider he obtains only the marginal benefit of care relative to the inferior provider but often must pay the full cost of any off-network treatment (not just the marginal costs). Arlen and MacLeod 2003. Beyond this, medical providers who invest less than is optimal in quality may not face pressure to charge a lower price because insured patients do not comparison shop for providers based on price. Thus, a medical provider who delivers sufficiently good care to have a profitable practice may not suffer a financial penalty if he underinvests in quality.

quality is not observable. Medical providers do not profit from investing in the level of care that patients would be willing to pay for – this being the level that maximizes the benefit to patients of care minus the cost of care – unless medical providers suffer losses as great as their patients when they injure patients through avoidable negligence (as measured by patients' willingness to pay to reduce the risk of medical error).[15] Malpractice liability potentially operates to give medical providers this incentive to invest in quality by ensuring that medical providers who deliver negligent care bear their patients' losses. Under such a system, medical caregivers minimize costs (and maximize profits) by investing in cost-effective care (i.e., optimal care).

Malpractice liability is needed to ensure adequate investment in quality even when caregivers genuinely care about their patients and want to deliver optimal care.[16] Patients' health depends not only on whether a physician wants to provide good care but also on the physician's *ability* to provide good care. This in turn depends on whether the physician (and the institutions within which he practices) invested adequately in the "expertise"[17] (and health information technology) needed to provide good care: including the expertise needed to correctly diagnose patients, accurately assess available treatments, and provide treatment free from avoidable error. Absent this investment, even well-intentioned medical providers will accidentally provide substandard care.[18] Patients want physicians to invest in the expertise that is cost-effective given the full cost to patients of medical error.

Physicians determine expertise based on the cost to themselves of error. Absent liability, the cost to a physician of error (the sadness and reputation loss they suffer when a patient is injured or killed) generally is less than the cost to the patient of the injury. Physicians thus will not spend as much on reducing error as patients would like them to (and would be willing to pay for), absent liability for patient injuries. Malpractice liability potentially operates to remedy this insufficient incentive to invest in error reduction by imposing financial sanctions for negligence. Liability can ensure that medical

---

[15] Arlen and MacLeod 2003, 2005. Patients' injuries should be evaluated based on patients' willingness to pay to avoid injuries because patients currently must pay for the care they receive, directly or indirectly.

[16] Similarly, MCOs and hospitals will not invest optimally in care if the financial impact to them of injuring a patient (e.g., through loss of reputation) is less than the cost to the patient of the injury. Arlen and MacLeod 2003.

[17] The term "expertise" is used to refer to all investments that affect a physician's ability to provide the quality of treatment he would like to provide. Thus, expertise includes investments that improve a physician's capacity to diagnose, select treatment, and provide treatment. It also includes other investments that reduce the likelihood of accidental error, such as hospitals' investment in computerized physician order entry systems for drugs and carbon dioxide monitors on anesthesiology equipment. Expertise also includes MCOs' investments in the quality and speed of their utilization review systems. Id.

[18] Id.

providers suffer losses equivalent to those of their patients (as measured by patient willingness to pay for safety) when they injure a patient through medical negligence.[19]

Accordingly, a well-designed system of malpractice liability benefits both patients and caregivers by giving medical providers financial incentives to deliver optimal care. Providers benefit from the resulting ability to credibly commit to delivering the quality of care patients are willing to pay for because this enables them to price their services based on the assumption that quality is optimal, even when patients cannot observe quality. Patients benefit from getting the quality of care they value most.[20]

Existing Problems

Although a well-designed malpractice liability system could induce efficient medical care, the current malpractice system is rife with problems.[21] Malpractice liability, for example, does not provide sufficient incentives for caregivers to invest in quality because negligent medical providers do not bear the full cost of the injuries they cause. Negligent physicians are not forced to pay for most of the harm they cause because most patients injured by physician negligence do not sue,[22] and those who do sue do not receive supercompensatory damages.[23] Moreover, most physicians purchase malpractice liability insurance that is not fully "experience-rated" to reflect a physician's patient outcomes or claims experience. As a result, malpractice liability may not be able to effectively encourage investment in quality because physicians who do provide good quality care may face the same costs (through insurance) as those who do not.[24] Furthermore, federal law insulates MCOs from malpractice liability for their negligent decisions even though MCOs' actions directly and indirectly affect the quality of care patients receive.[25]

---

[19] Id. at 1961–79; Arlen and MacLeod 2005. Efficient medical care requires that malpractice liability be extended to MCOs, both for physician negligence and for their own negligent treatment coverage decisions. Arlen and MacLeod 2003, 2005.

[20] For a formal proof, see Arlen and MacLeod 2005.

[21] In addition, the existing standard for determining negligent care (custom) may encourage excessive treatment. Danzon 1997; see Kessler and McClellan 1996; see also Arlen and MacLeod 2005 (deriving an alternative standard for medical negligence).

[22] See, e.g., Andrews et al. 1997, 312 (only 13 of the 175 patients who suffered a serious error filed suit); Weiler 1991, 12–13 (only one in eight of potentially valid claims of medical malpractice was actually filed).

[23] Arlen 2000. For an interesting empirical study of tort damages for serious injuries, see Sharkey 2005.

[24] For an excellent discussion of problems created by malpractice insurance, see, for example, Geistfeld 2005; Chapter 15 in this volume.

[25] *Aetna Health Inc. v. Davila*, 542 U.S. 2003. See Arlen and MacLeod 2003 (providing an economic argument for MCO liability); Sage 1997.

Problems also arise because malpractice liability in effect binds all patients to the same standard of care. Tort liability hurts some patients because it applies a common standard of care to all patients, at least in theory. This can hurt patients whose willingness to pay for safety is less than that reflected in the standard of care. These patients may be unable to pay for the higher quality care resulting from tort liability and might prefer lower quality care.

Malpractice liability cannot achieve its promise unless these problems (and others) are remedied. The issue is whether to reform malpractice liability from within or abandon it in favor of liability determined by contract.

ECONOMIC ARGUMENTS FOR CONTRACTUAL LIABILITY

Proponents of contractual liability assert that the best way to reform malpractice liability is to replace tort liability with a system that permits patients and providers to determine the scope of liability by contract.[26]

The strongest proponents of contractual liability assert that a move to contract is superior to efforts to reform malpractice liability because contractual liability is superior to even the best malpractice liability system. Thus, any malpractice liability reform should grant patients the ability to contract over liability, they argue.

The economic claim that contractual liability is superior to even a well-designed malpractice liability system rests on a simple, and initially attractive, proposition. Granting patients the right to contract over liability necessarily makes patients better off because some patients would be better off when allowed to contract out of liability, whereas no patient would be made worse off. Contractual liability would not make any patient worse off, it is argued, because any patient who would have benefited from the imposition of malpractice liability can (and will) simply impose malpractice liability by contract, thereby achieving the same welfare as under the tort system. Contracting thus affects only those patients who benefit from the ability to contract out of the existing tort system. These patients are better off with contracting.[27]

Many patients would benefit from the ability to contract out of tort liability, even under a well-designed malpractice liability regime. No single malpractice liability rule can serve the interests of all patients because patients differ substantially in their willingness to pay for safety. Similarly, no single damage rule can serve each patient's interests because patients also differ

[26] See, e.g., Epstein 1976, 119–28 (supporting contractual liability for individual physicians); Abraham and Weiler 1994 (favoring enterprise liability of hospitals for all medical errors); Danzon 1997 (MCO liability should be determined by contract); cf. Havighurst 2000 (justifying contractual enterprise liability of MCOs on both economic and pragmatic grounds).

[27] Professor Richard Epstein has most clearly articulated this view both as to contractual physician liability and as to why MCO liability should be contractual. Epstein 1976; Epstein and Sykes 2001.

in their views as to how much compensation they would like to receive if injured.[28] Accordingly, although most patients benefit when tort liability is used to induce optimal care, not all patients do. Those patients with a less than average ability to pay for safety may not be willing to pay for the care that tort liability induces. These patients might be better off if allowed to contract into an alternative liability rule, which produces lower cost (and lower quality) care.

Given this, contracting would appear to enhance patient welfare by allowing those patients who do not benefit from standard tort liability to contract out of it.[29] Contracting does not necessarily enhance patients' welfare, however, if it adversely affects those patients who would benefit from tort liability (as it is shown it may).

EVOLUTION OF CONTRACTUAL MALPRACTICE LIABILITY PROPOSALS

The earliest economic proposals for contracting over malpractice liability favored allowing physicians to contract with patients over the scope (and existence) of malpractice liability.[30] These were followed by proposals to channel liability through large medical institutions, such as MCOs, which could then contract with patients over the malpractice liability regime to be imposed on all of a patient's medical providers.[31]

Physician Contracting Out of Liability

Early proposals to permit physicians to contract with patients at the point of service were rejected both in academic theory and judicial practice. Physicians also initially did not rally around them.

Courts consistently have invalidated exculpatory provisions (which waive liability) in physicians' contracts with patients. Courts reject contracting out of liability in part out of concern that patients in need of medical care may agree to insulate physicians from liability in order to get needed care. Courts thus object to waivers, particularly absent evidence that the patient had a

---

[28] Patients also differ in their desire for, and willingness to pay for, compensation for injuries that result in serious permanent injury or death. For example, whereas some patients may wish to insure through the tort system against the risk of being killed by malpractice, many others may not. See, e.g., Arlen 2000; Cook and Graham 1977 (demonstrating that people may prefer less than full ex post compensation against nonpecuniary losses).

[29] This belief that contracting over liability is clearly superior to tort liability when customers (here patients) can act in their own best interests at the moment of contracting runs through the economic literature on contracting over both malpractice liability and products liability. See, e.g., Epstein 1976; Danzon 2000; Hylton 2000; Epstein and Sykes 2001; A. Schwartz 1988; see also G. Priest 1981.

[30] Epstein 1976.

[31] See, e.g., Danzon 2000; Abraham and Weiler 1994b (hospital enterprise liability); see also Havighurst 2000 (MCO contractual liability).

meaningful option to obtain services from the provider without a waiver (albeit at a higher price).[32]

In addition, many malpractice experts argue that patients may not be well enough informed about the benefits of liability to contract over malpractice liability effectively. Information problems are likely to be particularly great in the case of patient contracting with individual physicians. In-office physician contracting raises special concerns because patients cannot easily comparison shop for physicians based on contract terms. A patient contracting with a physician often does not ascertain the physician's contract terms until he arrives for his appointment, which often occurs long after the patient decided he needed care.[33] After this long wait, a patient presented with an undesirable physician contractual liability provision nevertheless may agree to it, because the cost of searching for a new physician is so high (introducing additional delay) and the potential benefit uncertain (because he does not know which other physicians offer better terms). High search costs thus could result in physicians obtaining liability waivers even when they are inefficient.[34]

Finally, physicians often cannot offer patients large enough financial incentives to induce patients to contract over liability. Physicians often cannot easily encourage patients to sign exculpatory provisions by offering to charge less for service because insured patients do not pay most of the costs of the treatment they receive. Thus, physicians often cannot induce patients to contract over liability, so long as courts prevent physicians from refusing to treat patients who reject exculpatory provisions.[35]

---

[32] See, e.g., *Tunkl v. Regents of University of California*, 60 Cal.2d 92, 32 Cal.Rptr. 33, 383 P.2d 441, 446–447 (1963) (invalidating a clause releasing a charitable hospital from liability for future negligence in part because of the hospital's superior bargaining power and the lack of a clause permitting the patient to pay a higher fee in return for imposing liability); *Ash v. New York Univ. Dental Center*, 164 A.D.2d 366, 564 N.Y.2d 308 (1990); *Smith v. Hosp. Authority of Walker, Dade and Catoosa Cos.*, 160 Ga.App. 387, 287 S.E.2d 99 (1981); *Cudnik v. William Beaumont Hospital*, 525 N.W.2d 891, 895–6 (Mich. App. 1994) (invalidating an exculpatory agreement between a patient and hospital in part because of the hospital's superior bargaining power and patient's inability to negotiate for liability).

[33] Patients also may not have adequate incentives to ascertain liability terms when offered a standard form contract in a physician's office because they have little reason to read the contract unless they are willing to leave if they find an unattractive clause. For a discussion of why rational parties may not investigate all contracting terms prior to contracting, see Katz 1998, 504.

[34] Indeed, when search costs are high, voluntary contracting may result in all medical providers insisting on liability waivers, even when this is inefficient, if patient search costs are sufficiently high that it is optimal for patients to simply accept a suboptimal contract because the expected marginal gain of seeking a new physician is not positive. See Schwartz and Wilde 1983, 1397, 1409–10 (discussing the circumstances under which search costs may produce inefficient contract terms).

[35] Danzon 2000, 1382. This problem is particularly great with fee-for-service insurance.

Entity-Level Contractual Liability

Contractual malpractice liability was given new life in the 1990s with the rise of large entities that can both contract with patients in advance of care and coordinate contracting across many providers. Of particular importance, the 1990s saw the rise of a new form of medical insurer, the MCO.[36] MCOs both finance and provide care. They thus enter into contracts with both patients and medical providers.

The second generation of contractual liability proposals generally favor placing all malpractice liability on medical entities (such as MCOs), which can then determine the ultimate financial responsibility of individual medical providers. These proposals permit the responsible entities to contract freely with patients (and medical providers) as to the extent of liability to be imposed. This right to contract includes the right to contract out of liability altogether.[37]

Contractual liability channeled through an entity capable of influencing and coordinating care – e.g., an MCO – avoids many of the problems of physician contractual liability. Patients contracting annually with an entity are less likely to agree to inefficient waivers as a result of duress, because they can contract when they are not in need of immediate medical care.

Large entities such as MCOs also are better able than many physicians to provide patients with appropriate financial incentives to alter liability terms. For example, MCOs can offer to reduce premiums in return for liability waivers or reductions.[38]

Patients engaged in periodic contracting for health care also may be better able to compare the contractual liability terms offered by different entities because they can obtain the terms in advance of needing medical services as part of their regular annual consideration of medical insurance or care. Search costs may be particularly low for patients employed by large employers because large employers need not "search" for contract terms but instead can simply tell medical entities wishing to contract with them which contractual liability terms they prefer.[39]

---

[36] MCOs now cover 70% to 98% of all Americans with health insurance. Glied 2000, 708–10. This chapter uses the term MCO to refer to any plan that uses either financial incentives or pretreatment utilization review to attempt to influence treatment cost.

[37] Abraham and Weiler 1994b (proposing enterprise liability for hospitals for all injuries caused by medical treatment without regard to fault); Sage, Hastings, and Berenson 1994 (supporting enterprise liability for medical malpractice); Havighurst 2000 (proposing enterprise liability for MCOs for all injuries caused by medical treatment without regard to fault); see also Danzon 2000 (supporting contractual MCO liability). But see Arlen and MacLeod 2003 (proposing entity-level liability for MCOs for MCO and physician negligence without granting MCOs the right to freely negotiate waivers).

[38] Danzon 2000.

[39] Scholars who make this argument in the malpractice context include Danzon 2000, 1382; Epstein and Sykes 2001, 644, 647–8; see also Havighurst 2000, 8–9.

Finally, some argue that MCO contractual liability presents less of a risk that patients will contract in error because most MCO contracts are actively negotiated by employers that can assess the benefits of liability. Employers will provide optimal terms, it is argued, because employers maximize profits when they provide their employees the most cost-effective health benefits.[40]

Accordingly, entity-level contractual liability, it is asserted, solves the problems of physician-based contractual liability. Any malpractice liability reform that includes entity-level contractual liability necessarily is superior to even the best-designed malpractice liability system implemented through the tort system.[41]

POTENTIAL COST TO PATIENTS OF CONTRACTUAL LIABILITY

The economic claim that contractual liability is superior to even the best malpractice liability system rests on the claim that patients cannot be hurt by a move to contracting because any patient who would have been well-served by tort liability will simply replicate tort by contract. This section evaluates this claim that any patient who would have been well-served by tort liability will impose malpractice liability by contract and shows that it is not correct.[42] The problems identified here afflict both individual physician and entity-level contracting.

This section shows that contractual liability may make some patients worse off because patients who would have benefited from malpractice liability will not necessarily elect to impose liability by contract, because contractual liability provides patients with lower benefits than does malpractice liability in many circumstances. Thus, patients who would have benefited from tort liability (and thus voted for it, if offered the option) nevertheless may prefer not to pay for contractual liability because they do not obtain sufficient benefit from liability obtained by contract to justify its cost. In addition, patients who benefit from malpractice liability may contract out of liability because they underestimate the benefit of contractual liability.[43]

Accordingly, contractual liability does not necessarily enhance patients' welfare. It may make some patients better off, but others worse off.

---

[40] See Epstein and Sykes 2001; Havighurst 2000.

[41] See, e.g., Epstein 1976; Epstein and Sykes 2001 (expressing faith in patient contracting).

[42] This chapter only considers proposals to permit patients to contract over liability. It does not examine contracts which require arbitration (compare with Hylton 2000), or which only shift liability from physicians to entities without altering its terms. Compare with Sage and Jorling 1994.

[43] This section focuses only on the relative potential deterrence benefits potentially available through tort liability and contractual liability for malpractice. For a full consideration of the relative costs as well as the benefits of malpractice liability and contractual liability, see Arlen 2005.

Lawmakers accordingly should not introduce contracting unless they can be sure that, in the aggregate, the benefits exceed the costs.

Lower Benefits of Contractual Liability

Proponents of contractual liability assume that patients who benefit from tort liability will replicate it by contract because they also assume that liability obtained by contract affords patients the same benefits as liability imposed by tort. This is not the case. Medical providers often will be unable to design contracts that enable patients to obtain the same benefit from contracted-for liability as they can from tort liability.

The benefit to each patient of tort liability flows not only from liability for his own injuries, but also from his providers' aggregate expected liability for injuries to other patients, both now and in the future. By contrast, contracted-for liability generally restricts a patient to determining his providers' liability for injuries to himself for the period of the contract.

Under tort liability, each patient benefits from expected liability for injuries to other patients because each medical provider determines how much to invest in measures to improve outcomes for all of his patients (such as expertise or computerized drug order entry systems) based on his total expected liability for all patients. Similarly, each patient benefits from expected liability in future periods (beyond the life of the contract), because each provider's incentives to invest in durable care that benefits current and future patients – such as physician expertise and computer systems that detect errors – depends on total expected liability both now and in the future. Thus, the benefit to each patient of well-designed malpractice liability derives not only from the threat of liability for injuries to himself, but also from the threat of liability for other patients and injuries in future periods.

Patients required to obtain liability by contract, by contrast, are limited to a much more restricted form of liability. Each patient only can impose liability for injuries to themselves and then only for the period of the contract.[44] This more restricted form of liability provides lower incentives for medical providers to take care than does tort liability, thus resulting in less improvement in quality than is potentially available through tort liability (as will be shown). As a result, informed patients who would benefit from tort liability (and thus vote for it, if given the option) nevertheless may rationally waive liability imposed by contract because the benefits of this form of liability do not exceed the costs. For these patients, the move from tort to contract is welfare reducing, eliminating their preferred choice (tort liability) in favor of a less valuable form of liability they do not want.

---

44 In the case of MCO contracting, employees may be able to contract collectively through their employers, but they may not be able to contract collectively with patients employed by other employers. Moreover, employers may not bargain for the contract terms that best serve employees, if employees are not fully informed about the benefits of liability.

Contracting Problems When "Care" Is a Collective Good. Patients do not
have efficient incentives to impose liability by contract to the extent that the
benefit generated by liability is a "collective good."

A central purpose of malpractice liability is to induce investments in higher
quality medical care. Many of these investments are a "collective good," in
that they increase medical providers' ability to provide good quality care
to any and all patients. For example, increased physician expertise in diagnosing patients benefits all of the physician's patients, whether any given
patient imposed liability or not. Similarly, health information technology
that reduces the likelihood of error in administering drugs also is a collective
good in that it benefits all of a hospital's patients.

All patients benefit when a medical provider increases his investment in
"collective care"; all are hurt when he underinvests in this collective care.
The incentives the tort system provides each medical provider to invest in
such care result not from liability to any individual patient but instead from
potential liability for all of the provider's patients. To induce optimal investment in collective care, tort liability imposes liability on medical providers
for harms to all of their patients. Each patient benefits from liability imposed
for harms to other patients.[45]

Patients who benefit from this collective imposition of liability may be
worse off under contractual liability because it transforms the collective
decision to impose liability for medical negligence (embodied in malpractice liability) into an individual decision. Individuals often cannot use individual contracting to obtain collective benefits because people often have
inadequate incentives to spend money on investments that benefit others.

Contractual liability will not result in each patient contracting into liability (even when they all would benefit if everyone did so), because each patient
gains too little from a decision to impose liability. Each patient has too little
incentive to contract into liability because he decides whether to impose liability by contract based only on the benefit to him of the resulting increase in
care. He does not take into account the benefit to other patients of providers'
increased care. Thus, a patient may contract out of welfare-enhancing liability because he does not take into account the benefit to others of the increase
in quality resulting from liability for harms to himself.

Beyond this, each patient may rationally waive liability in the hope of
"free-riding" on the higher quality care induced by the liability contracts
of other patients. When medical providers have many patients, each patient
may be able to waive liability without significantly affecting "collective"
quality because each medical provider's incentives to invest in collective care
depends on his total expected liability across all his patients. This would not
be significantly affected by a single waiver. Accordingly, each patient may
waive in the hope of free-riding on financial incentives provided by other

[45] Arlen and MacLeod 2003, 2003–4.

patients. If each patient does this, however, then no patient will impose liability, to the detriment of all.

Accordingly, contractual liability can reduce patients' welfare when patients benefit collectively from malpractice liability, because patients contracting individually may rationally waive liability even when collectively they are better off if liability is imposed. Thus, introducing individual contracting over liability may reduce patients' welfare relative to the collective determination of liability through the tort system.[46]

Contracting to Induce Precontractual Care. Contracting may be inefficient even when care is not a collective good because patients may not obtain sufficient benefit from the use of contractual liability to regulate investments in quality that affect multiple periods to justify the cost of contractual liability, even when tort liability would be efficient.

Malpractice liability benefits patients by providing medical caregivers an incentive to invest in durable care (e.g., expertise) for the benefit of patients they will have in the future. It encourages providers to invest in care precontract, long before the provider meets the patient. This precontractual investment in care is one of the important benefits patients derive from the imposition of malpractice liability. Indeed, for some patients, malpractice liability is welfare enhancing only because it increases providers' precontractual investments in care.[47]

Tort liability regulates precontractual care because medical providers anticipate the threat of malpractice liability for injuries to future patients. Contractual liability can provide this equivalent benefit only if medical providers expect patients to accept their future offers to impose liability by contract. Patients whose health depends primarily on precontractual care may not want to pay to impose liability by contract, however, because contractual liability may not enable them to obtain care from physicians who have invested more in precontractual care. Whereas the tort system benefits patients by providing medical caregivers with incentives to invest in precontractual quality, patients often cannot use their decision to contract into liability to provide their caregivers incentives to invest in precontractual care because, at the moment of contracting, medical providers' precontractual investments in care have already been made. Patients thus cannot use contracted-for liability to induce greater precontractual care. Contractual liability thus may result in suboptimal care, as medical caregivers will base their care decisions on the assumption that many future patients will waive liability.[48]

---

[46] Id.
[47] Id.
[48] Id. Keith Hylton's conclusion that informed patients waive liability only if liability is wealth-reducing rests on his assumption that the plaintiff's decision of whether to impose liability

Patients might have adequate incentives to contract into liability if they can use medical providers' decisions to offer contractual liability to identify which medical providers have invested more in precontractual care. Economic analysis of product warranties has shown that customers may be willing to pay for warranties (or liability) even when quality is fixed, if they can use the imposition of the warranty to distinguish high-quality producers from low-quality ones, because low-quality producers cannot afford to offer liability for product defects. In this situation, it is argued, high-quality producers will offer liability to signal their quality; consumers contract into liability to identify the higher quality producers.[49]

Yet reasons exist to doubt that contracting over malpractice liability will result in high-quality providers signaling quality through the offer of liability. First (for reasons discussed later), patients may not be well enough informed to accurately estimate the signal of quality provided by a provider's offer to bear liability. Accordingly, they may not be willing to pay the higher price charged by providers who offer liability, even when it would be in their best interests to do so.[50]

Second, providers may not be able to use liability to signal quality even if patients are informed, because contracting over liability often occurs in situations where a patient can negotiate with a provider over liability after selecting the provider. The standard analysis of signaling through warranties assumes that producers make take-it-or-leave it offers to consumers; consumers cannot offer to purchase the product for less without the warranty.[51] This assumption is reasonable as applied to many product markets because consumers rarely purchase products directly from the manufacturer. By contrast, in the medical care context, patients and employers contracting over liability often can negotiate directly with providers (either physicians or MCOs). A patient need not accept a provider's offer to assume liability as a final offer. This ability to negotiate may undermine medical providers' ability to use liability to signal quality because patients who have selected, and agreed to contract with, a provider based on the signal provided (i.e., the offer to assume liability) can enhance the value of the contract to both parties by agreeing to waive liability.

To see this, consider an informed patient who only benefits from contractual liability through its effects on precontractual care (for example,

---

will affect the injurer's care. Hylton 2000, 213, 220–2. This is not the case when care is determined precontract.

[49] See Spence 1977; Grossman 1981.

[50] Signaling will not produce a separating equilibrium if patients do not purchase liability offered by high-quality firms because they underestimate the benefit of liability. See Spence 1977, 564; see also Geistfeld 1995a, 248; Geistfeld 1994, 813 n. 35.

[51] See, e.g., Grossman 1981; see also Spence 1977; Geistfeld 1995a.

a patient seeking immediate treatment from a compassionate surgeon)[52]. In this circumstance, the patient only cares about the provider's offer to assume liability for the signal it provides. He does not benefit from the actual decision to impose liability at the moment of contracting once he has obtained the signal, because quality is already fixed precontract (and thus is unaffected by whether liability is actually imposed). Accordingly, a patient who has obtained what he believes is a credible signal of quality has little reason to actually insist that liability be imposed. Indeed, at this point, he gains nothing from paying the additional cost to impose liability and has every incentive to request that the provider offer a lower price in return for a liability waiver. This offer, if fairly priced, would benefit the provider and thus would be accepted.[53]

Yet, if too many patients negotiate around providers' offers to assume liability, contractual liability cannot function as a credible signal of quality because low-quality providers will be able to mimic high-quality providers at no additional cost by offering to assume liability, confident that patients will later seek a contract that does not impose liability. Accordingly, patients may not obtain a signaling benefit from the use of contractual liability to identify those who have invested more in precontractual care.[54]

Contractual liability, therefore, does not necessarily provide patients with the same benefit as malpractice liability because patients may not benefit from the use of contractual liability to affect precontractual investment in

---

[52] Signaling models of warranties assume that consumers accept fair warranty provisions whenever they are offered because these models assume that consumers value warranties as insurance against product defects. Producers thus can easily use warranties to signal product quality because consumers are willing to pay for warranties even if there is no signal. See, e.g., Grossman 1981; see also Spence 1977. By contrast, patients risking serious permanent injury do not necessarily want to pay to obtain compensation (i.e., insurance) through the tort system. First, patients can obtain insurance at lower cost outside of the tort system. Second, absent deterrence, patients might not want tort liability imposed for serious injuries (like death or coma) because they must pay the expected cost of such liability (through higher prices) but obtain little benefit from compensation paid to them should they suffer a serious injury (like death or coma). See, e.g., Epstein 1985; G. Priest 1987; A. Schwartz 1988; see also Cook and Graham 1977 (deriving the conditions for optimal insurance against nonpecuniary losses); Arlen 2000 (discussing optimal damages for death and serious permanent injury). Thus, any signaling analysis of contractual malpractice liability must assume that many patients do not value liability for the compensation (insurance) it provides.

[53] Patients may benefit from negotiating out of liability if they can negotiate after they are committed to dealing with a particular provider when liability is not a cost-effective way of insuring against injuries.

[54] Fudenberg and Tirole 1990 examined the effects of renegotiation on principals' ability to use contracts to remedy moral hazard problems. By contrast, the present analysis examines adverse selection (signaling) and considers problems arising from the ability to negotiate at the moment of contracting. Negotiation undermines signaling when consumers can negotiate after they have committed to dealing with a particular provider.

care. Accordingly, patients who would have benefited from the effects of malpractice liability on precontractual care may be worse off under contractual liability because they may not obtain sufficient benefit from contractual liability to justify its costs.[55] These patients' reduced willingness to contract into liability also hurts other patients because, as explained previously, patients benefit from the threat of liability for other patients.

Impact on Postcontractual Care. The preceding problem is less serious to the extent that patients benefit from the use of contractual liability to regulate postcontractual investments in care. If this incentive is sufficiently great, patients may benefit from accepting providers' offers to assume liability, even if they do not value the right to be compensated for nonpecuniary losses. Nevertheless, the effect of liability on postcontractual care may not be sufficiently great to justify contracting into liability, even when contractual liability can optimally regulate postcontractual care.

Moreover, patients do not necessarily obtain as much benefit from the use of contractual liability to regulate postcontractual care as they do from tort liability used for this purpose. Patients benefit from malpractice liability in part because it induces greater investment in durable postcontractual care (such as expertise). Patients know they will benefit in future periods from present-day incentives to invest in durable care, whether or not they switch medical providers in the future, because all medical providers are governed by malpractice liability. Tort liability thus gives all providers incentives to invest today to protect current and future patients.

By contrast, patients benefit from the use of contractual liability to induce postcontractual durable care only for as long as they obtain care from providers regulated by the contract. Given this, patients do not obtain the full benefit of the use of contractual liability to regulate durable care if they expect to switch providers in the future to those not governed by the contract.[56] Patients thus benefit less from contractual liability than from tort liability the greater the probability that the current contract does not apply to the providers from whom they will obtain care in the future. Patients may anticipate changing providers, even if they would rather not do so, if (1) their employer switches health insurers, for example to save costs or because the employer has merged with another company, or if (2) the patient changes (or loses) his job.[57] As a result, patients obtain less benefit from the incentives

---

[55] See supra note 43.

[56] Moreover, annual contracting over liability may not be efficient if patients' incentives to contract out of liability in the final period undermines the effectiveness of contracting in initial periods. Arlen and MacLeod 2003; see also Fudenberg and Tirole 1990.

[57] Patients may lose their existing health insurance when long-term illness results in patients losing their jobs and thus their health insurance. See Himmelstein et al. 2005.

provided by contractual liability than from the incentives provided by well-designed malpractice liability.

Accordingly, many patients who would have benefited from the use of malpractice liability to regulate postcontractual care will not derive sufficient benefit from contracted-for liability to induce them to contract into liability. The move to contractual liability hurts these patients.

Information Problems

Contractual liability also may harm patients who benefit from tort liability when patients are not sufficiently well-informed about the benefits and costs of liability to contract in their own best interests. In order to contract effectively, patients must know (or have incentives to learn) the contractual liability terms their providers' contracts contain, they must understand the costs and benefits of the terms, and they must know enough about terms offered by other providers to be able to comparison shop based on differences in contractual liability terms.

Patients contracting for malpractice liability often are not sufficiently well-informed to contract on their own behalf. Information problems may result in many patients contracting out of liability, even when they would be better off insisting that liability be imposed.

Patients required to contract over liability may contract out of liability even when it is not in their interests to do so if they underestimate the net personal benefit of imposing liability.[58] Malpractice liability imposes a direct and immediate cost on patients in the form of higher health insurance payments (and out-of-pocket medical costs). To make an informed choice about whether to pay this cost, patients must compare it against the benefit they obtain from using liability to induce greater medical provider investment in quality. Patients may underestimate this benefit if they underestimate either their need for serious medical care or the effect of sanctions for negligence on the expected quality of care provided.

Patients face little threat from medical negligence so long as they remain healthy and do not need serious care.[59] Accordingly, patients who underestimate their likelihood of needing serious medical care – as evidence suggests most do – also may underestimate the benefit to them of using liability to improve the quality of medical care.[60] Many patients also may underestimate the benefit of liability because they assume that their medical providers

---

[58] Spence 1977, 563; see also Schwartz and Wilde 1983, 1387, 1389, 1425–46.

[59] Thus patients cannot easily assess the benefit of liability collectively because it is patient-specific, as the value of care is likely to depend on both the probability that the patient becomes ill and the type of illness and treatment required.

[60] See Weinstein 1987, 494–6 (discussing evidence that patients underestimate the probability they will fall ill).

can be relied on to deliver the best care possible, even without liability. Even though patients regularly receive negligent care,[61] many patients assume that their own medical providers will deliver nonnegligent care regardless of their financial incentives. Indeed, this assumption may help explain why most patients injured by medical negligence do not sue. Patients injured by medical negligence may fail to pursue litigation because they trust their provider to deliver good care and thus incorrectly attribute their injuries to a non-actionable cause (such as background risks). Contractual liability thus may hurt patients if patients often underestimate the benefit to them of liability.

Some contractual liability proponents argue that information problems would not be significant if contractual liability provisions are negotiated on behalf of employees by sophisticated and informed employers, contracting with large entities such as MCOs.[62] Yet, employer contracting cannot eliminate problems presented by misinformed employees. Employers benefit from providing employees with the benefits package their employees value most. Thus, employers will negotiate for the contractual liability provisions that they expect their employees to *believe* to be in their best interests, and not the terms they know to be in their employees' best interests. Accordingly, if employees substantially underestimate the benefit of malpractice liability, then employers will contract out of liability even if they know that this does not enhance their employees' welfare.[63]

Contracting and Commitment

Accordingly, shifting liability from tort to contract can make patients worse off than they would be under malpractice liability because many patients obtain less benefit from liability imposed by contract than from liability imposed by tort. Thus, patients required to contract over liability may rationally reject contractual liability even when they would have benefited from (and, thus, been willing to vote for) malpractice liability for physician negligence. The choice that contract offers patients thus does not increase their options. It alters them, by changing the form of liability imposed. For patients who are well-served by malpractice liability, this change is likely to make them worse off.

---

[61] See supra note 1.

[62] See Epstein and Sykes 2001.

[63] Employers, moreover, may not have adequate incentives to attempt to educate employees. To the extent that employers bear the cost of health care, they do not benefit from encouraging employees to insist on higher quality care if employers derive less benefit than their employees from superior employee health. This is likely for many reasons, including employee turnover and the burden employers bear from providing benefits to retired employees. Moreover, not all employers will be better informed than their employees. Small firms, for example, may not have the expertise needed to accurately assess the expected costs and benefits to patients of waiver.

Contractual liability thus may be inferior to tort liability as a method for inducing optimal care, to the extent that contracting parties cannot use contract to replicate tort because tort liability better enables them to coordinate their collective incentives across patients and across time (and thus providers). A central issue for contractual liability proponents, accordingly, is to determine whether medical providers can (and will) solve these contracting problems in order to allow contractual liability to obtain the full benefits of tort liability while retaining the advantages of contractual liability.

In theory, medical providers could facilitate signaling and reduce collective action problems if each provider could credibly commit to offer only one contractual liability term to all patients both now and in the future. This would reduce free-riding problems, as each patient would know that all patients make the same decision. It also would enable providers to better use liability to signal quality, as patient-specific negotiation would not be allowed.

Although medical providers' ability to solve the commitment problem warrants serious consideration, there are reasons to be concerned. It is far from clear that medical providers have either the incentives or ability to remedy commitment problems under contractual liability. Medical providers may not have adequate incentives to commit to standard form contracts unless patients are sufficiently well-informed to understand the benefits of provider precommitment. Moreover, patients must have sufficiently accurate information about providers to detect providers who agree to negotiate around liability provisions (for example, with a large employer).

Moreover, even if medical providers can reduce contracting problems – for example, through the use of standard form contracts that bind all patients to a single contract – these solutions may reduce the benefit of contractual liability and increase the risk of misinformed contracting. The use of standard form contracts may reduce patients' ability to obtain contractual liability terms tailored to their individual preferences, thereby eroding one of the benefits of contractual liability. Indeed, patients in many areas may find themselves with only one effective choice to the extent that patients obtain insurance through employers that offer only one health plan.

In addition, contracting through standard form contracts may increase costs because patients are less likely to be informed when offered standard form contracts, as they may rationally not even read the contract. Accordingly, standard form contracts may increase the likelihood that patients are not sufficiently well-informed to contract on their own behalf.[64]

Accordingly, reasons exist to be concerned that medical providers either may not be able to develop contractual liability provisions that have benefits similar to tort liability or may not be able to do so at an acceptable cost. The

[64] See, e.g., Katz 1998.

concern thus remains that switching from malpractice liability to contractually based liability may reduce patients' welfare.

CONCLUSION

This chapter examines the standard economists' case for contractual liability, focusing on the argument that choice cannot hurt patients because any patient who benefits from malpractice liability will replicate malpractice liability by contract. This chapter shows that this claim does not hold. Patients who benefit from tort liability often will be worse off under contractual liability.

Patients may be worse off if they are not sufficiently well-informed to contract in their own best interests. They may choose to waive welfare-enhancing liability because they underestimate the benefits of liability. This problem cannot be solved by channeling contracting through employers.

In addition, informed patients who would have benefited from malpractice liability may be worse off under contractual liability because they may be unable to replicate malpractice liability by contract. Many of the benefits patients potentially derive from tort liability flow from the ability to provide stable incentives across time, across patients, and across providers (both current and future). Patients cannot necessarily obtain these benefits – many of which flow from commitment – through periodic contracting with current providers. Thus, many patients may be worse off under contractual liability to the extent that it effectively substitutes an inferior (narrower) form of liability for the broader liability that they prefer.

Accordingly, the argument for contractual liability cannot assume that patients are better off when allowed to contract over liability. Contractual liability should not replace tort liability unless it can be shown to enhance aggregate welfare, taking into account the negative effect of contracting on those patients who are better served by a tort liability regime. Whether it is indeed beneficial depends both on whether contracting parties can solve the problems with contractual liability identified here and on whether welfare-enhancing malpractice liability reform is possible. In the meantime, reformers should not rush to remedy existing problems by contract. There is no guarantee that the cure will not be worse than the disease.

14

Medical Malpractice Insurance Reform

"Enterprise Insurance" and Some Alternatives

Tom Baker

Medical malpractice has been a white-hot topic in state legislatures during three periods in recent history: the mid-1970s, the mid-1980s, and again in the early 2000s. Each time, the precipitating cause was the same: dramatic increases in medical liability insurance premiums, particularly in high-risk specialties and locations. For that reason alone, medical liability insurance deserves careful attention in any discussion of medical malpractice reform.

This chapter has three goals: to explain the pricing cycle that has driven these increases in medical liability insurance premiums, to evaluate the relative merits of potential public policy goals for medical liability insurance reform, and to consider ways to achieve those goals. As the title of this chapter suggests, I am most interested in promoting a reform that I call "enterprise insurance," but the discussion of policy goals will provide a set of conceptual tools that are useful for evaluating other medical liability insurance reforms. Thus, this chapter has something to offer beyond an argument for enterprise insurance.

I begin with a brief explanation of the medical liability insurance pricing cycle, focusing on aspects of medical liability that make the cycle so volatile. The main lesson here is that volatility in the medical liability insurance market results from the interaction between the cyclical nature of the insurance business generally and the comparatively high and concentrated nature of the uncertainties involved in predicting future medical liability losses in particular.

I then consider five potential goals for medical liability insurance reform: reducing medical liability insurance premiums, reducing volatility in medical practitioners' insurance premiums, ensuring access to medical liability insurance, enhancing the injury prevention role of medical liability insurance institutions, and reallocating the burden of insurance premiums. In response,

Thank you to Yan Hong, John Maroney, and Kathleen Santoro for able research assistance. Many of the ideas in this chapter are developed more fully in T. Baker 2005a.

I have two significant claims: First, reducing total medical liability insurance premiums is not a worthy public policy goal, unless we at the same time provide a new and better approach to prevention and compensation for medical injuries. Second, "enterprise insurance" is the most promising way to achieve most of the other, more worthy policy goals.

Enterprise insurance would obligate hospitals and similar organizations to provide insurance covering all liabilities arising out of services performed, or to be performed, in their facilities. For example, a birth is a procedure that, ordinarily, takes place in a hospital. Liability arising out of any services related to a birth would be covered by the liability insurance provided by the hospital in which a medical provider plans to deliver the baby. This approach places the medical liability insurance burden on organizations that provide facilities for much of the most risky patient care.

The term "enterprise insurance" is borrowed from the term "enterprise liability."[1] The difference between enterprise *insurance* and enterprise *liability* is that the enterprise does not as a formal matter become liable for the mistakes of the medical provider under the insurance approach; all the enterprise has to do is provide liability insurance. Nevertheless, an enterprise insurance regime would provide much of the deterrence benefit of an enterprise liability regime. The crucial differences are that the insurance responsibility of the enterprise for the medical provider's mistake would be capped at the level of the mandated insurance; the legal responsibility, and corresponding moral authority, would continue to rest with the individual provider.

Many medical schools and some HMOs and hospitals already have adopted a similar approach to liability insurance for their physicians.[2] As these organizations have found, they are better able than physicians to manage the volatility of insurance premiums and better able to obtain insurance or to make alternative risk transfer arrangements under even the most difficult market conditions. Enterprise insurance also enhances the injury prevention incentives for these organizations and their medical liability insurance – by concentrating the financial responsibility for liabilities – in contrast to the diffused responsibility of the individualized insurance approach.[3]

Enterprise insurance would not entirely replace the current individualized approach to medical liability insurance, but it would reduce the impact of future liability insurance crises on the specialists who have borne the brunt

[1] See generally Sage 1997.
[2] American Medical Association 1998, 33–44; Haugh 2003, 47; Larkin 2004, 44. See also Sage 1997, 174–5. Note that in at least some of the current arrangements individual physicians are responsible for paying all or part of their share of the premiums.
[3] Cf. Association of the Bar of the City of New York 1990, 579–80 (urging the expansion of voluntary "channeling" insurance programs in which physicians have the option to purchase liability insurance at a lower cost through a hospital, in part on the basis of the loss prevention benefits).

of prior crises. Medical providers with office-based practices would continue to need liability insurance for claims that do not arise out of an admission or a procedure to be performed in an enterprise facility. Historically, price, volatility, and access have not been as difficult for office-based practices as for hospital-based specialists. One demonstration of the easier time that office-based practices have had during insurance crises can be seen in the fact that some OB/GYNs reduced their medical malpractice premiums in recent years by giving up the obstetrical part of their practice.[4]

THE MEDICAL LIABILITY INSURANCE UNDERWRITING CYCLE

Insurance markets are subject to a business cycle that consists of periods in which insurance is priced above cost (a "hard" market) and periods in which insurance prices gradually decline relative to costs (a "soft" market).[5] Notably, coverage is plentiful and nonprice terms are favorable to policyholders during the soft market whereas coverage is restricted and nonprice terms are unfavorable to policyholders during hard markets.

A defining characteristic of the shift from a soft to a hard market is a sharp increase in insurers' accounting judgments regarding the costs of paying future claims. The increase is particularly dramatic in the medical liability area because of the "long tail" of medical liability insurance (meaning that claims often are not paid until five years or more after the policies are sold). Because of the long tail, loss cost revisions affect not only claims that will be paid under future policies but also the many claims that remain to be paid on policies sold in the past. It is too late to collect new premiums for policies already sold, but reserves under the old policies do need to be increased, with the result that a relatively modest change in expectations can have a dramatic impact on calendar year results due to the compounding effect of the long tail.

These hard market accounting revisions have misled many people into believing that the hard market results from a dramatic change in the underlying liability environment. As a result, they mistakenly conclude that a hard market signals a "litigation explosion" or a sudden change in either the frequency or severity of medical malpractice claims.

As I have explained elsewhere in detail, the medical malpractice insurance "crises" of the mid-1970s, the mid-1980s, and the early 2000s did not reflect a sudden or dramatic change in either litigation behavior or malpractice payments.[6] What changed instead were insurance market conditions and the investment and cost projections built into medical malpractice insurance premiums. Insurers that offered low prices based on optimistic scenarios in

[4] Strunk and Esser 2004, 3.
[5] This section of this chapter summarizes the analysis from T. Baker 2005b.
[6] Ibid.

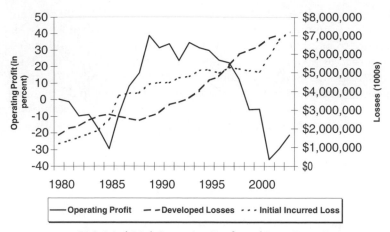

FIGURE 14.1. U.S. Med Mal Operating Profit and Loss Experience, 1980–2003.

1970, 1981, and 1997 switched to high prices based on pessimistic scenarios in 1975, 1986, and 2001. There has been a long-term upward trend in medical malpractice claim payments, but that trend has been far smoother than the swings of the pricing cycle would suggest.

Figure 14.1 provides one graphical depiction of the medical liability insurance underwriting cycle, using three important industrywide insurance accounting measures. The first measure is "operating profit," the solid line in Fig. 14.1.[7] Operating profit has a technical definition, but the basic idea is that years with positive operating profit percentages are profitable years for medical liability insurers and years with negative operating profit years are unprofitable years. Operating profit is measured in percentage terms, so the operating profit line in the figure should be read using the percentage numbers on the axis on the left side of the figure. The operating profit line depicts the well-known features of the underwriting cycle: a profit "valley" in the final years of both the 1980s and the 1990s soft markets, followed soon after by significant improvements.

The second insurance accounting measure shown in Fig. 14.1 is "initial incurred loss." This is the dotted line in the figure, and it shows the total dollar value of the losses that the medical liability insurance industry expected to pay on policies sold in the indicated year at the time those policies were sold. Initial incurred losses are predictions; they are not dollars paid to claimants or lawyers. Nevertheless, initial incurred losses have a real effect on profit and loss. As a matter of prudence (and by legal requirement in most instances), insurers must set "reserves" that are equal to the amount

---

[7] Data for Fig. 14.1 were taken from *Best's Aggregates and Averages, Property/Casualty* (2004 and earlier editions).

needed to pay future claims under any policies it sells and then must set aside assets to offset those reserves. Those assets are real money, which cannot be used for any purpose other than earning investment income.

The third insurance accounting measure displayed in Fig. 14.1 is "developed loss." This is the dashed line in the figure, and it shows the total dollar value of the losses that the insurance industry had paid or expected to pay for policies sold in the indicated year, as of ten years after the policies were sold (or as of the end of 2003 for policies sold since 1995). In other words, the number for 1982 comes from data available only as of the end of 1991, and the number for 1994 comes from data available only as of the end of 2003. Well over 90 percent of medical liability claim payments are made within ten years after the policies are sold, so the developed loss figures for the years 1994 and earlier come very close to the total losses that will be paid under policies sold for each of those years. The developed loss line becomes increasingly less "developed" the closer it gets to 2003.

One proof that medical liability insurance crises do not reflect sudden or dramatic changes in the frequency and severity of medical malpractice claims comes from the relationship between the three lines shown in the figure. The next two paragraphs walk readers through that exercise in detail.

The first step is to compare the rate of change over time in the initial incurred loss line (the dotted line) and the developed loss line (the dashed line). Notice how the *developed* loss line shows a slow but steady increase in medical malpractice insurance losses, with the exception of a relatively flat period from 1986 to 1989 (reflecting a decline in the supply of insurance sold during the hard market of that time as well as the effects of the 1980s tort reforms). Now notice how the *initial incurred* loss line jumps dramatically at the low point in the profit cycle and grows very slowly at all other times. This first step tells us that it is insurers' predictions about loss payments that increase dramatically at the onset of a hard market, not developed losses or actual claim payments.

The second step is to examine the relationship between the initial incurred loss line and the developed loss lines in Fig. 14.1. Notice how the initial incurred loss line is below the developed losses toward the end of each of the soft market periods shown in the chart (1980–1984 and 1987–2001). This means that the insurance industry *under*predicted its eventual loss costs during those years. Now notice how the initial incurred loss crosses and then rises above the developed loss line following the onset of the hard market in 1985. It is too soon to be absolutely sure about very recent developed losses, but it seems very likely that we will later be able to observe the same phenomenon with regard to initial and developed losses for policies sold beginning in 2001 or 2002. This later relationship means that the insurance industry *over*predicted losses during the hard market and the initial years of the soft market (1986–1995).

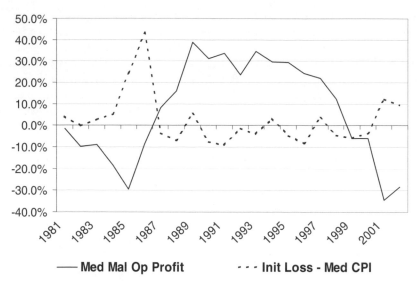

FIGURE 14.2. U.S. Med Mal Initial Incurred Loss, Controlling for Medical Inflation, 1980–2002.

Figure 14.2 shows the effect of the underwriting cycle on insurers' loss projections in a slightly different way: the rate of change in initial incurred loss over time, controlling for the effect of medical inflation.[8] As with the first figure, the solid line shows the operating profit and the dotted line shows the initial incurred losses. In this chart, however, the initial incurred loss line shows the rate of change in initial incurred losses on a year-by-year basis, accounting for medical inflation, so it should be read using the percentage figures on the left axis. When the initial incurred loss line is at zero, that means that initial incurred loss increased at exactly the rate of medical inflation. When the dotted line is above zero, initial incurred loss increased faster than medical inflation. And, when the dotted line is below zero, initial incurred loss increased more slowly than medical inflation. As is now evident, Fig. 14.2 presents quite a dramatic picture of the relationship between initial incurred losses and the underwriting cycle. Initial incurred loss increases significantly more than medical inflation *only* during the initial hard market years. At all other times, initial incurred loss increases at a rate that is at or below the rate of medical inflation.

---

[8] The rate of change was calculated using data from Fig. 14.1. Medical inflation data are from the Bureau of Labor Statistics annual Medical Care CPI reading. Bureau of Labor Statistics, U.S. Department of Labor, Consumer Price Index – All Urban Consumers Medical Care Services (2004). The rate of change for each year in Fig. 14.2 was computed by calculating the raw rate of change between year 1 and year 2 and subtracting from that rate the medical inflation rate for year 1.

We should not be misled by either of these charts into thinking that insurance industry executives necessarily change their understanding of loss costs in the dramatically cyclical fashion shown in these charts. There is great room for judgment in evaluating incurred losses, and the research in this area confirms the intuition that there is some income smoothing going on. In other words, insurance industry executives use optimistic loss cost predictions when prices are low because they do not want their profits to be too low in those years, and they use pessimistic loss cost predictions when prices are high because they do not want their profits to be too high in those years. Other factors that contribute to this income smoothing are the relative influence of the more conservative departments in insurance companies (claims and actuarial) over the course of the underwriting cycle and the role that emotion plays in perception of senior executives.[9]

There is nothing nefarious about some degree of income smoothing. The competitive dynamics of the insurance market drive the underwriting cycle. Even medical liability insurers with a dominant market share in a particular state are subject to national market conditions because of the importance of reinsurance in the medical liability market. The market sets the price; all the insurer can do is decide whether or not to offer the insurance and how to account for future losses. Predicting future losses involves a high degree of uncertainty, particularly in medical liability, and it would be unreasonable for us to expect insurers to ignore the market when accounting for those losses. Underpredicting losses at the end of the soft market and overpredicting losses at the start of a hard market allow insurers to manage their bottom line in a manner that preserves insurance capital.

With that said, the role of conscious income smoothing should not be overstated. There are real changes in perceptions over the course of the cycle. Because pricing medical malpractice insurance involves a great deal of judgment, the high, concentrated nature of uncertainty in medical liability insurance means that those changes in perception will have greater effect in medical liability insurance than in comparatively more predictable lines of insurance such as auto or homeowners' insurance. A variety of institutional and behavioral dynamics combine to shape this uncertainty into the reserving pattern illustrated in the two figures. These dynamics include competition based on market share, limits on insurance capacity, the moral hazard of limited liability and insurance guarantee funds, and herd behavior, along with the other factors explored in my extended treatment of this subject.[10]

One of the best ways to appreciate the heightened degree of uncertainty in medical liability insurance is to compare the "developments risk" posed by medical and auto liability insurance. There are five basic components to developments risk in liability insurance: injury developments, injury costs

---

[9] Fitzpatrick 2004, 257.
[10] T. Baker 2005b; Harrington 2004.

developments, standard of care developments, claiming developments, and legal developments.[11] For each component, medical liability risks are both higher and more variable than auto liability risks.

Medical liability poses higher and more variable injury development risk because the rate of change is more rapid for medical technology than auto technology and also because the health care sector of the economy is growing much faster than the number of autos or miles driven. Medical liability poses higher and more variable injury cost development risk than auto liability principally because of the greater average severity of medical liability claims and because norms regarding noneconomic damages appear to be less stable in medical liability than in auto liability. Medical liability poses higher and more variable standard of care development risk because of the comparatively rapid rate advances in medical care and because of the possibility that the physician-centered standard of care currently in place may give way to a potentially less forgiving "reasonable person" standard. Medical liability poses higher and more variable legal developments risk than auto liability because of the greater room for advances in the ability of plaintiffs' lawyers to select, finance, and prepare medical malpractice cases, as compared to the relative stability of auto litigation. Finally, medical liability faces higher and more variable claiming developments risk because the rate of medical liability claiming is presently so low in comparison to the rate of injuries from medical negligence, whereas the rate of auto liability claiming is so high that there is almost no room for growth.[12]

As this comparison makes plain, the future costs of medical liability insurance are far more uncertain than the future costs of automobile liability insurance. The greater the uncertainty is, the greater the range of future loss scenarios; therefore, the more room there is for loss scenarios to be affected by the competitive and behavioral dynamics of the underwriting cycle.

REDUCING MEDICAL LIABILITY INSURANCE PREMIUMS: AN UNWORTHY GOAL

Reducing total medical liability insurance premiums is not a worthy policy goal. No doubt this will seem a shocking statement to many. Yet, a clear-eyed policy analyst would have to agree that reforms directed principally at cutting insurance premiums would transfer wealth from victims of medical malpractice to health care providers.[13] "Welfare for doctors" would be an

---

[11] T. Baker 2004.

[12] T. Baker 2005b.

[13] See generally Geistfeld 2005 (explaining why "the general level of malpractice premiums does not create any unfairness" for medical providers). Cf. Pace et al. 2004 (documenting the extent to which damage caps shift costs of medical malpractice from defendants to plaintiffs).

antagonistic and therefore unhelpful label for efforts to cut medical malpractice liability in order to reduce medical liability insurance premiums, but that label would not be far off the mark.

The reason is simple: Medical liability insurance premiums represent the costs of medical malpractice that are borne by medical providers. Whether we understand those insurance premiums as a form of collective responsibility for malpractice or as an incentive for loss prevention, they are "too high" in an absolute sense only if they exceed the costs of medical malpractice or if injured patients are being overcompensated – or perhaps, if there is a severe disconnect between claim payments and liability.

Medical liability insurance premiums that exceeded the costs of medical malpractice would be too high from an efficiency perspective because of the risk of overdeterrence. They would be too high from a corrective justice perspective because the financial burden of medical providers would be out of proportion to their responsibility. We need not worry about this problem from either perspective, however, because total medical liability insurance premiums do not exceed the costs of medical malpractice. Only a small fraction of medical malpractice victims are compensated. Moreover, the price of medical malpractice insurance is far less than either the price of workers' compensation insurance or automobile insurance, despite the fact that medical malpractice kills more people each year than workplace and automobile accidents combined.[14] If anything, total medical liability insurance premiums are too low from either perspective.

Patients could be overcompensated if the total compensation that they received from liability insurance and other sources (such as health or disability insurance) exceeded the costs of their injuries. In that event, medical liability insurance premiums could be understood as too high from a corrective justice perspective because the injured patients would not need all the compensation that they were receiving. Even then, however, the proper response from either a corrective justice or an efficiency perspective might well be subrogation (i.e., allowing health and disability insurers to recover their costs through the liability action) rather than reducing medical liability. Moreover, overcompensation of some patients is not inconsistent with efficient deterrence, as long as there is an offsetting underenforcement of medical malpractice liability. In any event, we need not worry about overcompensation for medical injuries either, because the empirical research shows that injured patients are not being overcompensated. Most injured patients are not compensated at all,[15] except to the extent that they have health insurance that covers the costs of additional medical care. The de facto liability of physicians and other individual providers is limited to the amount of their liability insurance, which typically is inadequate to cover serious

[14] T. Baker 2005a, 62.
[15] See, e.g., Weiler et al. 1993.

disabilities.[16] And plaintiffs who are the beneficiaries of jury verdicts generally collect only a discounted amount of those verdicts; generally, the higher the verdict is, the greater the discount will be.[17]

A severe disconnect between claim payments and "true" liability might also lead us to conclude that medical liability premiums are too high, on the theory that any price is too high for a medical liability regime that is broken. I am not sure that I subscribe to that view, because there would be deterrence and corrective justice benefits even with a very high degree of randomness in liability, as long as the patients who benefit are injured as a result of a medical procedure.[18] Nevertheless, there is no need to evaluate whether I am correct, because the research strongly suggests that there is a satisfactory, if imperfect, link between claim payments and "true" liability.[19]

Empirical studies uniformly reject the claim that large payments are regularly made to large numbers of obviously undeserving patients.[20] With the possible exception of the Harvard public health group's studies (which were not designed to evaluate the link between payments and liability),[21]

---

[16] T. Baker 2001.

[17] Vidmar, Gross, and Rose 1998.

[18] While there would be a loss of legitimacy if a *de jure* fault-based system were exposed as a *de facto* strict liability system with random enforcement, that would not mean that the system could not be justified on efficiency or corrective justice grounds. The basic intuition is that liability without fault (which also can be referred to as "strict" or "enterprise" liability) can be consistent with both deterrence and corrective justice (Geistfeld 2005, 18) and that, in a world in which high rates of enforcement are not possible, random enforcement produces greater deterrence than predictable enforcement. Recent preliminary research suggests that there are efficiency gains from increasing uncertainty with regards to enforcement and that uncertainty does not violate corrective justice concerns as long as that uncertainty is not imposed for its own sake. See T. Baker, Harel, and Kugler 2004.

[19] Danzon 2000, 1357–9.

[20] Ibid.

[21] The Harvard study was well designed to estimate the incidence of medical malpractice but not the accuracy of medical malpractice claims. See Studdert, Brennan, and Thomas 2000, 1665 ("Just as claims or process focused studies can say little about the relationship between the epidemiology of negligence and claims, a population-based study like the UCMPS is not specifically designed to evaluate the performance of the malpractice system once a claim is initiated"). To estimate the incidence of medical malpractice, the Harvard team reviewed an astonishing 32,000 hospital records. But to estimate the accuracy of medical malpractice claims, the Harvard team reviewed a paltry fifty-one claim records. See Brennan, Sox, and Burstin 1996, 1963–7 (reporting that among the fifty-one malpractice claims identified in the New York study, "the severity of the patient's disability, not the occurrence of an adverse event or an adverse event due to negligence was predictive of payment to the plaintiff"). For a critique of the Harvard New York study conclusion regarding the accuracy of medical malpractice claim payments, see Saks 1994, 715–16 (concluding that "a closer look at the data seems to suggest that the legal process, even at the filing stage, is remarkably accurate" and that "the odds of a patient filing a claim without any basis, without a hint of an adverse event, appear to be about four in 10,000"); White 1994, 81 (reporting that the accuracy of claiming conclusions of the Harvard New York study differs from the other

all the relevant research supports the conclusion that most medical liability insurance compensation dollars go to claimants who have been injured by substandard care.[22] Moreover, even the Harvard researchers have concluded that the real medical malpractice claiming problem is that too many deserving people fail to bring malpractice claims, not that too many undeserving people make claims.[23]

None of this is to say that we should abandon efforts to reduce the administrative costs of medical malpractice dispute resolution or to explore more efficient and effective ways of compensating injured patients. What it does say, however, is that medical providers are not obviously the most deserving beneficiaries of any resulting cost savings. Legislative efforts to reduce or shift the burden of medical liability insurance premiums are "off-budget" transfer payments that need to be given the same level of moral and political scrutiny as other kinds of transfer payments.

REDUCING VOLATILITY IN INSURANCE PREMIUMS: ANOTHER UNWORTHY GOAL?

Even if reducing total medical liability insurance premiums may not be a worthy public policy goal, surely there must be merit in diminishing the volatility

---

studies and concluding that because the Harvard group studied such a small number of claims, "it seems a frail reed upon which to base major public policy recommendation").

The Harvard Colorado/Utah study used the same methods as the New York study. For this study, the researchers based their conclusions about the accuracy of medical malpractice claims on only eighteen medical malpractice claim records (Thomas et al. 2000). All of the other accuracy of claiming studies reviewed a much larger sample of medical malpractice claim records. Although the Harvard researchers acknowledge that their findings differ from those of the other studies and that their research design is less well suited to measuring the accuracy of claims (ibid., 1665), they continue to publish papers stating that most paid medical malpractice claims are without merit and confine mention of the other studies to footnotes. In addition, members of the Harvard team regularly make presentations to academic audiences stating that most paid medical malpractice claims lack merit and do not mention the contrary studies. I do not believe that they have responded to Professor Saks' reinterpretation of their data. See generally T. Baker 2005c.

[22] Taragin et al. 1992, 780 (evaluating 8,231 closed cases comprising the entire caseload from 1977 to 1992 of the largest medical malpractice insurer in New Jersey); Cheney et al. 1989 (evaluating 1,175 closed cases comprising the entire caseload of claims against anesthesiologists between 1985 and 1988 of seventeen medical malpractice insurers); Farber and White 1990 (evaluating 258 closed claims, comprising the entire caseload of claims against a large hospital that were initiated in 1977 or later and resolved by the end of 1989); Peeples, Harris, and Metzloff 2002. See also Sloan and Hsieh 1990 (evaluating 6,612 closed claims, comprising all claims reported under Florida's mandatory reporting system from 1985–8, but drawing conclusions about liability based on very skeletal information). See generally T. Baker 2005c.

[23] Weiler et al. 1993. See also Geistfeld 2005 (concluding that the severe underenforcement means that the number of malpractice claims brought against a provider is not a good proxy for the rate of malpractice committed by that provider).

of those premiums. Medical liability insurance is essentially a special-purpose group savings plan for medical providers. What rational savings plan would dramatically increase contribution requirements at random intervals that bear no connection to the income of those who are making the contributions?

Here, too, I challenge the common wisdom, though admittedly with somewhat less assurance. The real problem with medical liability is that it does not provide enough incentive for patient safety, because of the low enforcement rate. If volatile insurance premiums magnify the impact of medical liability – and there is reason to believe they do[24] – then smoothing the insurance cycle could reduce medical providers' loss prevention efforts. Not all efforts to reduce liability losses are socially productive, but efforts to prevent adverse medical events surely are.

This book is part of the proof that a medical liability insurance crisis focuses attention on medical malpractice. Whether that increased attention produces increased investment in loss prevention is harder to assess. Nevertheless, the available evidence is sufficient to justify more careful and thorough research before attempting to dampen the medical liability insurance pricing cycle.

There does not appear to have been any research documenting the rate of investment in loss prevention efforts over time. Nevertheless, behavioral decision research suggests that an attention-focusing "crisis" would lead to more significant changes in health care systems' loss prevention efforts than continuous, low-level attention. The basic idea is that a crisis makes the threat of medical liability more salient and thus "leverages" the deterrent impact of that potential liability. In prior work, I documented that the frequency of articles about medical malpractice in the medical journals shows a remarkable correlation with the insurance underwriting cycle. There is a long-term trend of increasing numbers of articles, a trend that increases significantly during each malpractice insurance crisis.[25]

Research on medical malpractice provides one of the mechanisms through which the crisis-induced salience of medical malpractice may produce action on the hospital floor. The California Medical Society commissioned the first large-scale effort to measure medical malpractice during the crisis of the mid-1970s, and the State of New York commissioned the famous Harvard study of New York hospital records during the crisis of the mid-1980s.[26] These studies and a follow-up study of Colorado and Utah hospital records provided the empirical foundation for the Institute of Medicine's influential report, *To Err Is Human*.[27] That report is widely credited with focusing

---

[24] T. Baker 2005b. Like part 1, this section presents highlights from that more detailed analysis.
[25] Ibid.
[26] Mills, Boyden, and Rubsamen 1977; Weiler 1991, xi. See also Mello and Brennan 2002.
[27] Thomas et al. 2000; also see Institute of Medicine 2000.

health care providers and health care researchers on protecting patient safety.[28]

Although this evidence does not prove that medical malpractice insurance crises have led to greater improvements in patient safety than would have occurred otherwise, it suggests that efforts to control the insurance cycle (assuming they are possible) could have undesirable unintended consequences. For this reason, any effort to dampen the medical malpractice insurance underwriting cycle should be coupled to programs to support injury prevention. Even if the underwriting cycle provides less spur to injury prevention than this evidence suggests, the low rate of medical malpractice enforcement means that there is very little risk that a new injury prevention program would "overdeter" medical malpractice.

Volatility and Enterprise Insurance

Although enterprise insurance would not reduce the volatility of the medical liability insurance underwriting cycle, it would eliminate the worst effects of that volatility for individual physicians. As discussed later, our present, individualized approach to medical liability insurance places the burden of coping with the underwriting cycle disproportionately on physicians in high-risk specialties and in high-risk locations. Enterprise insurance would shift that burden to organizations that are much better equipped to manage it. Hospitals, nursing homes, rehabilitation centers, and other large health care facilities provide a more diversified range of services than any type of physician and, thus, face more diversified risks. This greater diversity allows hospitals to spread the costs of liability insurance across both high- and low-risk services, so that increased premiums do not place as severe a stress on a narrow range of higher risk services, such as obstetrical care.

ENSURING ACCESS TO MEDICAL LIABILITY INSURANCE

For many health care providers, particularly those working in hospitals or other institutional settings, access to medical liability insurance is a necessity. Some states, and many hospitals and other health care institutions, require medical providers to obtain medical liability insurance as a condition for practice. Moreover, medical providers as a group have assets that would make medical liability insurance a practical necessity even if it were not otherwise required.

Without liability insurance to protect those assets, medical providers may make choices that reduce their exposure to medical liability. Many of those choices would be socially unproductive. For example, hiding assets is

---

[28] See, e.g., Studdert, Mello, and Brennan 2004, 5; Blendon et al. 2002.

socially unproductive because it turns medical liability into an empty gesture unable to serve loss prevention, corrective justice, or victim compensation purposes. Abandoning locations with liability insurance availability problems is socially unproductive because people in those locations need medical providers. Abandoning high-risk medical specialties is socially unproductive, except in the unusual situation in which the "unavailability" of medical liability insurance results from the incompetence of a particular medical provider.

Indeed, the only social benefit that I can imagine coming from reducing access to medical liability insurance is the concentration of high-risk medical care in the hands of fewer, higher volume providers. Research suggests that there is an inverse correlation between the frequency with which a physician performs a procedure and the error rate, meaning that higher volume medical providers have a lower rate of errors than providers who perform the procedures less frequently.[29] Thus, rationing medical malpractice insurance according to practice volume could reduce the rate of patient injury. But that benefit could be obtained with much less disruption from medical liability insurance pricing practices that reflect the fact that error rates decline with volume.[30]

For these reasons (and no doubt others), there has been widespread agreement across the spectrum of stakeholders in the health care field that ensuring access to medical liability insurance is a worthwhile policy goal. As reflected in the chapter by Sloan and Eesley, there have been a variety of regulatory approaches to achieving that goal. Among those approaches, residual market mechanisms (such as joint underwriting associations and assigned risk plans[31]) hold the most potential for addressing the short-term availability problems that can accompany the turn to a hard market.

There are three points that I would like to add to Professors Sloan and Eesley's discussion. First, it is important to keep questions about the long-term affordability of medical liability insurance analytically distinct from questions about access to medical liability insurance. Medical liability

---

[29] Halm, Lee, and Chassin 2002, 511–20.

[30] The common practice of charging uniform, specialty-based annual premiums that do not depend on the activity level of the provider effectively charges a higher per-exposure price for lower volume providers than higher volume providers. Nevertheless, my understanding is that this practice is based on administrative convenience and the perceived difficulty of determining who is and who is not a part-time practitioner, rather than a considered judgment regarding the relationship between volume and exposure.

[31] A joint underwriting association is an entity that exists to provide insurance when it is not available on the private market. Typically, the association provides the insurance at a price that is somewhat below the expected cost (otherwise, a private market insurer would presumably be willing to provide the insurance), and shortfalls between premiums and losses are covered by assessments on private market insurers according to their market share. An assigned risk program is a mechanism for forcing private market insurers to share the burden of insurance for medical providers who cannot find insurance on the private market.

premiums are a cost of medical care. Like an increase in the cost of rent for a prime downtown office location, an increase in the cost of medical malpractice premiums represents an occasion for the market for medical services to determine who will bear those costs. Legislators would be very unlikely to respond favorably to a request by the New York Medical Association to control office rental rates in Manhattan in order to maintain access to medical care. If medical liability insurance prices become so high that medical providers truly cannot make a living, the answer is for health care financing organizations to increase the prices that they pay for the affected services, not to require the victims of medical malpractice to subsidize those prices.[32]

Second, using residual market mechanisms to relieve short-term affordability problems could increase medical injuries if these mechanisms reduce the ability of medical liability insurers to refuse to insure health care providers who pose an unacceptably high risk. If a doctor cannot get insurance from the open market because insurers reasonably believe that he or she is less competent than most other doctors, then providing insurance through the residual market mechanism will have negative consequences for patient safety.

Third, an enterprise insurance requirement would reduce the demands on residual market mechanisms. The high-risk specialties that are most affected by the hard market price increases and reductions in supply tend to involve hospital-based procedures. Hospitals have greater access than physicians to private market alternatives to traditional medical liability insurance and, thus, will place fewer demands on residual market mechanisms even when traditional liability insurers reduce the supply of medical liability insurance at the onset of a hard market.

ENHANCING THE INJURY PREVENTION ROLE OF MEDICAL LIABILITY INSURANCE

In conceptual terms, there are four main ways that health care providers can reduce their exposure to potential liability.[33] They can share the risk of liability with others, most typically by taking advantage of the diversification or risk-pooling benefits of liability insurance or similar arrangements (such as risk retention groups). They can attempt to reduce the frequency or severity of injuries that can lead to liability claims. They can attempt to reduce the likelihood that injuries will lead to claims or that claims will lead to expensive settlements or judgments. And they can work to change liability law to reduce their exposure to liability, as medical societies have undertaken with

---

[32] Cf. Danzon 2000, 1369 (reporting that medical liability premiums are about 1% of the costs of health care).

[33] The analysis in this section is largely an extension into the medical liability insurance context of the ideas developed by George Cohen (1997/8).

some success on behalf of their members.[34] Medical liability insurers have these same tools at their disposal, plus the ability to refuse to insure very high-risk health care providers or to exclude coverage for high-risk procedures.

As this review suggests, not all efforts to manage medical liability benefit patients at risk from adverse medical events. Some do. Injury prevention clearly benefits patients, unless the cost of prevention exceeds the benefits.[35] Risk pooling can benefit patients who are injured by enabling providers to make good on their legal responsibilities. Refusing to insure high-risk providers and rationing insurance for high-risk procedures also can benefit patients – by channeling risky medical procedures to more competent, higher volume providers – as long as these efforts do not limit access to needed medical care.

On the other hand, efforts to limit liability by suppressing or managing claims or by changing the law are less likely to benefit patients. Patients who are injured clearly do not benefit from these efforts. Although it is theoretically possible that other patients benefit through reduced prices for health care, there is sound basis for concluding that they generally do not.

Liability-limiting tort reform would benefit patients as a class only if we were able to conclude that liability raises costs without any corresponding benefit. I discussed and rejected this possibility earlier (in the section explaining why reducing medical liability premiums was not a worthy public policy goal). Suppressing or managing claims could provide some benefit to patients with good outcomes, but only to the extent that those efforts weed out undeserving claims or exaggerated damage allegations in a manner that improves incentives to prevent injuries. Some claims suppression and management efforts surely meet those requirements. After all, we would not want liability insurers to write large checks to anyone who asks. Nevertheless, any fair-minded risk manager or insurance claims professional would concede that claims suppression efforts are directed at potentially legitimate claims as well as illegitimate claims, and that claims management efforts are directed at both deserving and undeserving claimants.

Historically, medical liability insurance institutions have invested far more efforts in claims management than in helping their insureds prevent injuries or even in helping their insureds suppress claims. The reason is simple: Claims

---

[34] Ibid. Perhaps because Cohen was writing about legal malpractice liability, which has not been subject to efforts to reduce or limit liability, he did not consider tort reform in his review of liability loss reduction strategies.

[35] This is one aspect of the problem of "defensive medicine." There is some research supporting the claim that the threat of liability leads physicians to engage in unproductive defensive medicine, though the presence of managed care seems to reduce that effect. See, e.g., Kessler and Rubinfeld 2004, 23. Also, there is some doubt whether the heart disease context of that research is generalizable because other research has failed to find a substantial amount of detrimental defensive practice. See generally T. Baker 2005a.

management produces an immediate and obvious financial payback for insurers. A million-dollar claim that goes away saves the insurer $1 million minus the costs of claims management. A million-dollar claim that becomes a $150,000 settlement or judgment saves the insurer almost as much. In addition, because liability insurers are directly in control of claims management efforts, they have greater confidence that investments in claims management will not be wasted.

As compared to claims management, even claims suppression is an uncertain investment for a medical liability insurer. Because the medical malpractice claiming rate is so low, the odds are very much against an adverse event becoming a claim, even without claims suppression efforts. Moreover, most claims suppression efforts have to be carried out by the health care provider, not insurer personnel, increasing the uncertainty between an insurer's investment and return.

This uncertainty of return is multiplied when it comes to injury prevention. The chain of probabilities linking a medical liability insurer's investment in injury prevention to any reduction in the liability insurer's loss expenses is simply too remote.[36] For this reason, it is hardly surprising that medical liability insurance does not offer the kind of safety discounts routinely offered in auto insurance. At most, a medical liability insurer will consider an applicant's patient safety practices during the underwriting process (i.e., when deciding whether to offer insurance) or the insurer might provide patient safety information as a free service, as much for marketing as loss prevention purposes.[37]

For these reasons medical liability insurers are not in the injury prevention business today, nor are they likely to get into that business in the future. How can any benefit come from trying to push them in that direction? Even if we had reason to believe that there was a benefit, how would we encourage them effectively?

The answer comes from looking more carefully at patient safety efforts (briefly rehearsed just above) then considering how the institutional advantages of medical liability insurers might give them a special role in preventing injuries. Recall that those patient safety efforts are (1) considering patient safety practices in underwriting and (2) providing patient safety information as a service to policyholders.

Incorporating patient safety information into underwriting decisions could promote patient safety – if that information is accurate and if health

---

[36] Mello and Hemenway 2004, 40 (explaining that because of underenforcement, "providers should not expect to cut their rate or overall number of claims very significantly by substantially reducing the rate of negligent injuries among their patients").

[37] This paragraph is based on informal interviews with risk management specialists at leading medical malpractice liability insurers.

care institutions change their practices in order to qualify for insurance. Providing this information to health care institutions also could promote patient safety – once again, if the information is accurate and if the institutions change their practices in response. Obviously, these are important caveats. Obtaining accurate information about health care institutions and effective patient safety measures is no simple matter. Nor is making sure that health care institutions act in response to that information.

Liability insurers have a number of institutional advantages that increase the likelihood of their obtaining accurate information and persuading health care institutions to act on that information. The first such institutional advantage is informational. No matter how much experience a hospital or practitioner has with medical malpractice claims, almost any medical liability insurer will have more. Much of this informational advantage relates to claims suppression and management – activities that we may not wish to encourage. But this informational advantage exists for injury prevention measures as well, especially when we compare liability insurers to individual health care providers and smaller health care institutions. This is not to say that liability insurance is the only institution that is positioned to see the injury prevention "big picture" more clearly than individual practitioners (health insurers are another[38]), simply that liability insurance is one institution that is so positioned.

The second institutional advantage is behavioral. A liability insurer does not have the same psychological stake in providing health care that a practitioner has. Whether the appropriate psychological term is "cognitive dissonance" or the "availability heuristic," the message from the research is the same: People are not good at paying attention to information that challenges their view of the world. For people in insurance companies, information that calls into question the safety of existing health care practices does not challenge their identity or self-esteem to the same extent that it may challenge the identities or self-esteem of a medical provider. As a result, medical liability insurance personnel may have an advantage over health care providers in recognizing when a medical liability claim indicates that the provider needs to make some changes in order to prevent future injuries. (Of course, health care providers may be better positioned than outsiders to improve safety practices in many situations; this comparative advantage is not inconsistent with the institutional advantage just described.)

The third institutional advantage relates to the relative weakness of administrators in institutions dominated by high-prestige professionals. "Because the insurance company says we have to" is an easier explanation for a highly paid, mobile surgeon to accept from a hospital administrator than "Because I'm in charge and I say so" and probably an easier explanation

---

[38] See the William Sage discussion in Chapter 2 of this volume.

to accept from a hospital risk manager than "Because I'm an expert and I say so."

The fourth institutional advantage derives from the fact that liability insurers, unlike most other injury prevention advisors, have their own money at stake. "Because the insurance company says we have to" is a satisfactory explanation, not only because it defuses power and status tensions within a health care organization, but also because the insurance company is a credible source of loss control information. This credibility comes not only from the informational and behavioral advantages just discussed but also from the fact the insurance company's money is on the line if an injured patient sues. The credibility that comes from bundling risk transfer and loss prevention services distinguishes liability insurers from consultants and other potential sources of injury prevention information. As long as risk transfer is the main service that liability insurers are selling, there is less temptation to take the edge off the loss prevention information in order to avoid losing or alienating the client.

What all this means is that medical liability insurers are to some degree already in the medical injury prevention business and that there is reason to believe that they should be good at it. What would it take to get them to do more?

The surest way to get liability insurers more invested in medical injury prevention is to raise the stakes. Automobile insurers are more intensely involved in preventing and minimizing the costs of accidents than medical liability insurers because of the very high rate of automobile insurance claims from automobile accidents. Fewer or less costly accidents mean fewer or less costly automobile claims, on a nearly one-to-one basis.[39]

One way to similarly focus medical liability insurers on accident prevention would be to reduce the very high barriers to medical malpractice claiming. Alternatively, policy makers could increase damage awards to counteract the low rate of claiming. As a political matter, however, there is little point in proposing reductions in the barriers to claiming or deliberate increases in damage awards, notwithstanding the sound theoretical basis for these approaches to addressing the problem of underenforcement.[40] Two more realistic approaches are injury prevention rewards and, once again, enterprise insurance.

Injury Prevention Rewards

The idea here is to create financial incentives for insurers to devote more effort to prevent injuries than it is economically rational for them to do

---

[39] Browne and Schmit 2004 (documenting high rate of auto claiming).
[40] Polinsky and Shavell 1998.

at present. Rewards could come in any number of ways. In states such as New York, which regulate premiums more aggressively, insurance companies could be permitted to earn a higher return on investment that would be proportional to their success in meeting specified injury prevention goals. In states that rely more on competition to set rates, insurers could be rewarded with premium tax credits or government grants. These tax credits or grants could be funded through special taxes on medical care, thereby internalizing the costs of medical injury prevention.

The real challenge here lies not in designing rewards but rather in identifying objective and effective injury prevention goals that medical liability insurers would be willing and able to meet. These goals should not be dreamed up in a law school faculty office. Instead, they should emerge from the health care and liability insurance industries, perhaps from a public competition in which the very first rewards are paid to the people or entities that identify workable injury prevention goals.

Enterprise Insurance

As compared to the current individualized approach to medical liability insurance, enterprise insurance increases loss prevention incentives for organizations and their liability insurers. Because an organization has to pay for the providers' liability insurance, it has greater incentive to monitor and improve providers' loss prevention efforts. So does the organization's liability insurer.

REALLOCATING THE BURDEN OF MEDICAL LIABILITY INSURANCE

Commentators have criticized the current approach to medical liability insurance premiums on two distributional grounds. First, physicians and other health care practitioners bear the burden of funding the medical liability system in a manner that is disproportionate to their share of health care revenues. William Sage reports that physicians bear most of the costs of medical liability despite the fact that they receive less than 15 percent of health care revenues and that "the medical profession is insufficiently capitalized to fund insurance for such a multiple of earnings, particularly when the burden falls mainly on a few specialties."[41]

Second, health care practitioners in high-risk specialties and high-risk locations bear the burden of medical liability insurance premiums that is out of proportion to their ability to prevent medical injury. These higher premiums correspond to real differences in risk, but they discourage practitioners

---

[41] Sage 2004b, 15.

from locating in high-risk locations or choosing high-risk specialties in a way that is said to be socially unproductive.[42]

In a perfectly competitive market, we would not worry about either of these problems. If physicians' share of medical liability premiums was disproportionate to their share of medical revenues, they could raise their prices in response. So, too, with physicians in high-risk specialties or locations. But the medical market lies very far from the world of perfect competition. Large government and private financing organizations set prices administratively, and consumers are largely indifferent to prices for specific medical procedures. Health care providers are not entirely pawns in this process, but we appear to be in a period of gradual reduction in physician income relative to other professionals. As a result, physicians have little or no ability to raise prices in response to increased costs. With the onset of a hard market in medical liability insurance, the burden of these sticky medical prices falls disproportionately on physicians in high-risk specialties and locations.

An enterprise insurance approach would address both of these distributional concerns. Enterprise insurance places the obligation to insure on institutions that command a higher percentage of health revenues and that employ or house medical providers with a broad range of risk exposures – making them better able to spread the high liability costs of some procedures. Although enterprise insurance would not address the problem of geography, it would place the obligation to insure on larger institutions that may be in a better position to negotiate higher prices in response to increases in medical liability insurance costs.

CONCLUSION: RESPONDING TO POTENTIAL OBJECTIONS TO ENTERPRISE INSURANCE

There are a number of potential critiques of enterprise insurance. It could be objected that enterprise insurance would

- interfere with the health care market,
- create a windfall for physicians with hospital practices,
- force hospitals to bear too much of the cost of medical liability,
- reduce the autonomy of physicians and other practitioners,
- lead to an increase in medical malpractice claiming, and
- present insurmountable administrative complications.

In addition (and in conflict with some of the other objections), it could be argued that there is no need to mandate enterprise insurance because the health care market is already moving in that direction.

I will address each of these objections in turn.

[42] See generally Geistfeld 2005.

Interference with the Health Care Market

The objection that enterprise insurance would interfere with the health care market may well be the easiest to rebut. The pervasive role of private and public health insurance means that the health care market already is far from an ideal world of free competition. Indeed, the present individualized approach to medical liability insurance is as likely to be the result of a market failure as of a well-functioning market. Given the superior ability of hospitals and other health organizations to obtain medical liability insurance, it is surprising that these organizations have not already assumed that responsibility on behalf of doctors who use their facilities.

Windfall to Physicians and Burden to Hospitals

Initially, enterprise insurance could provide a windfall to physicians and a difficult new burden for hospitals. But that windfall and burden eventually will dissipate through adjustments in prices and reimbursement rates. Moreover, the added burden to hospitals should not be overstated. The medical liability insurance burden already is shifting to hospitals, both through contracting (e.g., medical schools and HMOs providing insurance to their physicians) and through litigation efforts that target hospitals for liability. Increasing numbers of physicians are going without insurance,[43] and the comparatively low limits in physicians' malpractice policies results provides tremendous incentive to shift liability to hospitals.[44]

Reduction in Physician Autonomy

Enterprise insurance shares with enterprise liability the injury prevention benefits that follow from concentrating the financial responsibility for medical malpractice on the enterprise and its insurers. Enterprise insurance differs from enterprise liability, however, by leaving the liability on the physician and by limiting the enterprise's obligation to purchasing insurance. Enterprise insurance will increase the enterprise's incentive to manage the liability-causing activities. But, because the legal liability remains that of the physician (and other practitioners), the practitioner retains the moral authority that comes with that responsibility.[45] That moral authority will help individual practitioners retain their autonomy. This is not to say that there will be no conflicts of interest between doctors and the institutions that provide their insurance, but rather that retaining liability gives doctors greater moral and

---

[43] In addition to the Mello and Studdert chapter that opens this volume, see, e.g., Howard 2004; L. Johnson 2003.
[44] For an insightful illustration of this dynamic, see Werth 1998.
[45] See generally T. Baker 2002.

legal authority in addressing those conflicts than would straight enterprise liability.[46] Doctors currently insured through hospitals and medical schools appear to be managing those conflicts adequately.[47]

Increase in Claiming

The concern here is that enterprise insurance will reduce social barriers to malpractice claiming by further severing the link between physicians and claim payments. If so, this would be welcome a development on both corrective justice and efficiency grounds.

Administrative Complications

Administrative complication arguments almost always are "make-weight" arguments, hauled in to camouflage less savory interest-based objections. This situation is no exception. Compared to the burdens involved in shifting to DRG-based reimbursement and to adjusting to managed care, the administrative complications involved in setting up an enterprise insurance regime would be minimal. The most significant complications will involve physicians who practice both inside and outside of institutions and who therefore must purchase both individual and enterprise liability insurance policies. Because the enterprise insurance will cover liability arising only out of services related to procedures that will take place in an enterprise facility, and not liability arising out of other services, it will be necessary to draw lines. That line-drawing exercise certainly will result in insurance contract disputes. Nevertheless, this kind of litigation is routine in liability insurance; it always subsides once key precedents are established.[48] Clearly, there will be other complications as well, but physicians who presently obtain their liability insurance from a hospital or other entity are managing.[49]

Clearly, enterprise insurance would help alleviate the worst effects of the medical liability insurance underwriting cycle. Whether I have succeeded in making a persuasive case for enterprise insurance or not, I hope that I have adequately explained why medical liability insurance – and not medical liability itself – should be the focus of reforms that are directed

---

[46] For example, because the same liability insurer will be defending both the doctor and the hospital, the hospital's liability insurer will be less likely to blame the doctor, both because the liability insurer will also be responsible for paying the doctor's damages and because of the incentives created by the liability insurer's duty to settle in a situation in which the damages are in excess of the doctor's insurance limits (T. Baker 1997–8).

[47] American Medical Association 1998, 33–44.

[48] T. Baker 2003.

[49] American Medical Association 1998, 33–44.

at alleviating the next medical liability insurance crisis. Insurance market dynamics cause insurance crises, and the ill effects of those crises play out through the insurance market. Tort reform is an indirect and inefficient way to resolve an insurance problem. Insurance problems need insurance solutions.

15

Governments as Insurers in Professional and Hospital Liability Insurance Markets

Frank A. Sloan and Charles E. Eesley

Insurance issues rarely dominate the front page in public discussions of medical malpractice. Sharply rising premiums and nonavailability of coverage[1] have been the main precipitating factors in each medical crisis that has occurred in the United States in the past three decades. Whatever long-run trends in claims frequency and amounts paid per claim may be ("claims severity"), the immediate causes of premium increases and lack of supply can be found in the workings of the market for medical malpractice insurance.

Beginning with the rationale for public provision, this chapter describes the forms such provision has taken. Some public insurance is designed to mitigate fluctuations in the insurance cycle, which is characterized by periodic sharp increases in premiums and reductions in insurer capacity and availability of insurance to individual health care providers. This objective is accomplished by providing coverage for large claims. Other forms of public insurance focus directly on assuring availability of medical malpractice insurance through public risk-pooling arrangements or on protecting policy-holders from insurer bankruptcy. Next, we discuss lessons learned from the states' experiences with public provision of medical malpractice insurance coverage.

Although common themes emerge, some lessons only pertain to a single type of public insurance. One common theme is moral hazard, including reducing the potential deterrent effect of tort liability for health care providers to implement precautions to avoid injuries. Additionally, because combining public provision and patient safety may be efficient, we examine the relationship between public provision and patient safety in the following section. States have implemented insurance reform as well as various tort

---

[1] Nonavailability was less important in the crisis that occurred during the mid-1980s.

reforms in response to rising premiums and withdrawal of coverage from the market. We address whether there is a logical link between insurance and tort reform. We conclude that public provision of insurance can be in the public interest, but success is critically dependent on the details of program design. A poorly designed program may be worse than having no program at all.

RATIONALE FOR PUBLIC PROVISION

The rationale for public provision of medical malpractice insurance is that the public sector is able to provide affordable uninterrupted coverage in situations in which the private sector is unable to provide it. A reason for the interruptions in private coverage is the volatility of medical malpractice losses, particularly those from high-loss claims.

Large Claims and the Insurance Cycle

Growth of large claims, many of which take years to resolve, and trends that are difficult for insurers to predict ex ante can result in substantial increases in premiums as well as reductions in capacity to issue insurance.

Causes of Increased Premiums and Decreased Availability of Coverage: The Role of Large Claims. The dominant customers in the medical malpractice insurance market are physicians and hospitals. The vast majority of physicians purchase coverage from a primary insurer. Such insurers in turn may purchase *reinsurance* to reduce their direct exposure to high-cost claims or to losses in the aggregate above a specific dollar threshold of loss. Although much of the primary medical malpractice insurance market is state oriented, the market for reinsurance is international. Most major reinsurers are not domiciled in the United States.

Many hospitals, especially larger hospitals, self-insure for much of their medical malpractice loss. Self-insuring hospitals often purchase *excess insurance* to cover losses above a certain threshold. Such excess coverage is obtained from many of the same organizations that provide reinsurance to primary insurers. As with reinsurance, excess coverage may be obtained from several different organizations in "layers" with the excess coverage package being assembled by a broker.

Reinsurance and excess coverage are rarely, if ever, important subjects of debate over medical malpractice reform. However, large claims in a long-tail line of insurance, such as medical malpractice coverage, drive premiums, influence premium volatility, and accentuate the insurance cycle. The tail is long in this line because it often takes years after the injury occurs before a claim is filed, and additional years from the time the claim is filed to the time the claim is closed.[2] By contrast, the tail in such lines as automobile liability and collision and in health insurance is much shorter. Slow resolution of claims adds to uncertainty in premium setting as many events (e.g., judicial decisions) can intervene before the claim is resolved. Large claims are a problem for insurers if they drain reserves,[3] and for self-insured entities, such a claim may seriously affect the entities' operating performance. In the most serious cases, a large payment may threaten the financial viability of the insurer or self-insured entity.

A reinsurer/excess insurer similarly faces risks from insuring large claims. By definition, large claims are rare. When claims are infrequent, it is more difficult to judge whether the claim is a random event or represents an underlying change in claiming; the latter, but not the former, would require a change in the premium. The fact that claims are resolved in the far-distant future is problematic for the reinsurer/excess insurer because it increases the likelihood that events affecting claim resolution will intervene. For example, a high jury verdict in a jurisdiction may be precedent-setting, affecting how juries decide other claims as well as settlements that mirror jury verdicts. To the extent that the precedent affects all large claims in the jurisdiction, that is, the correlation in claims outcomes increases, the price of coverage is likely to increase to reflect this risk. In fact, in markets for coverage of catastrophic risk, the premium may be several times the expected value of the loss for the policy year.[4] For these reasons, a few large payouts may lead to substantial increases in reinsurance/excess insurance premiums, which in turn are paid directly by self-insured entities or are shifted forward by primary insurers in the premiums they charge physicians and other primary insurance premiums.

Medical malpractice is only one line in the global market for reinsurance and excess insurance. The recent (early 2000s) "hardening" (increased premiums, decreased supply) of the markets for reinsurance globally was not unique to medical malpractice, but rather was experienced by the market more generally. Thus, the underlying causes of the crisis are more likely to have been general as well rather than being medical malpractice specific.

Is the Market for Reinsurance and Excess Insurance Broken? The rationale for public intervention in a market is the presence of "market failure." The presumption in a mixed capitalist economy is to leave most activities to the working of private markets, absent specific evidence that private markets

---

[2] Medical malpractice insurers have solved the problem of the lag between the date of injury and claim filing by switching to claims made from occurrence coverage. Under claims made, the insurer covers losses from all claims filed during the policy year. Under an occurrence policy, the insurer covers losses from injuries occurring during the policy year.

[3] Sloan, Bovbjerg, and Githens 1991.

[4] Gron 1994.

cannot adequately achieve social objectives. In the context of medical mal-practice, the social objectives include, but are not limited to, maintaining patient access to affordable care. Medical malpractice insurance is one input in the production function for personal health services. Normally, in the context of product liability, if the underlying risk of an activity increases, this increased risk leads to a higher premium for product liability insurance. For example, the probability of an injury from an accident with a lawn mower leads to higher insurance premiums, which leads to a higher product price. Presumably, with higher priced lawn mowers, people would either plant substitutes for grass or let the grass in their yards grow taller. In addition, lawn mower manufacturers have an incentive to produce safer lawn mowers, which may come at a higher product price. The price increase reflects the added cost of producing a safer lawn mower although the manufacturing cost increase may cause the product liability premium to fall somewhat. In these ways, the risk from lawn mowing is reduced.[5]

If, on the other hand, in the case of medical malpractice insurance, higher premiums for reinsurance lead primary insurers to raise premiums for medical malpractice insurance and physicians raise prices, absent an ability of physicians to raise their fees, they may cease to provide services that frequently result in medical malpractice litigation or even stop practicing altogether. This is generally viewed as an undesirable outcome.

An important characteristic of insurance markets, especially the low-frequency, high-tail lines such as medical malpractice insurance, is the phenomenon of the insurance or underwriting cycle. At one point of the cycle, profits and reserves are low, premiums are low and stable, and the quantity of insurance is abundant. In response to increases in claims, particularly large claims, insurers may raise premiums substantially or, alternatively, withdraw from the market or at least threaten to do so. With higher premiums and fewer competitors, profits rise, attracting additional investment into the previously disrupted market. Partly as a result of the infusion of capital, capacity to write insurance recovers.[6] Availability of coverage expands; insurers seek out new markets, as occurred in medical malpractice insurance markets during the quiescent period of the 1990s. During such periods, insurers tend to forget past downturns and become more aggressive in promoting their products. To gain market share, insurers may offer coverage at attractive prices. With entry and lower prices, the cycle begins again.

Although inadequate prices (premiums below expected loss) is one reason for the return of the crisis phase of the cycle, there are other explanations,

---

[5] Shavell 1982.

[6] Even though external capital enters the industry when capacity is low, insurers appear to prefer to allow accumulation of retained earnings to compose part of the increase in capacity. For this reason, capacity may not increase as rapidly as one might otherwise expect (see Gron 1994).

including shocks to capacity from natural disasters or terrorism that affect the property-casualty industry generally;[7] naïve loss forecasting by insurers, resulting in loss forecast errors;[8] demand shocks driven by changes in actuarially expected losses;[9] and/or public policies, such as lags introduced by the lengthy process of rate making and rate regulation.[10] Regulatory lags cannot explain cycles in the reinsurance market, which is global; losses from terrorism have recently provided a shock to capacity.[11] Shocks could possibly be correlated across lines of property-casualty insurance within a country, reflecting, for example, judicial decisions or changes in the litigation-proneness of the population, but it seems less likely that the correlations would exist across countries. Following the year 2000, there were reductions in reinsurer capacity and increases in premiums globally and across lines of insurance, not just for medical malpractice coverage in the United States.[12]

In sum, market forces tend to correct the steep rises in premiums and reductions in availability that occur periodically. Such cycles, common in insurance markets, are also common in other markets, such as commodity markets. One would not say that such markets have "failed" just because there is volatility. However, the adjustment process to a competitive equilibrium may cause major, albeit temporary, disruptions in markets for medical care. In addition, part of the crisis may be the result of poorly constructed public policies, including but not limited to regulatory lags.

One important indicator of a well-functioning market in the long run is whether price, output, and returns to investment are similar to what would prevail under competition. Given the lack of data on reinsurers, there is no evidence on this segment of the insurance market. One reason that so many reinsurers are not located in the United States is to escape insurance regulation and statutory data reporting requirements. A study using data on medical malpractice coverage data for the years 1975–85 concluded that profitability of primary medical malpractice insurers on a risk-adjusted basis was about at the level one would expect in a competitive industry.[13] Unfortunately, there is no evidence whatsoever on profitability of reinsurers.

The Rationale for Public Provision of Coverage for Large Claims. The main rationale for government intervention in general and public provision in particular is that the cycle imposes substantial adjustment costs on policyholders. Unanticipated, large increases in premiums and withdrawal of

[7] Doherty, Lamm-Tennant, and Starks 2003; Gron 1994; Winter 1988.
[8] Venezian 1985.
[9] Froot and O'Connell 1997.
[10] Cummins and Outreville 1987.
[11] Congressional Budget Office 2004.
[12] *Reinsurance Magazine* 2004.
[13] Sloan, Bovbjerg, and Githens 1991.

supply can be very disruptive to physicians, hospitals, and other health care providers even though, during some periods, premiums are in a competitive equilibrium. It appears to be increasingly difficult for health care providers to shift higher premiums forward to consumers in the form of higher prices for their services. Large claims are difficult to predict and frequency of such claims may be correlated because of some common factor, such as judicial precedents. Reinsurers/excess insurers raise premiums markedly in response to demand shocks or (increased rates of penetration of the high layers of coverage) or shocks to capacity; such shocks are transmitted to the end user.

Although data to document returns accruing to reinsurers/excess insurers are lacking, conceptually, the required return on equity is high when non-diversifiable risk is high. Risk is nondiversifiable when it cannot be eliminated by adding insureds or adjusting the firm's portfolio of assets and liabilities. When such risk is perceived by suppliers of capital to have increased, so does the required return. Apparently, from patterns observed repeatedly in various lines of property-casualty insurance, premiums temporarily rise to levels above the required rate of return. This elicits capital flows to the industry, and capacity and supply increases and premiums fall, remaining approximately level for a time.

Publicly supplied insurance, at least in the forms that have emerged to date, does not change the underlying long-run risk. Rather, it changes the identity of the risk bearers. The policyholders, who are the health care providers themselves rather than private insurers, are placed at financial risk of overruns. Yet, by reducing volatility, there may be a welfare gain. It is possible, but by no means assured, that the risk bearers, physicians, hospitals, and other health care providers, who in the public plans are placed at risk of overruns, are willing to supply capital on more favorable terms than are investors worldwide.

Dealing Directly with Adjustment Costs

Rather than focus on the causes of instability in the market for medical malpractice insurance, another approach deals directly with the consequences. Residual markets serve customers regarded as undesirable by private insurers, such as high-risk persons or organizations likely to incur substantial losses. In general, the demand for coverage in residual markets organized by governments increases with decreases in insurer capacity and availability. Another approach is guaranty funds that cover the liability of insolvent insurers. Once an insurer is declared to be insolvent, the state insurance department assesses all licensed insurers in that state to contribute to the fund.

The general presumption in a competitive market is that insurance purchasers who are at greater risk of loss pay higher premiums for coverage.

At some price, there is likely to be a willing supplier. In fact, in such lines as automobile liability insurance, many surplus line insurers routinely cover such risks. In medical malpractice, private surplus line carriers also exist, but they are small relative to the size of the industry as a whole.[14] Public intervention in provision of insurance to high-risk persons or organizations exists when it is judged that there is an entitlement to coverage and there is concern that disadvantaged individuals or organizations cannot bear the full burden (premium) of their higher risk.

The rationale for public intervention following insurer insolvency is somewhat different from that for risk pools to provide insurance for individuals otherwise unable to obtain insurance. As in other markets, the probability of insolvency should be reflected in the premiums that policyholders are willing to pay. Policyholders should be willing to pay a higher premium to a company that can offer a higher degree of assurance that it can pay its obligations. If a policyholder obtains cheaper insurance from an insurer with a high insolvency risk, then this is a risk that the policyholder has decided to willingly bear, in the same sense that the purchaser of an old automobile benefits from a lower purchase price but faces a higher probability of repair. However, the argument for public provision is that the underlying risk of insolvency is difficult for consumers to judge ex ante. Thus, government should provide protections. Funds to cover losses are one form of protection. Solvency regulation of insurance is another.

FORMS OF PUBLIC LIABILITY INSURANCE
THAT HAVE BEEN IMPLEMENTED

Overview

There are two important ways in which state governments have actually supplied insurance for loss from medical injuries: patient compensation funds (PCFs) and medical no-fault programs. In contrast to Joint Underwriting Associations (JUAs) and guaranty funds, which require pooling of resources among private insurers, PCFs and no-fault programs involve direct public provision of insurance. To date, there has been no federal involvement in any of these types of programs.

Forms That Deal with the Causes of Volatility in Premiums
and Availability of Coverage

Patient Compensation Funds. Initially created in the 1975–6 crisis as part of more comprehensive malpractice reform, PCFs attempt to assure availability

---

[14] W. B. Schwartz and Mendelson 1989.

of malpractice insurance by paying for only the large losses that seldom occur. PCFs are organized as either a state agency or a trust fund and are funded from premium income and investment returns, not from state subsidies. Some PCFs were initially financed on a pay-as-you-go basis, assessing premiums as funds are expended, whereas others maintain reserves on unpaid claims. Only Pennsylvania's PCF continues to be funded on a pay-as-you-go basis.

These state funds usually cover liability that is above threshold amounts covered by primary insurance policies or qualified self-insurance plans. To lower the risk assumed by PCFs, they are often packaged with other statutory changes, which fall under the general category of "tort reform," such as damage caps. Although some PCFs offer unlimited excess coverage, most cover an incremental layer of $500,000 to $1,000,000 per occurrence.[15] Reinsurance may be provided on a per incident basis or for an aggregate of losses. The PCFs implemented to date base payment on the former.

As of 2004, eleven states had established PCFs: Florida (1975), Indiana (1975), Kansas (1976), Louisiana (1975), Nebraska (1976), New Mexico (1978), New York (1986), Pennsylvania (1975, 2002), South Carolina (1976), Wisconsin (1975), and Wyoming (1977). Florida's program closed in 1983, having underpriced coverage,[16] but was still paying claims as of April 2003. Pennsylvania passed legislation in 2002 that schedules a phase-out of its program by 2009. As of mid-2004, Ohio had not implemented a PCF.[17]

Interviews of representatives of the PCFs still in operation conducted by a team of researchers at Duke University, including one of the authors, during late 2003 and early 2004, revealed two major motivations for forming PCFs.[18] The first is to provide physicians and hospitals with affordable and reliable medical malpractice insurance coverage by reducing volatility in losses from large claims. The second is to provide adequate compensation for insured patients in the state. The first objective is a primary concern of medical interest groups; the second is primarily a concern of organizations representing the trial bar.

State PCFs differ from private liability insurers in four major ways. First, some states require insurer or self-insured entities' participation whereas in other states, participation is voluntary. However, even when PCF participation is mandatory, providers have their choice of private primary insurer. Second, public provision by a PCF ensures availability of coverage when private insurers become drawn to other states or different lines of insurance. Third, unlike private insurance for which some form of regulatory oversight

---

[15] Sloan 2004.
[16] Sloan et al. 1991, 123.
[17] Academy of Medicine of Cleveland, http://amcnoma.org/webpages/main.asp, accessed Sept. 14, 2004.
[18] Sloan et al. 2004.

exists in all states, in some states there is a lack of regulatory oversight or involvement in assuring adequacy of PCF rates. Fourth, as explained more fully later, some PCFs have used pay-as-you-go financing rather than standard actuarial principles generally used in the private sector.[19]

Because medical malpractice insurance is usually not experience rated, adverse selection can be a problem for voluntary insurance markets if premiums do not precisely match risk. If high-loss physicians or hospitals are able to obtain coverage at average rates, adverse selection is likely. Premiums of private reinsurers/excess insurers are highly experience rated. Mandatory participation in a PCF can avoid adverse selection; however, effectively subsidizing high-risk participants out of the pockets of low-risk participants may be viewed as unfair.

A state-run PCF has the benefit that it can keep excess coverage available because its decision to supply coverage is not guided by prospective rates of return. Demand for private reinsurance by primary medical malpractice insurers is directly related to the volatility of loss.[20] Private reinsurance is in turn volatile in terms of availability and premiums because reinsurers cover large, infrequent losses and can withdraw from the market during crisis periods.

PCFs usually are exempt from regulatory oversight that is otherwise typical of the insurance industry because arguments for regulatory oversight of insurers are thought not to apply to PCFs. As public organizations, PCFs plausibly lack an incentive through the profit motive to exploit their dominant market position by charging monopoly-level premiums or engaging in risky financial decisions that may lead to insolvency. Nonetheless, political pressures often lead to risky behavior. State budgetary constraints may cause understaffing and civil service rules may limit the ability to compete with the private sector for personnel.

Reinsurance is not the only approach used by insurers to protect themselves against large losses. In recent years, insurers have begun to use hedge instruments in which tail risk is transferred to investors. These instruments include catastrophe bonds, catastrophe options, and catastrophe puts.[21] Unlike reinsurance, in which very large losses are absorbed by a very large, but single property-casualty insurance industry, it should be easier to absorb such losses in a multi-trillion-dollar global capital market.

For these instruments to be used in the context of medical liability, a loss pooling mechanism, probably organized by the federal government, would be needed. Also, the threshold for such losses would be aggregate losses, not losses from single injuries.

---

[19] Private medical malpractice insurers have not always followed actuaries' advice in setting their premiums (see Sloan et al. 1991).

[20] Hoerger, Sloan, and Hassan 1990.

[21] Doherty and Smetters 2002; Congressional Budget Office 2002, Box B-1, p. 45; Varian 2001.

There are other parallels between losses attributable to medical liability and losses from catastrophes, such as hurricanes, floods, earthquakes, and terrorism. First, in both, public intervention may reduce incentives to prevent loss. Although a hurricane cannot be prevented, homes can be built to be hurricane-resistant and away from areas in which hurricanes are likely to occur. Second, as for medical liability, there is a social choice about how much risk-bearing should remain with private insurance versus how much should be covered from public funds. In the case of natural disasters, the U.S. Federal Emergency Management Agency (FEMA), for example, provides public assistance grants to state and local governments to repair damaged infrastructure. A parallel to medical liability would be federal grants-in-aid to states when a certain aggregate threshold of loss is exceeded. Such a program would require sharing of current information on losses. Individual states could implement a similar program. It is noteworthy that FEMA is financed from a broad general tax revenue base, not payments from insurance companies or parties at particular risk of incurring losses from natural disasters.

Medical No-Fault Programs. At its core, a no-fault system is a replacement of the tort system's case-by-case determination of fault with a system compensating all injuries caused by medical care without regard to negligence. The main benefits gained under no-fault are the reduction of the expense involved in payments to lawyers, dispute resolution, and reduced time in resolving claims.

Other countries employing no-fault programs, such as Sweden and New Zealand, broadly distribute compensation to injury victims using these savings in administrative expenses and lawyers' fees.[22] Other advantages proponents of medical no-fault in the United States point to are the possibility of more expert resolution of claims and improved injury deterrence along with greater incentives to exercise precaution if no-fault is in some form combined with experience rating.[23]

Implemented along with a package of statutory changes during the medical malpractice crisis of the 1980s, the only no-fault programs in the United States are Virginia and Florida's birth injury compensation funds. The primary objective of medical no-fault was to improve affordability of medical liability insurance for obstetricians; enhancing efficiency in claims resolution and improved compensation of injury victims were secondary objectives. Although the programs may assess liability insurers of all sorts up to one-quarter of 1 percent of net premiums to cover overruns, in neither state

[22] M. Rosenthal 1988.
[23] Bovbjerg and Sloan 1998; Weiler et al. 1993.

do the no-fault programs have access to general state revenues and there is no formula in the enabling statutes for raising premiums. The eligibility criteria were designed to include only cases that otherwise would have a high probability of being paid in tort and result in large monetary awards.

Virginia and Florida have the only medical no-fault programs in the United States. By contrast, broad no-fault coverage is provided for accidental injuries in Australia, New Zealand, and Sweden.[24] These plans key eligibility for coverage to accidental injuries rather than to medical conditions in general, while providing for a wider range of benefits than is typical of first-party health and disability insurance.

Forms That Deal with the Consequences of Volatility in Premiums and Availability

Joint Underwriting Associations. One role government has played is in the pooling of resources among private insurers. Programs of this type have come under the categories of Joint Underwriting Associations (JUAs) and state guaranty funds, and both cases are public entities that provide insurance as a last resort. JUAs serve providers who are unable to obtain coverage from other sources. They accomplish this by requiring participation by all medical malpractice insurers in a state, and then each member company is assessed a pro rata share of the shortfall if the JUA's premium income is not sufficient to cover losses. Beginning in the mid-1970s, states authorized JUAs to address gaps in coverage arising from the withdrawal of private insurers from the market.[25] To serve the public objectives of assuring availability of coverage and protecting consumers against insurer insolvency, state governments facilitate transactions within the private insurance sector to form risk pools. It is doubtful insurers would coordinate to establish high-risk pools without state action because these pools would be unprofitable. Though often conceived as temporary measures, some JUAs established in the 1970s remain active.[26]

State Guaranty Funds. Guaranty funds provide a mechanism for taxing financially healthy insurers to pay the obligations of insolvent insurers to their policyholders. To pay claims that are in excess of the assets of a particular insolvent insurer, member insurers are assessed a fixed percentage of premium volume.[27] In this way, guaranty funds offer physicians and other

[24] E. Cohen and Korper 1976; Gellhorn 1988; Palmer 1979, 1994; M. Rosenthal 1988.
[25] Nutter 1985.
[26] Council of State Governments 2003; New York State Department of Insurance 1997; G. Robinson 1986.
[27] S. Lee et al. 1997; Sloan et al. 1991, 55–6.

health care providers protection from insurer insolvency and indirectly keep compensation available for injured patients. Between 1969 and 1981, all states established guaranty funds covering all types of property-casualty insurance, including medical malpractice and life-health insurance.[28] They are all postinsolvency assessment funds, except for the New York fund. A similar system applies to banks as well.[29]

LESSONS LEARNED FROM PUBLIC PROVISION OF MEDICAL MALPRACTICE INSURANCE

Overview

Public programs are learning from experience and making progress in more effectively achieving their goals as time passes.[30] The experiences of states that have implemented various programs are potentially valuable to others with such programs and to other states considering implementing them. Unfortunately, there is very little sharing of experiences among the states. Rather, states seem to operate their programs in isolation from one another.

Several recurring themes emerge among the lessons learned. It is not possible to demonstrate that any of these public programs have decreased medical malpractice premiums or made such insurance more available to health care providers. They have succeeded in delivering their product at a low administrative cost. The conventional wisdom that the private sector is more efficient does not seem to apply in this context. Although "crowding out" of private coverage is a inherent risk of public provision, with some important exceptions described later, there is no indication that this has occurred to a large extent.

Patient safety is a concern in general and when insurance is offered in particular. There is no indication that public provision has improved patient safety. Nor is there any evidence that it has decreased it either. Administrators of public programs have not been involved in patient safety activities.

How public programs are funded is critical to their success. Program evaluation at regular intervals is essential to insure implementation is achieving the stated objectives. Some of the programs have probably suffered by lack of oversight and periodic monitoring and evaluation. Because pertinent issues differ somewhat depending on the type of public provision and to structure the discussion, we use a question-and-answer format in this section.

---

[28] Downs and Sommer 1999.
[29] Merton 1977.
[30] See, e.g., Sloan et al. 2004.

Patient Compensation Funds

Have PCFs Achieved the Dual Purposes That Motivated Their Formation?
A conclusive demonstration of whether medical malpractice insurance is
more available and affordable as a result of PCFs is not possible with data
currently available. Nonetheless, one can piece together some evidence from
a few available sources to get a preliminary evaluation.[31]

One indicator is from the Duke University survey mentioned previously.
Representatives of all nine PCFs currently operating in late 2003 and early
2004 were interviewed, and this survey was supplemented with financial data
and other information on these PCFs. None of the representatives could provide direct evidence that availability and affordability were improved because
a PCF existed in their states. But they did argue that as excess insurers, the
PCFs reduced the volatility of losses experienced by others. This we can
take at face value; this is almost certainly true inasmuch as the PCFs, with
the notable exception of the PCF in Pennsylvania, are handling the largest
claims.

Second, respondents said that PCFs have limited the exposure of primary
insurers to high losses, making their states more attractive to primary insurers even in states without statutory limits on liability. There is no direct
empirical evidence that this has, in fact, attracted primary insurers. Brokers
and private excess insurers also surveyed in late 2003 and early 2004 were
not enthusiastic about the PCF concept overall, which may be because the
public insurers are competitors; however, these respondents did indicate that
some of the states with PCFs were attractive to private insurers. Evidently, the
existence of a PCF has not completely eliminated demand for their products.

Third, PCF respondents pointed to low administrative expense compared
with private insurers. Empirical evidence in five of the states with PCFs
does support the claim that PCF staffing is lean.[32] Even though comparable
information from private insurers is lacking, it seems unlikely that their
staffing is as lean. On the other hand, PCFs may be providing fewer services.

Another indication of PCF performance comes from claims data filed with
the National Practitioner Data Bank (NPDB). Trends in claims frequency are
very similar between PCF and non-PCF states, and claims frequency during
1995 to 2002 was systematically higher in the PCF states. However, PCF
payments were not included in the NPDB data, so calculation of mean total
severity of loss or total losses incurred by private and public insurers in
PCF states was not possible. Based on available data on losses paid by PCFs
during 1998–2002, expressed in 2002 dollars using the general Consumer
Price Index, there was considerable variation in recent trends in losses among

[31] Ibid.
[32] Ibid., Fig. 1.

the five PCF states for which trends could be measured.[33] Losses increased appreciably for South Carolina's PCF and to a lesser extent for Wisconsin. By contrast, losses for the Pennsylvania PCF were almost unchanged. Those for the Kansas PCF declined (all measured in 2002 dollars). Other factors may have been responsible for these trends. Thus, it is difficult to attribute the trends solely to the presence of a PCF.

Furthermore, health care providers remain vulnerable to very high claims as most PCFs have a ceiling on coverage and most states have not established upper limits on liability. In Pennsylvania, the state with a PCF that no longer provides upper layers of coverage, it is not uncommon for juries in Philadelphia to award amounts exceeding the PCF layer of coverage.[34] It is unknown how frequently private reinsurance is purchased in states with PCFs, but in Pennsylvania, the lack of indexing of both the lower and upper bounds on coverage has resulted in the PCF covering a middle layer of insurance rather than the upper layer that the original law intended. At a certain threshold of claims, PCFs are intended to crowd out private excess/reinsurance. However, this may not occur for the simple reason that legislatures have not updated the limits of coverage.

Does the Method of Funding PCFs Matter and How? The method of funding PCFs is vital to the fund's long-term viability. There are several choices of funding mechanisms, which include pay-as-you-go financing, making actuarial projections, reserving for anticipated losses as all PCFs except Pennsylvania's now do, and, in the case of New York, subsidizing excess/reinsurance rather than publicly providing it.

At one time, several state PCFs used pay-as-you-go funding.[35] Almost none have retained it, with Pennsylvania as the exception. Under pay-as-you-go financing, as applied to PCFs, providers are assessed on the basis of currently incurred PCF outlays. Thus, although a claim may have originated many years in the past, current providers are assessed for such claims. In the states that implemented pay-as-you-go financing for PCFs, none have used general revenues.

By design, pay-as-you-go financing involves inequitable intergenerational transfers. Financing generally comes entirely from premiums paid by physicians and hospitals and investment income. Therefore, those health care providers who remain or enter subsidize providers who retire or leave the state. The former realized the benefits of excess coverage through the PCF while they were in practice in the state but were not assessed a full premium for such coverage. Conversely, providers who enter practice are among the financial losers. Because the trend in malpractice losses far exceeds changes

[33] Ibid., Fig. 2.
[34] Bovbjerg and Bartow 2003.
[35] Hofflander and Nettesham 2001.

in the cost of living, health care providers retiring or leaving the state receive a substantial net subsidy. Empirical evidence is lacking on the issue, but the desire to avoid these obligations arguably deters younger providers from entering practice in the state and induces older providers to retire early or move elsewhere.[36]

Pay-as-you-go has political appeal because payment obligations are deferred; thus, under a mandatory PCF pay-as-you-go plan, many of the political officials who are in office at the time the claims' obligations are incurred will not be around at the time these liabilities must be financed. There is the appearance of having been responsive to a crisis without having to pay the bill. It helps to solve short-term crises because initially losses tend to be low as claims are infrequent and those that have occurred are slow to be resolved. Eventually, as losses mount, however, PCFs often have to raise premiums – creating demands for another round of medical malpractice reform.

The alternative approach, standard in the private insurance sector, is to set premiums on the basis of anticipated future payments from claims filed in a particular policy year.[37] This eliminates the intergenerational transfer and possibly the problem of inevitably increasing funding requirements as time progresses. On the other hand, loss reserving involves educated guesses with premiums being set on the basis of these predictions. There is understandably some reluctance to pay increased premiums based on possibly inaccurate projections. Yet, this practice has stood the test of time.[38]

A pay-as-you-go system that guarantees insurability and does not base assessments on a provider's claims history helps insulate providers from nonmeritorious claims. This only holds true if juries frequently make errors in their findings of liability and determinations of damages. However, the arguments for loss reserving over pay-as-you-go financing appear much stronger, especially because if there is an eventual insolvency risk in the government PCF then health care providers remain vulnerable. For example, health care providers in South Carolina, where the PCF is chronically

---

[36] Albert (2003) tells the story of one physician's decision to move from Pennsylvania to Wisconsin based on the different medical malpractice environments in each state.

[37] Kansas, New Mexico, Wisconsin, and Louisiana have used loss reserving in funding their PCFs (Kansas Health Care Stabilization Fund 2002; Louisiana Patient Compensation Fund, http://www.lapcf.state.la.us/; New Mexico Public Regulation Commission 2001; Wisconsin Patient Compensation Fund, http://oci.wi.gov/pcf/htm). Still, choosing to hold reserves in and of itself does not assure adequate financing. Though the reasons may differ, public and private insurers that have actuarial evaluations performed do not always follow their recommendations (Kansas Health Care Stabilization Fund 2002; New Mexico Medical Society 2003; Sloan et al. 1991, 157). Additionally, reserves are vulnerable to utilization for unrelated purposes, as has occurred in Wisconsin (Wisconsin Insurance Report 2001, http:/oci.wi.gov/ann rpt/bus-2001/anrpttoc.htm; Wisconsin Hospital Association 2003).

[38] Sloan et al. 1991, 123–44.

underreserved, may be sued for the full amount individually if the PCF's funds are insufficient.[39]

The only state to subsidize reinsurance and excess coverage is New York. The subsidy is transparent and avoids the intergenerational inequities inherent in the pay-as-you-go approach. The underlying assumption is that medical care is a merit want.[40] To assure access to affordable medical care, it is desirable to subsidize an important input in the production of such services. In a less regulated environment than in New York, such subsidies may be expected to increase the demand for coverage, resulting in an increase in total premiums (prior to the subsidy).

Finally, voluntary PCFs suffer from an adverse selection problem where providers who are at low risk for future claims will drop out of the PCF, leaving only high-risk providers enrolled. Low-risk providers can opt out in favor of private coverage and avoid a full assessment by not renewing after the PCF's premiums increase.

Do PCFs Affect Deterrence of Medical Injuries? Moral hazard is a major problem in insurance in general. In the context of PCFs, moral hazard takes the form of reduced incentives to prevent injury, to reduce claims frequency conditional on an injury having occurred, and to reduce payment conditional on a claim being filed. Public provision may exacerbate moral hazard for several reasons, including lack of experience rated premiums. With experience rating, failure to take precautions in the current period leads to anticipated increases in premiums for future policy years. Thus, substituting non–experience rated public insurance may substantially increase moral hazard unless other actions are taken to improve patient safety and loss mitigation.

Experience rated assessments are used in three of the PCF states – South Carolina, Louisiana, and New Mexico. South Carolina providers are experience rated on claims frequency. Louisiana attaches a specific percentage increase to the assessment for those providers with high numbers of cases. Depending on the number of claims a provider has received (one, two, three, or four or more), there is a standardized increase in the surcharge. The 2002 PCF statute in Pennsylvania included the concept of experience rating, but this provision has not been implemented to date. As a partial substitute for experience rating, Wisconsin uses a peer review process to monitor physicians with a high number of claims.[41]

Interestingly, PCF respondents to the Duke University survey saw little or no connection between the PCF's activities and patient safety, loss

---

[39] South Carolina Legislative Audit Council 2000, 10.
[40] A merit want is a good that society deems should be available to all and its allocation should not be subject to normal market forces (see Musgrave 1957; Margolis 1982).
[41] Wisconsin Patient Compensation Fund, http://oci.wi.gov/pcf/htm 2003.

prevention, and claims management.[42] Respondents seem to view the PCF as a passive financial intermediary with patient safety and loss prevention responsibilities left to primary insurers or self-insured entities and not affected by the PCF's policies. Conceptually, it seems likely that any non–experience rated excess coverage would lead to moral hazard, but empirical evidence that this has truly occurred is lacking.

Joint Underwriting Associations

What Factors Explain the High JUA Market Share in Some States? The goal of JUAs is to provide availability of coverage to providers who cannot obtain it from private sources. Yet in some states, JUAs have become an important if not the dominant source of medical malpractice insurance coverage.

One factor in explaining a high or increasing market share is that JUA coverage is attractively priced relative to its private competitors. If the JUA's premium income is insufficient to cover losses and administrative expense, each member company is assessed a pro rata share of the shortfall. In competitive insurance markets, owners of companies demand a reasonable rate of return on the capital they supply. The only way to earn this return is for companies that subsidize the JUA (either all malpractice insurers or all property-casualty insurers) to increase premiums to their policyholders. As a result, privately obtained medical malpractice insurance becomes more expensive relative to JUA coverage, leading more physicians to substitute JUA-obtained coverage for private coverage.

Pooling arrangements therefore may "crowd out" private medical malpractice insurance, as occurred in some states with JUAs in the 1980s.[43] At that time, JUAs dominated the market in Massachusetts and Rhode Island, which like other New England states lacked physician-sponsored medical malpractice insurers.[44]

However, pricing is not the only determinant of the JUA market share. A growing share may be an indication of nonavailability of private insurance. Pennsylvania is a case in point. During the crisis in Pennsylvania that occurred after 2000, and following the exit of several private insurers from the medical malpractice insurance market in this state, hospitals and physicians increasingly relied on coverage through the state's JUA and on other alternative coverage sources such as risk retention groups.[45] In 2002, Pennsylvania's JUA had 1,700 physician policies in force, up from 351 in 2001.[46] Between 1999 and 2002, the number of health care providers

---

[42] Sloan et al. 2004.
[43] Kenney 1988.
[44] Sloan et al. 1991.
[45] Bovbjerg and Bartow 2003; Health and Hospital Association of Pennsylvania 2002a; Hinderberger 2003; Mello, Kelly, et al. 2003.
[46] Health and Hospital Association of Pennsylvania 2002b.

in Pennsylvania obtaining coverage through the JUA increased by more than a factor of seven.[47] In 2002, 12 percent of hospitals in Pennsylvania had their primary coverage through the Pennsylvania Joint Underwriting Association.[48] These increases occurred even though coverage from the JUA tends to be relatively expensive.[49] In Florida, there also has been a substantial increase in the number of physicians enrolled in the state's JUA, but it still represents only a small fraction of physicians in the state.[50]

What Effect, If Any, Do JUAs Have on Patient Safety? Health care providers often cannot get private insurance, at least at premiums that they deem to be affordable, because they have adverse claims histories. When physicians with many past claims are able to obtain coverage at standard rates through JUAs, subsidized by physicians with better track records, they lack incentive to improve (or leave practice). The major focus of JUAs has been on insuring physicians, not on developing programs to reduce the probability of claims. One exception is legislation introduced in Missouri requiring the JUA administrator to formulate, implement, and monitor a risk management program for all policyholders.[51]

As with PCFs and medical no-fault programs, the impetus for JUAs has not been a perception that patient safety levels were inadequate. Rather, these organizations are political responses to increased premiums and lack of available coverage. JUAs have been designed to fix a lack of availability problem, not a patient safety problem. However, by focusing on one issue, the solution may create or exacerbate others. In the context of JUAs, existing knowledge of how the programs operate in practice is so meager that we cannot state with any degree of certainty that they have exacerbated other problems.

Guaranty Funds

Even less is known about the performance of state guaranty funds than about JUAs, either in the context of medical malpractice insurance or in other lines of property-casualty insurance more generally. Here the discussion of risks must totally be based on theory.

What, If Any, Impacts Do State Guaranty Funds Have on Patient Safety? The moral hazard arising from guaranty funds is seen most directly in the conduct of private insurers. By insulating managers from the consequences

[47] Bovbjerg and Bartow 2003.
[48] Health and Hospital Association of Pennsylvania 2002a.
[49] Eskin 2003; Mello, Studdert, and Brennan 2003.
[50] State of Florida 2003.
[51] State of Missouri 2002, 2003.

of insurer bankruptcy, guaranty funds reduce market pressure on insurers to be prudent in their business decisions.

With the existence of a guaranty fund, policyholders have a greater incentive to select companies with lower premiums but with a higher bankruptcy risk. To avoid bankruptcy, insurers may try to avert injuries, but it seems more likely that they would be more selective in the risks they are willing to insure and in claims management. Thus, when the cost of bankruptcy is reduced by the presence of a guaranty fund, one would expect at most a minor effect on patient safety.

Might State Guaranty Funds Exacerbate Rather Than Reduce Insurance Cycles? State guaranty funds may exacerbate the effects of a capacity shortage. Large numbers of insolvencies are correlated with the crisis phase of the insurance cycle.[52] Assessing solvent insurers will reduce net worth and further reduce industry capacity. In protecting a few consumers from insurer insolvencies, guaranty funds may increase the premium levels throughout the industry via reducing net worth just when the industry is already capacity constrained. These problems could be avoided through a prefunded system, such as New York's.[53]

Redistributional effects arise in these programs, which are not transparent to consumers of health care or to citizens in general. To cover the bankruptcy of insurance firms on medical malpractice claims, it may be necessary and is permitted for insurers of other types of liability insurance to be assessed a tax. This could raise the premiums for consumers of other types of liability insurance, creating redistributional effects. Redistribution may occur in the opposite direction as well if auto liability insurers fail and their claims must be met with funds from medical liability insurers.

What is less apparent is that shocks to various property-casualty lines of insurance are correlated. Assessments may rise just at the point in the cycle when the line being assessed is experiencing losses. In this way, guaranty funds may exacerbate the insurance cycle. In addition to the moral hazard described previously, this may be a second way in which guaranty funds may cause economic inefficiency. As in other contexts, there are tradeoffs in insurance between risk protection and efficiency.

Medical No-Fault Programs

The Florida and Virginia no-fault programs – again, the only versions of medical no-fault that ever have been implemented in the United States – provide interesting evidence of what no-fault is likely to look like after the political compromises, including sources of program funding, have been made and trial lawyers are able to successfully advocate for the status quo after such

---

[52] Gron 1989, 1990.
[53] Gron 1994.

programs are implemented. The actual operating experience stands in sharp contrast to theoretical no-fault programs that can and have been devised by scholars.

Is Medical No-Fault a Substitute for Tort? The two medical no-fault programs were implemented as part of packages to reduce the threat of large obstetrical tort claims and hence increase access to obstetrical care. Compensating victims of obstetrical injuries, whether or not the injury was attributable to provider negligence, was at most a secondary concern of proponents of medical no-fault in these two states. Thus, one indicator of success is the effect of implementation of medical no-fault on frequency of tort claims. Because the programs covered an extremely narrow set of tort claims, empirical analysis must focus on the set of tort claims involving the same type of injuries.[54]

Since 1975, Florida has required that medical tort claims be reported to the state Department of Insurance after resolution. Virginia, like the vast majority of states, has no similar reporting requirement. Thus, this question can only be addressed with data from Florida.

In Florida, there is no evidence that implementation of medical no-fault reduced tort claim frequency of the injuries that the medical no-fault statute covers.[55] The bar to suing is not airtight because of judicial decisions favorable to the trial bar, and plaintiffs' attorneys drove a wedge through the cracks in the limitation on suing. One tactic that plaintiffs' attorneys have used is to argue that the patient's obstetrician had not adequately informed patients of his or her participation in the (voluntary) no-fault program. Consequently, patients only learned the details of the program and the physician's participation in it after the injury occurred.[56]

Tort claims frequency did not decrease after the no-fault program was implemented. This is not necessarily a bad result because some families were compensated who otherwise would not have been compensated and the overhead of these programs is far less than under tort,[57] but the result is inconsistent with an important goal of proponents of no-fault. Another reason that the program proved not to be a substitute for tort is that the definition of injuries was so narrow, an issue we address next.

Why Were So Few Injury Victims Compensated by the Programs? In Virginia, from 1987 to 2002, only seventy-two claimants received payment.[58]

---

[54] Sloan et al. 1999.
[55] Sloan, Whetten-Goldstein, et al. 1997, 1998.
[56] Failure to give adequate notice is understandable in that few expectant mothers want to contemplate life with a child with cerebral palsy before the fact, and this outcome has a low probability outcome of occurring.
[57] Sloan, Bovbjerg, and Rankin 1997.
[58] Joint Legislation Audit and Review Commission 2002, 83.

As of early 2003, fewer than twelve cases per year had been accepted for payment in the fourteen years that Florida's no-fault program has been operating.[59] The first reason that few injury victims were compensated is that the definitions of covered injuries were so narrow. In Virginia, as originally specified, only cases in which a live infant is permanently disabled and in need of assistance in all activities of daily living (ADLs) are eligible for coverage. In Florida, only infants weighing at least 2,500 grams at birth and "permanently and substantially mentally and physically" impaired are covered.[60] Eligibility criteria for program benefits were narrowly defined to keep assessments on physicians and hospitals low.

The programs were mainly funded by assessments on voluntarily participating physicians ($5,000 annually), licensed physicians who decide not to participate ($250 annually), and hospitals.[61] Participating providers continue to pay medical malpractice insurance premiums. There is no provision in either statute for raising premiums, and in neither state do the no-fault programs have access to general state revenues. In both states, however, the programs may assess liability insurers of all sorts up to one-quarter of 1 percent of net premiums written in the state. Private insurers, not the states, therefore bear the risk of overruns.[62]

Another reason is that the major stakeholders had no reason to publicize its existence, and plaintiffs' laws had a clear incentive to divert the most lucrative cases to litigation. Health care providers had no collective interest in publicizing the program as growth in enrollments would increase their assessments, and medical no-fault was implemented to reduce provider outlays for such expense, not to increase it. They had a private incentive to publicize the program in Florida in the sense that "failure to give notice" was used by attorneys to steer cases to tort. Yet, this was not apparent until years after the program was implemented. The administrators of the programs operated on tight budgets, making them reluctant to publicize the availability of benefits for families with birth-related injured children.

For no-fault to flourish, it must *not* be implemented in an environment of tort reform, which aims to reduce premiums and increase availability of coverage. The goals of no-fault are adequate compensation of injury victims quickly and efficiently. Because the number of injuries during the course of receipt of medical care far exceeds the number of valid tort claims, one must be prepared to pay more, not less, than under tort. Savings in administrative

---

[59] State of Florida 2003.

[60] Sloan 2004.

[61] Participating hospitals in Virginia at $50 per birth up to a maximum of $150,000 per hospital per year, and all hospitals in Florida at $50 per birth.

[62] The insurance lobby in both states opposed assessments on the premiums they collect, but subsequent attempts to repeal the provision failed (see Bovbjerg and Sloan 1998, 94).

cost are considerable under tort,[63] but such savings do not generally appear to be sufficient to offset the increase in injury compensation. No-fault cannot support many more claims than tort without relying on a much broader financing base, either general revenues or a dedicated tax funded from a much larger group than health care providers.

Does Medical No-Fault Reduce Deterrence of Medical Injuries? Conceptually, no-fault may reduce incentives for injury prevention by not penalizing injuries caused by negligence. For this reason, proposals for no-fault have included provisions for experience-rating providers based on no-fault claims frequency and implementation of other patient safety measures, including peer review.[64]

Neither Florida's nor Virginia's program included experience rating or other explicit patient safety measures. Experience rating is infeasible for a program with a very low number of paid claims. Patient safety measures could have been linked to implementation of no-fault, but this did not happen. As the programs are currently constituted, injuries are not attributed to fault; physicians and hospitals linked to particular injuries would only know that a claim had been filed because the agencies request patients' medical records.

Although patient safety measures have not been implemented, in part because of the programs' small size, it has been possible to manage benefits on an individualized basis. Thus, there is a considerable amount of care management for claimants' ongoing medical needs, conditional on compensation having occurred for an injury.

PUBLIC PROVISION AND TORT REFORM: CAN GOVERNMENT PLAY
A CONSTRUCTIVE ROLE IN LIABILITY COVERAGE WITHOUT
CHANGING THE TORT LIABILITY SYSTEM?

Until very recently, in the political environments in which tort reforms have been implemented, the "culprits" have largely been seen as overly generous juries and judges and greedy trial lawyers. The fact that injuries arise in the course of receipt of medical care is not denied. However, the causal role of provider actions or inactions is often denied. To this extent, there is no perceived need to link tort reform to patient safety.

Except for guaranty funds, public provision of medical malpractice arose from crises in medical malpractice that led to more general medical liability

---

[63] Sloan, Bovbjerg, and Rankin 1997.
[64] Weiler et al. (1993) argued that the savings from not having to prove negligence in medical liability cases could save a large amount of resources now spent on lawyers, expert witnesses, and courts. They contended that the savings might allow more injury victims to be compensated and to be compensated much more quickly.

tort reform.[65] Removing tort claims was the primary motive for medical no-fault. Caps on damages were an alternative to creating PCFs.[66] Or, at least, PCFs may have resulted in caps that were higher than they otherwise would have been. JUAs arose out of the lack of availability of medical malpractice insurance in the mid-1970s.[67]

More general tort reforms, often implemented along with PCFs, have an effect on the risk assumed by these state funds. From the vantage point of an insurer, limiting exposure to risk is desirable.[68] Of course, in the limit, if there is little exposure to risk, there will be little demand for the insurer's product. Nevertheless, it is not surprising that among the PCFs surveyed in late 2003 and early 2004, statutory limits on the size of awards were considered to be desirable.[69]

In the end, the decision about whether to implement statutory changes, such as limits on noneconomic or total damages, should be based on a number of considerations. Potential effects on public provision of insurance are likely to be of secondary importance.

PATIENT SAFETY AND RISK MANAGEMENT AND PUBLIC PROVISION
OF MEDICAL MALPRACTICE INSURANCE

Other factors being equal, provision of insurance changes the incentives of those insured. Likewise, removing the threat of tort liability may affect providers' incentive to exercise care. Thus, it is important to consider whether or not government can play a constructive role in liability coverage without incorporating patient safety and risk management activities. As with caps on damages, government's decision to regulate patient safety involves much broader issues than its potential effects on public provision. By contrast, policies affecting claims frequency and claims resolution, conditional on injuries having occurred, are much more clearly insurance issues.

What Are Public Insurers Doing Currently?

Of the various innovations outlined previously, most is known about patient safety and risk management of PCFs. Medical no-fault programs do not address patient safety. They do manage expenditures on behalf of the families

---

[65] Sloan, Mergenhagen, and Bovbjerg 1989.
[66] Zuckerman, Bovbjerg, and Sloan 1990.
[67] Sloan 1985.
[68] Biondi and Gurevitch (2003) concluded, based on their analysis, that in Pennsylvania caps would reduce that state PCF's average excess coverage by 42%.
[69] One PCF, Wisconsin, attributed its success in part to the existence of limits on noneconomic damages and damages in wrongful death cases (see Sloan et al. 2004).

who receive compensation, but this process is substantially different from claims management under tort. State guaranty funds have so far played no role in patient safety or risk management activities. Rarely in the literature on JUAs is there any mention of loss prevention.[70]

A few states have included patient safety activities in their PCF legislation. Although Pennsylvania's PCF has a hands-off role in promoting patient safety, the state did impose mandatory reporting and process standards as well as other specific patient safety requirements. These have been viewed as having an important impact on the patient safety climate in Pennsylvania. New York has made the strongest efforts by mandating risk management training for all recipients of the PCF subsidy. Wisconsin's PCF has a Risk Management Committee to provide patient safety guidance to PCF participants in addition to using a peer review process to monitor physicians with a high number of claims.

Incorporating experience rating into premium assessments is a more indirect approach that PCFs have used to encourage patient safety improvements. Experience rating has mostly been a recent addition to state PCF legislation. In Pennsylvania, the 2002 PCF statute included experience rating. South Carolina and New Mexico charge a higher rate based on the number of claims a provider has experienced. Finally, Louisiana adds a percentage increase to the assessment for providers with high numbers of cases. In Kansas, the Board of Governors is vested with the authority to eliminate providers from PCF coverage, and the Board receives lists of providers with high claims frequency. However, this has only happened once, as it is a lengthy process.

Once an injury has occurred, policies affecting claims frequency and claims resolution lie closer to the domain of insurers. Attempts to affect claims frequency include loss prevention activities aimed at reducing the probability that a potential accusation ends up filed as a claim. The goal of claims management is to lower the total potential payment from the resolution of any specific claim.

Although Pennsylvania has offered assistance if requested, to date loss prevention is not actively offered by any of the PCFs.[71] Pennsylvania's PCF has made an effort to both reduce the size of losses and the frequency of claims filed in the tort system by offering arbitration or mediation according to the Rush model.[72] However, the hospital must ask for help prior to the filing of a claim, and with 75 percent of cases tendered within thirty days

---

[70] Missouri is a notable exception, as legislation in that state requires the JUA administrator to implement and monitor a risk management program for all policyholders (see State of Missouri 2002, 2003).

[71] Sloan et al. 2004.

[72] Brown 1998.

of a trial/settlement, it is difficult for the PCF to engage in a more proactive role.[73]

Once a claim has been filed, the PCF may have a role in the resolution process because the size of the outcome will affect its costs. The problem is that claims resolution becomes more complex as the number of decision makers increases. PCFs have differed in how actively they have participated in claims management. Whereas Pennsylvania, Kansas, Wisconsin, and New Mexico closely monitor claims that are filed with the PCF, other PCFs have only been passive participants in the process, and three states with PCFs play no role in claims resolution. New York's public subsidy program has encouraged better coordination by urging physicians to use the same insurer for primary and excess coverage. In Wisconsin, PCF legislation dictates that the primary insurer defend the PCF and then once it tenders the claim to the PCF, claims resolution becomes solely the responsibility of the PCF. The PCF must continually monitors claims that may potentially be "bad faith" cases against the insurer. In South Carolina, the JUA manages claims for the PCF.

The PCF's role in claims management seems to be most controversial in Pennsylvania. Hospitals, brokers, and primary insurers surveyed all expressed similar views that settlements have been delayed, resulting in higher payouts because of the PCF's role in claims management.[74] Respondents (other than the PCFs) often stated that there was conflict with the PCF's own separate claims management activities, especially in cases where the PCF refused to settle and insisted on a trial. Primary insurers noted frustration with the PCF's decision-making authority regarding claims resolution when they still have a financial stake in the legal fees.

Close coordination appears to be critical in claims management and the process may be best left in the hands of insurers, with monitoring as an option to avoid "bad faith" cases where insurers may pursue cases above the PCF threshold less aggressively.

Is New Legislation Needed?

Claims management is best left to insurers. Except in their general oversight role of performance of public agencies, legislatures should avoid micromanaging insurers' activities in mitigating losses. There may be a role for legislation regarding patient safety, but one should be mindful that public provision of medical malpractice insurance is only a small part of the patient safety issue.

---

[73] Conover et al., n. d.
[74] Ibid.

BOTTOM LINE: IS PUBLIC PROVISION OF MEDICAL MALPRACTICE INSURANCE PART OF THE PROBLEM OR PART OF THE SOLUTION TO RECURRING MEDICAL MALPRACTICE INSURANCE CRISES?

Statutes creating public insurers have generally been part of larger packages of tort and insurance legislation. They have been considered part but never a central part of the solution to a medical malpractice insurance crisis. In this sense, public provision of medical malpractice practice insurance is much less important than are the major public programs, Medicare and Medicaid, in the provision of health insurance.

Proposals for a single public health insurer, for example, Medicare expanded to the U.S. population as a whole, have frequently been offered. No one has suggested universal public provision of medical malpractice insurance. Rather, public provision has been limited to coverage of large claims and JUA and guaranty fund pooling arrangements. That the discussion of Florida's innovative medical no-fault program is only 7 pages of a 345-page report of the Governor's Commission on Medical Malpractice is indicative of the perceived unimportance of this program among many leaders and stakeholders in that state.[75] In Pennsylvania, the PCF has received much more attention, but this is attributable to the large unfunded liability that has accumulated under its pay-as-you-go system. Because they are small organizations and there have been lengthy periods in which medical malpractice markets are quiescent, PCFs have not attracted much scrutiny from researchers either. Much of the existing evidence on performance is qualitative.

None of the public programs offer short-term solutions to an immediate crisis. Design and implementation takes time. Programs have learned from experience and have improved over time.[76]

For the longer run, PCFs may serve a useful role in reducing the volatility of the insurance cycle. Unless it is implemented on a much larger scale than in Florida and Virginia, medical no-fault does not have any potential as a policy instrument for dealing with crises in medical malpractice insurance. Otherwise, in compensating injury victims at low administrative cost, the programs have achieved much of what they were set out to do. Although offering risk protection, guaranty funds, by contrast, may actually exacerbate swings in the insurance cycle.

As of mid-2004, the crisis in reinsurance/excess insurance was largely over,[77] following large increases in premiums and decreases in availability during the previous two years. Even in a crisis state such as Pennsylvania, such insurance was generally available, although premiums remained at a much higher level than previously.

[75] State of Florida 2003.
[76] See, e.g., Sloan et al. 2004.
[77] *Reinsurance Magazine* 2004.

A few questions should be central to a state's decision about adopting a PCF. First, how serious are the short-run costs of downturns in the insurance cycle to providers and citizens as patients? This is largely a political question, particularly as much of the pain of the insurance cycle is of a relatively short duration and felt by a small but vocal constituency. Also, in spite of the large number of anecdotes, disruptions to patients attributable to either the insurance cycle or high medical malpractice premiums have not been documented empirically.

Second, how do PCFs compare to their counterparts in the private market? In terms of the cost of administering the insurance plan, although a direct quantitative head-to-head comparison is not available, it seems unlikely that private insurers are as efficient as PCFs. However, PCFs generally impose risks of overruns on policyholders. Private reinsurers/excess insurance companies, and ultimately the suppliers of equity to such companies, bear the risk in the short run. In the longer run, policyholders pay for adverse experience in the form of higher premiums. In this sense, the end result is much the same, and it is unclear whether the cost of equity capital to public insurers is really less than that to private organizations. Pennsylvania is stuck with its PCF for at least a decade because of the program's large unfunded liabilities. Finally, there is the issue of whether the transactions cost of primary insurer or self-insured entity is lower than that of dealing with a well-run public PCF. Because situations differ, this question will have to be answered on a state-by-state basis.

JUAs can provide insurance when it is not available from other sources. However, by underpricing such coverage, JUAs may unintentionally become the major insurer in a state. Guaranty funds potentially play a useful role, but knowledge about how they function in practice is very limited. Currently, there is much too little information about them available in the public domain.

The desirability of any of these public programs depends on how they are designed. Too often, legislators, governors, and stakeholders have focused on policy objectives rather than on program structure. The devil is in the details of implementation.

16

Medicare-Led Malpractice Reform

William M. Sage and Eleanor D. Kinney

There is increasing interest among policy makers in an integrated approach to patient safety and medical liability.[1] This chapter proposes and develops a breakthrough medical malpractice reform: a system of medical error identification, patient notification, rapid compensation, and safety improvement within the Medicare program. The reform would provide Medicare beneficiaries with better safety, improved communication in event of error, preservation of therapeutic relationships, timely settlement, and fair compensation at lower administrative cost. Disputes in the reformed system would be adjudicated by Medicare's existing administrative appeals system, which would work together with Medicare's quality improvement regulation and payment policy to reduce errors and compensate injured patients. Testing reform within Medicare would also make it possible to extend future reforms to the Medicaid population, which is also less likely than younger, nonindigent patients to bring malpractice claims.

WHY MEDICARE-LED MALPRACTICE REFORM?

Medical malpractice policy has been in suspended animation for decades. Nonacademic proponents of reform have hardly budged in their recommendations since 1975, and opponents by and large have countered those proposals without offering promising alternatives. The principal cause of stagnation is that medical malpractice policy has never integrated with overall health policy. In particular, the Medicare and Medicaid programs – which have shaped health policy and molded health politics since the 1960s – have never been engaged in malpractice reform.

The authors' research in Medicare's role in malpractice reform is supported by a grant from the Commonwealth Fund.

[1] Institute of Medicine 2000, 2002; Joint Commission on Accreditation of Healthcare Organizations 2005.

Medicare Can Reconnect Malpractice Policy to Health Policy

Because malpractice has not been connected to health policy, the politics of medical liability has been co-opted by the politics of general (nonmedical) tort reform. Thus, the public hears mainly rhetoric intended to persuade them that lawsuits destroy or preserve America's economy and social fabric, and not reasoned discussion of the effect of liability on the quality, cost, and availability of medical care.[2] Furthermore, malpractice reform remains preoccupied with replicating California's Medical Injury Compensation Reform Act (MICRA) – which caps noneconomic damages and limits lawyers' contingent fees in order to eliminate "junk and frivolous lawsuits" – not only because organized medicine has championed those reforms for decades, but also because those reforms are easily transferable to other legal arenas of greater importance to nonhealth care political stakeholders. Even seemingly innovative proposals, such as "medical courts," rely on stand-alone, reactive institutions for resolving traditional malpractice claims that might be more efficient than conventional litigation but would do little to enhance patient safety, spread the costs of avoidable injury, or help patients and physicians deal with adverse outcomes of care.

The existing reform debate ignores critical failings of conventional medical malpractice as a means of improving both patient care and insurance risk pooling. The current malpractice system treats patients like strangers, subjecting them and their physicians to a painfully slow, highly adversarial process that denies them information, compassion, and, where appropriate, compensation. Far too many medical errors occur, resulting in too many avoidable injuries, with malpractice litigation generally working at cross-purposes with timely, self-critical, systems-based performance improvement. Fragmented, volatile markets for liability insurance subject physicians and patients to periodic financial and political upheavals; induce perverse, "defensive" medical practice; and potentially decrease access to care for vulnerable populations.

Having Medicare play a principal role could dramatically change the politics of medical malpractice. Framing liability reform around Medicare shifts power from legislative committees primarily concerned with the judicial system to committees primarily concerned with the health care system. Medicare-led malpractice reform also may recruit new political voices, such as AARP, who have much more of a stake in health care generally and Medicare specifically than the general business and "consumer" lobbyists who currently control the debate. Finally, as occurred twenty years ago with respect to provider payment reform, it is highly likely that a successful Medicare malpractice initiative can be leveraged into systemwide reform as private payers and health care providers – particularly

---

[2] HHS, ASPE 2002.

hospitals – realize the advantages of a uniform approach to managing medical errors.

Common Law Tort Serves the Medicare Population Poorly

An integrated approach to injury prevention and compensation is particularly important in Medicare because conventional medical malpractice law serves Medicare beneficiaries poorly. There is persuasive evidence that injured aged or disabled individuals are less likely than other patients to obtain compensation in the existing common law tort system.

In the early 1990s, both the U.S. General Accounting Office (GAO) and the congressional Office of Technology Assessment conducted studies of the claiming behavior of Medicare and Medicaid patients, with similar findings.[3] In its review of the literature to date as well its analysis of independent data, GAO found that hospital malpractice awards paid on behalf of Medicare and Medicaid patients accounted for a relatively small share of total hospital malpractice losses. For a five-year period ending in September 1990, Medicare and Medicaid patients received about one-fourth of the $2.3 billion of hospital malpractice awards, although they represented more than 45 percent of hospital patients during this period. Medicare patients received a smaller proportion than Medicaid patients. GAO also found, based on earlier work of the National Association of Insurance Commissioners, that when Medicare and Medicaid patients were successful in litigation, they received awards half as large as privately insured patients.[4]

More recent studies have confirmed these findings.[5] Burstin and colleagues found that poor patients, uninsured patients, and the elderly were significantly less likely to file malpractice claims. Similarly, in a study of injuries and claims in Utah and Colorado, Studdert and colleagues found that nonclaimants were more likely to be Medicare or Medicaid recipients and more than seventy-five years of age. These investigators concluded that the elderly may be said to suffer a kind of "double jeopardy" because they also experience higher rates of medical injury.[6]

There are several reasons for this phenomenon. Long delays resolving claims – typically five years or more for serious injuries – disadvantage elderly patients. Elderly plaintiffs and potential plaintiffs suffer from greater difficulty proving causation of injury given their often complex medical histories, lower economic damages because most are retired and have relatively short projected lifespans, lesser capacity to recognize medical error because of the

[3] U.S. OTA 1992; U.S. GAO 1993.
[4] U.S. GAO 1987, 1993.
[5] Burstin et al. 1993; Studdert, Brennan, and Thomas 2000; Sager et al. 1990.
[6] Studdert, Thomas, et al. 2000; Thomas et al. 2000.

pressures of illness in advanced age, and emotional reluctance to alienate physicians on whom they depend. According to one plaintiffs' lawyer:

The death of a senior citizen...presents a vexing problem.... [C]oexistent disease and a relatively short life expectancy usually reduce these cases' value to a level below trial threshold. This is almost an absolute admonition where...your plaintiffs are only the surviving children. Here, jury sympathy...often gets very thin.[7]

There is also reason to believe that claims rates and malpractice payments for elderly patients may be increasing. Nursing home litigation has become commonplace in states that have enacted elder abuse laws over the past decade, accustoming personal injury lawyers to serving elderly clients. A growing elderly population makes seniors' experiences and needs more salient with judges, juries, and legislatures. And ever-rising health care costs following injury put financial pressure on seniors and their families to seek compensation, while enhancing potential returns to lawyers working on contingency. The threat of greater future litigation involving seniors adds to the urgency of reform, in large part because many physicians already find treating elderly patients relatively unrewarding and may reduce their Medicare caseloads if litigiousness is added to the mix.

Malpractice Adjudication Fits Well Within Medicare

An administrative alternative to medical malpractice litigation, linked to quality oversight and improvement, attracted widespread support in the late 1980s.[8] However, interest in comprehensive reform waned as malpractice insurance markets recovered and physicians' political attention turned to managed care. In 2005, there appear to be three available avenues for integrating malpractice policy with health policy, thereby focusing medical liability on patient safety while taking account of cost and access. One possibility is a state-level system of administrative compensation linked to health care regulation, much as workers' compensation dovetails with occupational safety regulation, as proposed by the Institute of Medicine in 2002.[9] A second possibility is for sponsors of employment-based health insurance to use their authority under ERISA to create a private system of limited compensation, with supervision by the U.S. Department of Labor. No formal proposals taking this approach have been circulated.

The third possibility – arguably the most promising – is for the federal government to pioneer a regulatory program of administrative adjudication of malpractice claims for Medicare beneficiaries that would improve compensation for injury and encourage performance improvement. As Harris

[7] Kaplan 2001.
[8] AMA/Specialty Society Medical Liability Project 1988; Johnson et al. 1989.
[9] Institute of Medicine 2002.

has observed, the scope and scale of the Medicare program make it well positioned to accomplish broad public goals in health care.[10] Medicare has displayed a strong interest in patient information, in technical patient safety improvements, and in overall quality enhancement. Medicare operates various programs aimed at ensuring and improving the quality of health care for beneficiaries. It also has the requisite infrastructure for the management of claims through its network of health insurers that administer the Medicare program nationwide and through its existing adjudication system for disputes over Medicare benefits.

Because Medicare is the nation's largest health care payer, bringing malpractice policy into Medicare also may promote direct coverage of economic losses and more careful incorporation of liability costs into reimbursement formulas. As medical care improves, future medical expenses become the most important component of malpractice damages and comprehensive health insurance constitutes a critical part of malpractice reform for both patients and providers. In addition, the federal government has unique capacity to absorb shocks to insurance markets and therefore can blunt the harshest effects of malpractice crises on health care providers.

Medicare frequently tests innovations through pilot programs and demonstration projects. Consequently, Medicare can institute malpractice reform selectively, starting with medical groups, hospitals, and other organized health care providers capable of improving patient safety and promptly compensating avoidable injury. The importance of Medicare to the hospital sector makes Medicare a particularly credible and effective catalyst for enterprise-based malpractice reform. For example, Medicare can impose conditions of participation on providers designed to ensure that patients who exchange their traditional rights under state malpractice reform for novel federal remedies are adequately protected.

These features enable a Medicare-led malpractice reform to connect the handling of individual injury claims to other initiatives currently under way within the Medicare program and to important health policy issues affecting that program. The former category includes Medicare's recently revamped quality improvement program, patient safety and disclosure requirements adopted by JCAHO, consumer information and provider "report card" efforts, and pay-for-performance innovations. The latter category includes attracting physicians to the Medicare program, taking provider liability costs into better account when updating Medicare reimbursement formulas, ensuring adequate coverage for Medicare beneficiaries of health care needs consequent to unexpected injury, and improving accountability within Medicare managed care (Medicare Advantage). In this regard, Medicare also has the capacity to proactively detect and disclose unanticipated events rather than

---

[10] Harris 2003.

waiting passively for lawsuits to be filed and pursued, and thus could avoid caseloads or expenditures that would create budgetary or administrative problems.[11]

EXISTING ADMINISTRATIVE INFRASTRUCTURE FOR MEDICARE-LED MALPRACTICE REFORM

Medicare has an extensive administrative structure in place that could be used to implement Medicare-led malpractice reform. Medicare has the authority, which it has used, to require health care institutions to implement quality improvement strategies. Medicare has a network of contractors that can receive claims and conduct medical reviews. Finally, Medicare has an administrative appeals system to adjudicate disputed cases.

Medicare's Relationship with Physicians, Hospitals, and Other Providers

The Medicare program's relationship with health care professionals and institutional providers is one that a provider enters voluntarily in order to be paid for services to Medicare beneficiaries. It is on the basis of these consensual, often contractual relationships that any Medicare-led malpractice reform must be implemented.

Medicare Conditions of Participation for Institutional Providers. An important issue is the latitude available to the federal government to impose contractual obligations on health care institutions relating to patient safety and compensation. The Medicare statute states the specific types of health care institutions that can provide services to Medicare beneficiaries and sets forth the conditions upon which these institutions can participate in the Medicare program. These "conditions of participation" define basic characteristics needed to assure accessible, high-quality care.

The Medicare statute empowers the Medicare program to adopt regulatory conditions of participation for hospitals and specifically states: "The Secretary may impose additional requirements if they are found necessary in the interest of the health and safety of the individuals who are furnished services in hospitals."[12] The Medicare program has historically taken this mandate literally and has imposed important quality improvement measures on hospitals. Most recently, Medicare modified its conditions of participation for hospitals to require hospitals to institute the so-called Quality Assessment and Performance Improvement (QAPI) program.[13] The QAPI

---

[11] Studdert et al. 1997.
[12] 42 C.F.R. 421.1(1)(a)(i) (2005), referring to 42 U.S.C. § 1995x(e) (2005).
[13] Hospital Conditions of Participation: Quality Assessment and Performance Improvement, 68 Fed. Reg. 3435 (Jan. 24, 2003) (42 C.F.R. Part 482) (Final Rule).

program requires hospitals to implement many of the patient safety strategies that have developed in recent years: tracking incidents, analyzing their causes, taking preventive actions, and instituting mechanisms for information sharing, feedback, and learning throughout the facility.

Medicare Contracts with Medicare Advantage Health Plans. Medicare's relationship with health maintenance organizations (HMOs) and other health plans that serve Medicare beneficiaries under the Medicare Advantage program (formerly called Medicare+Choice) is also contractual and voluntary. Again, the Medicare statute and regulations impose a variety of conditions on HMOs and other health plans that they must meet to provide care to Medicare beneficiaries who choose to enroll in managed care, as opposed to receiving their benefits and health care through the traditional fee-for-service Medicare program.[14]

Medicare's Relationship with Physicians. Medicare's relationship with physicians is different. Theoretically, the Medicare program does not contract directly with physicians for their services to Medicare beneficiaries. Rather, Medicare's relationship is with the beneficiary enrolled in Medicare's Part B Supplementary Medical Insurance program.[15] Medicare has a formal relationship only with physicians who actively "accept assignment" of the beneficiary's claim for payment under the Medicare program.[16] If a physician accepts assignment, the physician must regard Medicare payment as full payment for the services in the claim.[17]

However, over the years, mainly in an effort to gain control over the inflation in physician payment, the Medicare program has made it extremely difficult for physicians to serve Medicare beneficiaries and not accept assignment. In the Omnibus Budget Reconciliation Act of 1989 (OBRA), Congress established a new fee schedule for physician services. Implemented in 1992, the Resource-Based Relative Value Scale (RBRVS) reformed Medicare physician payment to better reflect the resources used by each physician specialty to care for Medicare patients with specific conditions.[18] OBRA required physicians to submit bills to Medicare on behalf of Medicare patients and greatly limited the degree to which physicians could charge beneficiaries fees in excess of Medicare payment levels. These provisions made it highly advantageous for physicians to accept assignment for all Medicare claims. Thus, as a practical matter, Medicare does have a direct contractual relationship with most physicians.

[14] 42 U.S.C. § 1395w-21 (2005); 42 C.FR 422.2 and 489 (2005).
[15] 42 U.S.C. § 1395u(b)(3)(c) (2005).
[16] 42 U.S.C. § 1395cc (2005).
[17] 42 U.S.C. § 1395hh (2005).
[18] Omnibus Budget Reconciliation Act of 1989, § 6102, Pub. L. No. 101–239, 103 Stat. 2111, 2169 (codified as amended at 42 U.S.C. § 1395w-4(a)).

Medicare Claims Management and Medical Review Capacity

The Medicare program is administered through a network of insurance companies and physician organizations nationwide. These perform different functions in determining coverage of medical services, managing claims for payment for services, and overseeing the quality of services. Medicare's Quality Improvement program operates a national network of fifty-three Quality Improvement Organizations (QIOs). The QIOs, located in each state, territory, and the District of Columbia, review the provision of Medicare services in hospitals and other health care institutions, especially for underserved populations. The QIO program ensures that Medicare payments are made only for medically necessary services and investigates beneficiary complaints about quality of care.

A short history of Medicare's quality improvement authority is instructive for a potential malpractice reform initiative. Immediately after the inception of the Medicare program, Medicare expenditures began rising at an alarming rate. In 1969, out of concern for escalating costs, Congress required utilization review of hospital services[19] and began to investigate the volume and quality of care for Medicare beneficiaries. In 1972, finding utilization review by hospitals ineffective,[20] Congress inaugurated the Professional Standards Review Organization (PSRO) program.[21] This program required the Medicare program to contract with independent, physician-dominated organizations to review the utilization of health care services for Medicare beneficiaries. Pursuant to statute, services to Medicare beneficiaries would be paid under the following circumstances:

(1) only when, and to the extent, medically necessary, as determined in the exercise of reasonable limits of professional discretion; and (2) in the case of services provided by a hospital or other health care facility on an inpatient basis, only when and for such period as such services cannot, consistent with professionally recognized health care standards, effectively be provided on an outpatient basis or more economically in an inpatient health care facility of a different type, as determined in the exercise of reasonable limits of professional discretion.[22]

In 1982, Congress established the Medical Utilization and Quality Control program to replace the PSRO program.[23] Section 1395y(g) of the Medicare statute mandates that the Secretary, in making determinations of whether items or services meet coverage criteria and "for the purposes of promoting

---

[19] Social Security Amendments of 1969, as amended Oct. 30, 1972, Pub. L. No. 92–603, §201(a)(2), 86 Stat. 1371 (codified as amended at 42 U.S.C. § 1395x(k)).

[20] S. Rep. No. 92-1230, 92d Cong., 2d Sess. 254 (1972).

[21] Social Security Amendments of 1972, Pub. L. No. 92–603 tit. II, §249F, 86 Stat. 1329 (codified as amended at 42 U.S.C. § 1320c-1 – c-19).

[22] 42 U.S.C. Sec. 1320c (2005).

[23] Tax Equity and Fiscal Responsibility Act of 1982, Pub. L. No. 97-248 § 96 Stat. 324 (codified as amended at 42 U.S.C. § 1320c-3(a)(1)).

the effective, efficient, and economical delivery of health care services, and of promoting the quality of services," "shall enter into contracts with [peer review organizations]."[24]

The powers of peer review organizations (now called quality improvement organizations [QIOs]) are broad. QIOs can retroactively deny Medicare payment for services not meeting their utilization or quality standards.[25] The QIO can also initiate proceedings before the Office of the Inspector General (OIG) of the Department of Health and Human Services (HHS) to fine or exclude providers or practitioners from receiving payment under the Medicare program if they are found guilty of gross and flagrant violations of their obligation to provide care of acceptable quality, or are guilty of substantial violations in a substantial number of cases.[26] In 1986, Congress also required QIOs to review all written complaints about the quality of services not meeting professionally recognized standards of health care.[27]

In recent years, CMS has launched specific quality initiatives for the major classes of providers. These involve the collection of data on quality measures and the implementation of strategies to improve quality and promote safety in hospitals and, to a lesser extent, health plans. One project is the Premier Hospital Incentive Demonstration, which recognizes and provides financial rewards to acute-care hospitals that demonstrate high-quality performance in a number of areas.[28] Medicare also launched the National Health Information Infrastructure (NHII), a comprehensive knowledge-based network to enhance clinical decision making by providing health information when and where it is needed, with the ambitious goal of improving the efficiency, effectiveness, and overall quality of health care in the United States.[29] The Food and Drug Administration (FDA), also part of HHS, promulgated a rule to reduce medication errors by requiring bar coding of drugs used in hospitals and by instituting safety reporting requirements for drugs and biologics.[30]

These programs all require health care providers to collect data on quality of care, including medical errors, for Medicare beneficiaries treated in their institutions. If data on medical malpractice claims, collected in a closed Medicare system, were joined with data on Medicare beneficiaries from these other programs, much could be learned about the epidemiology of medical injury and malpractice claims.

---

[24] 42 U.S.C. § 1395y(g) (2005).
[25] 42 U.S.C. § 1320c-3(a)(2) (2005).
[26] 42 U.S.C. § 1320c-5(b) (2005).
[27] Omnibus Budget Reconciliation Act of 1986, Pub. L. No. 99-509, § 100 Stat. 1874 (codified as amended at § 1320c-3(a)(14)).
[28] U.S. HHS, CMS 2005.
[29] U.S. HHS, ASPE 2004.
[30] Bar Code Label Requirement for Human Drug Products and Biological Products, 69 Fed. Reg. 9119 (Feb. 26, 2004) (21 C.F.R. Parts 201, 606, and 610) (Final Rule).

Medicare's Beneficiary Appeals Process

Medicare operates a national administrative appeals system to adjudicate disputes between Medicare beneficiaries and the program. Because these disputes involve coverage, existing appeals processes include an independent medical review component that marshals medical expertise to resolve contentious clinical issues. This framework is potentially adaptable to adjudicate malpractice cases.

The Medicare program is organized into four parts, with separate systems for early stages of appeals. Parts A and B of Medicare, which finance hospital care and physician (and other outpatient) services respectively on a fee-for-service basis, share an appeals system. Part C, Medicare's longstanding HMO program now called Medicare Advantage, has a grievance system with independent medical review. Part D, the new Medicare prescription drug benefit, also has a grievance system that is integrated into Part C's system if the beneficiary is appealing a Medicare Advantage plan's determination. For all parts, there is a common framework for administrative review within CMS and judicial review in federal district court.

In recent years, Congress and CMS have reformed the Medicare appeals process in important respects, partly in response to criticism of the prior procedures.[31] Several of the reforms facilitate use of the Medicare appeals process for adjudicating malpractice claims. First, the reforms have added independent medical review for fee-for-service Medicare at the state level and independent review for Medicare Advantage and Prescription Drug Plans at the national or regional level. Second, Congress has insulated administrative review of appeals from CMS policy makers, who have historically sought to influence appeal outcomes to save funds. However, these reforms have yet to be fully implemented because of financial and resource constraints on CMS.[32]

Fee-for-Service Medicare. Congress established the current appeals process for Part A and Part B beneficiary appeals in 2000.[33] Appeal follows a denied claim for coverage and/or payment submitted to a Medicare contractor – fiscal intermediaries in the case of Part A and carriers in the case of Part B. For each claim, the Medicare contractor makes an initial determination on coverage and/or payment. If the beneficiary is dissatisfied with the initial determination, a hearing is available before an employee of the contractor, and the contractor makes a final decision.

---

[31] Foote et al. 2004; Kinney 2003; U.S. House 1999.

[32] U.S. GAO 2003b.

[33] Medicare, Medicaid, and SCHIP Benefits Improvement and Protection Act of 2000 § 522 (2000) in Pub. L. No. 106-554, Consolidated Appropriation – FY 2001, Appendix F, § 522 (2000), 114 Stat. 2763, 2763H-72 – H-85 (codified at 42 U.S.C. §1935 ff); Medicare Program: Changes to the Medicare Claims Appeal Procedures, 70 Fed. Reg. 11,420 (Mar. 8, 2005) (42 C.F.R. Parts 401 and 405) (Interim Final Rule).

Independent review is available for reconsideration of the contractor's determination before a qualified independent contractor (QIC). QICs are independent organizations comprised of panels of physicians and other health care professionals who can consider medical, technical, and scientific evidence associated with the appeal. The QIC's reconsideration must include a detailed explanation of its decision, a discussion of pertinent facts and regulations, and, where the issue is whether services are "reasonable and necessary," an explanation of the scientific rationale.

This process involving Medicare contractors is important. Even before there is administrative review before an administrative law judge (ALJ), the system mandates independent medical review. This approach would be useful for Medicare-led malpractice reform because it provides an informal review of medical issues before the initiation of more structured proceedings.

Medicare Advantage and Prescription Drug Plans. The appeals system for the Medicare Advantage program is largely the same as for its predecessor, the Medicare+Choice program.[34] All Medicare Advantage plans must have meaningful grievance procedures to adjudicate beneficiary complaints. Because prepaid health plans do not process "claims" per se, the precipitating event for an appeal can be any adverse action against a Medicare beneficiary – although most appeals involve denials of treatment on coverage grounds. The plan must also accord beneficiaries a hearing as part of its grievance process.

External review for reconsideration of a health plan's final determination is available before an independent entity. These entities are required to have medical expertise available for reviews involving medical issues.

The appeals process for the prescription drug benefit is the same as for health plans because Medicare Advantage plans administer the Part D drug benefit for their enrollees.[35] Other prescription drug plans serving fee-for-service Medicare beneficiaries must have a similar appeals process with comparable steps, timetables, and other characteristics. To initiate an appeal, the beneficiary must request a coverage determination from the plan.

Administrative Review for Medicare Beneficiary Appeals. Regardless of the part of Medicare in which their appeal is generated, all beneficiaries are entitled to administrative review by a corps of administrative law judges within CMS. After reconsideration, the beneficiary's appeal proceeds to an ALJ, with further review by the HHS Departmental Appeals Board (DAB). The

[34] 42 U.S.C. 1395w-21(e)–(g) (2005); Establishment of the Medicare+Choice Program, 63 Fed. Reg. 34968, 35021 (1998) (Final Rule) (42 C.F.R. Part 422).

[35] Pub. L. No. 108-173, § 101, 17 Stat.2066 (2003) (to be codified at 42 U.S.C. 1395w-104); Medicare Prescription Drug Benefit, 70 Fed. Reg. 4194 (Jan. 28, 2005) (Final Rule) (42 C.F.R. Subpart 423M); Medicare Prescription Drug Benefit; Interpretation (70 Fed. Reg. 13397, March 25, 2005) (Final Rule) (42 C.F.R. Subpart 423M).

DAB's decision constitutes final agency action, following which the beneficiary can seek judicial review in federal court.

In the MMA, Congress moved the Medicare administrative appeals system from the Social Security Administration (SSA) to an independent office within HHS.[36] MMA also specified with unusual detail what the transfer should entail. The most important requirement is that ALJs must be independent from CMS and its contractors, which was accomplished by locating Medicare ALJs in an office "organizationally and functionally separate." The ALJ office is responsible to the Secretary but "shall not report to, or be subject to supervision by" any other officer in HHS. The Secretary must also provide for an appropriate geographic distribution of ALJs throughout the United States to ensure timely access for beneficiaries.

A beneficiary is entitled to an ALJ hearing within a statutorily established time period if the amount in controversy is $100 or more. If the deadline is not met, the beneficiary may seek review directly by the DAB. In fee-for-service Medicare, the QIC becomes a party in the ALJ hearing and prepares information required for the appeal, including an explanation of the issues and the relevant policies. The DAB reviews each case de novo. If the deadline for DAB review is not met, the beneficiary may seek judicial review if the amount in controversy is $1,000 or more.

Judicial Review of Medicare Administrative Adjudications. Judicial review in federal district court is available for all claims under all parts of the Medicare program. The standards for judicial review are those for Social Security program appeals under Title II of the Social Security Act.[37] As to facts, the standard of review is whether the agency decision is supported by substantial evidence. The court can order the agency to take new evidence if there is good cause for its prior exclusion under limited conditions. In addition, there are limits on the court's review of national coverage determinations that might be relevant in a malpractice case.[38]

Medicare's Beneficiary Ombudsman Program

The MMA established within HHS a Medicare Beneficiary Ombudsman to assist beneficiaries with complaints, grievances, and requests for information

[36] Pub. L. No. 108-173, § 931, 17 Stat. 2066 (2003) (to be codified at 42 U.S.C. §1935 ff note); Medicare Program: Changes to the Medicare Claims Appeal Procedures, 70 Fed. Reg. 11,420 (Mar. 8, 2005) (Interim Final Rule) (42 C.F.R. Parts 401 and 405).

[37] 42 U.S.C. § 405(g) (2005).

[38] 42 U.S.C. § 1395ff(b) (2005). These limits preclude judicial review of Medicare's national coverage determinations as well as procedural challenges of national coverage determinations for failure to comply with APA and other statutory rulemaking procedures. Also, a court must remand a challenged NCD back to CMS for amplification before invalidating it on any grounds.

with respect to any aspect of the Medicare program, including appeals from adverse determinations by Medicare contractors. The ombudsman may not advocate increases in payment or expanded coverage of services but may identify issues and problems in payment or coverage policies. An ombudsman could play a key role in a Medicare malpractice adjudication system by helping beneficiaries identify claims for medical injury and putting beneficiaries in touch with relevant personnel in a provider, plan, or Medicare contractor who could assist with claim resolution.

A PROPOSED MEDICARE MALPRACTICE ADJUDICATION AND COMPENSATION SYSTEM

The guiding principle for Medicare-led liability reform is to use established institutions within the Medicare program to adjudicate and compensate malpractice claims. This approach would be suitable either for a Medicare demonstration project or for outright programwide implementation, but a demonstration is a logical first step. Placing the resolution of malpractice claims within Medicare also provides unique opportunities for integrating malpractice data with other data collected for quality assurance and improvement. This combination would enable earlier identification and compensation of medical injury, avoidance of malpractice litigation, and improvements in patient safety as medical injuries are identified and analyzed by the review process.

Medicare-led malpractice reform involves four fundamental issues: legal authority, substantive and procedural mechanics, integration of liability reform with other Medicare policy initiatives, and evaluation of the reform's outcome. Unless specified to the contrary, the discussion that follows assumes that Medicare-led malpractice reform would be developed as a demonstration project and tested with selected health care providers in limited geographic areas.

Legal Authority

Medicare-based malpractice reform grounded in federal law offers a path through the thicket of state constitutional objections that have often blocked, or been perceived to preclude, comprehensive overhaul of malpractice litigation by state legislatures.[39] An important threshold question is whether a federal administrative agency can assume jurisdiction over state common law tort claims, especially if the adjudication of the common law tort claims is not required for its effective discharge of the agency's current statutory assignment.

---

[39] Witt 2004.

Issues of authority divide into federal constitutional and statutory categories. Constitutional concerns must be anticipated and addressed but should not present insuperable barriers to a Medicare-based malpractice program. In American federalism, Article I of the U.S. Constitution limits federal legislative authority to enumerated powers and, reinforced by the Tenth Amendment, reserves residual authority to state government. Although legal analysis is warranted, federal spending powers and regulatory powers over interstate commerce should be sufficient to authorize federal litigation rights that supersede state malpractice claims under the supremacy clause.

Congress has enacted laws that supersede state tort law. One important example is the Employee Retirement Income Security Act of 1974 (ERISA), which established a federal scheme for the adjudication of claims against employer-sponsored benefit plans.[40] In *Pilot Life Insurance v. Dedeaux*,[41] the Supreme Court emphatically ruled that the existence of a federal scheme for adjudicating claims preempted state tort law in a case involving the tort of bad faith breach of insurance contract. As a result, ERISA plan participants or beneficiaries must adjudicate their tort claims under the ERISA scheme rather than the common law tort system even though the statutory scheme does not provide equal damages by way of remedy.

The issue of federal preemption of tort remedies has arisen in other contexts. With respect to the Federal Employees Health Benefit Plan, the federal government typically asserts that state law tort causes of action are preempted by federal law. However, courts are split as to whether such preemption exists.[42] Some courts also have recognized that Medicare beneficiaries may bring state tort claims against Medicare HMOs, notwithstanding the regulatory scheme contained in the Medicare statute.[43]

A different constitutional issue requiring more extensive analysis is Congress's ability under Article III and the Seventh Amendment to limit recourse to federal courts and jury trials in favor of intraagency administrative adjudication with deferential judicial review, especially for federal claims that replace traditional state claims. The United States Supreme Court has permitted such delegations within limits.[44]

Crowell v. Benson[45] is the early case regarding delegation of the authority to adjudicate state tort causes of action to a federal administrative agency.[46] *Crowell* concerned a federal workers' compensation program for seamen

---

[40] Employee Retirement Income Security Act of 1974, § 503, Pub. L. No. 93-406, 88 Stat. 832 (codified as amended at 29 U.S.C. § 1001 et seq.).
[41] 481 U.S. 41 (1987).
[42] Jost 1999.
[43] Ibid.
[44] Struve 2005.
[45] 285 U.S. 22 (1932).
[46] Asimow et al. 1998.

in which a federal administrative agency adjudicated compensation claims. The Court upheld the delegation but, because "private rights" such as common law tort liability were implicated, held that Article III judges reviewing agencies' decisions must have independent power to decide all issues of law and "jurisdictional fact" (facts that determine the agency's jurisdiction over the matter).[47]

The important aspect of *Crowell v. Benson* for purposes of Medicare-driven malpractice reform is that the Supreme Court sanctioned a federal regulatory scheme to supplant state common law tort suits and similar claims brought in federal court. The fact that recourse to Article III courts was available in the statutory scheme was critical to the scheme's validity. Because *Crowell v. Benson* concerned admiralty law, the issue of entitlement to a jury trial under the Seventh Amendment was not adjudicated.

The Supreme Court revisited this issue of delegation of judicial powers of Article III courts to other governmental bodies in *Northern Pipeline Construction Co. v. Marathon Pipe Line Co.*[48] and, more recently, in *Thomas v. Union Carbide Agricultural Products Co.*[49] and *Commodity Futures Trading Commission v. Schor.*[50] In *Marathon Pipe Line*, the Court invalidated a statute that assigned breach of contract issues in bankruptcy proceedings to bankruptcy judges, who are not appointed pursuant to Article III, chiefly because of the breadth of the judicial power delegated to the bankruptcy judges. In both *Thomas* and *Schor*, by contrast, the Court upheld legislative delegation of authority to adjudicate common law claims where such delegation was closely related to an underlying regulatory scheme, participation in the adjudication scheme was voluntary, and case outcomes were subject to some kind of judicial review.

Regarding the Seventh Amendment guarantee of a right to trial by jury, the leading modern case is *Atlas Roofing Co. v. Occupational Safety and Health Review Commission*,[51] in which petitioners challenged the authority of the enabling statute to allow the agency to impose civil money penalties, enforceable in federal court, on employers for unsafe working conditions. The Supreme Court concluded that the Seventh Amendment had not been violated because the imposition of the penalty sought to enforce a public rather than a private right. The Court also explained in a footnote that the agency's decisions could be reviewed by the federal courts of appeals; thus, the case did not present the question whether Congress could commit the adjudication of fines to the agency "without any sort of intervention by a

[47] Ibid.
[48] 458 U.S. 50 (1982).
[49] 473 U.S. 568 (1985).
[50] 478 U.S. 833 (1986).
[51] 430 U.S. 442 (1977).

court at any stage of the proceedings."[52] However, other cases suggest that the constitutional authority to substitute administrative adjudication for jury trials is still uncertain.[53]

Other constitutional due process concerns include the defendant's private liberty interest, arbitrary deprivation of property, fair notice to parties, and vagueness in decision making.[54] However, comprehensive reform that rationally balances the interests of both plaintiffs and defendants within a major federal program such as Medicare seems likely to survive legal challenge on these grounds. In *Association of American Physicians and Surgeons v. Weinberger*,[55] for example, the plaintiff medical organization challenged the PSRO program on the ground that it violated rights guaranteed the plaintiff physicians and their patients by the First, Fourth, Fifth, and Ninth Amendments to the Constitution. These constitutional arguments would likely be invoked in a legal challenge to Medicare-led malpractice reform. The United States District Court for the Northern District of Illinois ruled that the PSRO program was constitutional and was affirmed by the U.S. Supreme Court six months later, suggesting that there exists wide latitude to establish quality improvement programs within Medicare.[56] Similarly, in *Rasulis v. Weinberger*,[57] the Seventh Circuit Court of Appeals upheld regulations setting requirements for physical therapists in hospitals that had been attacked as unduly restricting medical practice in violation of the Fifth Amendment. The Court relied on Medicare's statutory authorization for conditions of participation to impose "such additional requirements as . . . necessary in the interest of the health and safety of individuals who are furnished services in the institution."[58]

Assuming that there are no significant constitutional barriers to the establishment of Medicare-led malpractice reform, at least on a voluntary or demonstration basis, the second question is whether HHS has the requisite statutory authority to establish a demonstration and, ultimately, a permanent reform. In other words, can HHS modify aspects of the Medicare program to institute a malpractice adjudication system without specific direction by Congress?

There is a very strong case for such statutory authority. Various demonstration authorities exist, some of which plausibly empower HHS to experiment with alternatives to malpractice litigation. CMS has general authority

---

[52] 430 U.S. at 1269 and n. 13. See Asimow et al. 1998.
[53] Struve 2005.
[54] Geistfeld 2005.
[55] 395 F.Supp. 125 (N.D.Ill. 1975), aff'd per curium, 423 U.S. 975 (1975).
[56] *Association of American Physicians and Surgeons v. Mathews*, 423 U.S. 975 (1975).
[57] 502 F.2d 1006 (7th Cir. 1974).
[58] 502 F.2d at 1010, citing 42 U.S.C. § 1395x(e)(9) (2005).

for demonstrations and studies regarding improvements in Medicare payment methodologies and other matters related to the operation of the Medicare program.[59] CMS is currently using this authority, for example, to launch a demonstration of reinsurance payment for prescription drug plans and Medicare Advantage organizations participating in the prescription drug benefit.[60] HHS also has specific authority under Section 646 of the MMA to offer "incentives to improve safety of care provided to beneficiaries" on a demonstration basis.[61] However, the design and approval of a Section 646 demonstration is a lengthy and complex process. Consequently, Medicare's general demonstration authority may present a more expeditious path to malpractice reform, at least in the short term.

Certain aspects of Medicare-led malpractice reform are nonetheless likely to require explicit congressional authorization. Most important, it is unlikely that CMS could certify hospitals as immune from state tort claims because of their participation in a malpractice demonstration project without legislation conferring federal preemption. Legislation would also probably be necessary to extend reform beyond the demonstration stage to encompass the entire Medicare population, and to make participation in an administrative adjudication system mandatory rather than voluntary for beneficiaries.

Other aspects of developing and implementing Medicare-led malpractice reform will require HHS rulemaking, including any economic analysis mandated by the Office of Management and Budget. The statute is clear that the Secretary has broad authority to make rules for the Medicare program.[62] An important issue is whether the CMS, by regulation, could impose participation in a malpractice adjudication system for Medicare beneficiaries on institutional or professional providers through the various contractual relationships that currently bind these providers to the Medicare program. As discussed previously with respect to the QAPI program, the Medicare program has been able to mount important provider-based quality assurance and improvement programs as a condition of participation in the Medicare program.

Substantive Components of Medicare-Led Reform

In the remainder of this chapter, we specify the basic components of Medicare-led malpractice reform, identify options for policy makers in the

---

[59] 42 U.S.C. § 1395ll (2005).
[60] CMS, Medicare Program; Part D Reinsurance Payment Demonstration, 70 Fed. Reg. 9360 (Feb. 25, 2005) (Notice).
[61] Medicare Prescription Drug, Improvement and Modernization Act of 2003, Pub. L. 108-173, § 646 (codified as amended at 42 U.S.C. § 1395cc-3).
[62] 42 U.S.C. § 1395hh(b) (2005).

design of each component, and connect those options to the achievement of goals such as patient safety, compensation for injury, and open communication with patients and beneficiaries. Some components are substantive, including provider and beneficiary participation, triggering events, and safety and compensation outcomes. Other components are procedural, involving the process of presenting evidence and adjudicating claims.

Provider "Earn-In." A persistent fallacy in health policy generally, and in medical liability specifically, is that all health care providers have equal capacity to deliver high quality care. Single-threshold forms of professional qualification with pro forma renewal, such as state licensing and specialty board certification of physicians, and multiple-year, nearly-everyone-passes seals of approval, such as JCAHO accreditation of hospitals, perpetuate the uniformity myth. Greater reliance on market and consumerist mechanisms in recent decades has created interest in measuring quality on an ongoing basis, disclosing information in public "report cards," and matching health system characteristics to consumer preferences. Medicare-led malpractice reform presents an opportunity to reward the subset of health care providers that have systems in place to keep patients safe and redress avoidable injuries fairly, while creating incentives for the rest to develop that capacity.

What types of health care provider should be eligible to utilize federal standards for medical liability instead of being subject to conventional tort litigation? What structures and behaviors should earn them qualified immunity from conventional lawsuits? The patient safety literature attaches greater potential for safety to larger provider organizations that can evaluate processes of care and support comprehensive medical informatics and communications systems than to individual physicians. For that reason, and because they are already subject to payment-related conditions of participation in the QAIP program for providers and payers described previously, hospitals and closed-panel HMOs seem best positioned to participate in a demonstration of Medicare-led malpractice reform.

For example, participation might be limited to hospitals that provide malpractice coverage for at least 50 percent of their medical staffs. Participating hospitals should also follow identified clinical and informational "best practices" for safety and quality measured by such national data systems as HEDIS and CAHPS and similar systems developed by organizations such as the National Quality Forum, National Patient Safety Foundation, and the Leapfrog group. All physicians caring for Medicare patients at participating hospitals would be covered by the demonstration rules in connection with that care, including for services provided outside of the hospital with respect to the same episode of care. Large physician group practices would also be strong candidates for participation, with similar conditions attached.

A critical issue is ensuring that health care providers participating in reform and therefore "immune" from tort litigation will be the best providers, considering their care as a whole, not the worst. As Gosfield wrote:

If a health plan, integrated system, or large physician group is generally working to improve quality and is willing to be held accountable in this rigorous way, then when patients are harmed, these entities ought to be able to opt out into an alternative liability system.... Patients choosing a plan, system, or clinician ought [sic] be put on prior notice that the high performance of the entity generally will create this different approach.[63]

There has been a dramatic increase in the number of physicians per capita with nearly all growth in medical specialties.[64] Not all physicians are closely connected with medical enterprises, although the number of solo practitioners has declined since the 1970s. Only a small percentage of physicians are employed by hospitals, and these cluster in a few specialties such as radiology and emergency medicine. According to Cunningham, 62 percent of nonfederal, postresidency, patient care physicians practiced in noninstitutional settings in 2001, and in most fields only 20 to 25 percent of physicians belonged to a group with more than eight physicians.[65] Furthermore, smaller, undiversified practices are harder hit by downturns in malpractice insurance markets, particularly if they represent high-liability fields such as obstetrics, neurosurgery, or orthopedics. Offering crisis relief to many of these physicians is essential for any malpractice reform proposal to succeed in either political or pragmatic terms.

How would physicians not part of a corporate enterprise participate in liability reform? To a degree, malpractice crises automatically lead physicians to seek shelter from hospitals where they admit patients simply because hospitals have greater capital, better bargaining skills, and a multispecialty practice base that helps them weather harsh conditions in liability insurance markets.[66] However, antifraud regulators have been uneasy about casual arrangements that might enable hospitals to channel kickbacks to admitting physicians, and the financial benefits of hospital-sponsored malpractice coverage are substantial. Therefore, one must carefully define circumstances under which enterprises eligible for Medicare-led malpractice reform may bring independent physicians under their liability umbrella. In general terms, these are situations in which a physician's participation in overall patient safety activities and agreement to report, disclose, and remediate specific medical errors improve collective performance at the institutional level. A useful analogy is "clinical integration" in antitrust law, a

[63] Gosfield 2000.
[64] Grumbach 2002, Table 1.
[65] Cunningham 2004.
[66] Mello et al. 2005.

concept newly endorsed by the federal antitrust enforcement agencies as indicating that otherwise independent providers are not merely engaged in financial collusion but rather working to offer a better quality product to patients.

Incentives for Physician and Provider Participation. A related question is how to make a reformed liability system sufficiently and immediately attractive to both physicians and hospitals. What financial inducements might be necessary to generate sufficient provider interest? A noteworthy feature of the ongoing malpractice crisis, in comparison to its twentieth-century predecessors, is that state-level reforms have included direct subsidies as well as traditional tort reforms. Among other things, this dynamic reflects the degree to which physician fees have become constrained by public and private health insurance practices. However, financial strains from volatile liability costs differ between physicians and hospitals when insurance actuaries turn pessimistic. The former, at least in the most exposed specialties, struggle to maintain affordable primary coverage, while the latter can self-insure routine litigation costs and are more concerned with excess layers of insurance that protect against the occasional case that generates a $10 million or $20 million damage award. The cost of these layers is very volatile and may not be priced competitively.

Therefore, a strong argument exists for federal subsidy. It is even possible that direct federal reinsurance of hospital liability, with appropriate corridors of shared risk (something that is difficult to do for individual physicians), would offer the best value for the public's investment. Moreover, a properly designed demonstration project will surface more injuries eligible for compensation than the current tort system, while compensating those injuries more predictably. Because the total cost of compensation is uncertain and is a major criterion for evaluation of the reform being tested, the federal government should also provide stop-loss coverage to participating hospitals if their total liability costs during the demonstration period exceed historical benchmarks.

Medicare-led malpractice reform is highly consistent with the "pay for performance" concept. A consensus appears to have emerged among both public and private payers that a substantial portion of provider payment should be contingent on meeting process-based or outcome-based standards for quality. The Medicare program is aggressively pursuing pay for performance initiatives, some of which involve carefully selected provider organizations that meet specific quality standards, such as the Premier Hospital demonstration described previously. Similarly, health care providers might earn the right to bypass conventional tort litigation for an important subset of their patients (Medicare beneficiaries) and to receive financial assistance with their overall liability costs by demonstrating compliance with patient safety standards and providing better support for injured patients.

This perspective on malpractice reform reinforces the idea of creating a better system of injury detection, prevention, and compensation and not merely reducing access to the current, flawed system by erecting further barriers to filing claims and receiving payment.

Beneficiary "Opt-In." A Medicare-led demonstration of malpractice reform would provide an exclusive administrative remedy for selected Medicare beneficiaries injured by medical care. Conventional state law tort claims would be preempted. A critical issue is whether Medicare patients treated by participating providers should be obligated to accept a limited federal remedy in lieu of filing a conventional state tort claim. What opportunities, if any, should there be to opt out of the new system, or should patients expressly opt in? These difficult questions require triangulation among legal, political, and policy considerations.

In policy terms, mandatory participation would likely work best. Potential for evaluation is a central concern for any demonstration project, and selection bias is an ever-present risk in social science research. If decisions to participate are nonrandom, so that claims channeled into administrative resolution are not a representative sample of events or disputants, evaluation becomes more difficult. Furthermore, strategic incentives to bring particular claims in the forum likely to prove most lucrative can undermine the actual as well as the measurable benefits of malpractice reform. Although nominally mandatory for patients whose physicians elect to participate, the "no-fault" alternatives to malpractice suits that are available to victims of neonatal injury in Florida and Virginia have been underutilized in large part because plaintiffs and their lawyers can manipulate descriptions of particular cases so as to exclude them from coverage if conventional tort litigation seems promising.[67]

Finally, testing reform using Medicare patients in selected settings with strong federal sponsorship allows the terms of compensation to be generous. As discussed previously, data suggest that Medicare patients file many fewer tort claims than younger patients relative to the injuries they suffer, receive less in damages both in average terms and in likelihood of a very large payout, and experience similar delays in payment. Nonmonetary benefits such as timely, honest disclosure of error and injury and a less adversarial process that permits therapeutic relationships with familiar physicians and hospitals to continue are likely to be valued greatly by seniors and their families. In addition, explicit reform demonstrations with federal funding are not as constrained by politically motivated estimates of budget impact than would be the case for across-the-board federal legislation of a similar character or for uncoordinated demonstration projects using scarcer state or local dollars.

[67] Bovbjerg and Sloan 1998.

On the other hand, there are strong political reasons to make participation in Medicare-led malpractice reform voluntary for patients to the greatest degree compatible with a successful demonstration. Limiting individuals' access to courts for personal injury is a highly polarized issue in health care and in American society generally. For both emotional and financial reasons, few issues rival tort reform in terms of aggressive partisanship, overheated rhetoric, and suspicion of new ideas. Although Medicare's central role in health policy is undeniable, even a constrained demonstration proposal is likely to provoke tests of political allegiance on both sides, which might delay or derail meaningful reform. Requiring mandatory participation by patients would allow anti–tort reform constituencies to caricature the proposal as merely another attempt to further enrich corporate and professional groups by stripping vulnerable seniors of their legal rights (and would provoke a predictable response accusing trial lawyers of exploiting the public for personal advantage). If a mandatory reform were adopted over these objections, it would almost certainly become mired in litigation challenging its constitutionality. Debating reform in these terms ignores the plain fact that seniors fare poorly both as patients in a health care system with suboptimal safety and as potential plaintiffs in a litigation system financed with contingent fees. Enhancing reform with a patina of voluntary choice might sustain a demonstration program until it can credibly establish its effects on participants and on the health care system as a whole.

There are several ways to make participation in a Medicare malpractice adjudication system voluntary. For example, Medicare beneficiaries living in the geographic area served by participating hospitals could be given notice of the demonstration rules and could make a onetime election to proceed with any claims that arise through the Medicare appeals system instead of the common law tort system, with subsequent opportunities to opt out for medical care not yet received. Hospitals and physicians that have entered a Medicare demonstration could notify existing patients that they will be asked to consent to adjudication of claims through the Medicare appeals system, and new patients could be asked to consent upon initiation of care if they had not already made such an election. Patients incapable of election or consent, such as those receiving emergency services, would retain their existing legal rights but might be offered an opportunity to enter the reformed system for follow-up care. Similarly, the system might allow patients to retain the ability to litigate in exceptional circumstances, such as willful misconduct.

Event Detection and Disclosure. Under a Medicare malpractice system, unlike the existing tort system, patients would not be solely responsible for determining that they had a claim for medical injury. A major premise of Medicare-led reform is that it should actively root out medical errors rather than assuming the reactive posture of conventional litigation. Participating hospitals should have in place some constellation of adverse event detection systems, such as mandatory reporting of designated events and unanticipated injuries, voluntary reporting of near misses, and computerized screening for drug side effects. These systems should have government or self-regulatory oversight. For example, JCAHO standards, which already require hospitals to have a patient safety infrastructure, might be modified to connect those processes to patient compensation mechanisms. Similarly, voluntary or mandatory reporting systems for medical errors, such as those contemplated by recent federal legislation modeled on the Aviation Safety Reporting System, should be configured to capture categories of events potentially eligible for compensation, in order to provide a check on providers' efforts both to identify errors and to implement and share improvements. This process could be leveraged through existing Medicare quality of care initiatives. Specifically, when a medical injury is identified using the processes that Medicare now mandates for participating providers and health plans to review and report patient safety problems discussed previously, that problem would be referred to the relevant Medicare contractor or health plan for assessment of potential for compensation. If injured beneficiaries were not satisfied with determinations by Medicare contractors, they could appeal to the Medicare administrative appeals system and ultimately obtain limited judicial review.

Reform would also aim to improve how patients and families learn about medical errors. Although JCAHO merely urges but does not require notification of patients regarding medical errors, the American Medical Association has stated that disclosure is ethically required of physicians and a handful of states mandate it for hospitals.[68] Health care providers participating in a Medicare malpractice demonstration should be required promptly to disclose serious, unanticipated outcomes of care to patients (or, when appropriate, families) in writing. Pennsylvania's statute, which requires written disclosure within seven days, is a good model.[69] With disclosure mandatory, participating hospitals and physicians would have a strong interest in productive conversations that air concerns, relate information valuable for patient safety, and reach settlements in as many cases as possible. A demonstration project might therefore require participating hospitals to train physicians in basic mediation skills, create a consultation service of error communication experts, and offer patients early, facilitative mediation promptly after the initial disclosure of error.[70] In some instances, it is likely that patients and families would be satisfied with an apology, open discussion, and payment of out-of-pocket expenses and would not pursue even an administrative remedy beyond that point.

---

[68] Liebman and Hyman 2005.

[69] Medical Care Availability and Reduction of Error (MCare) Act § 302 , Pa. Act of Mar. 20, 2002, Pub. L. 154, No. 13.

[70] Liebman and Hyman 2005.

Information derived from these activities would also feed into other Medicare programs. Unlike tort litigation, with its tendency toward confidential settlement and spotty reporting to regulators even when mandatory (e.g., the National Practitioners Data Bank), both dispute-related data and underlying clinical information would be available to quality regulators. In addition to Medicare's QAIP program, CMS has launched specific quality initiatives, described previously, for the major classes of providers.

Compensable Events. Eligibility for and amount of payment are the key questions for any administration compensation system. It is generally accepted that the negligence-based standard of care used in tort litigation functions poorly. Conceptually, a finding of professional negligence denotes a departure from customary and reasonable practice.[71] Because physicians often practice medicine unscientifically, relying on habit rather than clinical evidence,[72] this standard excuses substantial suboptimal care. At the same time, an accusation of negligence constitutes a personal affront and reputational threat that many physicians fiercely resist because it connotes egregious conduct that violates the norms of their professional community.[73]

Practically, a negligence standard turns the compensation decision into a battle of expert medical witnesses whose qualifications vary according to local procedural rules and whose demeanor tends to count more than the scientific underpinnings of their testimony. Juries may reach reasonable conclusions in most cases, but their determinations do not correlate systematically with good or bad medical care and are seldom incorporated into provider-based or regulatory quality improvement initiatives. Moreover, the vast majority of cases are dropped or settle without generating usable information regarding physician or hospital quality, often with explicit gag clauses that prevent the facts of the dispute as well as the amount of the payment from reaching the public.

For these reasons, most advocates of administrative compensation favor a standard of "avoidability" or "preventability" judged by scientific experts.[74] Certain events might be automatically compensable, on the theory that their occurrence is almost always avoidable. A Medicare administrative review system would facilitate the use of designated events schemes to determine liability and require compensation without further consideration of fault. These "accelerated compensation events," first developed by Bovbjerg and Tancredi, initially would be identified and updated by an expert process upon which a Medicare administrative review system would rely.[75] More recently,

[71] Peters 2001, 2002.
[72] Institute of Medicine 2002; Chassin and Galvin 1998.
[73] Sage 2004a.
[74] Studdert and Brennan 2001a; Institute of Medicine 2002.
[75] Tancredi and Bovbjerg 1991; Bovbjerg et al. 1991; American Bar Association 1979.

a forum of stakeholders has established a consensus list of events that should "never" happen in the provision of care.[76] In these instances, the hospital or physician group would notify the patient of the event, report the event to the appropriate quality oversight bodies within Medicare and elsewhere, and offer compensation without contesting eligibility.

Where avoidability is contested, a Medicare administrative review would begin using the claims systems and procedures described previously, modified appropriately for malpractice disputes as outlined later. In most cases, as in the current tort system, providers and patients would settle the case at preliminary stages, but with two distinct advantages over conventional litigation. First, strict timetables for mediation and adjudication would ensure prompt resolution. Second, information would be captured immediately and used for quality improvement purposes. Early disclosure and settlement could be rewarded, similar to the incentives that O'Connell and colleagues have proposed to identify claims early and encourage payers to make early offers and injured patients to accept those offers.[77]

This approach would also force the health care system to deal better with unavoidable but serious injuries than occurs in tort. For example, the largest malpractice payments typically involve severely compromised newborns requiring lifetime medical care. These tragic situations increase the volatility of malpractice insurance markets, threaten the reputations of well-intentioned health care providers, and induce widespread defensive medical practice. Though potentially related to gestational and perinatal events that compromise oxygen and blood flow to the fetus, most of these cases are not considered avoidable.[78] An administrative compensation system based on avoidability will not pay the extraordinary cost of treating and maintaining these individuals, leading the Medicare program to evaluate the adequacy of its benefit package and possibly leading to an improved coverage system for catastrophic illness. Neonatal injury is not currently a problem for Medicare beneficiaries (though assistive reproductive technology may eventually make it one!). But it is a major issue for state Medicaid programs, which pay for more than one-third of births in the United States.[79] Furthermore, unexpected complications requiring significant out-of-pocket expenses may arise for other medical conditions affecting seniors, not all of which are necessarily covered by the current Medicare benefit.

Compensation Amounts (Damages). A Medicare-based administrative compensation system would be more uniform and predictable in its damages determinations than tort litigation because it would rely heavily on prospective guidelines (schedules) and would avoid both the exaggerations of partisan

[76] National Quality Forum 2002.
[77] O'Connell and Eaton 1999; O'Connell 1982, 1986.
[78] American College of Obstetrics and Gynecology 2003.
[79] Kaiser Foundation 2004, Table 7.

expert witnesses and the emotions of lay jurors. Administrative processes would also be able to approach the damages issues dispassionately whether or not liability was at issue. One might even expect situations to arise in which an acknowledged preventable event has occurred but the parties cannot agree on an appropriate payment and turn to the ALJ process for a binding determination. By contrast, defendants in malpractice litigation are often unwilling to present evidence about damages during trial for fear of appearing to the jury as conceding liability.

The specifics of calculating damages in a Medicare-led malpractice system are open to debate but should be culturally easier than would be the case in a stand-alone forum such as a state court. Medicare ALJs, like many other administrative officers, are accustomed to awarding damages or benefits pursuant to schedules. In a demonstration project, compensation would likely include all provable economic damages, such as lost wages (typically low for Medicare beneficiaries) and future medical expenses. Periodic payment of future medical expenses would be allowed. Compensation would also include lump-sum noneconomic damages. The maximum amount of noneconomic damages for the most severely and persistently injured could not exceed a preset figure.

Agency rulemaking and advisory committee processes would probably be required to draft initial schedules and create a process for revising and updating them. With respect to economic damages, Medicare ALJs are accustomed to dealing with survival, degree of disability, and lost wages, and the federal government is likely to have considerable advantages over individual litigants in local courtrooms when estimating the cost of future medical care. The Medicare program can also deal directly with medical costs by expanding benefits to injured patients and waiving subrogation rights against liable providers. With respect to noneconomic damages, reformers have long suggested scheduling damages as a means of bringing rationality and consistency to injury compensation in medical malpractice.[80] Medical injuries invoke the same issues as other statutory compensation schemes – the nature, severity, and permanency of the injury. Most public compensation programs administered by agencies, such as the Social Security Disability Insurance program, Department of Labor workers' compensation programs, and veterans' disability programs, award benefits pursuant to schedules that have already predetermined what benefits should be awarded for specific types and degrees of injury or illness.[81]

A final consideration is the threshold degree of injury that merits payment. In the tort system, the vast majority of negligent injuries never receive compensation because the result would not be worth the effort. Anecdotal reports suggest that, because of the necessary investment in expert witnesses and the delay and uncertainty in obtaining a final judgment, patients who

[80] Blumstein et al. 1991; Bovbjerg et al. 1989.
[81] Kinney 2005.

suffer less than $100,000 in compensable injury cannot find a competent lawyer who will accept the case on contingent fee. As noted, lower potential damages are one reason why seniors are poorly served by the current system of malpractice litigation. An administrative compensation system, by contrast, might find itself with the opposite problem: becoming swamped by small-dollar claims. For this reason, proposals for "no-fault" compensation in medical malpractice typically include an injury threshold, below which compensation is unavailable regardless of injury causation.[82] Again, ALJs are accustomed to enforcing injury thresholds. Moreover, because a Medicare-led malpractice system is proactive rather than reactive with respect to event detection, it will capture a much larger number of small claims than occurs in tort and can convey that information to institutional and regulatory quality improvement efforts.

Procedural Components

Medicare has two principal procedural advantages over generic "medical courts" for resolving malpractice claims. First, Medicare can be proactive with respect to error and injury reporting rather than simply reacting to filed claims. Second, Medicare already has in place a tested system for adjudicating beneficiary appeals, onto which a malpractice adjudication system can be grafted. Still, critical procedural elements remain to be determined. These include (1) how a claim for medical malpractice as opposed to a claim for coverage or payment would be presented, (2) what parts of the Medicare appeals system would be involved with adjudicating malpractice claims, and (3) how evaluating claims with respect to malpractice liability and damages would differ from evaluating benefits claims.

Initiation of Complaints. As discussed previously, in most cases Medicare beneficiaries or their families would receive information about unanticipated outcomes of medical care from participating providers. Discussions would ensue, with or without formal mediation, in hopes of reaching a consensual settlement. Beneficiaries, with or without counsel, who had not reached a settlement with the appropriate provider with respect to liability or damages, or who felt aggrieved by care that was not identified by the provider as unexpectedly injurious, would file their claim with a Medicare fee-for-service program contractor. Generally, it would be the same Medicare contractor to whom they would appeal a coverage denial or raise another issue with the Medicare program. The Medicare contractor would evaluate the claim to determine whether it was essentially a grievance about the provider's conduct toward the beneficiary or it involved a medical injury that would benefit from medical review. In the first instance, the Medicare contractor would refer the claim first to the relevant provider and/or health plan. In the

---

[82] Studdert and Brennan 2001b.

second instance, the contractor would refer the claim to the QIC for medical review and possible settlement.

The Medicare Beneficiary Ombudsman, who handles a variety of beneficiary concerns, would be trained to identify complaints involving medical injuries. The ombudsman would connect the beneficiary to the relevant officials in the provider organization or plan that would handle a medical claim. The ombudsman could also assist the beneficiary in marshaling the information needed to present a claim and assist the beneficiary in the early stages of the process. The responsibilities of the new office of the Medicare Beneficiary Ombudsman have not been delineated. However, the ombudsman needs at a minimum to be able to recognize medical injury when beneficiaries bring complaints and to know where to refer those cases.

For beneficiaries enrolled in Medicare Advantage, claims would be filed using the grievance procedure of their Medicare managed care plan. The health plan would make essentially the same determination as the Medicare contractor. If the claim were essentially a grievance, the claim would remain in the plan's grievance system. But if the claim involved a medical injury, the plan would refer the claim to their external reviewer QIC for medical review.

Experience discussing both grievances and injuries with patients and families might lead providers and health plans to utilize similar mediation skills and mechanisms for both categories of dispute. Medicare is already introducing mediation at the QIC level for beneficiary complaints as an alternative to medical record review.[83] Empirical research found that 18 percent of patient complaints about care concerned communication problems with physicians and 7 percent pertained to the provider's "humaneness."[84] Another study of malpractice suits over prenatal injuries found that nearly a quarter of subjects (24%) sued because the physician did not tell the truth about the injury and another one-fifth (20%) sued because they could not find out what happened to their child.[85]

Participating providers might be required to offer patients mediation not less than sixty days following disclosure of a serious event, with the goal of promoting voluntary settlement in the majority of cases. Cases not already subjected to structured discussion following disclosure of error could be referred back to the participating hospital, physician group, or health plan, with oversight from the ombudsman or QIC. A nonadversarial process that convenes the parties as soon after the episode of care as possible enables the parties to resolve situations through explanation, apology, system improvement, or monetary compensation is useful for both technical lapses and failures of communication, with one often serving as a marker for another.[86]

[83] Giammona 2003; Scully-Hayes 2002.
[84] Hickson et al. 1997.
[85] Hickson et al. 1992.
[86] Hickson et al. 2002.

Presentation of Evidence and Bases for Decision. In situations involving technical subject matter, including medical care, American civil procedure relies on partisan expert witnesses selected and paid by the litigants to present evidence to a lay jury. This convention has been criticized as both unreliable and expensive and often requires the judge to exert greater control over expert testimony than he or she is comfortable with.[87] Malpractice litigation commonly presents difficult issues regarding the standard of care, causation of injury, and extent of damages. In a study of malpractice disputes, Poythress and colleagues found that the adversarial system was not always perceived as the most just and fair model.[88] They compared the conventional adversarial model, in which the parties developed medical expert testimony, with two hybrid models in which the judge took greater control over the development of expert testimony. In one hybrid model, the judge selected the expert; and in the other, the judge arranged for an empirical survey of physicians in the relevant field and geographic area to determine breach of the standard of care. Both hybrid models were perceived to be more just and fair than the purely adversarial model, in which the disputants arranged for their own expert testimony. Quasi-inquisitorial procedures of this sort differ from the common law tradition by emphasizing truth-finding over political rights of litigants but comport with traditional principles of equity courts.[89] Furthermore, unlike disputes over Medicare benefits, the government does not have a clear financial interest in the outcome of a malpractice decision but values both safe and cost-effective medical services for beneficiaries.

Proposals to create specialized, stand-alone medical courts respond principally to concerns over lack of technical expertise on the part of both judges and juries, but raise other concerns.[90] By contrast, use of common medical review through the QIC provides an excellent opportunity to marshal required medical expertise in a fair and expeditious manner. As described previously, regulations listing accelerated compensation events would conclusively establish liability for certain avoidable injuries. In less clear cases of medical injury, a Medicare malpractice system could facilitate the use of medical practice guidelines to establish a standard of avoidability. Where expert testimony is needed, an ALJ could invite written submissions from the parties' experts, or HHS by regulation might empower the ALJ to appoint an impartial clinical or actuarial expert, with the cost covered by Medicare demonstration funding. As an experienced decision maker, moreover, the ALJ would be authorized and competent to consult relevant HHS reports, advisory opinions, best-practice documents, or other reports of federal health care agencies for "legislative facts."[91]

---

[87] Shuman 2001; *Journal of Health Politics, Policy and Law* 2001.
[88] Poythress et al. 1993.
[89] Kessler 2004.
[90] Struve 2003, 2004.
[91] Kinney 2005.

Medical practice guidelines are "systematically developed statements of recommendation for patient management to assist practitioner and patient decisions about appropriate health care for specific clinical circumstances."[92] Another definition is a "standardized specification for care developed by a formal process that incorporates the best scientific evidence of effectiveness with expert opinion."[93] Since their emergence on a widespread basis in the 1980s, medical practice guidelines became increasingly more widespread and sophisticated. The guidelines have moved from statements of procedures that constitute good-quality care to detailed decision trees that guide steps in care depending on patient-specific variables. Medical practice guidelines, medical standards of care, and the theoretical foundation of evidence-based medicine are now well accepted in medical circles.[94] They are also widely accessible through the National Guideline Clearinghouse (NGC), a public resource for evidence-based clinical practice guidelines within the Agency for Healthcare Research and Quality (AHRQ), which is part of HHS.

SSA ALJs are accustomed to working with guidelines and decision trees to apply expert opinion that is codified in an administrative rule and also to adjudicate medical conditions. There is conceptually little difference in applying these coverage and disability guidelines than applying a detailed medical practice guideline to determine the standard of care or to determine that a medical injury is included in a list of designated events. Moreover, SSA ALJs are specifically trained to evaluate degree of disability using medical-vocational guidelines, which are analogous in some respects to determinations of life expectancy, degree of injury, and forgone earnings in malpractice cases.[95] Medical–vocational guidelines are basically decision trees to be followed in determining whether jobs exist in the national economy for individuals with specific characteristics with respect to degree of impairment, age, education, and work experience. SSA promulgated these regulations in the 1980s in order to bring more consistency to the determination of qualification for disability benefits at a time when demand for benefits was growing dramatically and SSA had great concerns about inequities resulting from inconsistent testimony of vocational experts.[96]

Results of Decision, Appeals, and Use as Precedent. As discussed previously, creating an information-rich environment for patient safety, quality improvement, and fairness of compensation is one of the major reasons for pursuing malpractice reform through Medicare. Unlike the common law

---

[92] Institute of Medicine 1990.
[93] Leape 1990.
[94] Williams 2004.
[95] 43 Fed. Reg. 55349 (1978), 20 C.F.R. Subpart 404 P (2005).
[96] 42 U.S.C. § 423(d)(2)(A).

of tort, health care providers who participate in a Medicare malpractice demonstration are obligated to disclose medical errors to patients or their families in order to foster systematic improvement as well as to vindicate individual rights. Similarly, the public interest in safe medical care and reasonably equal treatment of Medicare beneficiaries dictates that results of ALJ decisions as well as settlements reached in lieu of decision should be publicly available. ALJs should issue written decisions in all cases. Confidential settlements would be prohibited, except when an independent privacy interest such as the protection of a minor requires that certain information be withheld.

On the other hand, the individual patient's personal interest in the outcome of an administrative determination regarding medical liability is much more direct than any single beneficiary's claim on Medicare benefits. Therefore, rights of appeal and of federal judicial review should be more liberal for malpractice cases than for national coverage decisions. Nonetheless, the standard for review should be based on established administrative law rather than on civil procedure, with reversal only for abuse of discretion for legal questions or lack of substantial evidence for factual questions. Otherwise, incentives will exist for parties to look to courts inappropriately for ultimate relief and shortchange the administrative process.

Whether ALJ determinations should constitute precedent in subsequent cases presenting similar facts is an open question. Because clinical circumstances vary widely in cases of medical injury, and situations requiring administrative resolution often will not involve ACEs or treatment subject to guidelines, past decisions offer valuable guidance to hearing officers. Furthermore, all prior decisions will be readily available as will information about settlements, reducing the risk that precedents will be invoked selectively. However, it seems prudent, at least for demonstrations of malpractice reform, to use prior decisions to improve the regulatory infrastructure of Medicare's malpractice system such as identification of ACEs, scheduling of damages, and referral of clinical questions for guideline development rather than to constrain individual ALJs during periods in which experimentation and innovation are desirable. For example, HHS should review ALJ determinations annually to inform its best-practice reporting. A separate mechanism should be in place to monitor Medicare ALJ performance, which has been suggested by administrative law experts observing ALJs generally.[97] Records of settlements and hearing outcomes may also be useful in any federal clearinghouse of patient safety information that is developed.

Finally, information regarding case outcomes will be essential for evaluating the success or failure of Medicare-based malpractice reform, including estimating the costs and benefits of expanding reform to a larger population

---

[97] Gifford 1997; Koch 1994; Administrative Conference of the United States 1992.

of Medicare beneficiaries. Evaluation of a demonstration should include, at a minimum, the following:

Comparison groups:

- Pre- and postdemonstration comparisons of Medicare beneficiaries at participating hospitals
- Comparison of participating hospitals to matched, nonparticipating hospitals
- Comparison of Medicare beneficiaries to other patients at participating hospitals

Comparison metrics:

- Event detection and mandatory reporting rates
- Voluntary event reporting rates
- Qualitative evaluation of error disclosure conversations
- Qualitative evaluation of changes in hospital patient safety practices
- Time required to resolve disputes and/or pay compensation following injury
- Payment frequencies and amounts
- Liability insurance costs and availability
- Patient satisfaction with process
- Physician and hospital satisfaction with process

CONCLUSION

A promising option for malpractice reform is for the federal government to propose a comprehensive restructuring of malpractice claims involving Medicare, and eventually Medicaid, which could then set the standard for the rest of the health care system. This would solve a chronic problem for liability reform – it is perceived more as a legal than as a health policy issue. The surest way for malpractice to be placed on the national health policy agenda is for Medicare to take ownership of it. Medicare-led reform, which could take advantage of Medicare's established systems of administrative adjudication, would link the process of identifying and compensating avoidable injuries to Medicare's other quality improvement initiatives. Prompt resolution of claims would be hugely advantageous to seniors compared to suffering delays of several years in courtroom proceedings. Making malpractice policy through Medicare policy would also focus the political process on the health policy impact of liability reform, rather than allowing lobbyists on both sides of the aisle to exploit public concern over health care for general partisan advantage. Federal demonstrations of this approach should begin immediately.

Bibliography

Abraham, Kenneth S., 1992. "What Is a Tort Claim? An Interpretation of Contemporary Tort Reform." *Maryland Law Review* 51.

Abraham, Kenneth S., and Paul C. Weiler, 1994a. "Enterprise Medical Liability and the Choice of the Responsible Enterprise." *American Journal of Law and Medicine* 20.

———, 1994b. "Enterprise Medical Liability and the Evolution of the American Health Care System." *Harvard Law Review* 108.

Academy of Medicine of Cleveland/Northern Ohio Medical Association, 2004. "Medical Malpractice Commission Meets to Learn More About a Patient Compensation Fund." At http://amcnoma.org/webpages/main.asp (last accessed Sept. 14, 2004).

Adams, E. Kathleen, and Stephen Zuckerman, 1984. "Variation in the Growth and Incidence of Medical Malpractice Claims." *Journal of Health Politics, Policy and Law* 9.

Administrative Conference of the United States, 1992. "Recommendations and Statements of the Administrative Conference Regarding Administrative Practice and Procedure." *Federal Register* 57: 61759.

Agency for Healthcare Research and Quality (AHRQ), 2005. "Medical Errors and Patient Safety." At http://www.ahrq.gov/qual/errorsix.htm (last accessed July 11, 2005).

Agresti, Alan, 1996. *Introduction to Categorical Data Analysis*. New York: Wiley.

Albert, Tanyax, 2003. "A Tale of Two States." *American Medical News* 12.

Allred, Keith G., 2000. "Anger and Retaliation in Conflict: The Role of Attribution." In Morton Deutsch and Peter T. Coleman, eds., *The Handbook of Conflict Resolution*. San Francisco: Jossey-Bass.

American Bar Association (ABA), 1979. "Designated Compensable Event System: A Feasibility Study." Chicago: ABA.

American College of Obstetrics and Gynecology (ACOG), 2003. "Neonatal Encephalopathy and Cerebral Palsy: Defining the Pathogenesis and Pathophysiology." Chicago: ACOG.

American College of Physicians, 2003. "Reforming the Medical Professional Liability Insurance System." Washington, DC: American College of Physicians. At http://www.acponline.org/hpp/pospaper/liability ins.pdf (last accessed Aug. 15, 2004).

———, 1995. "Beyond MICRA: New Ideas for Liability Reform." *Annals of Internal Medicine* 122.

American Enterprise Institute–Brookings Joint Center for Regulatory Studies, 2002. "Fear of Litigation Study: The Impact on Medicine." Study conducted for Common Good. At http://cgood.org/assets/attachments/68.pdf (last accessed Oct. 28, 2004).

American Law Institute (ALI), 1991a. *Enterprise Responsibility for Personal Injury, Volume I: The Institutional Framework*. Philadelphia: ALI.

———, 1991b. *Enterprise Responsibility for Personal Injury, Volume II: Approaches to Legal and Institutional Change*. Philadelphia: ALI.

American Medical Association (AMA), 2004. "Medical Liability Reform – Now!" At http://www.ama-assn.org/ama1/pub/upload/mm/450/mlrnowdec032004.pdf. (last accessed Oct. 10, 2005).

———, 1998. *Medical Professional Liability Insurance: The Informed Physician's Guide to Coverage Decisions*. Washington, DC: AMA.

———, 1970. "Malpractice." *American Medical News* 13 (Feb. 9).

American Medical Association (AMA), Council on Ethical and Judicial Affairs, 2004. *Code of Medical Ethics: Current Opinions with Annotations, 2004–2005*. Chicago: American Medical Association. Current opinions available at http://www.ama-assn.org/ama/pub/category/2503.html (last accessed July 10, 2005).

American Medical Association (AMA)/Specialty Society Medical Liability Project, 1988. "A Proposed Alternative to the Civil Justice System for Resolving Medical Liability Disputes: A Fault-Based Administrative System." Chicago: AMA.

Anders, G. T., R. A. Berenson, R. L. Egger, C. Havighurst, W. L. Kissick, S. E. McGraw, and S. K. Murata, 1993. "What the Clinton Health Plan Means to You." *Medical Economics* 70.

Anderson, Richard E., 2005. "Effective Legal Reform and the Malpractice Insurance Crisis." *Yale Journal of Health Policy Law and Ethics* 5.

Andrews, Lori B., Carol Stocking, Thomas Krizek, Lawrence Gottlieb, Claudette Krizek, Thomas Vargish, and Mark Siegler, 1997. "An Alternative Strategy for Studying Adverse Events in Medical Care." *Lancet* 349.

Arlen, Jennifer, 2005. "Contracting Over Malpractice Liability." Unpublished manuscript in possession of editors.

———, 2000. "Tort Damages: A Survey." In Boudewijn Bouckaert and Gerrit De Geest, eds., *Encyclopedia of Law and Economics*. Cheltenham: Edward Elgar.

Arlen, Jennifer, and Reinier Kraakman, 1997. "Controlling Corporate Misconduct: An Analysis of Corporate Liability Regimes." *New York University Law Review* 72.

Arlen, Jennifer, and W. Bentley MacLeod, 2005. "Torts, Expertise, and Authority: Liability of Physicians and Managed Care Organizations." *RAND Journal of Economics* 36.

———, 2003. "Malpractice Liability for Physicians and Managed Care Organizations." *New York University Law Review* 78.

Arrow, Kenneth, Robert H. Mnookin, Lee Ross, Amos Tversky, and Robert Wilson, eds., 1995. *Barriers to Conflict Resolution*. New York: W. W. Norton.

Asimow, Michael R., Arthur E. Bonfield, and Ronald M. Levin, 1998. *State and Federal Administrative Law*. 2d ed. St. Paul, MN: West Group.

Associated Press, 2004. "Some Maryland Doctors, Irked by Costs, Consider Going 'Bare,' Shifting Liability to Hospitals." *Insurance Journal* at http://www. insurancejournal.com/news/east/2004/11/01/47323.htm (last accessed July 26, 2005).

Association of American Medical Colleges, 2002. "Number of U.S. Medical Schools Teaching Selected Topics." Table from *Liaison Committee on Medical Education Part II Annual Medical School Questionnaire for 2000–2001.* At http://services.aamc.org/currdir/section2/LCMEHotTopics.pdf (last accessed Oct. 28, 2004).

Association of the Bar of the City of New York, 1990. *Medical Malpractice Recommendations for the State of New York.* New York: City Bar Association.

Aulisio, May T., 2001. "Medical Malpractice, Mistake Prevention, and Compensation." *Kennedy Institute Ethics Journal* 11.

Babcock, Linda, and Greg Pogarsky, 1999. "Damage Caps and Settlement: A Behavioral Approach." *Journal of Legal Studies* 28.

Baicker, Katherine, and Amitabh Chandra, 2004. "The Effect of Malpractice Liability on the Delivery of Health Care." NBER Working Paper 10709 (August).

Baker, Laurence, Howard Birnbau, Jeffrey Geppert, David Mishol, and Erick Moyneur, 2003. "The Relationship Between Technology Availability and Medical Spending." *Health Affairs* Web Exclusive W3–537 (Nov. 5).

Baker, Peter, 2005. "Bush Campaigns to Curb Lawsuits; President Says 'Junk' Litigation Is Driving Small-Town Doctors out of Business." *Washington Post* (Jan. 6).

Baker, Thomas, forthcoming. "Making Sense With Numbers: The Uses and Abuses of Empirical Research on the Validity of Medical Malpractice Claims." Unpublished paper in possession of editors.

———, 2005a. *The Medical Malpractice Myth.* Chicago: University of Chicago Press.

———, 2005b. "Medical Malpractice and the Insurance Underwriting Cycle." *DePaul Law Review* 54.

———, 2005c. "Reconsidering the Harvard Medical Practice Study Conclusions about the Validity of Medical Malpractice Claims." *Journal of Law, Medicine, & Ethics* 33.

———, 2004. "Insuring Liability Risks." *Geneva Papers* 29.

———, 2003. *Insurance Law and Policy: Cases, Materials and Problems.* New York: Aspen Publishers.

———, 2002. "Risk, Insurance and the Social Construction of Responsibility." In Tom Baker and Jonathan Simon, eds., *Embracing Risk: The Changing Culture of Insurance and Responsibility.* Chicago: University of Chicago Press.

———, 2001. "Blood Money, New Money and the Moral Economy of Tort Law in Action." *Law & Society Review* 35.

———, 1997–8. "Liability Insurance Conflicts and Defense Lawyers: From Triangles to Tetrahedrons." *Connecticut Insurance Law Journal* 4.

Baker, Thomas, Alon Harel, and Tamar Kugler, 2004. "The Virtues of Uncertainty in Law." *Iowa Law Review* 89.

Baldus, David, John C. MacQueen, and George Woodworth, 1994. "Improving Judicial Oversight of Jury Damages Assessments: A Proposal for the Comparative Additur/Remittitur Review of Awards for Nonpecuniary Harms and Punitive Damages." *Iowa Law Review* 80.

Baldwin, Laura-Mae, Gary L. Hart, Michael Lloyd, Meredith Fordyce, and Roger A. Rosenblatt, 1995. "Defensive Medicine and Obstetrics." *Journal of the American Medical Association* 274.

Barach, Paul, 2003. "The End of the Beginning: Lessons Learned From the Patient Safety Movement." *Journal of Legal Medicine* 24.

Barger-Lux, M. Janet, and Robert P. Heaney, 1986. "For Better and Worse: The Technological Imperative in Health Care." *Social Science & Medicine* 22.

Bayley, Carol, 2004. Email communication to Chris Stern Hyman (October 26).

———, 2001. "Turning the Titanic: Changing the Way We Handle Mistakes." *HEC Forum* 13.

Beckman, Howard B., Kathryn M. Markakis, Anthony L. Suchman, and Richard M. Frankel, 1994. "The Doctor–Patient Relationship and Malpractice: Lessons From Patient Depositions." *Archives of Internal Medicine* 154.

Belfiglio, G., 2003. "Partnering for Malpractice Reform." *Healthplan* 11.

Berenson, Robert A., Kelly Devers, Hoangmai Pham, and Gigi Liu, forthcoming. "Physicians' Role in Hospital Patient Safety Efforts." Unpublished paper in possession of editors.

Berenson, Robert A., D. A. Hastings, and William G. Kopit, 1996. "The Legal Framework for Effective Competition." *Baxter Health Policy Review* 1996.

Berenson, Robert A., Sylvia Kuo, and Jessica H. May, 2003. "Medical Malpractice Liability Crisis Meets Markets: Stress in Unexpected Places." Center for Studying Health System Change Issue Brief, no. 68.

Berg, Miriam, 2004. "Hospitals Implement Programs That Encourage Clinicians to Apologize for Mistakes." *Nursing Executive Watch* 5 (Dec. 10).

Berlinger, Nancy, 2005. *After Harm: Medical Error and the Ethics of Forgiveness.* Baltimore: Johns Hopkins University Press.

———, 2004. "Fair Compensation Without Litigation: Addressing Patients' Financial Needs in Disclosure." *ASHRM Journal* 24.

———, 2003. "Avoiding Cheap Grace: Medical Harm, Patient Safety, and the Culture(s) of Forgiveness." *The Hastings Center Report* 33.

Berwick, Donald M., 2005. "Health Services Research as a Citizen in Improvement." *Health Services Research* 40.

———, 2000. Testimony before the Subcommittee on Health of the Committee on Veterans' Affairs and the Subcommittee on Health and the Environment and the Subcommittee on Oversight and Investigations of the Committee on Commerce. U.S. House of Representatives (Feb. 9). At http://veterans.house.gov/hearings/schedule106/feb00/2-9-00/DBerwick.htm (last accessed July 27, 2005).

———, 1989. "Continuous Improvement as an Ideal in Health Care." *New England Journal of Medicine* 320.

Biondi, Richard S., and Arthur Gurevitch, 2003. *Citizens Allied for Pennsylvania Patients: Projected Effect of Capping Non-economic Damages on Pennsylvania Physician Professional Liability Costs.* New York: Milliman USA.

Black, Bernard S., Charles M. Silver, David A. Hyman, and William M. Sage, 2005. "Stability, Not Crisis: Medical Malpractice Claim Outcomes in Texas, 1988–2002." *Journal of Empirical Legal Studies* 2.

Blendon, Robert J., Catherine M. DesRoches, Mollyann Brodie, et al., 2002. "View of Practicing Physicians and the Public on Medical Errors." *New England Journal of Medicine* 347.

Bloche, M., and David Studdert, 2004. "A Quiet Revolution: Law as an Agent of Health System Change." *Health Affairs* 23.

Blumenthal, Ralph, 2004. "Texas Company Removes Web List of Malpractice Plaintiffs." *New York Times* (Mar. 11).

Blumstein, James F., Randall R. Bovbjerg, and Frank A. Sloan, 1991. "Beyond Tort Reform: Developing Better Tools for Assessing Damages for Personal Injury." *Yale Journal on Regulation* 8.

Boehm, Geoff, 2005. "Debunking Medical Malpractice Myths." *Yale Journal of Health Policy Law and Ethics* 5.

Bogner, Marilyn Sue, 1994. *Human Error in Medicine*. Hillsdale, NJ: Lawrence Erlbaum Associates.

Boodman, Sandra G., 2004. "When Malpractice Premiums Jump, Some Docs Ask Patients to 'Donate' to the Cause." *Washington Post* (Sept. 21).

Boothman, Richard C., 2004. Interview with Scott Simon. Weekend Edition. National Public Radio (Dec. 18). At http://www.npr.org/templates/story/story.php?storyId=4234901 (last accessed Jan. 7, 2005).

Borfitz, Deborah, 2003. "Malpractice: Is Going Bare the Only Option?" *Medical Economics* 80.

Boumil, Marcia, Clifford E. Elias, and Diane Bissonnette Moes, 2003. *The Law of Medical Liability in a Nutshell*. 2d ed. St. Paul, MN: West Publishing Co.

Bourgeois, Martin J., Irwin A. Horowitz, Lynne Forster Lee, and Jon Grahe, 1995. "Nominal and Interactive Groups: Effects of Preinstruction and Deliberations on Decisions and Evidence Recall in Complex Trials." *Journal of Applied Psychology* 80.

Bovbjerg, Randall R., 2005a. "Malpractice Crisis and Reform." *Clinics in Perinatology* 32.

———, 2005b. "Liability Problems and Transparent Disclosure to Patients as a Solution: Final Narrative Report to the Changes in Health Care Financing and Organization Program." Washington, DC: Urban Institute Press.

———, 2003. "Alternative Models of Federalism: Health Insurance Regulation and Patient Protection Laws." In John Holahan, Alan Weil, and Joshua M. Weiner, eds., *Federalism and Health Policy*. Washington, DC: Urban Institute Press.

———, 1994. "Promoting Quality and Preventing Malpractice: Assessing the Health Security Act." *Journal of Health Politics, Policy and Law* 19.

———, 1989. "Legislation on Medical Malpractice: Further Developments and a Preliminary Report Card." *University of California-Davis Law Review* 22.

———, 1986. "Medical Malpractice on Trial: Quality of Care Is the Important Standard." *Law and Contemporary Problems* 49.

———, 1975. "The Medical Malpractice Standard of Care: HMOs and Customary Practice." *Duke Law Journal* 1975.

Bovbjerg, Randall R., and Anna Bartow, 2003. "Understanding Pennsylvania's Medical Malpractice Crisis: Facts About Liability Insurance, the Legal System, and Health Care in Pennsylvania." Philadelphia: Pew Charitable Trusts. At http://medliabilitypa.org/research/report0603/UnderstandingReport.pdf (last accessed Apr. 23, 2005).

Bovbjerg, Randall R., L. Dubay, G. M. Kenney, and S. A. Norton, 1996. "Defensive Medicine and Tort Reform: New Evidence in Old Bottles." *Journal of Health Politics, Policy and Law* 21.

Bovbjerg, Randall R., and Robert H. Miller, 2000. "Physician Groups and Medical Errors: Models and Lessons for Law." Paper presented at APHA annual meeting, Boston (Nov. 14).

Bovbjerg, Randall R., Robert H. Miller, and David W. Shapiro, 2001. "Paths to Reducing Medical Injury: Professional Liability and Discipline vs. Patient Safety – and the Need for a Third Way." *Journal of Law, Medicine & Ethics* 29.

Bovbjerg, Randall R., and Brian Raymond, 2003. "Kaiser Permanente, Patient Safety, Just Compensation and Medical Liability Reform." At http://www.kpihp.org/publications/briefs/patient_safety.pdf (last accessed July 28, 2005).

Bovbjerg, Randall R., and Frank A. Sloan, 1998. "No Fault for Medical Injury: Theory and Evidence." *University of Cincinnati Law Review* 67.

Bovbjerg, Randall R., Frank A. Sloan, and James F. Blumstein, 1989. "Valuing Life and Limb in Tort: Scheduling 'Pain and Suffering.' " *Northwestern University Law Review* 83.

Bovbjerg, Randall R., Frank A. Sloan, Avi Dor, and Chee Ruey Hsieh, 1991. "Juries and Justice: Are Malpractice and Other Personal Injuries Created Equal?" *Law and Contemporary Problems* 54.

Bovbjerg, Randall R., Frank A. Sloan, and Peter J. Rankin, 1997. "Administrative Performance of 'No-Fault' Compensation for Medical Injury." *Law and Contemporary Problems* 60.

Bovbjerg, Randall R., Laurence R. Tancredi, and Daniel S. Gaylin, 1991. "Obstetrics and Malpractice: Evidence on the Performance of a Selective No-Fault System." *Journal of the American Medical Association* 265.

Boyle, Leo V., 2002. "Are Malpractice Damage Caps Unfair to Patients?" *Physicians Weekly* (Mar. 18). At http://www.physweekly.com/pc.asp?issueid=12&questionid=12 (last accessed Feb. 3, 2003).

Bradley, Colin P., 1992. "Factors Which Influence the Decision Whether or Not to Prescribe: The Dilemma Facing General Practitioners." *British Journal of General Practice* 42.

Brennan, Troyen A., 1991. *Just Doctoring: Medical Ethics in the Liberal State.* Berkeley: University of California Press.

Brennan, Troyen A., L. L. Leape, N. M. Laird, et al., 1991. "Incidence of Adverse Events and Negligence in Hospitalized Patients: Results of the Harvard Medical Practice Study, I." *New England Journal of Medicine* 324.

Brennan, Troyen A., and Michelle M. Mello, 2003. "Patient Safety and Medical Malpractice: A Case Study." *Annals of Internal Medicine* 139.

Brennan, Troyen A., Colin M. Sox, and Helen R. Burstin, 1996. "Relation Between Negligent Adverse Events and the Outcomes of Medical-Malpractice Litigation." *New England Journal of Medicine* 335.

Brown, Max D., 2003. Vice President and General Counsel, Rush University Medical Center, Chicago. Telephone conversation with Chris Stern Hyman (Nov. 13).

———, 1998. "Rush Hospital's Malpractice Mediation Program: An ADR Success Story." *Illinois Bar Journal* 86.

Browne, Mark J., and Joan T. Schmit, 2004. "Patterns in Personal Automobile Third Party Bodily Injury Litigation: 1977–1997." At http://ssrn.com/abstract=588481 (last accessed July 25, 2005).

Budetti, Peter P., and Teresa M. Waters, 2005. "Medical Malpractice Law in the United States." Report prepared for the Kaiser Family Foundation. At http://www.kff.org (last accessed June 24, 2005).

Bureau of Labor Statistics, 2004. "Consumer Price Index: All Urban Consumers Medical Care Services." Washington, DC: Bureau of Labor Statistics, U.S. Department of Labor.

Burstin, Helen R., William G. Johnson, Stuart R. Lipsitz, and Troyen A. Brennan, 1993. "Do the Poor Sue More? A Case-Control Study of Malpractice Claims and Socioeconomic Status." *Journal of the American Medical Association* 270.

Bush, George W., 2005. "President Discusses Medical Liability Reform." Press Release, White House (Jan. 5). At http://www.whitehouse.gov/news/releases/2005/01/print/20051015-4.html (last viewed October 12, 2005).

Cabana, Michael D., 1999. "Why Don't Physicians Follow Clinical Practice Guidelines? A Framework for Improvement." *Journal of the American Medical Association* 282.

Calabresi, Guido, 1970. *The Cost of Accidents*. New Haven, CT: Yale University Press.

Califano, Joseph A., Jr., 1986. *America's Health Care Revolution: Who Lives? Who Dies? Who Pays?* New York: Random House.

Californians Allied for Patient Protection, 2005. "Sample Recent Medical Malpractice Awards in California Under MICRA." At http://micra.org (last accessed June 27, 2005).

Cantor, Joel C., Robert A. Berenson, Julia S. Howard, and Walter Wadlington, 1997. "Addressing the Problem of Medical Malpractice." In *To Improve Health and Health Care*. Princeton, NJ: The Robert Wood Johnson Foundation. At http://www.rwjf.org/reports/anthologies/1997chap6.htm (last accessed July 29, 2005).

Cappello, A. Barry, and G. James Strenio, 2000. "Juror Questioning: The Verdict Is In." *Trial* 36.

Casalino, Lawrence P., Kelly J. Devers, Timothy K. Lake, Marie Reed, and Jeffrey J. Steddard, 2003. "Benefits of and Barriers to Large Medical Group Practice in the United States." *Archives of Internal Medicine* 163.

Catholic Healthcare West, Quality Committee, 2001. "Philosophy of Mistake Management." At http://www.sorryworks.net/media24.phtml (last accessed Oct. 26, 2004).

Cecil, Joe S., Valerie P. Hans, and Elizabeth C. Wiggins, 1991. "Citizen Comprehension of Difficult Issues: Lessons From Civil Jury Trials." *American University Law Review* 40.

Centers for Medicare and Medicaid Services (CMS), 2005a. "Acronym List." At http://www.cms.hhs.gov/acronyms/listall.asp?Letter=A (last accessed June 7, 2005).

———, 2005b. "National Health Accounts, National Health Expenditures by Type of Service and Source of Funds: Calendar Years 1960–2003." At http://www.cms.hhs.gov/statistics/nhe/ (last accessed July 26, 2005).

Chandra, Amitabh, Shantanu Nundy, and Seth A. Seabury, 2005. "The Growth of Physician Medical Malpractice Payments: Evidence from the National Practitioner Data Bank." *Health Affairs* Web Exclusive W5–240 (May 31).

Charles, Sara C., Jeffrey R. Wilbert, and Kevin J. Franke, 1985. "Sued and Nonsued Physicians' Self-Reported Reactions to Malpractice Litigation." *American Journal of Psychiatry* 142.

Chassin, Mark R., and Robert W. Galvin, 1998. "The Urgent Need to Improve Health Care Quality." *Journal of the American Medical Association* 280.

Cheney, Frederick W., Karen Posner, Robert A. Caplan, and Richard J. Ward, 1989. "Standard of Care and Anesthesia Liability." *Journal of the American Medical Association* 261.

Chernew, Michael E., Peter D. Jacobson, Timothy P. Hofer, Keith D. Aronson, and A. Mark Fendrick, 2004. "Barriers to Constraining Health Care Cost Growth." *Health Affairs* 23.

Christenson, John F., Wendy Levinson, and Patrick M. Dunn, 1992. "The Heart of Darkness: The Impact of Perceived Mistakes on Physicians." *Journal of General Internal Medicine* 7.

Cirincione, Sandra, 1986. "The History of Medical Malpractice in New York State." *New York State Journal of Medicine* 86.

Cohen, Eva D., and Samuel P. Korper, 1976. "The Swedish No-Fault Patient Compensation Program: Provisions and Preliminary Findings." *Insurance Law Journal* 637.

Cohen, George, 1997/8. "Legal Malpractice Insurance: A Comparative Analysis of Economic Institutions." *Connecticut Insurance Law Journal* 4.

Cohen, Jonathan R., 2002. "Legislating Apology: The Pros and Cons." *University of Cincinnati Law Review* 70.

————, 2000. "Apology and Organizations: Exploring an Example from Medical Practice." *Fordham Urban Law Journal* 27.

————, 1999. "Advising Clients to Apologize." *Southern California Law Review* 72.

Cohen, Neil P., and Daniel R. Cohen, 2003. "Jury Reform in Tennessee." *University of Memphis Law Review* 34.

Cohen, Thomas H., 2004. "Medical Malpractice Trials and Verdicts in Large Counties, 2001." U.S. Department of Justice, NCJ No. 203098. At http://www.ojp.usdoj.gov/bjs/pub/pdf/mmtvlco1.pdf (last accessed July 27, 2005).

Committee on Federal Courts of the New York State Bar Association, 1988. "Improving Jury Comprehension in Complex Civil Litigation." *St. John's Law Review* 62.

Committee on Government Operations, 1969. "Medical Malpractice: Patient vs. Physician." Report of the Subcommittee on Executive Reorganization. 91st Congress, 2d session. Washington, DC: Government Printing Office.

Common Good, 2002. "Fear of Litigation." Report on Harris Interactive Study. At http://cgood.org/healthcare-reading-cgpubs-polls-6.html (viewed July 20, 2005).

Commonwealth of Pennsylvania Patient Safety Authority (CPPSA), 2005. 2004 Annual Report. Harrisburg: CPPSA.

Congressional Budget Office (CBO), 2004. "Limiting Tort Liability for Medical Malpractice." Washington, DC: CBO.

————, 2002. "Federal Reinsurance for Disasters." Washington, DC: CBO.

Connor, J. T. H., 2004. "The Victorian Revolution in Surgery." *Science* 304.

Conover, Christopher J., F. A. Sloan, C. E. Eesley, C. A. Mathews, and W. M. Sage, n.d. "Excess Coverage and the Medical Malpractice Crisis: A Study of Pennsylvania." Unpublished manuscript in possession of editors.

Cook, Philip, and Daniel Graham, 1977. "The Demand for Insurance and Protection: The Case of Irreplaceable Commodities." *Quarterly Journal of Economics* 91.

Cook, W. Rupert, and Charlotte Neff, 1994. "Attitudes of Physicians in Northern Ontario to Medical Malpractice Litigation." *Canadian Family Physician* 40.

COPIC Insurance Company, 2000–4. *COPIC's 3Rs Program: Participation Manual for Physicians and Other Providers*. Denver, CO: COPIC.

Cote, Charles J., Daniel A. Notterman, Helen W. Karl, Joseph A. Weinberg, and Carolyn McCloskey, 2000. "Adverse Sedation Events in Pediatrics: A Critical Incident Analysis of Contributing Factors." *Pediatrics* 105.

Council of State Governments, 2003. "Medical Malpractice Crisis: TrendsAlert." At http://www.csg.org/NR/rdonlyres/ek7a03dfatxrcgh656amm6vnlw2owndpku4rp3 xhss32rzeche5ggb4j4mbwdozh4zsobfboqxysz3bnp5corc6rrae/Medical+ Malpractice+%28May+Revised%29.pdf (last accessed July 28, 2005).

Coyte, Peter C., Donald N. Dewees, and Michael J. Trebilcock, 1991. "Medical Malpractice: The Canadian Experience." *New England Journal of Medicine* 324.

Cramm, Tim, Arthur J. Hartz, and Michael D. Green, 2002. "Ascertaining Customary Care in Malpractice Cases: Asking Those Who Know." *Wake Forest Law Review* 37.

Craswell, Richard, and John Calfee, 1986. "Deterrence and Uncertain Legal Standards." *Journal of Law, Economics and Organization* 2.

Crawford & Co., 2004. "Alternative Risk Financing: A Growing Answer to the Volatile Insurance Marketplace." At http://www.crawfordandcompany.com/ pdf/021-04%20AltRiskWP%208.pdf (last accessed July 30, 2005).

Croley, Steven P., and Jon D. Hanson, 1995. "The Nonpecuniary Costs of Accidents: Pain-and-Suffering Damages in Tort Law." *Harvard Law Review* 108.

Cruse, Donna, and Beverly A. Browne, 1987. "Reasoning in a Jury Trial: The Influence of Instructions." *Journal of General Psychology* 114.

Cuellar, Alison Evans, and Paul J. Gertler, 2004. "How the Expansion of Hospital Systems Has Affected Consumers." *Health Affairs* 24.

———, 2003. "Trends in Hospital Consolidation: The Formation of Local Systems." *Health Affairs* 22.

Cummins, D., and F. Outreville, 1987. "An International Analysis of Underwriting Cycles in Property-Liability Insurance." *Journal of Risk and Insurance* 54.

Cunningham, Robert, 2004. "Professionalism Reconsidered: Physician Payment in a Small-Practice Environment." *Health Affairs* 23.

Curran, William J., and A. Moseley, 1975. "The Malpractice Experience of Health Maintenance Organizations." *Northwestern University Law Review* 70.

Cushing, Harvey, 1938. *The Doctors Welch of Norfolk*. Boston: [no publisher listed].

Dann, B. Michael, 1993. "'Learning Lessons' and 'Speaking Rights': Creating Educated and Democratic Juries." *Indiana Law Journal* 68.

Danzon, Patricia M., 2000. "Liability for Medical Malpractice." In Anthony J. Culyer and Joseph P. Newhouse, eds., *Handbook of Health Economics*. Amsterdam: Elsevier.

———, 1998. "Medical Malpractice Liability." In Robert E. Litan and Clifford Winston, eds., *Liability: Perspective and Policy 101*. Washington, DC: Brookings Institution Press.

———, 1997. "Tort Liability: A Minefield for Managed Care?" *Journal of Legal Studies* 26.

———, 1990. "Medical Malpractice: Incidence and Incentive Effects." Working Paper, Wharton School.

———, 1988. "Medical Malpractice Liability." In Robert E. Litan and Clifford Winston, eds., *Liability: Perspectives and Policy*. Washington, DC: Brookings Institution Press.

———, 1986. "The Frequency and Severity of Medical Malpractice Claims: New Evidence." *Law and Contemporary Problems* 48.

———, 1985. *Medical Malpractice: Theory, Evidence, and Public Policy.* Cambridge, MA: Harvard University Press.

Danzon, Patricia M., Andrew J. Epstein, and Scott Johnson, 2003. "The 'Crisis' in Medical Malpractice Insurance." Unpublished manuscript at http://fic.wharton.upenn.edu/fic/papers/04/Danzon%20%20Paper.pdf (last accessed July 29, 2005).

Danzon, Patricia M., and Mark V. Pauly, 2001. "Insurance and New Technology: From Hospital to Drugstore." *Health Affairs* 20.

Danzon, Patricia M., Mark V. Pauly, and Raynard S. Kington, 1990. "The Effects of Malpractice Litigation on Physicians' Fees and Incomes." *American Economic Association Papers and Proceedings* 80.

Dao, James, 2005. "A Push in States to Curb Malpractice Costs." *New York Times* (Jan. 5).

Dauer, Edward A., 2003. "A Therapeutic Jurisprudence Perspective on Legal Responses to Medical Error." *Journal of Legal Medicine* 24.

Dauer, Edward A., and Leonard J. Marcus, 1997. "Adapting Mediation to Link Resolution of Medical Malpractice Disputes with Health Care Quality Improvement." *Law and Contemporary Problems* 60.

Dauer, Edward A., Leonard J. Marcus, and Susan M. C. Payne, 2000. "Prometheus and the Litigators: A Mediation Odyssey." *Journal of Legal Medicine* 21.

Deason, Ellen E., 1998. "Court-Appointed Expert Witnesses: Scientific Positivism Meets Bias and Deference." *Oregon Law Review* 77.

DeGette, Diana, 2005. "Insurance Reform Must Be Part of Liability Debate." *Roll Call* (July 11).

Deprez, Ronald D., et al., 1997. "Impact of Obstetric Practice Guidelines on Physician Behavior." Final Report, Grant No. HS07294. Public Health Research Institute, Agency for Health Care Policy and Research, U.S. Department of Health and Human Services.

Devers, Kelly J., Hoangmai H. Pham, and Gigi Liu, 2004. "What Is Driving Hospitals' Patient-Safety Efforts?" *Health Affairs* 23.

De Ville, Kenneth, 1998. "Medical Malpractice in the Twentieth-Century United States: The Interaction of Technology, Law and Culture." *International Journal of Technology Assessment in Health Care* 14.

———, 1990. *Medical Malpractice in Nineteenth-Century America.* New York: New York University Press.

DHEW (Department of Health, Education, and Welfare), 1973. "Report of the Secretary's Commission on Medical Malpractice." Washington, DC: DHEW.

Diamond, Shari Seidman, Michael J. Saks, and Stephan Landsman, 1998. "Juror Judgments About Liability and Damages: Sources of Variability and Ways to Increase Consistency." *DePaul Law Review* 48.

Diamond, Shari Seidman, Neil Vidmar, Mary Rose, Leslie Ellis, and Beth Murphy, 2003. "Juror Discussions During Civil Trials: Studying an Arizona Innovation." *Arizona Law Review* 45.

Dobbs, Dan B., 1993. *The Law of Remedies: Damages, Equity, Restitution.* 2d ed. St. Paul, MN: West Publishing Co.

Doherty, Neil A., Joan Lamm-Tennant, and Laura T. Starks, 2003. "Insuring September 11th: Market Recovery and Transparency." *The Journal of Risk and Uncertainty* 26.

Doherty, Neil A., and Kent Smetters, 2002. "Moral Hazard in Reinsurance Markets." Working Paper No. 9050. National Bureau of Economic Research.

Downey, A. G., 1977. "Some Rights and Liabilities of 'Going Bare.'" *The Journal of Legal Medicine* 5.

Downs, David H., and David W. Sommer, 1999. "Monitoring, Ownership, and Risk-Taking: The Impact of Guaranty Funds." *Journal of Risk and Insurance* 66.

Dranove, David, and Anne Gron, 2005. "Effects of the Malpractice Crisis on Access to and Incidence of High-Risk Procedures: Evidence From Florida." *Health Affairs* 24.

Druckman, James N., and Kjersten R. Nelson, 2003. "Framing and Deliberation: How Citizens' Conversations Limit Elite Influence." *American Journal of Political Science* 47.

Dubay, Lisa, Robert Kaestner, and Timothy Waidmann, 2001. "Medical Malpractice Liability and Its Effect on Prenatal Care Utilization and Infant Health." *Journal of Health Economics* 20.

———, 1999. "The Impact of Malpractice Fears on Cesarean Section Rates." *Journal of Health Economics* 18.

Dubler, Nancy N., and Carol Liebman, 2004. *Bioethics Mediation: A Guide to Shaping Shared Solutions.* New York: United Hospital Fund.

Dumas, Bethany K., 2000. "Jury Trials: Lay Jurors, Pattern Jury Instructions, and Comprehension Issues." *Tennessee Law Review* 67.

Eddy, David M., 1998. "Performance Measurement: Problems and Solutions." *Health Affairs* 17.

Edlavitch, Stanley A., 1988. "Adverse Drug Event Reporting: Improving the Low U.S. Reporting Rates." *Archives of Internal Medicine* 148.

Ehrenzweig, Albert A., 1964. "Compulsory 'Hospital Accident' Insurance: A Needed First Step Toward the Displacement of Liability for 'Medical Malpractice.'" *University of Chicago Law Review* 31.

Eichhorn, John H., Jeffrey B. Cooper, David J. Cullen, Ward R. Maier, James H. Phillip, and Robert G. Seeman, 1986. "Standards for Patient Monitoring During Anesthesia at Harvard Medical School." *Journal of the American Medical Association* 256.

Elazar, Daniel J., 1972. *American Federalism: A View from the States.* 2d ed. New York: Crowell.

Elwork, Amiram, Bruce D. Sales, and James J. Alfini, 1982. *Making Jury Instructions Understandable.* Charlottesville, VA: The Michie Company.

———, 1977. "Juridic Decisions: In Ignorance of the Law or in Light of It?" *Law & Human Behavior* 1.

Encinosa, William E., and Fred J. Hellinger, 2005. "Have State Caps on Malpractice Awards Increased the Supply of Physicians?" *Health Affairs* Web Exclusive W5–250 (May 31).

Ennis, Maeve, A. Clark, and Jurgis G. Grudzinskas, 1991. "Change in Obstetric Practice in Response to Fear of Litigation in the British Isles." *Lancet* 338.

Ensign, John, 2005. "Medical Care Under Liability Crunch." *Roll Call* (July 11).

Entman, Stephen S., Cheryl A. Glass, Gerald B. Hickson, Penny B. Githens, Kathryn Whetten-Goldstein, and Frank A. Sloan, 1994. "The Relationship Between Malpractice Claims History and Subsequent Obstetric Care." *Journal of the American Medical Association* 272.

Epstein, Richard, 1985. "Products Liability as an Insurance Market." *Journal of Legal Studies* 14.

———, 1984. "The Legal and Insurance Dynamics of Mass Tort Litigation." *Journal of Legal Studies* 13.

———, 1976. "Medical Malpractice: The Case for Contract." *American Bar Foundation Research Journal* 1.

Epstein, Richard, and Alan O. Sykes, 2001. "The Assault on Managed Care: Vicarious Liability, ERISA Preemption, and Class Actions." *Journal of Legal Studies* 30.

Eskin, David J., 2003. Testimony Before the U.S. House Committee on Energy and Commerce, February 10.

Farber, Henry S., and Michelle J. White, 1994. "A Comparison of Formal and Informal Dispute Resolution in Medical Malpractice." *Journal of Legal Studies* 23.

———, 1990. "Medical Malpractice: An Empirical Examination of the Litigation Process." *RAND Journal of Economics* 22.

Feagles, Prentiss E., Betsy I. Carter, James A. Davids, Neal E. Tackabery, and Clay B. Tousey, Jr., 1975. "An Analysis of State Legislative Responses to the Medical Malpractice Crisis." *Duke Law Journal* 1975.

Federal Reserve Bank of Minneapolis, 2005. "Consumer Price Index Calculator." At http://minneapolisfed.org/Research/data/us/calc/index.cfm. (last accessed July 12, 2005).

Feinman, Jay M., 2005. "Unmaking and Remaking Tort Law." *Journal of High Technology Law* 5.

Fielding, Stephen L., 1999. *The Practice of Uncertainty: Voices of Physicians and Patients in Medical Malpractice Claims*. Westport, CT: Auburn House.

Fiesta, Janine, 1994. "Communication: The Value of an Apology." *Nursing Management* 25.

Finley, Lucinda M., 2005. "The Hidden Victims of Tort Reform: Women, Children, and the Elderly." *Emory Law Journal* 53.

Fitzpatrick, Sean M., 2004. "Fear Is the Key: A Behavioral Guide to Underwriting Cycles." *Connecticut Insurance Law Journal* 10.

Flango, Victor E., 1980. "Would Jurors Do a Better Job if They Could Take Notes?" *Judicature* 63.

Foote, Susan Bartlett, Douglas Wholey, Todd Rockwood, and Rachel Halpern, 2004. "Resolving the Tug-of-War Between Medicare's National and Local Coverage." *Health Affairs* 23.

ForsterLee, Lynne, Irwin A. Horowitz, and Martin J. Bourgeois, 1993. "Juror Competence in Civil Trials: Effects of Preinstruction and Evidence Technicality." *Journal of Applied Psychology* 78.

Froot, Kenneth A., and Paul G. J. O'Connell, 1997. "The Pricing of U.S. Catastrophe Reinsurance." Working Paper No. 6043. National Bureau of Economic Research.

Fudenberg, Drew, and Jean Tirole, 1990. "Moral Hazard and Renegotiation in Agency Contracts." *Econometrica* 58.

Furrow, Barry R., Thomas L. Greaney, Sandra H. Johnson, Timothy S. Jost, and Robert I. Schwartz, 2000. *Health Law*. 2d ed. St. Paul, MN: West Publishing.

Galanter, Marc, 2004. "The Vanishing Trial: What the Numbers Tell Us, What They May Mean." *Dispute Resolution Magazine* 10.

Gallagher, Thomas H., Amy D. Waterman, Alison I. Ebers, Victoria J. Fraser, and Wendy Levinson, 2003. "Patients' and Physicians' Attitudes Regarding the Disclosure of Medical Errors." *Journal of the American Medical Association* 289.

Galloway, Angela, 2004. "Lobbying Over Medical Malpractice Issue Heats Up." *Seattle Post-Intelligencer* (March 3).

Gandhi, Tejal K., Saul N. Weingart, Joshua Borus, et al., 2003. "Adverse Drug Events in Ambulatory Care." *New England Journal of Medicine* 348.

Gaster, Barak, 1993. "The Learning Curve." *Journal of the American Medical Association* 270.

Gatowski, Sophia I., Shirley A. Dobbin, James T. Richardson, Gerald P. Ginsburg, Mara L. Merlino, and Veronica Dahir, 2001. "Asking the Gatekeepers: A National Survey of Judges on Judging Expert Evidence in a Post-*Daubert* World." *Law and Human Behavior* 25.

Geistfeld, Mark, 2005. "Malpractice Insurance and the (Il)legitimate Interests of the Medical Profession in Tort Reform." *DePaul Law Review* 54.

———, 1995a. "Manufacturer Moral Hazard and the Tort-Contract Issue in Product Liability." *International Review of Law and Economics* 15.

———, 1995b. "Placing a Price on Pain and Suffering: A Method for Helping Juries Determine Tort Damages for Nonmonetary Injuries." *California Law Review* 83.

———, 1994. "The Political Economy of Neocontractual Proposals for Products Liability Reform." *Texas Law Review* 72.

Gellhorn, Walter, 1988. "Medical Malpractice Litigation (U.S.) – Medical Mishap Compensation (N.Z.)." *Cornell Law Review* 73.

Gendell, Murray, 2001. "Retirement Age Declines Again in 1990s." *Monthly Labor Review* 124 (October).

Giammona, Mary D., 2003. "Medicare Comes to the Mediation Table." Medical Board of California Action Report (July).

Gibson, Rosemary, and Janardan Prasad Singh, 2003. *Wall of Silence: The Untold Story of the Medical Mistakes That Kill and Injure Millions of Americans*. Washington, DC: Lifeline Press.

Gifford, Daniel J., 1997. "Federal Administrative Law Judges: The Relevance of Past Choices to Future Directions." *Administrative Law Review* 49.

Glassman, Peter A., John E. Rolph, Laura P. Petersen, Melissa A. Bradley, and Richard L. Kravitz, 1996. "Physicians' Personal Malpractice Experiences Are Not Related to Defensive Clinical Practices." *Journal of Health Politics, Policy and Law* 21.

Glied, Sherry A., 2005. "The Employer-Based Health Insurance System: Mistake or Cornerstone?" In David Mechanic, Lynn B. Rogut, David C. Colby, and James R. Knickman, eds., *Policy Challenges in Modern Health Care*. New Brunswick, NJ: Rutgers University Press.

———, 2000. "Managed Care." In Anthony J. Cuyler and Joseph P. Newhouse, eds., *Handbook of Health Economics*. New York: Elsevier.

Goold, Susan D., Timothey Hofer, Marc Zimmerman, and Rodney A. Hayward, 1994. "Measuring Physician Attitudes Toward Cost, Uncertainty, Malpractice, and Utilization Review." *Journal of General Internal Medicine* 9.

Gosfield, Alice G., 2000. "Liability for Quality: A Modest Proposal." *Managed Care & Cancer* 2.

Grady, Mark F., 1988. "Why Are People Negligent? Technology, Nondurable Precautions, and the Medical Malpractice Explosion." *Northwestern University Law Review* 82.

Greene, Edith, and Brian Bornstein, 2000. "Precious Little Guidance: Jury Instruction on Damage Awards." *Psychology, Public Policy, and Law* 6.

Greene, Edith, David Coon, and Brian Bornstein, 2001. "The Effects of Limiting Punitive Damage Awards." *Law & Human Behavior* 25.

Griffin, Larry P., Kenneth V. Heland, Linda Esser, and Susannah Jones, 1999. "Overview of the 1996 Professional Liability Survey." *Obstetrical and Gynecological Survey* 54.

Gron, Anne, 1994. "Capacity Constraints and Cycles in Property-Casualty Insurance Markets." *RAND Journal of Economics* 25.

———, 1990. "Capacity Constraints in Property-Casualty Insurance Markets." Mimeo, Massachusetts Institute of Technology.

———, 1989. "Property-Casualty Insurance Cycles, Capacity Constraints, and Empirical Results." Ph.D. dissertation, Department of Economics, Massachusetts Institute of Technology, Cambridge, MA.

Gronfein, William P., and Eleanor DeArman Kinney, 1991. "Controlling Large Malpractice Claims: The Unexpected Impact of Damage Caps." *Journal of Health Politics, Policy and Law* 16.

Grossman, Sanford, 1981. "The Informational Role of Warranties and Private Disclosure About Product Quality." *Journal of Law and Economics* 24.

Grow, Brian, 2004. "Expert Witnesses Under Examinations." *Chicago Tribune* (July 20).

Grumbach, Kevin, 2002. "Fighting Hand to Hand Over Physician Workforce Policy." *Health Affairs* 21.

Gutheil, Thomas G., Harold Bursztajn, and Archie Brodsky, 1984. "Malpractice Prevention Through the Sharing of Uncertainty: Informed Consent and the Therapeutic Alliance." *New England Journal of Medicine* 311.

Hacker, Jacob S., 1998. "The Historical Logic of National Health Insurance: Structure and Sequence in the Development of British, Canadian, and U.S. Medical Policy." *Studies in American Political Development* 12.

Haiduc, Amanda E., 1990. "A Tale of Three Damage Caps: Too Much, Too Little and Finally Just Right." *Case Western Reserve Law Review* 40.

Hall, Mark A., 1991. "The Defensive Effect of Medical Practice Policies in Malpractice Litigation." *Law & Contemporary Problems* 54.

Hall, Mark A., Roger Anderson, Rajesh Balkrishnan, Steven R. Feldman, Alan B. Fleischer, Jr., David Goff, and William Moran, 2002. "Measuring Medical Practice Patterns: Sources of Evidence From Health Services Research." *Wake Forest Law Review* 37.

Hallinan, Joseph T., and Rachel Zimmerman, 2004. "Malpractice Insurer Sees Little Savings in Award Caps." *Wall Street Journal* (Oct. 28).

Halm, Ethan A., Clara Lee, and Mark Chassin, 2002. "Is Volume Related to Outcome in Health Care? A Systematic Review and Methodologic Critique of the Literature." *Annals of Internal Medicine* 137.

Halvorson, George C., and George Isham, 2003. *Epidemic of Care: A Call for Safer, Better, and More Accountable Health Care*. San Francisco: Jossey-Bass.

Hamm, Ginny M., and Steve S. Kraman, 2001. "New Standards, New Dilemmas: Reflections on Managing Medical Mistakes." *Bioethics Forum* 17.

Hamm, William G., C. Paul Wazzan, and H. E. Frech, 2005. "MICRA and Access to Healthcare." At http://www.micra.org (last accessed Feb. 10, 2005).

Hammitt, James K., Stephen J. Carroll, and Daniel A. Relles, 1985. "Tort Standards and Jury Decisions." *Journal of Legal Studies* 14.

Hannaford, Paula L., Valerie P. Hans, and G. Thomas Munsterman, 2000. "Permitting Jury Discussions During Trial: Impact of the Arizona Reform." *Law and Human Behavior* 24.

Hans, Valerie P., Paula L. Hannaford, and G. Thomas Munsterman, 1999. "The Arizona Jury Reform Permitting Civil Jury Trial Discussions: The Views of Trial Participants, Judges, and Jurors." *University of Michigan Journal of Law Reform* 32.

Hanscom, Robert B., Michelle M. Mello, Robert P. Powers, Luke Sato, Mary A. Schaefer, and David M. Studdert, 2003. "Legal Liability and Protection of Patient Safety Data." Commissioned paper for the Institute of Medicine Committee on Patient Safety Data Standards (available from lead author on request).

Hargraves, J. Lee, and Hoangmai Pham, 2003. "Back in the Driver's Seat: Specialists Regaining Autonomy." Tracking Report No. 7 (January). Center for Studying Health System Change.

Harper, Fowler V., and Fleming James, 1956. *The Law of Torts*. Boston: Little, Brown.

Harrington, Scott E., 2004. "Tort Liability, Insurance Rates, and the Insurance Cycle." In Robert Litan and Richard Herring, eds., *Brookings-Wharton Papers on Financial Institutions*. Washington, DC.

Harris, Dean M., 2003. "Beyond Beneficiaries: Using the Medicare Program to Accomplish Broader Public Goals." *Washington & Lee Law Review* 60.

Harvard Medical Practice Study Group, 1990. *Patients, Doctors, and Lawyers: Medical Injury, Malpractice Litigation, and Patient Compensation in New York.* Cambridge, MA: Harvard University Press.

Haugh, Richard, 2003. "Surviving Medical Malpractice Madness." *Hospitals and Health Networks* 77.

Havighurst, Clark C., 2000. "Vicarious Liability: Relocating Responsibility for the Quality of Medical Care." *American Journal of Law and Medicine* 26.

———, 1997. "Making Health Plans Accountable for the Quality of Care." *Georgia Law Review* 31.

———, 1995. *Health Care Choices: Private Contracts as Instruments of Health Reform.* Washington, DC: AEI Press.

Havighurst, Clark C., and Laurence R. Tancredi, 1974. "Medical Adversity Insurance – A No-Fault Approach to Medical Malpractice and Quality Assurance." *Milbank Memorial Fund Quarterly* 51.

Health and Hospital Association of Pennsylvania (HAP), 2002a. "Professional Liability Coverage in Pennsylvania: Findings of a Statewide Survey." Harrisburg, PA: HAP.

———, 2002b. "An Overview of the Medical Liability Environment in Pennsylvania." Harrisburg, PA: HAP.

HealthGrades, 2004. "Patient Safety in American Hospitals." At http://www.healthgrades.com (last accessed June 12, 2005).

Heclo, Hugh, 1978. "Issue Networks and the Executive Establishment." In Anthony King, ed., *The New American Political System*. Washington, DC: American Enterprise Institute.

Heffler, Stephen, Katherine Levit, Sheila Smith, Cynthia Smith, Cathy Cowan, Helen Lazenby, and Mark Freeland, 2001. "Health Spending Growth up in 1999; Faster Growth Expected in the Future." *Health Affairs* 20.

Hellinger, Fred J., and William E. Encinosa, 2003. "The Impact of State Laws Limiting Malpractice Awards on the Geographic Distribution of Physicians." At http://www.ahrq.gov/research/tortcaps/tortcaps.htm (last accessed Apr. 13, 2005).

Hershey, Nathan, 1969. "An Alternative to Mandatory Licensure of Health Professionals." *Hospital Progress* 50.

Herzlinger, Regina E., 2004. *Consumer-Driven Health Care: Implications for Providers, Payers and Policy Makers*. San Francisco: Jossey-Bass.

Heuer, Larry, and Steven Penrod, 1994a. "Juror Notetaking and Question Asking During Trials: A National Field Experiment." *Law and Human Behavior* 18.

———, 1994b. "Trial Complexity: A Field Investigation of Its Meaning and Its Effects." *Law and Human Behavior* 18.

———, 1989. "Instructing Jurors: A Field Experiment With Written and Preliminary Instructions." *Law and Human Behavior* 13.

———, 1988. "Increasing Jurors' Participation in Trials: A Field Experiment With Jury Notetaking and Question Asking." *Law and Human Behavior* 12.

Hickson, Gerald B., Ellen W. Clayton, Stephen S. Entman, Cynthia S. Miller, Penny B. Githens, Kathryn Whetten-Goldstein, and Frank A. Sloan, 1994. "Obstetricians' Prior Malpractice Experience and Patients' Satisfaction With Care." *Journal of the American Medical Association* 272.

Hickson, Gerald B., Ellen W. Clayton, Penny B. Githens, and Frank A. Sloan, 1992. "Factors That Prompted Families to File Malpractice Claims Following Perinatal Injury." *Journal of the American Medical Association* 268.

Hickson, Gerald B., C. F. Federspiel, J. W. Pichert, C. S. Miller, J. Gauld-Jaeger, and P. Bost, 2002. "Patient Complaints and Malpractice Risk." *Journal of the American Medical Association* 287.

Hickson, Gerald B., James W. Pichert, Charles F. Federspiel, and Ellen W. Clayton, 1997. "Development of an Early Identification and Response Model of Malpractice Prevention." *Law & Contemporary Problems* 60.

Higgins, C. W., and E. D. Meyers, 1987. "Managed Care and Vertical Integration: Implications for the Hospital Industry." *Hospitals and Health Services Administration* 32.

Himmelstein, David U., Elizabeth Warren, Deborah Thorne, and Steffie Woolhandler, 2005. "Illness and Injury as Contributors to Bankruptcy." *Health Affairs* 24.

Hinderberger, Philip R., 2003. *Medical Liability Report Card 2000*. San Francisco: NORCAL Mutual Insurance Company.

Hoadley, John F., Debra A. Draper, Sylvia Kuo, et al., 2003. "Health Care Market Stabilizes, but Rising Costs and State Budget Woes Loom in Boston." Community Report No. 12 (Fall). Center for Studying Health System Change.

Hoerger, Thomas J., Frank A. Sloan, and Mahmud Hassan, 1990. "Loss Volatility, Bankruptcy, and Insurer Demand for Reinsurance." *Journal of Risk and Uncertainty* 3.

Hofflander, Alfred, and Jane D. Nettesham, 2001. *Report on the Medical Malpractice Insurance Delivery System in Pennsylvania*. Redwood City, CA: Stanford Consulting Group.

Hoffman, Bjorn, 2002. "Is There a Technological Imperative in Health Care?" *International Journal of Technology Assessment in Health Care* 18.

Hogan, Neal C., 2003. *Unhealed Wounds: Medical Malpractice in the Twentieth Century*. New York: LFB Scholarly Publishing.

Holzer, James F., 1990. "The Advent of Clinical Standards for Professional Liability." *Quality Review Bulletin* 16.

————, 1987. "Channeling Programs Aid MD-Hospital Cooperation." *Hospitals* 61.

Howard, Melanie, 2004. "'Going Bare': Physicians Seek Alternatives to Current Liability System." *Washington Hospital Center Physician* 10.

Howe, R. C., 1994. "How JCAHO, WEDI, ANSI, HCFA, and Hillary Clinton Will Turn Your Systems Upside Down." *Healthcare Information Management* 8.

Howell, Joel D., 1995. *Technology in the Hospital: Transforming Patient Care in the Early Twentieth Century*. Baltimore: Johns Hopkins University Press.

Hurley, Robert E., Bradley C. Strunk, and Justin S. White, 2004. "The Puzzling Popularity of the PPO." *Health Affairs* 23.

Hyams, Andrew L., David W. Shapiro, and Troyen A. Brennan, 1996. "Medical Practice Guidelines in Malpractice Litigation: An Early Retrospective." *Journal of Health Politics, Policy and Law* 21.

Hylton, Keith, 2000. "Agreements to Waive or to Arbitrate Legal Claims: An Economic Analysis." *Supreme Court Economic Review* 8.

Hyman, David A., and Charles Silver, 2005. "The Poor State of Health Care Quality in the U.S.: Is Malpractice Liability Part of the Problem or Part of the Solution?" *Cornell Law Review* 90.

Iglehart, John K., 2001. "America's Love Affair With Medical Innovation." *Health Affairs* 20.

Institute for Healthcare Improvement (IHI), 2004. "IHI Improvement Staff Call on 'To Err Is Human.'" At http://www.ihi.org/NR/rdonlyres/842DFE9D-2B72-4D21-91DE-00644AD25530/0/Transcript_111204_112204.pdf (last accessed Jan. 12, 2005).

Institute of Medicine (IOM), 2002. *Fostering Rapid Advances in Health Care: Learning from System Demonstrations*. Janet M. Corrigan, Ann Greiner, and Shari M. Erickson, eds. Washington, DC: National Academies Press.

————, 2001. *Crossing the Quality Chasm: A New Health System for the 21st Century*. Washington, DC: National Academies Press.

————, 2000. *To Err Is Human: Building a Safer Health System*. Linda T. Kohn, Janet M. Corrigan, and Molla S. Donaldson, eds. Washington, DC: National Academies Press.

————, 1990. *Clinical Practice Guidelines: Directions for a New Program*. Marilyn J. Field and Kathleen N. Lohr, eds. Washington, D.C.: National Academies Press.

Insurance Information Institute, 2005. "Hot Topics & Issues Updates: Captives and Other Risk-Financing Options." At http://www.iii.org/media/hottopics/insurance/test3/ (accessed June 3, 2005).

Ireland, Thomas R., Walter D. Johnson, and James D. Rodgers, 1992. "Why Hedonic Measures Are Irrelevant to Wrongful Death Litigation." *Journal of Legal Economics* 2.

Jacobi, John V., and Nicole Huberfeld, 2001. "Quality Control, Enterprise Liability, and Disintermediation in Managed Care." *Journal of Law, Medicine & Ethics* 29.

Jacobson, Peter D., and Scott D. Pomfret, 1999. "Establishing New Legal Doctrine in Managed Care: A Model of Judicial Response to Industrial Change." *University of Michigan Journal of Law Reform* 32.

Jacobson, Peter D., and C. John Rosenquist, 1996. "The Diffusion of Low Osmolar Contrast Agents: Technological Change and Defensive Medicine." *Journal of Health Politics, Policy and Law* 21.

———, 1988. "The Introduction of Low Osmolar Contrast Agents in Radiology: Medical, Economic, Legal, and Public Policy Issues." *Journal of the American Medical Association* 260.

Johnson, Kirk B., Phillips, Carter G., Orentlicher, David, and Martin S. Hatlie, 1989. "A Fault-Based Administrative Alternative for Resolving Medical Malpractice Claims." *Vanderbilt Law Review* 42.

Johnson, Lee J., 2003. "Go Bankrupt? Go Bare?" *Medical Economics* 80.

Johnson, William G., Troyen A. Brennan, Joseph P. Newhouse, Lucien L. Leape, Ann G. Lawthers, Howard H. Hiatt, and Paul C. Weiler, 1992. "The Economic Consequences of Medical Injuries: Implications for a No-Fault Insurance Plan." *Journal of the American Medical Association* 267.

Joint Commission on Accreditation of Healthcare Organizations (JCAHO), 2005. *Health Care at the Crossroads: Strategies for Improving the Medical Liability System and Preventing Patient Injury.* Oakbrook Terrace, IL: JCAHO.

———, 2003. In *Comprehensive Accreditation Manual for Hospitals: The Official Handbook.* Oakbrook Terrace, IL: JCAHO.

Joint Legislative Audit and Review Commission (JLARC), Commonwealth of Virginia, 2002. "Review of the Virginia Birth-Related Neurological Injury Compensation Program." Richmond, VA: JLARC.

Jones, T. M., and P. K. O'Hare, 1989. "Putting a Premium on Medical Staffs: A Novel Way to Insure Physician Liability (and Loyalty)." *Health Progress* 70.

Jost, Timothy Stoltzfus, 2004. "The Supreme Court Limits Lawsuits Against Managed Care Organizations." Health Affairs Web Exclusive W4–417 (Aug. 11).

———, 1999. "Governing Medicare." *Administrative Law Review* 51.

Journal of Health Politics, Policy and Law (JHPPL), 2001. Special Issue: Evidence: Its Meanings in Health Care and in Law. *Journal of Health Politics, Policy and Law* 26.

Kachalia, Allen J., N. K. Choudhury, and David M. Studdert, 2005. "Emerging Physician Responses to the Malpractice Crisis." *Journal of Law, Medicine & Ethics* 33.

Kacmar, Donald E. 1997. "The Impact of Computerized Medical Literature Databases on Medical Malpractice Litigation: Time for Another *Helling v. Carey* Wake-Up Call?" *Ohio St. Law Journal* 58.

Kaiser Family Foundation, 2003. "Public Opinion on the Medical Malpractice Debate." At http://www.kff.org/Healthpollreport/Archive_April2003/Index.cfm (last accessed July 2, 2005).

Kaiser Foundation, 2004. "Issue Brief: Medicaid's Role for Women" (November). At http://www.kff.org/womenshealth/upload/Medicaid-s-Role-for-Women.pdf (last accessed Jan. 8, 2005).

Kansas Health Care Stabilization Fund, 2002. "Indicated Liabilities at June 30, 2002: Surcharge Determination for FY2003." St. Louis: Tillinghast-Towers Perrin.

Kant, Immanuel, 1785 [1964]. *Groundwork of the Metaphysic of Morals.* H. J. Paton, trans. New York: Harper & Row.

Kaplan, Gerald F., 2001. "The Nuts and Bolts of the Medical Malpractice Case: Some Things to Do Before Filing Suit." Philadelphia: Pennsylvania Bar Institute.

Kassin, Saul M., and Lawrence S. Wrightsman, 1979. "On the Requirements of Proof: The Timing of Judicial Instruction and Mock Juror Verdicts." *Personality and Social Psychology* 37.

Katz, Avery, 1998. "Standard Form Contracts." In Peter Newman, ed., *The New Palgrave Dictionary of Law and Economics.* London: Macmillan Press.

Keeton, W. Page, Dan B. Dobbs, Robert E. Keeton, and David G. Owen, 1984. *Prosser and Keeton on the Law of Torts.* 5th. ed. St. Paul, MN: West Publishing.

Kelso, J. Clark, and Kari C. Kelso, 1999. "Jury Verdicts in Medical Malpractice Cases and the MICRA Cap." At http://www.mcgeorge.edu/government_law_and_policy_publications_ccglp_pubs_micra_cap_pdf.pdf (last accessed July 28, 2005).

Kenney, Roger K., 1988. *1986 Financial Condition of Medical Malpractice JUAs.* Schaumburg, IL: Alliance of American Insurers.

Kersh, Rogan, 2005. "Pennsylvania Medical Malpractice Politics, 1975–2005." Philadelphia: Pew Charitable Trusts.

Kersh, Rogan, and James A. Morone, 2005. "Obesity, Litigation, and the New Politics of Public Health." *Journal of Health Politics, Policy and Law* 30.

Kessler, Daniel P., 2004. "The Effects of the U.S. Malpractice System: A Review of the Empirical Literature." New York: Manhattan Institute. At http://www.pointoflaw.com/pdfs/kessler-malpractice-jced1.pdf (last accessed July 24, 2005).

Kessler, Daniel P., and Mark B. McClellan, 2002a. "Malpractice Law and Health Care Reform: Optimal Liability Policy in an Era of Managed Care." *Journal of Public Economics* 84.

———, 2002b. "How Liability Reform Affects Medical Productivity." *Journal of Health Economics* 21.

———, 1997. "The Effects of Malpractice Pressure and Liability Reforms on Physicians' Perceptions of Medical Care." *Law and Contemporary Problems* 60.

———, 1996. "Do Doctors Practice Defensive Medicine?" *Quarterly Journal of Economics* 111.

Kessler, Daniel P., and Daniel Rubinfeld, 2004. "Empirical Effects of the Civil Justice System." NBER Working Paper 10825; reprinted in A. Mitchell Polinsky and Steven Shavell, eds., *Handbook of Law and Economics.* New York: North-Holland.

Kessler, Daniel P., William M. Sage, and David J. Becker, 2005. "The Impact of Malpractice Reforms on the Supply of Physician Services." *Journal of the American Medical Association* 293.

Kidwell, Richard P., 2004. Managing Attorney for Claims and Litigation, The Johns Hopkins Health System Corp. Email communication to Chris Stern Hyman (Feb. 26).

Kim, Minah, Robert J. Blendon, and John M. Benson, 2001. "How Interested Are Americans in New Medical Technologies? A Multicountry Comparison." *Health Affairs* 20.

Kinney, Eleanor D., 2005. "Administrative Law Approaches to Medical Malpractice Reform." *Saint Louis University Law Journal* 49.

————, 2003. "The New Medicare Coverage Decision-Making and Appeal Procedures: Can Process Meet the Challenge of New Medical Technology?" *Washington & Lee Law Review* 60.

————, 1995. "Malpractice Reform in the 1990s: Past Disappointments, Future Success?" *Journal of Health Politics, Policy and Law* 20.

Klick, Jonathan, and Thomas Stratmann, 2003. "Does Medical Malpractice Reform Help States Retain Physicians and Does It Matter?" Unpublished manuscript at http://papers.ssrn.com/sol3/papers.cfm?abstract_id = 453481 (last accessed July 29, 2005).

Klingman, David, A. Russell Localio, Jeremy Sugarman, Judith L. Wagner, Phillip T. Polishuk, Leah Wolfe, and Jacqueline A. Corrigan, 1996. "Measuring Defensive Medicine Using Clinical Scenario Surveys." *Journal of Health Politics, Policy and Law* 21.

Koch, Charles H., 1994. "Administrative Presiding Officials Today." *Administrative Law Review* 46.

Kraman, Steven S., and Ginny Hamm, 1999. "Risk Management: Extreme Honesty May Be the Best Policy." *Annals of Internal Medicine* 131.

Kramer, Geoffrey P., and Dorean M. Koenig, 1990. "Do Jurors Understand Criminal Jury Instructions? Analyzing the Results of the Michigan Juror Comprehension Project." *University of Michigan Journal of Law Reform* 23.

Kressel, Kenneth, Cheryl Ann Kennedy, Elise Lev, Louise Taylor, and Jonathan Hyman, 2002. "Managing Conflict in an Urban Health Care Setting: What Do 'Experts' Know?" *Journal of Health Care Law and Policy* 5.

Lake, Timothy K., Kelly Devers, Linda R. Brewster, and Lawrence P. Casalino, 2003. "Something Old, Something New: Recent Developments in Hospital–Physician Relationships." *Health Services Research* 38.

Lamb, Rae M., David M. Studdert, Richard M. J. Bohmer, Donald M. Berwick, and Troyen A. Brennan, 2003. "Hospital Disclosure Practices: Results of a National Survey." *Health Affairs* 22.

Lande, John, 2004. "'The Vanishing Trial' Report: An Alternative View of the Data." *Dispute Resolution Magazine* 10.

Landon, Bruce E., James Reschovsky, and David Blumenthal, 2003. "Changes in Career Satisfaction Among Primary Care and Specialist Physicians, 1997–2001." *Journal of the American Medical Association* 289.

Landrigan, Christopher P., Jeffrey M. Rothschild, John W. Cronin, et al., 2004. "Effect of Eliminating Extended Work Shifts and Reducing Weekly Work Hours on Serious Medical Errors in Intensive Care Units." *New England Journal of Medicine* 351.

Lapetina, Elizabeth M., and Elizabeth M. Armstrong, 2002. "Preventing Errors in the Outpatient Setting: A Tale of Three States." *Health Affairs* 21.

Larkin, Howard, 2004. *Hospitals and Health Networks Magazine* 78.

Laugesen, Miriam J., and Thomas Rice, 2003. "Is the Doctor In? The Evolving Role of Organized Medicine in Health Policy." *Journal of Health Politics, Policy and Law* 28.

Lawrence, Richard D., 2004. "Primer on Wrongful Death Claims." *Trial* 40.

Lazare, Aaron, 1995. "Go Ahead, Say You're Sorry." *Psychology Today* 28.

Leape, Lucian L., 2005. "Preventing Medical Errors." In David Mechanic, Lynn B. Rogut, David C. Colby, and James R. Knickman, eds., *Policy Challenges in Modern Health Care*. New Brunswick, NJ: Rutgers University Press.

———, 1990. "Practice Guidelines and Standards: An Overview." *QRB Quality Review Bulletin* 16.

Leape, Lucian L., and Donald M. Berwick, 2005. "Five Years After 'To Err Is Human': What Have We Learned?" *Journal of the American Medical Association* 293.

Leape, Lucian L., Ann G. Lawthers, Troyen A. Brennan, and William G. Johnson, 1993. "Preventing Medical Injury." *Quality Review Bulletin* 19.

Lee, George, M. D., 2004. E-mail communication to Carol B. Liebman (October 25).

Lee, Jason S., Robert A. Berenson, Rick Mayes, and Anne K. Gauthier, 2003. "Medicare Payment Policy: Does Cost Shifting Matter?" *Health Affairs* Web Exclusive W3–480 (Oct. 8).

Lee, Soon-Jae, David Mayers, and Clifford W. Smith, Jr., 1997. "Guaranty Funds and Risk-Taking: Evidence From the Insurance Industry." *Journal of Financial Economics* 44.

Leebron, David W., 1989. "Final Moments: Damages for Pain and Suffering Prior to Death." *New York University Law Review* 64.

Lefevre, Frank V., Teresa M. Waters, and Peter P. Budetti, 2000. "A Survey of Physician Training Programs in Risk Management and Communication Skills for Malpractice Prevention." *Journal of Law, Medicine, & Ethics* 28.

Lester, Gregory W., and Susan G. Smith, 1993. "Listening and Talking to Patients: A Remedy for Malpractice Suits?" *Western Journal of Medicine* 158.

LeTourneau, Charles U., 1970. "Malpractice." *Hospital Management* 19.

Levi, Deborah L., 1997. "The Role of Apology in Mediation." *New York University Law Review* 72.

Levinson, Wendy, Debra L. Roter, John P. Mullooly, Valerie T. Dull, and Richard M. Frankel, 1997. "Physician–Patient Communication. The Relationship With Malpractice Claims Among Primary Care Physicians and Surgeons." *Journal of the American Medical Association* 277.

Liang, Bryan A., 2000. "Risks of Reporting Sentinel Events." *Health Affairs* 19.

———, 1997. "Assessing Medical Malpractice Jury Verdicts: A Case Study of an Anesthesiology Department." *Cornell Journal of Law and Public Policy* 7.

Lieberman, Joel D., and Bruce D. Sales, 1997. "What Social Science Teaches Us About the Jury Instruction Process." *Psychology, Public Policy and Law* 3.

Liebman, Carol B., and Christine S. Hyman, 2005. "Medical Error Disclosure, Mediation Skills, and Malpractice Litigation: A Demonstration Project in Pennsylvania." Philadelphia: Pew Charitable Trusts. At http://medliabilitypa.org/research/liebman0305/ (last accessed Nov. 2, 2005).

Liebman, Carol B., and Chris Stern Hyman, 2004. "A Mediation Skills Model to Manage Disclosure of Errors and Adverse Events to Patients." *Health Affairs* 23.

Lindblom, Charles, 1959. "The Science of Muddling Through." *Public Administration Review* 19.

Liptak, Adam, 2004. "Doctor's Testimony Leads to a Complex Legal Fight." *New York Times* (June 20).

Localio, A. Russell, Ann G. Lawthers, Joan M. Bengtson, Liesi E. Hebert, Susan L. Weaver, Troyen A. Brennan, and Richard J. Landis, 1993. "Relationship Between

Malpractice Claims and Cesarean Delivery." *Journal of the American Medical Association* 269.

Localio, A. Russell, Ann G. Lawthers, Troyen A. Brennan, Nan M. Laird, Leisi E. Hebert, Lynn M. Peterson, Joseph P. Newhouse, Paul C. Weiler, and Howard H. Hiatt, 1991. "Relation Between Malpractice Claims and Adverse Events Due to Negligence." *New England Journal of Medicine* 325.

Localio, A. Russell, Susan L. Weaver, J. Richard Landis, Ann G. Lawthers, Troyen A. Brennan, Liesi E. Hebert, and Tonya J. Sharp, 1996. "Identifying Adverse Events Caused by Medical Care: Degree of Physician Agreement in a Retrospective Chart Review." *Annals of Internal Medicine* 125.

Lohr, Steve, 2005. "Bush's Next Target: Malpractice Lawyers." *New York Times* (Feb. 27).

Louisiana Patient Compensation Fund, 2003. At http://www.lapcf.state.la.us/ (last accessed Dec. 29, 2003).

Luft, Harold S., James C. Robinson, Deborah W. Garnick, Susan C. Maerki, and Stephen S. McPhee, 1986. "The Role of Specialized Clinical Services in Competition Among Hospitals." *Inquiry* 23.

Marcus, M. B., 2002. "Healthcare's 'Perfect Storm.'" *U.S. News & World Report* (July 1).

Margolis, H., 1982. *Selfishness, Altruism and Rationality: A Theory of Social Choice.* Cambridge, UK: Cambridge University Press.

Mariner, Wendy K., 2000. "What Recourse? Liability for Managed-Care Decisions and the Employee Retirement Income Security Act." *New England Journal of Medicine* 343.

―――, 1996. "Liability for Managed Care Decisions: The Employee Retirement Income Security Act and the Uneven Playing Field." *American Journal of Public Health* 86.

Mays, Glen P., Robert E. Hurley, and Joy M. Grossman, 2003. "An Empty Toolbox? Changes in Health Plans' Approaches for Managing Costs and Care." *Health Services Research* 38.

Mazor, Kathleen M., Steven R. Simon, and Jerry H. Gurwitz, 2004. "Communicating With Patients About Medical Errors." *Archives of Internal Medicine* 164.

Mazor, Kathleen M., Steven R. Simon, Robert A. Yood, Brian C. Martinson, Margaret J. Gunter, George W. Reed, and Jerry H. Gurwitz, 2004. "Health Plan Members' Views About Disclosure of Medical Errors." *Annals of Internal Medicine* 140.

McCarthy, Thomas, 1985. "The Competitive Nature of the Primary Care Physicians' Services Market." *Journal of Health Economics* 4.

McGlynn, Elizabeth A., Steven M. Asch, John Adams, Joan Keesey, Jennifer Hicks, Alison Decristofaro, and Eve A. Kerr, 2003. "The Quality of Health Care Delivered to Adults in the United States." *New England Journal of Medicine* 348.

McGoldrick, Meg, 2004. Chief operating officer, Abington Memorial Hospital. Email communication to Chris Stern Hyman (Aug. 10).

McGuire, Thomas G., 2000. "Physician Agency." In Joseph P. Newhouse and Anthony J. Culyer, eds., *Handbook of Health Economics.* Amsterdam: Elsevier B.V.

Meadow, William, 2002. "Operationalizing the Standard of Medical Care: Uses and Limitations of Epidemiology to Guide Expert Testimony in Medical Negligence Allegations." *Wake Forest Law Review* 37.

Meadow, William, and Cass R. Sunstein, 2001. "Essay: Statistics, Not Experts." *Duke Law Journal* 51.

Medicare Payment Advisory Commission (MEDPAC), 2005. *Report to Congress: Physician-Owned Specialty Hospitals.* Washington, DC: MEDPAC.

Mehlman, Maxwell J., 2003. "Resolving the Medical Malpractice Crisis: Fairness Considerations." At http://medliabilitypa.org/research/mehlman0603 (last accessed July 5, 2005).

———, 1994. "Bad 'Bad Baby' Bills." *American Journal of Law, Medicine, and Ethics* 20.

Mello, Michelle M., and Troyen A. Brennan, 2002. "Deterrence of Medical Errors: Theory and Evidence for Malpractice Reform." *Texas Law Review* 80.

Mello, Michelle M., and David Hemenway, 2004. "Medical Malpractice as an Epidemiological Problem." *Social Science and Medicine* 59.

Mello, Michelle M., Carly N. Kelly, David M. Studdert, Troyen A. Brennan, and William M. Sage, 2003. "Hospitals' Behavior in a Tort Crisis: Observations From Pennsylvania." *Health Affairs* 22.

Mello, Michelle M., David M. Studdert, and Troyen A. Brennan, 2003. "The New Medical Malpractice Crisis." *New England Journal of Medicine* 348.

Mello, Michelle M., David M. Studdert, Catherine M. DesRoches, Jordon Peugh, Kinga Zapert, Troyen A. Brennan, and William M. Sage, 2005. "Effects of a Malpractice Crisis on Specialist Supply and Patient Access to Care." *Annals of Surgery* 242.

Mello, Michelle M., David M. Studdert, Catherine M. DesRoches, Jordon Peugh, Kinga Zapert, Troyen A. Brennan, and William M. Sage, 2004. "Caring for Patients in a Malpractice Crisis: Physician Satisfaction and Quality of Care." *Health Affairs* 23.

Mello, Michelle M., David M. Studdert, Eric J. Thomas, Catherine Yoon, and Troyen A. Brennan, 2004. "Is There a Business Case for Patient Safety? An Analysis of Hospital Adverse Event Costs and Where They Fall." Unpublished manuscript in possession of lead author.

Mencimer, Stephanie, 2003. "Malpractice Makes Perfect." *Washington Monthly* 35 (Oct.).

Merton, R. C., 1977. "An Analytic Derivation of the Cost of Deposit Insurance and Load Guarantees: An Application of Modern Option Pricing Theory." *Journal of Banking and Finance* 1.

Meyers, A. R., 1987. "'Lumping It' – The Hidden Denominator of the Medical Malpractice Crisis." *American Journal of Public Health* 77.

Millenson, Michael L., 2005. "Still Demanding Medical Excellence." In David Mechanic, Lynn B. Rogut, David C. Colby, and James R. Knickman, eds., *Policy Challenges in Modern Health Care.* New Brunswick, NJ: Rutgers University Press.

———, 2003. "The Silence." *Health Affairs* 22.

Miller, Marlene R., and Chunliu Zahn, 2004. "Pediatric Patient Safety in Hospitals: A National Picture in 2000." *Pediatrics* 113.

Miller, Robert H., and Randall R. Bovbjerg, 2002. "Efforts to Improve Patient Safety in Large, Capitated Medical Groups: Description and Conceptual Model." *Journal of Health Politics, Policy and Law* 27.

Mills, Don Harper, 1978. "Medical Insurance Feasibility Study: A Technical Summary." *Western Journal of Medicine* 128.

Mills, Don Harper, John S. Boyden, and David S. Rubsamen, 1977. *Report on the Medical Insurance Feasibility Study.* San Francisco: Sutter Publications.

Mintz, Beth, and Donald Palmer, 2000. "Business and Health Care Policy Reform in the 1980s: The 50 States." *Social Problems* 47.

Mnookin, Robert H., Scott R. Peppet, and Andrew S. Tulumello, 2000. *Beyond Winning: Negotiating to Create Value in Deals and Disputes.* Cambridge, MA: Belknap Press of Harvard University Press.

Mohr, James C., 2000. "American Medical Malpractice Litigation in Historical Perspective." *Journal of the American Medical Association* 283.

————, 1993. *Doctors and the Law: Medical Jurisprudence in Nineteenth Century America.* Baltimore: Johns Hopkins University Press.

Morlock, Laura L., and Faye E. Malitz, 1993. *Short-Term Effects of Tort and Administrative Reforms on the Claiming Behavior of Privately Insured, Medicare, Medicaid and Uninsured Patients.* Washington, DC: U.S. Congress, Office of Technology Assessment.

Musgrave, R. A., 1957. *Theory of Public Finance.* New York: McGraw-Hill.

Myers, Chris, and Todd Burchill, 2002. "The Short Life of a Medical Device." *Health Forum Journal* 45.

Myers, Chris, and Reuben Ehrlich, 2001. "Biotech Frontiers." *Health Forum Journal* 44.

Nance, John, 2005. "Changing Cockpit Culture: Why We Fired Captain Kirk – Airline Pilots No Longer Act Like They Have All the Answers, and We're Safer Because of It." ABC News Commentary (Mar. 29). At http://abcnews.go.com/Business/FlyingHigh/story?id = 602002 &page = 1 (last accessed June 7, 2005).

National Academy for State Health Policy (NASHP), 2000. *State Reporting of Medical Errors and Adverse Events: Results of a 50-State Survey.* Portland, ME: NASHP.

National Conference of Commissioners on Uniform State Laws, 2004. *Uniform Mediation Act.* At http://www.law.upenn.edu/bll/ulc/mediat/2003finaldraft.htm. (last accessed Oct. 28, 2004).

National Conference of State Legislatures, 2005. "State Medical Malpractice Reform Action 2005." At http://www.ncsl.org/standcomm/sclaw/medmalreform05.htm (last accessed July 20, 2005).

National Governors Association, 2003. "MCH Update 2002: State Health Coverage for Low-Income Pregnant Women, Children, and Parents." Washington, DC: NGA (Center for Best Practices).

National Journal Poll Track, 2005. "2005 Polling on Health Care." At http://nationaljournal.com/members/polltrack/2005/issues/05healthcare1.htm (last accessed July 5, 2005).

National Patient Safety Foundation (NPSF), 2005. "Patient Safety Bibliography." At http://www.npsf.org/html/bibliography.html (last accessed July 5, 2005).

National Practitioner Data Bank Public Use File, 2004. At http://Www.Npdb-Hipdb.Com/Publicdata.Html (last accessed Dec. 17, 2004).

National Quality Forum, 2002. "Serious Reportable Events in Healthcare: A National Quality Forum Consensus Report." Washington, DC: NQF.

Nelson, Eugene C., Paul B. Batalden, T. P. Huber, J. J. Mohr, M. M. Godfrey, L. A. Headrick, and J. H. Wasson, 2002. "Microsystems in Health Care, Part 1: Learning from High-Performing Front-Line Clinical Units." *Joint Commission Journal on Quality Improvement* 28.

Newman, Marc C., 1996. "The Emotional Impact of Mistakes on Family Physicians." *Archives of Family Medicine* 5.

New Mexico Medical Society, 2003. Council minutes of January 11, 2003 meeting. Unpublished document in possession of editors.

New Mexico Public Regulation Commission (NMPRC), 2001. "Annual Report of the Commission." Santa Fe, NM: NMPRC.

New York State Department of Insurance (NYSDI), 2004. "Underlying Individual Policy & New York Statutory Excess Medical Malpractice Insurance Coverage." At http://www.ins.state.ny.us/rg040413.htm (last accessed July 23, 2005).

_____, 1997. "The Status of the Primary and Excess Medical Malpractice Market and the Future Need for the Medical Malpractice Insurance Association." Albany, NY: NYSDI.

Nichols, Len M., Paul B. Ginsburg, Robert A. Berenson, Jon Christianson, and Robert E. Hurley, 2004. "Are Market Forces Strong Enough to Deliver Efficient Health Care Systems? Confidence Is Waning." *Health Affairs* 23.

Nixon, Richard M., 1971. "President Nixon's Economic Message to Congress." *Congressional Quarterly Almanac*, Book No. 27. Washington, DC: Congressional Quarterly Press.

Nutter, Franklin W., 1985. "The Second Time Around." *Best's Review: Property/Casualty Insurance* 86.

O'Connell, Daniel, Maysed Kemp White, and Frederic W. Platt, 2003. "Disclosing Unanticipated Outcomes and Medical Errors." *Journal of Clinical Outcomes Management* 10.

O'Connell, Jeffrey, 1986. "Neo-no-fault Remedies for Medical Injuries: Coordinated Statutory and Contractual Alternatives." *Law & Contemporary Problems* 49.

_____, 1982. "Offers That Can't Be Refused: Foreclosure of Personal Injury Claims by Defendants' Prompt Tender of Claimants' Net Economic Losses." *Northwestern University Law Review* 77.

O'Connell, Jeffrey, and Geoffrey Paul Eaton, 1999. "Binding Early Offers as a Simple, If Second-Best, Alternative to Tort Law." *Nebraska Law Review* 78.

Office of Inspector General, 2004. Advisory Opinion 04-19 (Dec. 30). At http://www.oig.hhs.gov/fraud/docs/advisoryopinions/2004/a00419.pdf (last accessed June 21, 2005).

Oren, E., E. R. Shaffer, and B. J. Guglielmo, 2003. "Impact of Emerging Technologies on Medication Errors and Adverse Drug Events." *American Journal of Health-System Pharmacy* 60.

Ostrom, Carol M., 2004. "Physicians Angry With Swedish for Hiring Own Doctors." *Seattle Times* (July 29).

Oxholm, Carl, 2004. General Counsel of Drexel University College of Medicine and of Drexel University. Email communication to Chris Stern Hyman (Aug. 10).

Pace, Nicholas M., Daniela Golinelli, and Laura Zakaras, 2004. "Capping Non-economic Awards in Medical Malpractice Trials: California Jury Verdicts Under MICRA." Santa Monica, CA: RAND Institute for Civil Justice.

Pacey, Arnold, 1983. *The Culture of Technology.* Oxford, UK: Basil, Blackwell.

Page, Leigh, 2002. "Indecent Exposure: Physicians Throw Caution to the Wind as Malpractice Premiums Skyrocket." *Modern Physician* 3.

Palmer, Geoffrey, 1994. "New Zealand's Accident Compensation Scheme: Twenty Years On." *University of Toronto Law Journal* 44.

———, 1979. *Compensation for Incapacity.* Wellington, NZ: Oxford Press.

Partnership for Patient Safety, 2004. "First Do No Harm, Part 3: Healing Lives, Changing Cultures" (video recording). Chicago: P4ps Ltd.

Pauly, Mark V., 1980. *Doctors and Their Workshops: Economic Models of Physician Behavior.* Chicago: University of Chicago Press.

Pauly, Mark V., Thomas Abbott, and Christy L. Thompson, 2004. "Do Higher Malpractice Premiums Depress Physician Incomes?" Working Paper, Wharton School.

Pauly, Mark V., and Mark Redisch, 1973. "The Not-for-Profit Hospital as a Physician's Cooperative." *American Economic Review* 63.

Pauly, Mark V., and Mark A. Satterthwaite, 1981. "The Pricing of Primary Care Physicians' Services: A Test of the Role of Consumer Information." *Bell Journal of Economics* 12.

Payne, Kathleen, 1995. "Linking Tort Reform to Fairness and Moral Values." *Detroit College of Law Review* 1995.

Peeples, Ralph, Catherine T. Harris, and Thomas B. Metzloff, 2002. "The Process of Managing Medical Malpractice Cases: The Role of Standard of Care." *Wake Forest Law Review* 37.

Penrod, Steven D., and Larry Heuer, 1997. "Tweaking Commonsense: Assessing Aids to Jury Decision Making." *Psychology, Public Policy, and Law* 3.

Perez-Peña, Richard, 2004. "Law to Rein in Hospital Errors Is Seen as Abused." *New York Times* (Sept. 29).

Peters, Philip G., 2002. "Empirical Evidence and Malpractice Litigation." *Wake Forest Law Review* 37.

———, 2001. "The Reasonable Physician Standard: The New Malpractice Standard of Care?" *Journal of Health Law* 34.

Petersen, Laura A., Troyen A. Brennan, Anne C. O'Neil, E. Francis Cook, and Thomas H. Lee, 1994. "Does Housestaff Discontinuity of Care Increase the Risk for Preventable Adverse Events?" *Annals of Internal Medicine* 121.

Peterson, Mark A., ed., 1999. "The Managed Care Backlash." *Journal of Health Politics, Policy and Law* 24 (symposium issue).

Peterson, Osler L., Leon P. Andrews, Robert S. Spain, and Bernard G. Greenburg. 1956. "An Analytical Study of North Carolina General Practice: 1953–1954." *Journal of Medical Education* 31.

Pew Project on Medical Liability in Pennsylvania, 2002. Pew Charitable Trusts. At http://medliabilitypa.org/research/survey1002/ (last accessed July 23, 2005).

Pham, Hoangmai H., Kelly Devers, Sylvia Kuo, and Robert A. Berenson, 2005. "Health Care Market Trends and the Evolution of Hospitalist Use and Roles." *Journal of General Internal Medicine* 20.

Pham, Hoangmai H., Kelly Devers, Jessica H. May, and Robert A. Berenson, 2004. "Financial Pressures Spur Physician Entrepreneurialism." *Health Affairs* 23.

Physician Insurers Association of America (PIAA), 2005. "About Us: History." At http://www.piaa.us/about_piaa/history.htm (last accessed Jan. 13, 2005).

———, 2002. *Breast Cancer Study.* 3rd. ed. Rockville, MD: Physician Insurers Association of America.

————, 2000. *Laparoscopic Injury Study*. Rockville, MD: Physician Insurers Association of America.

————, 1998. *Neurological Impairment in Newborns: A Malpractice Claim Study*. Rockville, MD: Physician Insurers Association of America.

————, 1995. *Breast Cancer Study*. Rockville, MD: Physician Insurers Association of America.

————, 1994. *Laparoscopic Procedure Study*. Rockville, MD: Physician Insurers Association of America.

Pierce, Ellison C., Jr., 1990. "The Development of Anesthesia Guidelines and Standards." *Quality Review Bulletin* 16.

Pierluissi, Edgar, Melissa A. Fischer, Andre R. Campbell, and C. Seth Landefeld, 2003. "Discussion of Medical Errors in Morbidity and Mortality Conferences." *Journal of the American Medical Association* 290.

Pierson, Paul, 2000. "Increasing Returns, Path Dependence, and the Study of Politics." *American Political Science Review* 94.

Pietro, Daniel A., Linda J. Shyavitz, Richard A. Smith, and Bruce S. Auerbach, 2000. "Detecting and Reporting Medical Errors: Why the Dilemma?" *British Medical Journal* 320.

Polinsky, A. Mitchell, and Steven Shavell, 1998. "Punitive Damages: An Economic Analysis." *Harvard Law Review* 111.

Porter, Michael E., and Elizabeth Olmsted Teisberg, 2004. "Redefining Competition in Health Care." *Harvard Business Review* 39.

Poythress, Norman G., Joseph E. Shumacher, Richard G. Wiener, and Mary Rose Murrin, 1993. "Procedural Justice Judgments of Alternative Procedures for Resolving Medical Malpractice Claims." *Journal of Applied Social Psychology* 23.

Preston, S. H., 1998. "Malpractice Danger Zones: Why Primary Care Is More Vulnerable Than Ever." *Medical Economics* 75.

Priest, Dana, 1993. "Clinton Advisers Discuss Plan to Shift Liability from Physicians." *Washington Post* (May 21).

Priest, George L., 1992. "Can Absolute Manufacturer Liability Be Defended?" *Yale Journal on Regulation* 9.

————, 1987. "The Current Insurance Crisis and Modern Tort Law." *Yale Law Journal* 96.

————, 1985. "The Invention of Enterprise Liability: A Critical History of the Intellectual Foundations of Modern Tort Law." *Journal of Legal Studies* 14.

————, 1981. "A Theory of Consumer Product Warranty." *Yale Law Journal* 90.

Raphael, David Daiches, 2001. *Concepts of Justice*. New York: Oxford University Press.

Rauch, Jonathan, 1994. *Demosclerosis*. New York: Times Books.

Rawls, John R., 1971. *A Theory of Justice*. New York: Oxford University Press.

Reason, James, 2000. "Human Error: Models and Management." *British Medical Journal* 320.

————, 1990. *Human Error*. New York: Cambridge University Press.

Redinbaugh, Ellen M., James M. Schnuerger, Leonard L. Weiss, Adam Brufsky, and Robert Ornold, 2001. "Health Care Professionals' Grief: A Model Based on Occupational Style and Coping." *Psychooncology* 10.

Reifman, Alan, Spencer M. Gusick, and Phoebe C. Ellsworth, 1992. "Real Jurors' Understanding of the Law in Real Cases." *Law and Human Behavior* 16.

Reinsurance Magazine, 2004. "Survey of Risk Managers and Reinsurance Buyers." At http://www.reinsurancemagazine.com (last accessed Sept. 4, 2004).

Rettig, Richard A., Peter D. Jacobson, Cynthia Farquhar, and Wade M. Aubry, 2005. *False Hope vs. Evidence-Based Medicine: The Failure of Bone Marrow Transplantation for Breast Cancer.* New York: Oxford University Press.

Riskin, Leonard L., 2003. "Decision-Making in Mediation: The New Old Grid and the New New Grid System." *Notre Dame Law Review* 79.

Robbennolt, Jennifer K, 2004. "Faculty Focus – Apologies and Legal Settlement: An Empirical Examination. *Issues and Interests* 5. University of Missouri-Columbia School of Law, Center for the Study of Dispute Resolution.

——, 2003. "Apologies and Legal Settlement: An Empirical Examination." *Michigan Law Review* 102.

Robinson, Andrew R., Kirsten B. Hohmann, Julie I. Rifkin, Daniel Topp, Christine M. Gilroy, Jeffrey A. Pickard, and Robert J. Anderson, 2002. "Physician and Public Opinions on Quality of Health Care and the Problem of Medical Errors." *Archives of Internal Medicine* 162.

Robinson, Glen O., 1986. "The Medical Malpractice Crisis of the 1970s." *Law and Contemporary Problems* 49.

Robinson, James C., 2004. "Reinvention of Health Insurance in the Consumer Era." *Journal of the American Medical Association* 291.

——, 2001. "The End of Managed Care." *Journal of the American Medical Association* 285.

——, 1994. "The Changing Boundaries of the American Hospital." *Milbank Quarterly* 72.

Rochefort, David A., and Roger W. Cobb, 1994. "Instrumental Versus Expressive Definitions of AIDS Policymaking." In *idem.,* eds., *The Politics of Problem Definition: Shaping the Policy Agenda.* Lawrence: University Press of Kansas.

Rock, S. M., 1988. "Malpractice Premiums and Primary Cesarean Section Rates in New York and Illinois." *Public Health Reporter* 58.

Roddis, Richard S. L., and Richard E. Stewart, 1975. "The Insurance of Medical Losses." *Duke Law Journal* 1975.

Rogers, Audrey S., Ebenezer Israel, Craig R. Smith, David Levine, A. Marshall McBean, Carmine Valente, and Gerald Faich, 1988. "Physicians' Knowledge, Attitudes, and Behavior Related to Adverse Drug Events." *Archives of Internal Medicine* 148.

Rogers, David, 1993. "Initial Clinton Medical Malpractice Reform Plans Pulled After Resistance From Entrenched Interests." *Wall Street Journal* (June 15).

Rosenhan, David L., Sara L. Eisner, and Robert J. Robinson, 1994. "Notetaking Can Aid Juror Recall." *Law and Human Behavior* 18.

Rosenthal, Alan, 2001. *The Third House: Lobbyists and Lobbying in the States.* Washington, DC: Congressional Quarterly Press.

Rosenthal, Marilynn M., 1988. *Dealing with Medical Malpractice: The British and Swedish Experience.* Durham, NC: Duke University Press.

Rovner, Julie, 2005. "Overdosing on Studies." *National Journal: Congress Daily* (June 9).

Rubin, Paul H., 2005. "Public Choice and Tort Reform." Emory Law and Economics Research Paper Series, No. 04-09.

Rubin, Robert, and Daniel Mendelson, 1994. "How Much Does Defensive Medicine Cost?" *Journal of American Health Policy* 4.

Rustad, Michael L., 1996. "Nationalizing Tort Law: The Republican Attack on Women, Blue Collar Workers and Consumers." *Rutgers Law Review* 48.

Rustad, Michael L., and Thomas H. Koenig, 2002. "Taming the Tort Monster: The American Civil Justice System as a Battleground of Social Theory." *Brooklyn Law Review* 68.

Sage, William M., 2005a. "Medical Malpractice Insurance and the Emperor's Clothes." *DePaul Law Review* 54.

_____, 2005b. "New Directions in Medical Liability Reform." In Richard Anderson, ed., *Malpractice and Medical Practice Handbook*. Totowa, NJ: Humana Press.

_____, 2004a. "Reputation, Malpractice Liability, and Medical Error." In Virginia A. Sharpe, ed., *Accountability: Patient Safety and Policy Reform*. Washington, DC: Georgetown University Press.

_____, 2004b. "The Forgotten Third: Liability Insurance and the Medical Malpractice Crisis." *Health Affairs* 23.

_____, 2003a. "Understanding the First Malpractice Crisis of the 21st Century." In Alice Gosfield, ed., *2003 Health Law Handbook*. St. Paul, MN: West Group. At http://medliabilitypa.org/research/law1103/chapter.pdf (last accessed July 27, 2005).

_____, 2003b. "Medical Liability and Patient Safety." *Health Affairs* 22.

_____, 2002. "Putting the Patient in Patient Safety: Linking Malpractice Complaints and Patient Risk." *Journal of the American Medical Association* 287.

_____, 2001. "The Lawyerization of Medicine." *Journal of Health Politics, Policy and Law* 26.

_____, 1997. "Enterprise Liability and the Emerging Managed Health Care System." *Law and Contemporary Problems* 60.

Sage, William M., Kathleen E. Hastings, and Robert A. Berenson, 1994. "Enterprise Liability for Medical Malpractice and Health Care Quality Improvement." *American Journal of Law and Medicine* 20.

Sage, William M., and James M. Jorling, 1994. "A World That Won't Stand Still: Enterprise Liability by Private Contract." *DePaul Law Review* 43.

Sager, Mark, S. K. Voeks, P. J. Drinka, E. H. Langer, and P. Grimstad, 1990. "Do the Elderly Sue Physicians?" *Archives of Internal Medicine* 150.

Saks, Michael J., 1994. "Medical Malpractice: Facing Real Problems and Finding Real Solutions." *William & Mary Law Journal* 35.

Saks, Michael J., Lisa A. Hollinger, Roselle L. Wissler, David Lee Evans, and Allen J. Hart, 1997. "Reducing Variability in Civil Jury Awards." *Law and Human Behavior* 21.

Sand, Leonard B., and Steven Alan Reiss, 1985. "A Report on Seven Experiments Conducted by District Court Judges in the Second Circuit." *New York University Law Review* 60.

Scheutzow, Susan O., 1999. "State Medical Peer Review: High Cost but No Benefit – Is It Time for a Change?" *American Journal of Law and Medicine* 25.

Schmitt, C. H., 2003. "A Medical Mistake." *U.S. News & World Report* (June 30/July 7).

Schoenbaum, Stephen C., and Randall R. Bovbjerg, 2004. "Malpractice Reform Must Include Steps to Prevent Medical Injury." *Annals of Internal Medicine* 140.

Schuck, Peter H., 1991. "Scheduled Damages and Insurance Contracts for Future Services: A Comment on Blumstein, Bovbjerg, and Sloan." *Yale Journal on Regulation* 8.

Schwartz, Alan, 1988. "Proposals for Products Liability Reform: A Theoretical Synthesis." *Yale Law Journal* 97.

Schwartz, Alan, and Louis L. Wilde, 1983. "Imperfect Information in Markets for Contract Terms: The Examples of Warranties and Security Interests." *Virginia Law Review* 69.

Schwartz, Greg T., 1994. "Reality in the Economic Analysis of Tort Law: Does Tort Law Really Deter?" *UCLA Law Review* 42.

Schwartz, Victor E., and Cary Silverman, 2004. "Hedonic Damages: The Rapidly Bubbling Cauldron." *Brooklyn Law Review* 69.

Schwartz, W. B., and D. N. Mendelson, 1989. "Physicians Who Have Lost Their Malpractice Insurance: Their Demographic Characteristics and the Surplus-Lines Companies That Insure Them." *Journal of the American Medical Association* 262.

Scott, H. Denman, Ann Thacher Reushaw, Sara E. Rosenbarm, William J. Waters, Michael Green, L. G. Andrews, and Gerald A. Faich, 1990. "Physician Reporting of Adverse Drug Reactions: Results of the Rhode Island Adverse Drug Reaction Reporting Project." *Journal of the American Medical Association* 263.

Scully-Hayes, Kathleen, 2002. "Mediation and Medicare Part A Provider Appeals: A Useful Alternative." *Journal of Health Care Law & Policy* 5.

Seabury, Seth A., Nicholas M. Pace, and Robert T. Reville, 2004. "Forty Years of Civil Jury Verdicts." *Journal of Empirical Legal Studies* 1.

Serviansky, Daniel, 2004. "Apologies and the Resolution of Disputes." Unpublished paper on file with the editors.

Sexton, J. B., and R. L. Helmreich, 2003. "Using Language in the Cockpit: Relationships with Workload and Performance." In R. Dietrich, ed., *Communication in High Risk Environments*. Hamburg: Helmut Buske Verlag GmbH.

Sharkey, Catherine, 2005. "The Unintended Consequences of Medical Malpractice Damages Caps." *New York University Law Review* 80.

———, 2003. "Punitive Damages: Should Juries Decide?" *Texas Law Review* 82.

Shavell, Stephen, 1982. "On Liability and Insurance." *Bell Journal of Economics* 13.

———, 1980. "Strict Liability Versus Negligence." *Journal of Legal Studies* 9.

Shortell, Steven M., R. R. Gillies, and D. A. Anderson, 1994. "The New World of Managed Care: Creating Organized Delivery Systems." *Health Affairs* 13.

Shuman, Daniel W. 2001. "Expertise in Law, Medicine, and Health Care." *Journal of Health Politics, Policy and Law* 26.

Silver, Charles, 2004. "Half-Baked Thoughts on Punitive Damages in Medical Malpractice Cases." Presentation at Judicial Symposium, AEI-Brookings Center for Regulatory Studies, Washington, DC, Sept. 24.

Silverman, Rachel Emma, 2004a. "So Sue Me: Doctors Without Insurance." *Wall Street Journal* (Jan. 28).

———, 2004b. "Database for Doctors Tracks Litigious Patients." *Wall Street Journal* (Mar. 5).

Sloan, Frank A., 2004. *Public Medical Malpractice Insurance*. Durham, NC: Duke University Center for Health Policy, Law and Management.

———, 1990. "Experience Rating: Does It Make Sense for Medical Malpractice Insurance?" *American Economics Association Papers and Proceedings* 80.

———, 1985. "State Responses to the Malpractice Insurance 'Crisis' of the 1970s: An Empirical Assessment." *Journal of Health Politics, Policy and Law* 9.

Sloan, Frank A., and Randall R. Bovbjerg, 1989. "Medical Malpractice: Crises, Response and Effects." *HIAA Research Bulletin* 1.

Sloan, Frank A., Randall R. Bovbjerg, and Penny B. Githens, 1991. *Insuring Medical Malpractice*. New York: Oxford University Press.

Sloan, Frank A., Randall R. Bovbjerg, and P. Rankin, 1997. "Administrative Performance of 'No-Fault' Compensation for Medical Injury: No-Fault Compared to Tort Systems." *Law and Contemporary Problems* 60.

Sloan, Frank A., Penny B. Githens, and Gerald B. Hickson, 1993. "The Dispute Resolution Process." In Frank A. Sloan, Penny B. Githens, Ellen Wright Clayton, Gerald B. Hickson, Douglas A. Gentile, and David F. Partlett, eds., *Suing for Medical Malpractice*. Chicago: University of Chicago Press.

Sloan, Frank A., and Chee Ruey Hsieh, 1990. "Variability in Medical Malpractice Payments: Is the Compensation Fair?" *Law and Society Review* 24.

Sloan, Frank A., Carrie A. Mathews, Christopher J. Conover, and William M. Sage, 2004. "Public Medical Malpractice Insurance: An Analysis of State-Operated Patient Compensation Funds." Durham, NC: Duke University Center for Health Policy, Law and Management.

Sloan, Frank A., Paula M. Mergenhagen, and Randall R. Bovbjerg, 1989. "Effects of Tort Reforms on the Value of Closed Medical Malpractice Claims: A Microanalysis." *Journal of Health Politics, Policy and Law* 14.

Sloan, Frank A., K. Whetten-Goldstein, S. Entman, E. Kulas, and E. Stout, 1997. "The Road From Medical Injury to Claims Resolution: How No-Fault and Tort Differ." *Law and Contemporary Problems* 60.

Sloan, Frank A., K. Whetten-Goldstein, E. Kulas, G. Hickson, and S. Entman, 1999. "Compensation for Birth Related Injury: No-Fault Compared to Tort Systems." *Archives of Pediatrics & Adolescent Medicine* 153.

Sloan, Frank A., K. Whetten-Goldstein, E. Stout, S. Entman, and G. Hickson, 1998. "No-Fault System of Compensation for Obstetric Injury: Winners and Losers?" *Obstetrics and Gynecology* 91.

Sloan, Frank A., et al., 1995. "Effects of the Threat of Medical Malpractice Litigation and Other Factors on Birth Outcomes." *Medical Care* 33.

Smarr, Lawrence E., 2003. Statement of the Physician Insurers Association of America Before the Joint Hearing of the United States Senate Judiciary Committee and Health, Education, Labor, and Pensions Committee. Washington, DC: U.S. Government Printing Office.

Smith, George P., 2001. "Setting Limits: Medical Technology and the Law." *Sydney Law Review* 23.

Smith, Vicki L., 1991. "Impact of Pretrial Instruction on Jurors' Information Processing and Decision Making." *Journal of Applied Psychology* 76.

Somers, Herman M., 1977. "The Malpractice Controversy and the Quality of Patient Care." *Milbank Memorial Fund Quarterly* 55.

South Carolina Legislative Audit Council, 2000. "A Review of the Medical Malpractice Patients' Compensation Fund." Columbia, SC: South Carolina General
Assembly.

Southwick, Arthur F., 1988. *The Law of Hospital and Health Care Administration.*
2d ed. Ann Arbor, MI: Health Administration Press.

———, 1983. "Hospital Liability: Two Theories Have Been Merged." *Journal of
Legal Medicine* 4.

Spaeth, Ronald G., Kelley C. Pickering, and Shannon M. Webb, 2003. "Quality Assurance and Hospital Structure: How the Physician–Hospital Relationship
Affects Quality Measures." *Annals of Health Law* 12.

Spence, Michael, 1977. "Consumer Misperceptions, Product Failure, and Product
Liability." *Review of Economic Studies* 44.

Starr, Paul, 1982. *The Social Transformation of American Medicine: The Rise of a
Sovereign Profession and the Making of a Vast Industry.* New York: Basic Books.

Starr, Paul, and Walter A. Zelman, 1993. "A Bridge to Compromise: Competition
Under a Budget." *Health Affairs* 12 (Supplement).

State of Florida, 2003. "Report of the Governor's Select Task Force on Healthcare Professional Liability Insurance." Florida Insurance Council. At http://www.
flains.org/public/ls_medmalreport25.html-ssi (last accessed Sept. 17, 2004).

State of Missouri, 2003. Senate Bill No. 1204 (introduced Feb. 25).

State of Missouri, 2002. Senate Bill No. 551 (introduced Feb. 20).

Steinmo, Sven, and Jon Watts, 1995. "It's the Institutions, Stupid! Why Comprehensive Health Insurance Always Fails in America." *Journal of Health Politics, Policy
and Law* 20.

Steffy, Loren, 2004. "Doctors Who Don't Treat Lawyers Are Own Worst Enemy."
Houston Chronicle (June 20).

Stevens, Rosemary, 1989. *In Sickness and in Wealth: American Hospitals in the
Twentieth Century.* New York: Basic Books.

Stevenson, David G., and David M. Studdert, 2003. "The Rise of Nursing Home
Litigation: Findings From a National Survey of Attorneys." *Health Affairs* 2.

Steves, Myron F., Jr., 1975. "A Proposal to Improve the Cost to Benefit Relationships in the Medical Professional Liability Insurance System." *Duke Law Journal*
1975.

Stoddard, Jeffrey J., J. Lee Hargraves, Marie Reed, and Allison Vratil, 2001. "Managed Care, Professional Autonomy, and Income: Effects on Physician Career Satisfaction." *Journal of General Internal Medicine* 16.

Stolberg, S. G., 2003. "Lobbyists on Both Sides Duel in the Medical Malpractice
Debate." *New York Times* (Mar. 12).

Stone, Douglas, Bruce Patton, and Sheila Heen, 1999. *Difficult Conversations.* New
York: Viking.

Strasser, Florian, J. Lynn Palmer, Monica Castro, Jie Willey, Loren Shen, Ki Shin,
Debra Sivesind, Estela Beale, and Eduardo Bruera, 2003. "Impact of Physician
Sitting (SIT) Versus Standing (STA) During Inpatient Oncology Consultations:
Patients' Preference and Perception of Compassion and Duration." *Proceedings of
the American Society of Clinical Oncology* 736.

Strunk, Albert L., and Linda Esser, 2004. "Overview of the 2003 ACOG Survey of
Professional Liability." *ACOG Clinical Review* 9.

Struve, Catherine T., 2005. "The FDA and the Tort System: Postmarketing Surveillance, Compensation, and the Role of Litigation." *Yale Journal of Health Policy, Law and Ethics* 5.

———, 2004. "Improving the Medical Malpractice Litigation Process." *Health Affairs* 23.

———, 2003. "Expertise in Medical Malpractice Litigation: Special Courts, Screening Panels, and Other Options." The Pew Charitable Trusts' Project on Medical Liability in Pennsylvania. At www.medliabilitypa.org (last accessed Aug. 14, 2005).

Studdert, David M., and Troyen A. Brennan. 2001a. "No-Fault Compensation for Medical Injuries: The Prospect for Error Prevention." *Journal of the American Medical Association* 286.

———, 2001b. "Toward a Workable Model of 'No-Fault' Compensation for Medical Injury in the United States." *American Journal of Law and Medicine* 27.

———, 2000. "The Problem of Punitive Damages in Lawsuits Against Managed-Care Organizations." *New England Journal of Medicine* 342.

Studdert, David M., Troyen A. Brennan, and Eric J. Thomas, 2000. "Beyond Dead Reckoning: Measures of Medical Injury Burden, Malpractice Litigation, and Alternative Compensation Models From Utah and Colorado." *Indiana Law Review* 33.

Studdert, David M., Michelle M. Mello, and Troyen A. Brennan, 2004. "Medical Malpractice." *New England Journal of Medicine* 350.

Studdert, David M., Michelle M. Mello, A. A. Gawande, and Troyen A. Brennan, 2006. "Disclosure of Medical Injury to Patients: An Improbable Risk Management Strategy." Unpublished manuscript.

Studdert, David M., Michelle M. Mello, William M. Sage, Catherine M. DesRoches, Jordon Peugh, Kinga Zapert, and Troyen A. Brennan, 2005. "Defensive Medicine Among High-Risk Specialist Physicians During a Malpractice Crisis." *Journal of the American Medical Association* 293.

Studdert, David M., Eric J. Thomas, Helen R. Burstin, Brett I. Zbar, E. John Orav, and Troyen A. Brennan, 2000. "Negligent Care and Malpractice Claiming Behavior in Utah and Colorado." *Medical Care* 38.

Studdert, David M., Eric J. Thomas, Brett I. W. Zbar, Joseph P. Newhouse, Paul C. Weiler, Jonathon Bayuk, and Troyen A. Brennan, 1997. "Can the United States Afford a 'No-Fault' System of Compensation for Medical Injury?" *Law and Contemporary Problems* 60.

Studdert, David M., Y. Tony Yang, and Michelle M. Mello, 2004. "Are Damage Caps Regressive? A Study of Malpractice Jury Verdicts in California." *Health Affairs* 23.

Sugarman, Stephen D., 1992. "A Restatement of Torts: An Essay Review of American Law Institute Reporters' Study, Enterprise Responsibility for Personal Injury." *Stanford Law Review* 44.

Suit, Collin, 2005. "Questionable Medicine: Why Federal Medical Malpractice Reform May Be Unconstitutional." *Arizona Law Review* 47.

Summerton, Nicholas, 1995. "Positive and Negative Factors in Defensive Medicine: A Questionnaire Study of General Practitioners." *British Medical Journal* 301.

Sunstein, Cass R., Reid Hastie, John W. Payne, David A. Schkcade, and W. Kip Viscusi, 2002. *Punitive Damages: How Juries Decide*. Chicago: University of Chicago Press.

Sutter, Russell L., 2003. *U.S. Tort Costs: 2003 Update – Trends and Findings on the Costs of the U.S. Tort System*. Atlanta, GA: Tillinghast-Towers Perrin.

———, 2002. "Kansas Health Care Stabilization Fund, Indicated Liabilities at June 30, 2002: Surcharge Determination for FY2003." St. Louis, MO: Tillinghast-Towers Perrin. At http://www.hcsf.org/insurers.htm (last accessed May 14, 2004).

Tancredi, Laurence R., and Randall Bovbjerg, 1991. "Rethinking Responsibility for Patient Injury: Accelerated-Compensation Events, a Malpractice and Quality Reform Ripe for a Test." *Law and Contemporary Problems* 54.

Taragin, Mark I., Katherine Martin, Sharona Shapiro, Richard Trout, and Jeffrey L. Carson, 1995. "Physician Malpractice: Does the Past Predict the Future?" *Journal of General Internal Medicine* 10.

Taragin, Mark I., Laura R. Willet, Adam Wilczek, Richard Trout, and Jeffrey L. Carson, 1992. "The Influence of Standard of Care and Severity of Injury on the Resolution of Medical Malpractice Claims." *Annals of Internal Medicine* 117.

Taylor, Leslie, 2003. 3R and program coordinator, COPIC Insurance. Telephone conversation with Chris Stern Hyman (Dec. 10).

Thomas, Eric J., Stuart R. Lipsitz, David M. Studdert, and Troyen A. Brennan, 2002. "The Reliability of Medical Record Review for Estimating Adverse Event Rates." *Annals of Internal Medicine* 136.

Thomas, Eric J., David M. Studdert, Helen R. Burstin, et al., 2000. "Incidence and Types of Adverse Events and Negligent Care in Utah and Colorado." *Medical Care* 38.

Thomas, Eric J., David M. Studdert, Joseph P. Newhouse, et al., 1999. "Costs of Medical Injuries in Utah and Colorado." *Inquiry* 36.

Thorpe, Kenneth, 2004. "The Medical Malpractice 'Crisis': Recent Trends and the Impact of State Tort Reforms." *Health Affairs* Web Exclusive (Jan. 21).

Thurston, Norman K., 2001. "Physician Market Power–Evidence From the Allocation of Malpractice Premiums." *Economic Inquiry* 39.

Tillinghast Towers-Perrin, 2002. *U.S. Tort Costs: 2002 Update*. New York: Tillinghast Towers-Perrin.

Tinker, J. H., D. L. Dull, R. A. Caplan, R. J. Ward, and F. W. Cheney, 1989. "Role of Monitoring Devices in Prevention of Anesthetic Mishaps: A Closed Claims Analysis." *Anesthesiology* 71.

Todd, James S., 1993. "Health Care Reform and the American Medical Association." *New England Journal of Medicine* 328.

Tussing, A. Dale, and Martha A. Wojtowycz, 1992. "The Cesarean Decision in New York State, 1986: Economic and Noneconomic Aspects." *Medical Care* 30.

Udell, Nancy, and David B. Kendall, 2005. "Health Courts: Fair and Reliable Justice for Injured Patients." Washington, DC: Progressive Policy Institute.

U.S. Congress, Office of Technology Assessment, 1994. "Defensive Medicine and Medical Malpractice." OTA-H-602. Washington, DC: U.S. Government Printing Office.

———, 1993. "Impact of Legal Reforms on Medical Malpractice Costs." OTA-BP-H-119. Washington, DC: U.S. Government Printing Office.

———, 1992. "Do Medicaid and Medicare Patients Sue Physicians More Often Than Other Patients?" Washington, DC: OTA.

U.S. Department of Health and Human Services (HHS), Centers for Medicare and Medicaid Services (CMS), "Quality Initiatives." At http://www.cms.hhs.gov/quality/ (last accessed Aug. 15, 2005).

U.S. Department of Health and Human Services (HHS), Assistant Secretary for Planning and Evaluation (APSE), 2004. "The National Health Information Infrastructure." At http://aspe.hhs.gov/sp/nhii/ (last accessed Aug. 21, 2005).

———, 2002. "Confronting the New Health Care Crisis: Improving Health Care Quality and Lowering Costs by Fixing Our Medical Liability System." At http://aspe.hhs.gov/daltcp/reports/litrefm.pdf (last accessed Feb. 1, 2004).

U.S. Department of Health and Human Services (HHS), 1987. "Report of the Task Force on Medical Liability and Malpractice." Washington, DC: HHS.

U.S. House of Representatives, Committee on Energy and Commerce, Subcommittee on Oversight and Investigations, 2003. *Hearing on Pennsylvania Medical Liability Crisis*. Washington, DC: U.S. Government Printing Office.

U.S. House of Representatives, 1999. "Medicare Appeals Process." Hearings before the Subcommittee on Health of the House Committee in Ways and Means. 105th Cong., 2d Sess. (April 23).

U.S. General Accounting Office (GAO), 2003a. "Medical Malpractice Insurance: Multiple Factors Have Contributed to Increased Premium Rates." GAO Report 03-702. Washington, DC: GAO.

———, 2003b. "Medical Malpractice: Implications of Rising Premiums on Access to Health Care." GAO Report 03-836. Washington, DC: GAO.

———, 2003c. "Specialty Hospitals: Geographic Location, Services Provided, and Financial Performance." GAO Report 04-167. Washington, DC: GAO.

———, 1997. "Managed Care: Explicit Gag Clauses Not Found in HMO Contracts, But Physician Concerns Remain." GAO Report HEHS-97-175. Washington, DC: GAO.

———, 1993. "Medical Malpractice: Medicare/Medicaid Beneficiaries Account for a Relatively Small Percentage of Malpractice Losses." GAO Report 93-126. Washington, DC: GAO.

———, 1987. "Medical Malpractice: Characteristics of Claims Closed in 1984." GAO Report HRD-87-55. Washington, DC: GAO.

Varian, Hal R., 2001. "Catastrophe Bonds Could Fill the Gaps in Reinsurance." *New York Times* (Oct. 25).

Veldhuis, Marjan, 1994. "Defensive Behavior of Dutch Family Physicians: Widening the Concept." *Family Medicine* 26.

Venezian, Emilio C., 1985. "Ratemaking Methods and Profit Cycles in Property and Liability Insurance." *Journal of Risk and Insurance* 52.

Vidmar, Neil, 1995. *Medical Malpractice and the American Jury: Confronting the Myths About Jury Incompetence, Deep Pockets, and Outrageous Damage Awards*. Ann Arbor: University of Michigan Press.

Vidmar, Neil, and Leigh Anne Brown, 2002. "Tort Reform and the Medical Liability Insurance Crisis in Mississippi: Diagnosing the Disease and Prescribing a Remedy." *Mississippi College Law Review* 22.

Vidmar, Neil, Felicia Gross, and Mary Rose, 1998. "Jury Awards for Medical Malpractice and Post-verdict Adjustment of Those Awards." *DePaul Law Review*
48.

Vidmar, Neil, Paul Lee, Kara MacKillop, Kieran McCarthy, and Gerald McGwin,
2005. "Uncovering the 'Invisible' Profile of Medical Malpractice Litigation:
Insights From Florida." *DePaul Law Review* 54.

Vimercati, Antonella, Pantaleo Greco, Anila Kardashi, Cristina Rossi, Veral Loizzi,
Marco Scioscia, and Giuseppe Loverro, 2000. "Choice of Cesarean Section and
Perception of Legal Pressure." *Journal of Perinatal Medicine* 28.

Vincent, Charles, 2003. "Understanding and Responding to Adverse Events." *New
England Journal of Medicine* 348.

Vincent, Charles, Magi Young, and Angela Phillips, 1994. "Why Do People Sue
Doctors? A Study of Patients and Relatives Taking Legal Action." *Lancet* 343.

Viscusi, W. Kip, 2004. "Tort Reform and Insurance Markets." *Risk Management
and Insurance Review* 7.

Viscusi, W. Kip, and Patricia Born, 2005. "Damages Caps, Insurability, and the Performance of Medical Malpractice Insurance." *Journal of Risk and Insurance* 72.

————, 1995. "Medical Malpractice Insurance in the Wake of Liability Reform."
Journal of Legal Studies 24.

Wachter, Robert M., 2004. "The End of the Beginning: Patient Safety Five Years
After 'To Err Is Human.'" *Health Affairs* Web Exclusive W4-534 (Nov. 10).

Wachter, Robert M., and Kaveh G. Shojania, 2004. *Internal Bleeding: The Truth
Behind America's Terrifying Epidemic of Medical Mistakes*. New York: Rugged
Land.

Wachter, Robert M., Kaveh G. Shojania, Sanjay Saint, Amy J. Markowitz, and Mark
Smith, 2002. "Learning From Our Mistakes: Quality Grand Rounds, a New Case-
Based Series on Medical Errors and Patient Safety." *Annals of Internal Medicine*
136.

Ward, Robert Edwin, 1955. *An Evaluation of Hospital Malpractice Insurance*.
Unpublished M.P.H. thesis, Yale University, New Haven, CT.

————, 1991. *Medical Malpractice on Trial*. Cambridge, MA: Harvard University
Press.

Weiler, Paul C., Howard H. Hiatt, Joseph P. Newhouse, William G. Johnson, Troyen
A. Brennan, and Lucian L. Leape, 1993. *A Measure of Malpractice: Medical Injury,
Malpractice Litigation, and Patient Compensation*. Cambridge, MA: Harvard Uni-
versity Press.

Weinstein, Neil D., 1987. "Unrealistic Optimism About Susceptibility to Health
Problems: Conclusion From a Community-Wide Sample." *Journal of Behavioral
Medicine* 10.

Weisman, Carol S., Laura L. Morlock, Martha Ann Teitelbaum, Ann C. Klassen,
and David D. Celentano, 1989. "Practice Changes in Response to the Malpractice
Litigation Climate: Results of a Maryland Physician Survey." *Medical Care* 27.

Weiss Ratings, Inc., 2003. "Medical Malpractice Caps: The Impact of Non-economic
Damage Caps on Physician Premiums, Claims Payout Levels, and Availability of
Coverage." At http://www.weissratings.com/malpractice.asp (last accessed Aug. 3,
2004).

Weissman, Joel S., Catherine L. Annas, Arnold M. Epstein, Eric C. Schneider, Brian Clarridge, Leslie Kirle, Constantine Gatsonis, Sandra Feibelmann, and Nancy Ridley, 2005. "Error Reporting and Disclosure Systems: Views From Hospital Leaders." *Journal of the American Medical Association* 293.

Werth, Barry, 1998. *Damages*. New York: Simon & Schuster.

White, Michelle J., 1994. "The Value of Liability in Medical Malpractice." *Health Affairs* 13.

White House Press Release, 2002. "President Calls for Medical Liability Reform and Worker Pension Protection" (Aug. 7). At http://www.whitehouse.gov/news/releases/2002/08/20020807-1.html (last accessed Feb. 3, 2003).

Williams, C. L., 2004. "Evidence-Based Medicine in the Law Beyond Clinical Practice Guidelines: What Effect Will EBM Have on the Standard of Care?" *Washington & Lee Law Review* 61.

Winter, Ralph, 1988. "The Liability Crisis and the Dynamics of Competitive Insurance Markets." *Yale Journal on Regulation* 5.

Wisconsin Department of Insurance, 2001. "Wisconsin Insurance Report Business of 2001." At http://oci.wi.gov/ann_rpt/bus_2001/anrpttoc.htm. (last accessed Dec. 29, 2003).

Wisconsin Hospital Association, 2003. "2003–2005 State Budget: Impacts on Wisconsin Hospitals." At http://www.wha.org/pubArchive/position_statements/pp2003issuesummary.pdf (last accessed Sept. 16, 2004).

Wisconsin Patient Compensation Fund, 2003. At http://oci.wi.gov/pcf.htm (last accessed Dec. 29, 2003).

Witman, Amy B., Deric M. Park, and Steven B. Hardin, 1996. "How Do Patients Want Physicians to Handle Mistakes? A Survey of Internal Medicine Patients in an Academic Setting." *Archives of Internal Medicine* 156.

Witt, John Fabian, 2004. "Lessons From History: State Constitutions, American Tort Law, and the Medical Malpractice Crisis." Philadelphia: Pew Charitable Trusts' Project on Medical Liability in Pennsylvania. At www.medliabilitypa.org (last accessed Aug. 14, 2005).

———, 2000. "From Loss of Services to Loss of Support: The Wrongful Death Statutes, the Origins of Modern Tort Law, and the Making of the Nineteenth-Century Family." *Law and Social Inquiry* 25.

Wolaver, Amy M., and Christopher S. P. Magee, n.d. "Law Firm, Insurance, and Health Care Lobbying Over Medical Liability Legislation." Unpublished paper in the possession of the editors.

Wu, Albert W., Thomas A. Cavanaugh, Stephen J. McPhee, Bernard Lo, and Guy P. Micco, 1997. "To Tell the Truth: Ethical and Practical Issues in Disclosing Medical Mistakes to Patients." *Journal of General Internal Medicine* 12.

Yackle, Larry W., 1989. "Choosing Judges the Democratic Way." *Boston University Law Review* 69.

Yoon, Albert, 2001. "Damage Caps and Civil Litigation: An Empirical Study of Medical Malpractice Litigation in the South." *American Law and Economics Review* 3.

Zelizer, Viviana A., 1985. *Pricing the Priceless Child: The Changing Social Value of Children*. New York: Basic Books.

Zelman, Walter A., and Robert A. Berenson, 1998. *The Managed Care Blues and How to Cure Them*. Washington, DC: Georgetown University Press.

Zhan, Chunliu, and Marlene R. Miller, 2003. "Excess Length of Stay, Charges, and Mortality Attributable to Medical Injuries During Hospitalization." *Journal of the American Medical Association* 290.

Zimmerman, Rachel, 2004. "As Malpractice Caps Spread, Lawyers Turn Away Some Cases." *Wall Street Journal* (Oct. 8).

Zuckerman, S., Randall R. Bovbjerg, and Frank A. Sloan, 1990. "Effects of Tort Reforms and Other Factors on Medical Malpractice Insurance Premiums." *Inquiry* 27.

Index